RATIO AND VOLUNTAS

Ratio and Voluntas

The Tension Between Reason and Will in Law

KAARLO TUORI
Helsinki University, Finland

Routledge
Taylor & Francis Group
LONDON AND NEW YORK

First published 2011 by Ashgate Publishing

2 Park Square, Milton Park, Abingdon, Oxon OX14 4RN
711 Third Avenue, New York, NY 10017, USA

Routledge is an imprint of the Taylor & Francis Group, an informa business

First issued in paperback 2016

British Library Cataloguing in Publication Data
Tuori, Kaarlo.
Ratio and voluntas : the tension between reason and will in
law. -- (Applied legal philosophy)
1. Law--History. 2. Law--Philosophy. 3. Semantics (Law)
4. Constitutional law.
I. Title II. Series
340.1'1-dc22

Library of Congress Cataloging-in-Publication Data
Tuori, Kaarlo.
Ratio and voluntas : the tension between reason and will in law / by Kaarlo Tuori.
p. cm. -- (Applied legal philosophy)
Includes bibliographical references and index.
ISBN 978-1-4094-2013-2 (hardback) -- ISBN 978-1-4094-2014-9 (ebook) 1. Law--Philosophy. I. Title.
K230.T86A37 2010
340'.1--dc22

2010033627

ISBN 978-1-4094-2013-2 (hbk)
ISBN 978-1-138-24988-2 (pbk)

Transferred to Digital Printing in 2014

Contents

EPILOGUE

Series Editor's Preface

The objective of the Applied Legal Philosophy series is to publish work which adopts a theoretical approach to the study of particular areas or aspects of law or deals with general theories of law in a way which focused on issues of practical moral and political concern in specific legal contexts.

In recent years there has been an encouraging tendency for legal philosophers to utilize detailed knowledge of the substance and practicalities of law and a noteworthy development in the theoretical sophistication of much legal research. The series seeks to encourage these trends and to make available studies in law which are both genuinely philosophical in approach and at the same time based on appropriate legal knowledge and directed towards issues in the criticism and reform of actual laws and legal systems.

The series will include studies of all the main areas of law, presented in a manner which relates to the concerns of specialist legal academics and practitioners. Each book makes an original contribution to an area of legal study while being comprehensible to those engaged in a wide variety of disciplines. Their legal content is principally Anglo-American, but a wide-ranging comparative approach is encouraged and authors are drawn from a variety of jurisdictions.

Tom Campbell
Series Editor
Centre for Applied Philosophy and Public Ethics
Charles Sturt University, Canberra

Preface

Iustitia, the Roman goddess of Law and Justice, is armed not only with the sword but also with the balance. From the ancient beginnings of Western legal tradition, law has been conceived as traversed by a fundamental tension: power (will) and reason. The symbolism of representations of Iustitia seems as familiar and decipherable to us as to the ancient Romans. The law remains ineffectual without the sword; to make a difference, the law cannot be mere *ratio*. But not only does the balance as the law's *ratio* need the sword as its complement; power could neither achieve its objectives nor organise itself without assistance from the law.

The tension between these two poles, reason and will, or – to use the Latin expressions – *ratio* and *voluntas* – is the main topic of this study. Although I try to locate it in time and place, I do not follow its vicissitudes from the very origins of our legal tradition but focus on the historical type of law we are accustomed to calling modern law. In *Critical Legal Positivism* (Ashgate 2002), I presented my view of the distinctive features of the ideal-typical mature modern legal system; this study builds on that view. My starting point is that modern law is essentially positive law, based on conscious human action, such as decisions of the legislator and the judges. This fundamental positivity and the decisionist element it implies seem to entail the clear supremacy of *voluntas* in law. But to show the vital role that *ratio* also plays, I have drawn a very different picture of the law's positivity than has been usual in twentieth-century legal positivism, dominated by the two main figures of Hans Kelsen and H.L.A. Hart.

I draw a distinction between two aspects of law or – if you wish – two meanings of the concept of law. Law is at once a symbolic-normative phenomenon and a social phenomenon: it consists both of a normative order – a *legal order* – and of specific social practices – *legal practices*, such as lawmaking, adjudication and legal scholarship. These two aspects of law constantly interact. Legal practices are social practices whose function lies in producing and reproducing law in its other aspect, as a legal order. Legal practices also provide the ontological support for law as a symbolic-normative phenomenon: without their backing we could not speak of the existence of a legal order. On the other hand, legal practices need support from legal norms. This goes especially for such institutionalised practices as lawmaking and adjudication, which receive their legal character from legal norms of competence, organisation and procedure – secondary rules in the sense defined by Hart.

The contribution of legal practices, especially of lawmaking and adjudication, lends modern law its positive character. However, the decisions on which law relies are not decisions 'out of nothing' (*aus Nichts*) but based on certain presuppositions. These presuppositions point to another crucial distinction in my conception of 'mature' modern law: a distinction between *levels of law* or – to be more exact – between levels of the legal order. I understand the law as a multi-layered normative phenomenon which, in addition to the *surface* of individual statutes, decisions and scholarly interventions, also includes 'sub-surface' *legal-cultural* elements, such as general legal concepts and principles, legal theories or doctrines, and patterns of argumentation. The legal-cultural layers stand in constitutive relation to events on the law's surface: they make up the normative, conceptual and methodological reservoir without which the legislator could not enact its laws, the judges issue their rulings, or the scholars write their articles and monographs. In legal practices, they mainly function in an unconscious, tacit way: they form an integral part of the hermeneutic *pre-understanding* through which legal actors approach their specific tasks. But the relationship between the law's surface and its legal-cultural infrastructure is of a recursive character: not only is the surface dependent on legal-cultural presuppositions but these, in turn, originate from individual contributions of the legislator, judges or legal scholars, to mention the main actors of modern law. The cultural, sub-surface elements of law result from a process of *sedimentation*, starting from what transpires on the surface. The relation of sedimentation also extends the law's positivity from its surface to its legal-cultural underpinnings, bringing the idea of modern law's multi-layered nature into harmony with its positivity.

It is precisely in relating modern law's positivity to its multi-layered nature that my critical positivism differs from Kelsen's and Hart's approach. Arguably, their hierarchical legal order is a surface-level phenomenon; they do not thematise its legal-cultural underpinnings. Kelsen, for example, was interested in the presuppositions of surface-level regulations merely as regards their conceptual infrastructure; the normative contents of the legal order were entirely dependent on the *voluntas* of the legislator. Emphasis on the law's sub-surface layers also makes it difficult to locate critical legal positivism within the distinctions related to the notions of *inclusive* and *exclusive positivism*, so very much in vogue in Anglo-American jurisprudential debates, especially in the 1990s: exponents of both inclusive and exclusive positivism seem to be interested mainly in the surface-level legal order. By contrast, in my view of 'mature' modern law, connections to morals and ethics are knit primarily on the law's sub-surface levels. According to my suggestion put forth in this study, modern law's *ratio* finds its main locus in the law's sub-surface, legal-cultural layers; *ratio* is sedimented or layered reason, which informs legal actors' pre-understanding and unfolds its influence primarily through this pre-understanding. And as legal practices, producing the material on the law's surface, depend on sub-surface presuppositions, so the *voluntas* of the law's decision-makers, the legislator and the judge, depends on this sedimented or layered reason.

This study also endeavours to locate the tension between *ratio* and *voluntas* in time and space; in fact, alterations in the law's *temporality* and *spatiality* constitute one of my central sub-themes. I focus on two ruptures: the one inaugurating the modern period (Chapter 2) and the other warranting the talk of late modernity (Chapter 9). In its temporal aspect, the modern era is characterised, first, by a linear conception of time which leaves the horizon of the future open and malleable, and, second, by increasing social acceleration. In its spatial aspect, in turn, modernity is characterised by liberation from the bounds of locality and the conquest of new space, first in the shape of the nation state then, in our late modernity, in the processes of globalisation and virtualisation. Development of law is inextricably bound to development of cultural conceptions of time and space as well as to temporal and spatial characteristics of social structures. In addition, it is vital to relate the law's time and space to its two dimensions – the legal order and legal practices – as well as to the layers of the legal order. Thus, the law's surface level is constantly changing, whereas its putative deep structure or deep culture represents legal *longue durée*. In spatial respect, in turn, the legal-cultural layers of modern law have never been so exclusively tied to the nation state as has been the case with the surface-level legal order.

However, my objective to heed the time and space of the law's *ratio* and *voluntas* does not merely imply attention to the law's general temporal and spatial coordinates. This study alternates between legal-theoretical and legal-historical discussions. I make three forays into the history of legal thinking. These are intended to highlight the manner in which the law's *ratio*, in particular, has been conceived. All three forays are directed to periods of transition: the first to the seventeenth- and eighteenth-century debates between classical common-law authors and the early representatives of legal positivism, such as Thomas Hobbes and Jeremy Bentham (Chapter 2); the second to the ideas of the German historical school of the early nineteenth century and its subsequent conversion into *Begriffsjurisprudenz* (conceptual jurisprudence) (Chapter 3); and the third to the twentieth-century realist and analytical criticism of legal conceptualism (Chapter 4). These historical forays make it plain how differently the law's *ratio* has been understood in different historical and cultural settings. Thus, the traditionalist, communal notion of reason, still espoused by the classical common-law doctrine, has not been able to withstand the pressure of cultural modernisation. Nonetheless, as I also try to argue, this historical and legal-cultural variety should not obscure the continuity of tasks that fall to the law's *ratio*. I distil these tasks from the English seventeenth- and eighteenth-century debates: providing legal actors with their indispensable hermeneutic pre-understanding; maintaining a certain coherence in law; keeping open the channels between law and the moral and ethical spheres of society; and disciplining the free reign of the law's *voluntas*. My legal-theoretical interests dictate my perspective on legal history; I am not engaged in an independent study in the history of ideas, but endeavour through my legal-historical forays to shed light on certain still pertinent legal-theoretical issues.

In fact, throughout the study I maintain a dialogue between the legal-theoretical and the legal-historical approach. This methodological choice is based on my belief in the profoundly historical nature of the law's *ratio* and *voluntas*, as well as their relationship. Within the modern period, I lay particular stress on two developments: the law's instrumentalisation, and the democratisation of lawmaking. The law's *instrumentalisation* in the service of the legislator's political aims already motivated the anti-conceptualist criticism which I discuss in my last historical foray (Chapter 4) and reached its zenith in the post-Second World War welfare state. Arguably, instrumentalisation augmented the weight of *voluntas* in law. But it also called for novel ways to control this *voluntas*, thus accounting for many twentieth-century developments within judicial and constitutional review (Chapters 7 and 8). At present, the law's instrumentalisation appears to have drifted into difficulties, mainly because of late modern temporal and spatial transformations, connected to globalisation (Chapter 9).

The impact of *democratisation* on the relationship between the law's *ratio* and *voluntas* has been ambivalent. On the one hand, democratisation has granted economically and socially depressed groups access to lawmaking, enabling them to promote their interests and remedy their particular problems by legislative means; this, of course, is a central backdrop to the legislative activism of the welfare state. But democratisation has not only further enhanced the law's instrumentalisation and strengthened the position of legislative *voluntas*; it has also at least potentially enriched the reason associated with this *voluntas*.

Voluntas should not be equated with irrationality or arationality. As Hobbes makes quite clear, the legislator is guided by a specific rationality: instrumental rationality, which conceives of the law as a means to achieve the legislator's political goals. What constitutes the problem with such a view of legislative *voluntas* is not a lack of rationality but rather its truncated nature. Hobbes' and Bentham's legislator acknowledges only one dimension in practical reason: namely, instrumental reason. Here, democracy alters the situation, at least potentially, by sensitising the lawmaking procedure to such discourses within civil society where even the ethical and moral aspects of legislative issues are addressed. In Kantian terms, democracy enables the legislative will to convert from a mere instrumentalist *Willkür* to a fully rational *Willen.*

Hence, it would be erroneous to link the perspective of *ratio* solely to legal scholarship and adjudication and see lawmaking as necessarily dominated by a *voluntas* which only attends to instrumentalist viewpoints. On the other hand, adjudication inevitably includes moments of fiat, as is shown particularly by analysis of hard cases that involve weighing and balancing principles and counter-principles; legal scholarship, too, is affected by the conscious or unconscious strategic motivations of schools and individuals, competing for academic and social recognition and influence. If it is mistaken to treat lawmaking as mere *voluntas*, it would also over-stretch the point to explore adjudication or academic legal scholarship exclusively in terms of a disinterested *ratio*. If the main focus of this study is on academic legal science, that does not imply a claim that legal scholars would be the only guardians of *ratio* in modern law. Rather, my choice of emphasis is based on the view that legal scholarship accomplishes vital tasks in modern law by articulating and elaborating the professional legal culture and in forming the pre-understanding of legal actors. I have tried to capture the particular role of legal scholarship in the catchword of its *dual citizenship*: legal scholarship is a citizen of both the realm of science and the realm of law. Accordingly, many of its distinctive features as an academic discipline flow from its participation in the functioning of the legal system while, vice versa, many of its peculiarities as a legal practice derive from its other citizenship as an academic discipline.

Ratio and *voluntas* also constitute two possible perspectives on law. As regards academic disciplines, the perspective of *voluntas* appears typical of the way social sciences, such as sociology or political science, approach the law. However, the respective emphasis on *ratio* and *voluntas* varies within legal scholarship, too. Legal positivists define the law's unity through the hierarchical order of legal norms and the authorities issuing them. Hence, they tend to privilege the position of *voluntas*, whereas those striving for principle-based coherence – say, Dworkin and Habermas – adopt the standpoint of *ratio*.

This study endeavours to apply some of the basic lessons of the contemporary conceptual approach to intellectual history, with Quentin Skinner as perhaps its most prominent exponent. These include due attention to the argumentative context of interventions in various types of discourse: discursive interventions always relate to previous interventions which they dispute, with which they argue, on which they concur or elaborate, and so on. Throughout the study, my main interlocutor will be a collective person who will be graced with female form and termed the *Critic*. Her main real-life models exist in the shape of some Critical Legal Studies researchers, such as Martti Koskenniemi, my colleague at the Law Faculty of Helsinki University. The Critic tends to reduce legal discourse to strategically motivated interventions which aim at promoting particular extra-discursive interests. I try to demonstrate the one-sidedness of the Critic's conception of legal discourse by taking recourse to the speech act theory of J.L. Austin and John Searle. The Critic absolutises the perlocutionary dimension of legal speech acts, with its focus on their extra-discursive effects. She allows no independence to the illocutionary dimension of speech acts where their claims to formal and substantive validity are located and discussed. Yet the very notion of legal discourse seems to require an understanding of the importance of the illocutionary dimension: it is the continuous mutual assessment of their claims to normative validity that links individual speech acts together and constitutes in the first place something we can call legal discourse. In addition, the Critic, zealous to disclaim any normative involvement, ignores what can be termed the *imposed normativity of all legal scholarship*. The normativity of legal scholarship concerns not only such overtly normative interpretive or systematic standpoints that are a vital element in the standard legal science which on the Continent is called legal dogmatics. In addition, all legal scholarship, including the type driven by the Critic, is subject to another kind of normativity, flowing from its dependence on legal-cultural preconditions, on a legal pre-understanding. Here, too, a certain recursivity is at work: legal scholarship contributes to the reproduction of its very presuppositions.

As should be evident by now, my own approach stresses the role of *ratio* in law. Just as the law itself, this *ratio* displays two aspects: it is inherent in law both as a symbolic-normative phenomenon – as a legal order – and as legal practices. Thus, the law's *ratio* should be understood not only as the sedimented, legal-cultural foundations of the legal order but also in procedural and discursive terms: as distinctive features of legal practices and legal discourse that allow due space for all the aspects of practical reason, without one-sidedly privileging the instrumental dimension. Nonetheless, I do not deny the possibility or legitimacy of examining legal discourse in strategic terms; throughout the study, I refer both to the Critic's standpoint and to 'external' sociological analyses, such as Pierre Bourdieu's depiction of the legal field. But – and here my divergence from the Critic or my social-scientific colleagues is evident – just as we may bracket out the illocutionary aspect, we may also suspend the perlocutionary aims and consequences of legal speech acts and confine our discussion to the normative claims that speech acts make in the illocutionary dimension. Indeed, the main thrust of this study lies in the latter dimension: my aim is not merely to reconstruct or describe particular features of modern law and legal discourse. I employ the means of the conceptual approach to intellectual history (see esp. Chapter 4), but unlike an intellectual historian *à la* Skinner, I do not usually content myself with locating the interventions in their argumentative context and identifying their claim to normative correctness. I also take an overt normative stand on these claims; on, for example, the merits of anti-conceptualist criticism (Chapter 4). My normative standpoints are premised on the continuing pertinence of such tasks of the *ratio* as maintaining the law's coherence and disciplining the instrumentalism of *voluntas*. This is also the backdrop to the Epilogue (Chapter 9) which addresses the globalisation or de-nationalisation of law.

I understand this study as a contribution to the legal theory of modern law and, as such, thus transcending the boundaries of particular legal cultures. But my own roots lie in the Continental, Romano-Germanic culture. This, of course, impregnates the pre-understanding with which I have tackled the issues I have chosen to discuss. I have included comparative and historical material to show the general purport of the issues – all in one way or the other connected to the many-faceted tensions between the law's *ratio* and *voluntas* – but, by the same token, also their culturally and historically varying guises. But it is apparent that my discussion of common-law culture is coloured by own legal-cultural prejudices ('prejudices' in Gadamer's sense). By far the most intricate chapter of this study for me has been Chapter 2, where I discuss common law and its inherent *ratio* as portrayed by the classical common-law authors of seventeenth- and eighteenth-century England. When drafting and re-drafting the text, I had to radically revise my preliminary view – a culturally dependent pre-understanding. The starting-point was to depict classical common-law ideology as epitomising a traditionalist, pre-modern view of law and, thus, to obtain a contrast, firstly, to the reflexive legal culture of a mature modern legal system and, secondly, to academic legal scholarship as the main articulator of that culture. But the more I tried to comprehend the specific common-law rationality, the more simplistic my initial conception, with its clear-cut distinctions, began to look. In Chapter 2, I still resort to the contrast between pre-modern and modern, but more in an ideal-typical way, thus – so I hope – avoiding at least the most obvious of the dichotomous pitfalls. It would, however, be a miracle, if the exposition of common-law thinking in Chapter 2 or the rule of doctrine in Chapter 8 were not affected by my legal-cultural subconscious. The same qualification goes for my discussion of American legal conceptualism (Chapter 3) and its realist criticism (Chapter 4).

In present-day debates of a putative convergence between Romano-Germanic and common-law legal cultures, I find myself in the camp of the sceptics. Despite evident deep-structural similarities, significant differences remain, say, in the doctrine of legal sources and in the respective position of legislator, courts and scholars as the main legal actors. In addition, since the latter part of the nineteenth century the US and English legal systems have in important respects followed different routes. For instance, as regards the role of academic legal scholarship, the United States stands closer to Continental Europe than the former mother country. Still, in the United States, too, the common-law heritage is clearly detectable in, for example, the elevated status of the courts.

Legal language is a pivotal element of legal culture; indeed, legal-cultural differences may even cause linguistic misunderstandings. Continental authors already come up against difficulties when trying to find proper terms for scholarly activities. In this study, I use '*legal scholarship*' as a synonym for '*legal science*'. However, at the same time I am conscious of the particular – and in respect of my own linguistic use, misleading – connotations of 'science'. In the Anglo-Saxon world, 'science' easily brings to mind the natural sciences, as opposed to the humanities, with their distinct understanding of scientific research. Furthermore, in the United States 'legal science' is often related to Christopher Columbus Langdell's late nineteenth-century endeavour to 'scientify' the law. I hope the reader keeps in mind the 'neutral' sense which I attach to 'legal science'.

In addition to 'legal scholarship' (or 'legal science'), I employ the term '*normative legal scholarship*', which may further confuse the reader. By this expression I refer to legal scholarship which presents overt normative standpoints, on, say, interpretation of statutes or precedents, the systematisation of law, or the significance and use of legal concepts and principles. The term covers both what on the Continent is called *legal dogmatics* and (normative) *legal theory*. 'Legal dogmatics' itself is a continuous headache for Continental scholars trying to express themselves in English; neither English nor American legal culture recognises the term. According to the standard definition, 'legal dogmatics' refers to scholarly activity focusing on interpreting and systematising legal norms (norm statements). I have chosen to use the term '*doctrinal research*' for such academic activities. In turn, the term '*doctrine(s)*' refers to the end product of doctrinal research, especially its systematising endeavours. Thus, the '*Allgemeine Lehren*' of distinct departments of law that play a pivotal role in Continental legal culture(s) will be called 'general doctrines'. However, I am aware of the polyvalence of 'doctrine' in the legal language of common-law cultures and the courts' central task in articulating and developing the normative whole called doctrine. Here, problems in translation noticeably reflect important differences in the respective status of the key legal actors of modern law.

Emphasis on the intractable culture-dependence of legal theory implies a response to the ever-recurring accusation of *ethnocentrism*: yes, my discussion of modern law is ethnocentric in the sense that my legal pre-understanding is permeated by the 'prejudices' (again, the term taken in its Gadamerian sense) of my own Continental European legal culture. But I also do believe that legal cultures, and not only those falling under the label of 'Western legal tradition', include sufficiently common elements to make cross-boundary discussion both possible and worthwhile. I try to be cautious against simplistic *evolutionary-theoretical assumptions* which such expressions as '*modern law*' and '*legal modernisation*' may evoke and which, in critical interventions, are often seen to go together with ethnocentrism. Still, I believe that it makes sense to anchor legal-theoretical discussions in a Weberian ideal type of 'mature' modern law which existing legal systems match to a greater or lesser extent. And I also believe that it makes sense to speak of legal modernisation as a process where the legal system acquires features related to this ideal type. But I do not conceive of legal modernisation as a uniform process which always and everywhere traverses the same successive stages and assumes identical guises.

This study is divided into three parts, preceded by a Prologue and succeeded by an Epilogue. The Prologue aims to situate and defend normative legal scholarship by responding to two challenges to its legitimacy and very possibility as an academic, scientific enterprise. The first challenger comes from social sciences: the claim is that normative legal scholarship is indelibly tainted by ideology and, because of its normative and discursive closure, cannot rise to the level of science; and that legal scholars make the fatal mistake of not acknowledging that norms really are facts. In my counterargument, I examine legal scholarship's dual citizenship and its participation not only in scientific but also in legal discourse; the divergent roles that norms and facts play in legal and social science; and the different nature and function of legal and social theories. Here, my discussion relates to the internal/external distinction which legal theorists – at least ever since publication of Hart's *The Concept of Law* – have invoked as both an account and a vindication of the specific legal standpoint. The other challenger with whom I dispute in Chapter 1 is not an outsider but an insider: a legal scholar but one who attempts to expel normative legal scholarship from the realm of academic research. My counterargument employs the concepts of speech act theory: I criticise the Critic for reductionism, for examining legal speech acts in a one-sided manner merely from the perspective of their perlocutionary, extra-legal effects and for ignoring the illocutionary dimension where claims of normative validity are raised and appraised. The Critic is also blind to the 'imposed normativity' which is inescapable because the Critic's research, too, necessarily depends on available legal-cultural resources and participates in reproduction of the prevailing legal culture.

Part I focuses on three instructive phases in the history of the law's *ratio*. Chapter 2 sketches the basic temporal and spatial parameters of modern law that frame the highly volatile tension between *ratio* and *voluntas*: modern law, at least on its surface, is constantly changeable law with the nation state as its privileged space. I introduce the discussion of legal modernisation by distinguishing between two concepts of *tradition*: a *philosophical* or *hermeneutical* concept, referring to the inevitable cultural situatedness of all human cognition and interpretation, and a *historical-sociological* concept, referring to particular arrangement of social beliefs and practices. The central argument is that in the course of legal modernisation, the law moves from the pole of a tradition (in the historical-sociological sense), firmly attached to time (the past) and place (the locale), towards the pole of an expert system, increasingly detached from temporal or spatial bounds. This implies significant alterations in the nature of the legal culture that provides legal actors with their pre-understanding. If tradition in the historical-sociological sense functioned in pre-modern, largely customary law also as a tradition in the philosophical-hermeneutical sense, then modern legal culture has opened up to reflexive assessment and elaboration, and reserved for legal scholarship a prominent role in legal-cultural change. However, my brief foray into the history of English common law should serve as a caution against hasty and sweeping – evolutionary! – generalisations.

In Chapter 2, I resort to English seventeenth- and eighteenth-century debates between common-law authors and the early legal positivists Hobbes and Bentham. The aim is not only to portray 'semi-traditional' classical common-law ideology as a contrast to my ideal-typical mature modern law, but also to distil the tasks of *ratio* which have not lost their importance in (further) cultural and societal modernisation. These tasks, such as maintaining the law's coherence and tempering the instrumentalism of its *voluntas*, structure many of the discussions in subsequent chapters.

Chapter 3 moves the focus from seventeenth- and eighteenth-century England to nineteenth-century Germany, where the law's modernisation was taking decisive steps. According to my judgement, the historical school of the first half of the century deserves merit for perceiving the particular role of legal scholarship in the development of law and for recognising its peculiar dual citizenship as both a scientific and a legal practice. I also claim that the historical school already gave expression to many of the tensions that have subsequently permeated modern law and its self-understanding and that are all in one way or another related to the precarious relationship between *ratio* and *voluntas*. These include the tension between modern law's positivity and its 'supra-positive' preconditions; the tension between the law's autonomy and its ineffaceable societal and cultural moorings; and the tension between the law's positivity and systematicity.

Chapter 4 brings us already to the threshold of our own time. The focus is on the realist and analytical criticism of German-oriented *Begriffsjurisprudenz* and its American conceptualist counterpart. This criticism, in line with its object, was an international phenomenon, although in its concrete manifestations, of course, depended on particular legal-cultural contexts. Against the backdrop of an examination of the methodological premises adopted in conceptual history, I make a foray to four critical debates: the German criticism from the positions of *Interessenjurisprudenz* and *Freirechtslehre*, already initiated by Rudolph von Jhering in the second half of the nineteenth century; American Legal Realism with its Golden Age in the 1920s and 1930s: the partly contemporaneous but largely independent Scandinavian Realism, whose dominance lasted well into the 1960s, if not even longer; and, finally, Finnish post-Second World War analytical scholarship. But even in Chapter 4, my main interest does not lie in the history of ideas as such. Rather, by assessing the merits of anti-conceptualist criticism I attempt to summarise lessons which would be of relevance for present-day and future post-realist and post-analytical legal scholarship. I dispute the relevance of formal-logical criticism of the conceptualists' constructive method. As regards the first, so-called inductive phase, I recall the significance for the historical school of the method of *Anschauung*; a method of grasping organic interdependencies which cannot be compressed into the logically-tuned categories of present-day philosophy of science. The historical school's notion of the law's organicity emphasised two features of law which their analytical critics in their formalism and universalism tend often enough to ignore: the law's substantive coherence, and its historicity. Slightly paradoxically, in logically-oriented criticism, legal conceptualism has been blamed not only for unwarranted inductivism but also for conceptual apriorism or Platonism, to resort to one of the critics' favourite denigrating expressions. And it is true that both the historical school and the subsequent *Begriffsjurisprudenz* construed their positivism on a supra-positive foundation. But here, too, the conceptualist argument displays a sound core: it draws attention to the legal-cultural presuppositions of the singular events on the law's surface: the legislator's laws, judges' rulings, and scholars' monographs and articles. The second, deductive phase of the conceptualists' constructive method can also be stripped of its quasi-logical attire and understood in terms of analogical and principle-based reasoning. But the requirement, raised especially by American Legal Realists, of tearing down the quasi-logical façade and of engaging in overt morals- or policy-based argumentation retains its strength even after such 'sympathetic' re-reading of the conceptualists' methodological premises. But, under my final counterargument directed both at empiricist re-definitions of basic legal concepts and at suggestions to integrate legal scholarship into social sciences, law remains a particular normative enterprise. Instead of attempting to reduce legal normativity to social facticity, we should explore law and society in their interdependency and, thus, (re-)connect with the tradition instigated by Savigny with his notion of *legal institutions*. The law possesses autonomy but this is merely of a relative, not an absolute character.

In our post-analytical and post-realist age, many analytical or realist insights have been sedimented into central elements of our legal pre-understanding. But, as I have tried to show with the discussions in Chapter 4, this should not obscure the still relevant aspects of the programme for legal scholarship of the historical school, such as striving for coherence and systematisation while simultaneously being sensitive to historical change. Part II focuses on the way legal scholarship, especially doctrinal research (legal dogmatics), can and should contribute to the law's coherence. Chapter 5 discusses the law's systematisation through its division into distinct fields: contract law, the law of torts, criminal law, administrative law, and so on. I argue that aspiration for *total coherence*, covering the legal order as a whole, has lost its pertinence, but that *local coherence* within diverse fields of law is still a relevant objective, as is shown by debates on such putative new fields as, say, information or communications law, medical law or environmental law. The traditional divisions, dating from the nineteenth century, have been disputed in the course of the law's increasing instrumentalisation and its resulting bifurcation, which has found its manifestation in such distinctions as F.A. Hayek's rule of just conduct and rules of organisation, or Jürgen Habermas' law as an institution and law as a medium. However, it would be overhasty to declare nineteenth-century systematisation wholly moribund; rather, it has been complemented by new divisions, following different criteria and cutting across traditional lines. In Chapter 5, I also present my argument for the continuing importance and achievability of the normative aim of coherence.

Arguably, the main instrument for achieving coherence in law consists in legal doctrine, in what Continental Europe calls general doctrines (*allgemeine Lehren*) of distinct fields of law. Particularly in Romano-Germanic legal cultures, the main responsibility for their articulation and elaboration falls to legal scholarship. Chapter 6 analyses general doctrines in terms of legal concepts, principles and theories.

Constitutional law holds a key position in managing the tension between law's *voluntas* and *ratio*. On the one hand, through its provisions on lawmaking, a constitution establishes the law's positivity and provides the political legislator's *voluntas* access to the law. But on the other hand, particularly through its provisions on basic rights and constitutional review, a constitution also imposes restrictions on this same *voluntas*. The law's *voluntas* is formed in the political system, while a constitution fulfils a peculiar intermediary function at the interface between the legal and political systems. Part III is devoted to discussing this function from the perspective of the former. Chapter 7 examines the common-law notion of the rule of law and the Continental notion of the *Rechtsstaat* as two legal-cultural ways of handling the tension between law's *voluntas* and *ratio*. My conclusion is that what I call the English *Sonderweg* with its emphasis on parliamentary supremacy and its rejection of constitutional review seems to be approaching its end. I also claim that in a mature modern legal system the law's *ratio* primarily exerts its tempering influence on the law's *voluntas* in everyday legal practices through the legal-cultural pre-understanding of legal actors, in, say, principle-based interpretation of policy-based statutes. Institutional constitutional review constitutes merely the last resort in monitoring the law's legitimate limits.

In Chapter 8, I present my last-resort argument for constitutional review in a more detailed way and by discussing the 'core case' against such review, boiling down to claims of its anti-democratic nature – what Alexander Bickel famously called the *counter-majoritarian difficulty* – and its tendency to juridify political issues. The critical observations do not annihilate the last-resort defence; instead, they serve as warning signs against a review exceeding its justifiable reach. I renounce the simplistic conception which reduces legislation to *voluntas* associated with instrumental reason and emphasise the potential of the democratic lawmaking procedure to embody a wider notion of practical reason and to include deliberations on the ethical and moral dimensions of legislative issues. Nonetheless, because the legislator's privileged perspective is – entirely legitimately! – instrumental, sidestepping or at least underrating basic-rights aspects cannot be excluded. The ongoing debates about constitutional review tend to assume the dichotomy of judicial or legislative supremacy and to reduce the alternatives in judicial review to the US-type diffused model and the German-type concentrated model. In Chapter 8, I argue that in fact the so-called hybrid forms, such as those included the *New Commonwealth Model of Constitutionalism* or – for that matter – the Finnish system, are best suited to avoiding those problematic consequences of constitutional review to which critical commentators have drawn our attention.

In Chapter 9, which constitutes the Epilogue to this study, I turn to those ongoing transformations in the law's temporal and spatial characteristics which have engendered discussion of law's de-nationalisation, even globalisation. I am especially interested in the implications these transformations might have with regard to the tension between the law's *ratio* and *voluntas*. I agree with critics of the traditional black-box model of international and municipal law and contend that it is impotent to serve as a framework for exploring such instances of a new type of transnational law as, for instance, EU law. But I also caution against a new version of black-box thinking where autopoietically functioning, mutually closed global social systems are all engendering their own 'law beyond the state'. I stress that our present legal experience should rather be depicted in terms of *interlegality*: overlapping and continuous discursive contacts between various legal orders and legal systems. We see a tendency of legal fragmentation but we should also be sensitive to the counter-tendencies of legal integration which lie behind Klaus Günther's tentative concept of the *universal code of legality*. As a result of the phenomena attesting to mounting legal pluralism, the nation-state legislator has lost its monopoly on the law's *voluntas* and, by the same token, new forms are called for, transcending nation-state boundaries, for achieving the tasks of the *ratio*. In addition to the coherence-creating processes to which Günther has alluded with his 'universal code of legality', we can point to tendencies of constitutionalisation, including a rights-dimension, which are detectable within at least some transnational legal systems. But the big issue remains: how to replace the normative and institutional arrangements of the democratic *Rechtsstaat* whose locus lies in the nation state and which the law's de-nationalisation has bereaved of much of their efficacy?

This study is a thoroughly revised version of one that I published in Finnish in 2007 (*Oikeuden ratio ja voluntas*, WSOYpro, Helsinki). I have detached the discussions from their Finnish contexts, although Finnish material is still used in illustrating the issues and, in some connections, in suggesting normative solutions with a wider pertinence. The manuscript to the Finnish edition was reviewed by many colleagues to whom I again address my collective thanks. In addition, I have received invaluable comments on the changes and additions I have made for the English edition. Here I want to mention especially Sabine Frerichs, Juha Lavapuro, Toni Malminen, Kimmo Nuotio, Tuomas Ojanen and Heikki Pihlajamäki. Most of them are members of the Centre of Excellence in European Law and Polity, with its main seat at the University of Helsinki, and their constructive criticism is a concrete sign of the benefits of such a research organisation. The Centre has enabled me to concentrate on scholarly work in the academic year 2008–2009. Hopefully, this study may also be of assistance in specifying the framework for approaching the particularities of European law, thus contributing to execution of the Centre's research plan.

PROLOGUE

Chapter 1
Two Challengers of Normative Legal Scholarship

The Requirement of Reflexivity

Modern culture is reflexive culture. It is able to assess itself, to reflect on itself, and to debate its own validity: continuous criticism and the contestability of its results characterise modern science; moral norms have lost their self-evident authority, guaranteed by tradition, and are in need of justification; and modernism makes art of art, literature of literature, and music of music. Modern law is positive law, resulting from conscious human action. Positive law would be unthinkable without cultural reflexivity: production of new law through explicit decisions presupposes existing law's openness to criticism. The idea of a *constitution*, which regulates production of new legal norms, is one of the major contributions of modern law. Modern law regulates the process of its own amendment and repeal and in so doing positivises its own reflexivity.

At the level of individual personality, reflexivity is manifest in subjective self-examination and self-criticism, in conscious moral and ethical choices, in thinking about one's thinking. The reflexivity of personality has its limits, which Freud, for instance, tried to chart with his concept of the subconscious. The self-awareness of culture is also based on something which remains unquestioned; this 'something' has been given various denominations, such as episteme (Foucault), cultural archetype or collective subconscious (Jung). But, paradoxically enough, pondering the boundaries of reflexivity forms part and parcel of the very reflexivity of modern culture.

Reflexivity consists in both cultural fact and cultural norm. This also holds for the field of culture we call science. Reflexivity as a cultural fact distinguishes modern science from, for example, late medieval scholasticism, which denied the possibility of criticising canonical writings and allowed merely for comments on and additions to established truth. Reflexivity as a cultural norm obliges researchers to situate themselves and their research in the context of social practices and scientific constructions. In this chapter, I try to defend normative legal scholarship before two types of challenges which have questioned not only its legitimacy but also its very possibility as a distinct scholarly enterprise. Common to these challenges is that they reject the distinction between the internal and the external point of view, so cherished by (normative) legal theory. Roger Cotterell does this in the role of social theorist, Martti Koskenniemi in that of legal scholar.

An integral part of my argument will rely on what I call the *dual citizenship of legal scholarship*.[1]

The Legal Practices of Modern Law

Modern law shows two faces to us: it can be examined both as a symbolic-normative phenomenon – a legal order – and as specialised social practices: legal practices, such as lawmaking, adjudication and legal scholarship. The emergence of the specific type of law we call modern law has been a centuries-long process. With, for example, Harold J. Berman, we can start a history of its appearance from the late eleventh and early twelfth century; from the comprehensive legal, as well as cultural, social and political, transformations which Berman has grouped together under the term 'Papal Revolution' (Berman 1983). This history can be written in terms of the shifting emphases between three main legal practices and the corresponding institutional sites: adjudication (courts), lawmaking (royal or parliamentary legislator) and legal scholarship (universities). Our history is traversed by both transnational and national plots. Modern law can be conceived as the result of certain cultural and social differentiations. Thus, in the formative period of modern law, a group of professional lawyers emerged, united amongst themselves and distinguished from legal laymen by their specific elite legal culture. This group provided the main actors for specialised legal practices, such as adjudication, legal scholarship and law-drafting. Here, a crucial role was played by the revival of Roman law after the discovery of Justinian's (482–565) compilation and the founding of universities, where Roman law was studied and taught. The universities, the first and foremost of which was in Bologna, not only constituted the institutional site for legal scholarship but also produced a transnational caste of legal professionals and a transnational, common European core of legal culture. University-based legal scholars, the glossators of the twelfth and the thirteenth centuries, and the commentators of the following centuries, filled Roman legal terms with abstract conceptual content, elaborated particular legal methods on the basis of the prevalent scholastic procedure of analysis and synthesis, and transmitted this legal-cultural heritage to students from different parts of Europe who made up Europe's transnational professional legal elite.

Despite the common cultural basis related to re-conceptualised Roman law and the scholastic methods of analysis and synthesis, the developmental paths of modern legal systems show significant national divergences. Thus, the respective weight of the main legal practices of adjudication, scholarship and lawmaking

1 In the following, I shall use 'legal scholarship' and 'legal science' as synonyms. I am aware of the specific, legal-cultural connotations of the term 'legal science'; in fact, some of these will be discussed in what follows. In my use of the term, I try to maintain a certain neutrality with regard to these alternative significations; I will, though, also argue for my own conception of the specifics of legal science.

varies in different countries and at different times. A glance at nineteenth-century England, Germany and France is instructive enough: in England, common-law courts still hold the dominant role they have occupied ever since the reign of Henry II (1133–1189) in the late twelfth century; in Germany, the ascendancy which university-based legal scholarship gained during the sixteenth-century reception of Roman law reaches its peak in the decades preceding adoption of the *Bürgerliches Gesetzbuch* (*BGB*, 1896); and in post-revolutionary France, with its exegetical school of legal science and its courts conceived as '*bouches de loi*', legislative supremacy goes almost unquestioned.

Subsequently, the differences between these modern legal systems have levelled down, and all of them have assigned a distinct role to the main legal actors – the legislature, the courts and legal scholars. If the *BGB* epitomised the triumph of German legal scholarship, it also marked the beginning of the end of its dominance; in the twentieth century, the role of the legislator and the judges clearly surpassed that of legal scientists. The development of modern society, such as the rise of the welfare state as a remedy to the dysfunctional economic and social consequences of the capitalist market economy, has led to increased instrumentalism in law and enhanced the position of the legislature. Common-law countries, including Britain, have not been spared this development. In post-Second World War Britain, legal scholarship, too, seems to have been able to carve for itself a niche among legal practices, although by no means is its status equal to that it enjoys in, say, Germany. And in France, legal academics have abandoned the (over-)deferential approach of the exegetical school, while publication of reasoned opinions of the highest courts has endowed them with an elevated precedential value (Dawson 1968, pp. 374ff.). Divergences remain: arguably, the position of the courts is still stronger in England than on the Continent, and in Continental legal systems, in turn, legislation and legal science play a more dominant role than in England. Continental observers are often inclined to lump together Britain and the United States as two common-law countries, but, actually, their legal systems display interesting disparities. During the nineteenth century, they clearly entered divergent routes of development: in the United States, legislation and university-based legal scholarship conquered much more ground than they have been allowed in Britain.

The doctrine of legal sources prevailing in a legal system records the respective positions of legal practices and the corresponding institutional actors. But, of course, it does not provide us with an explanation as to the status of lawmaking, adjudication and legal scholarship. Explaining legal modernisation is not my primary concern here. Let me only refer to such Grand Theorists as Max Weber (1864–1920) and Jürgen Habermas and suggest that long-term explanations be sought in general societal and cultural modernisation. Societal modernisation is epitomised by the formation of such 'objectified' societal structures as the capitalist economy and a centralised state; these were the economic and political structures to which Weber linked modern law's formal rationality. But modern law also reflects and exemplifies cultural modernisation, characterised by the differentiation and systematisation of such cultural spheres as science, morals and law, and art. However, the varieties of legal modernisation call for more detailed explanations. Clearly, the vicissitudes of political history have played their part. The political fragmentation of Germany goes a long way to accounting for the dominance of Roman law and the learned jurists during the long period of history beginning with the sixteenth-century reception and continuing all the way to unification of the country in 1870–1871, and the subsequent foundation of the *Reichsgericht* in 1879 and enactment of the *BGB* in 1896. In more general terms, political disintegration seems to be conducive to the high status of legal scholarship. In addition to Germany, reference can be made to Northern Italy and Southern France during the late Middle Ages (Van Caenegem 1993, pp. 84ff.). But we should not overestimate the role of political circumstances and ignore cultural factors, irreducible to political developments, in explaining the significance of scholarship among legal practices.

Despite the divergent paths to legal modernity and remaining disparities, cautious legal- and social-theoretical generalisations are warranted: in 'mature' modern legal systems, lawmaking, adjudication and legal scholarship each fulfil their specific functions with regard to one another and to the surrounding society. In this chapter, my main focus will be on contributions of legal science.

The history of legal modernisation testifies to the crucial contributions of legal scholarship. It was the achievements of university-based scholarship that led to creation of a European transnational legal-cultural basis, and it was in the universities that this basis was transmitted to the transnational corps of learned jurists. In some regions, such as Northern Italy and – from the sixteenth century onwards – Germany, legal scholars were even granted a formally recognised role in legal proceedings. In the German procedure of *Aktenversendung*, the record of a case was dispatched to a faculty of law for its collective opinion (Dawson 1968, pp. 200ff.). The procedure bore a conspicuous resemblance to the Roman practice of turning to learned jurists for their opinion (*responsa*). The prominent status of legal scholarship in Germany in the decades preceding adoption of the *BGB* could build on centuries-old antecedents. But it was only Friedrich Carl von Savigny's (1779–1861) and Carl Friedrich Puchta's (1798–1846) school of historical jurisprudence that clearly formulated legal scholarship's self-understanding of its dual citizenship: of its peculiar character as both a legal and scientific practice (see Chapter 3).

Legal practices are social practices which have specialised in production and reproduction of the law as a symbolic-normative phenomenon – as a legal order. Legal practices provide the framework for legal discourse and the individual speech acts making up this discourse. Different legal practices – such as lawmaking, adjudication and legal scholarship – fulfil different tasks in the legal system. Yet they all participate in a common discourse, and, as I will argue in this chapter, it is this discourse that links their particular contributions together.

Legal scholarship's functioning as a legal practice is most evident in doctrinal research; in what on the Continent is defined as the province of *legal dogmatics*.[2] Through its interpretive standpoints and systematisation proposals, doctrinal research contributes to production and reproduction of the legal order, and participates in ongoing legal discourse. But legal scholarship is not merely a legal practice. It is also a scientific practice and subject to the limitations and commitments ensuing from this, such as the requirement of reflexivity. Both legal and social scientists are often at a loss when attempting to define the characteristic features of legal science and its relationship to social science. It is the peculiar dual citizenship of legal science that accounts for this embarrassment.

The law as a legal order results from, and is supported by, the continuous productive and reproductive activities of legal practices, including legal scholarship. With regard to the symbolic-normative side of modern law, my main premise is its *multi-layered* nature. Law as a legal order does not consist merely of such explicit *surface-level* material as individual statutes and rulings or legal scholars' normative standpoints. The law also includes *legal-cultural* layers on which legal practices and legal discourse rely as indispensable presuppositions but which largely unfold their effects unconsciously, through legal actors' tacit pre-understanding. This legal-cultural infrastructure embraces normative, conceptual and methodological ingredients: general legal principles, concepts and theories; doctrines of legal sources; and distinct patterns of legal argumentation.

The prevailing legal culture can be conceived as sedimentation from surface-level interventions of the legislator, judges and legal scholars. Legal culture and legal practices stand in a recursive relation to each other. Legal culture is a sedimentary result of legal practices. However, with its normative, conceptual and methodological resources, it simultaneously constitutes the very possibility of future legislative, adjudicative and scholarly practices. Within the law's sedimented layers, we may discern a common core, something amounting to modern law's *deep structure*, and shared by different legal cultures. This common legal-cultural core – we could also call it modern law's *deep culture* – can be examined in terms of its normative, conceptual and methodological elements: modern law's fundamental principles and categories as well as its characteristic methods and patterns of argumentation. And the history of the appearance of modern law, starting from the turn of the eleventh century, could also be written in terms of the establishment of its normative, conceptual and methodological premises through the cumulative accomplishments of legal practices.

The Internal and External Perspective on Law

I shall begin with the challenge to the distinctiveness of normative legal scholarship posed from the direction of social science.

---

2 In what follows, I shall use the expressions 'doctrinal research' and 'legal dogmatics' as synonyms.

The distinction between the internal and external perspective on law was one of the main themes of H.L.A. Hart's (1907–1992) *The Concept of Law*. Hart had his predecessors but it is largely to his credit that this distinction has become almost a commonplace in legal theory: the legal scholar is supposed to adopt an internal, participant's point of view on law, whereas the sociologist is said to approach law from an external observer's perspective. In the view of many legal theorists, this divergence in perspective also explains the frequent breakdowns in communication between legal and social scientists. It is not uncommon for the former to blame the sociologists for completely losing sight of the law and for talking in their supposedly legal analyses about something other than law. Consequently, legal science often grants very little space for sociological insights. Sociologists are accorded merely the status of humble servants who are allowed to offer their services only on request and under conditions dictated by legal science.

In (legal) sociological debates, Niklas Luhmann (1927–1998) held a stance which comes close to the legal-theoretical distinction between the internal and external perspective. However, he arrived at his position within the framework of a systems-theoretical interpretation of society. According to his account, both jurists (legal scholars) and sociologists observe the law, but the former do this from the inside, the latter from the outside. Luhmann treats law and science as two different, autopoietically organised and operating social sub-systems, each with its own communicative network, and closed to its environment. Sociology's locus lies in the sub-system of science, and its discourse is scientific discourse. Legal scholarship, by contrast, participates in legal and not in scientific discourse. The binary code it relies on is that of law/non-law (*Recht/Unrecht*) and not that of true and untrue. Owing to its specific code, legal discourse is inevitably closed to communication taking place in other social sub-systems. But so, too, is scientific discourse; communicative closure characterises not only legal but also sociological discourse.

Luhmann (2004) concludes by sharply distinguishing between legal scholarship's self-description (*Eigenbeschreibung*) and sociology's external description (*Fremdbeschreibung*) of the law. Legal scholarship produces two types of theory, corresponding to the difference between legal dogmatics (doctrinal research) and legal theory. *Dogmatic* or *doctrinal theories* – say, of property or contract in private law or of the state as a legal person in public law – strive for conceptual consistency in law, and serve the internal norm of justice, which requires like cases to be treated alike and unlike cases unalike. In the evolution of law, that is, in the circular movement of variation, selection and stabilisation, the contribution of legal dogmatics lies in the last phase.

In Luhmann's conceptual scheme, dogmatic theories are based on self-observation of the legal system but they do not yet amount to its self-description. In *self-observation*, individual legal operations locate themselves within the structures and operations of the legal system; self-observation implies or explains that what is at issue is legal communication. When legal decisions refer to statutes or case-law, they practice self-observation and connect to previous operations of the legal system. *Self-descriptions*, in turn, are reflexive; in them, the unity of the system is reflected in the system itself. *Legal theory* is the form in which the legal system reflects itself, its unity (ibid., pp. 423ff.).

Legal theory addresses the legal system, whereas social theory functions in the scientific sub-system, with the scientific community as its audience. Luhmann is highly cautious about social theory's potential to serve the self-description of the legal system, i.e. legal theory. The reason for his caution is evident: legal and social theory are inserted into different communicative networks, into different operatively closed social sub-systems. Although legal and social theory have no opportunity for direct communication across the boundaries of the two social sub-systems of law and science, Luhmann does leave one channel open for their mutual influence.

The interaction between autopoietically operating, mutually closed social sub-systems constitutes a general problem in Luhmannian social theory. It also affects the theory of law: assuming the autopoietic functioning of social sub-systems, how can we account for the impact on law of other social sub-systems, and vice versa? One solution proposed by Luhmann is what he calls *structural coupling*. In structural coupling, individual operations – communicative acts – partake simultaneously in the functioning of two different social sub-systems: contracts are operations of the legal and economic sub-system, while a constitution establishes a structural coupling between the legal and political sub-systems (ibid., pp. 381ff.). Correspondingly, Luhmann hints at the possibility of theory acting as a medium for a structural coupling of the scientific sub-system with the reflexive self-descriptive theories of other sub-systems, such as legal theory in the system of law. The theory of which such coupling could be expected is, of course, the Luhmannian theory of autopoietic social systems (ibid., p. 459).

In sociological debates, Luhmann represents a minority position. The prevailing attitude towards the distinction between internal and external perspectives, so dear to legal scholars, appears to be rather critical. Cotterrell provides us with the opportunity to assess the critical argument.

Cotterrell is inclined to treat the distinction as a device with which normative legal theory tries to legitimise the ideological closure of legal discourse. It is this very closure which, in his view, prevents normative legal theory from attaining the level of a science. Ideology differs from science by its self-perception. It 'assumes its own completeness and its unassailable integrity, closes off inquiry because within its sphere answers are already known, specified in advance of any observations of the complexity and contradictions of experience' (Cotterrell 1996, p. 11). Because of the ideological closure of its discourse, legal scholarship tends to reject sociological information about extra-legal social reality. Legal ideology also postulates unity where, in reality, diversity, complexity and fragmentation hold sway.

For Cotterrell, Ronald Dworkin is the epitome of ideological legal thinking based on discursive closure: 'Dworkinian legal discourse generates its own closed world, observing morality, politics, and society only in its own discursive terms'.

It presents the legal sociologist with two options: 'either to accept the Dworkinian characterisation of law's discursive empire and share in legal knowledge as a participant in this discourse or else remain an outside observer unable to speak of "law" as such since law is accessible only as and through legal discourse' (ibid., pp. 103–104).

Cotterrell exhorts legal sociologists to examine the practices that reinforce, result from, and depend on the normative and discursive closure of law. But he also emphasises that legal sociology 'must ultimately deny or transgress internal-external or observer-participant distinctions'. Thus, 'in order to understand law, the legal sociologist has to understand it as a participant, or as a participant does, or rather as many different kinds of participants do – lawyers or citizens, for example, living in the world of law'. Different participants' positions exist, but none of them are 'pure': 'participation blends with observation; there are innumerable, continually shifting forms of involvement and distancing that make up the diversity of legal experience and understanding'. Legal sociology 'samples, inhabits, imagines, explores, compares, questions, and confronts different participant perspectives'. In sum, 'legal sociology is the enterprise of trying to broaden legal perspectives while understanding the narrower perspectives of particular professional or other encounterers of law' (ibid., pp. 369–370).

Thus – to summarise Professor Cotterrell's views – legal sociology is able to tell the truth of law, which ideological closure impedes legal discourse, including legal scholarship, from achieving. Sociology and legal scholarship relate to each other as science and ideology, and as science, sociology represents a superior form of knowledge in comparison with ideologically tainted legal scholarship.

In Cotterrell's account, sociology is also superior to legal scholarship in its reflexivity. Sociology is 'fundamentally reflexive, self-contextualising'; it 'must also embrace the examination of the social foundations of all disciplines and discourses, including its own'. Law (legal discourse), by contrast, lacks this inherently reflexive character; at least in normal conditions, it 'necessarily presents itself as authoritative and normatively secure' (ibid., pp. 109–110).

For his comparison between sociological and legal knowledge about law, Cotterrell takes yardsticks from scientific practices. His judgement is based on the assumption that legal scholarship – and legal discourse more generally – harbours scientific aspirations similar to those of sociology but, as a consequence of its ideological closure, is unable to live up to those aspirations. Sociology, by contrast, can open the law's normative and discursive closure and produce more adequate knowledge about social reality, including law and legal ideas. Cotterrell assesses legal scholarship merely as a scientific practice, and ignores the other side of its dual citizenship: its character as a legal practice.

Both Cotterrell and Luhmann draw a one-sided and defective picture of legal scholarship. If Cotterrell tends to reduce legal scholarship to a scientific practice, with scientific pretensions equivalent to those of sociology, Luhmann's reductionism lies in the opposite direction. He examines legal scholarship, both legal dogmatics and legal theory, merely as a legal practice and, in consequence, rejects any claims of its scientific nature. Cotterrell and Luhmann disagree on the justification of the internal–external distinction, but what they share is a reductionist view of legal scholarship. The peculiar dual citizenship of legal science should be given the attention it deserves. Legal scholarship is not misfired or deficient sociology with validity or knowledge claims identical to those of the latter; legal scholarship is not only a scientific, but also a legal practice. But nor does legal scholarship consist only of interventions in the ongoing communication about valid law, with validity claims comparable to those of lawmaking or adjudication; legal scholarship is not just a legal practice, it is also a scientific practice.

Legal Science in Legal Discourse

Legal science is a legal practice, and legal scholars participate in legal discourse with their interventions. I shall try to highlight the distinctive features of legal science and its theories through an analysis of legal discourse.

'Discourse' is a contested concept which is used in many divergent senses. Michel Foucault's (1927–1984) discourses (Foucault 1972) are not equivalent to Jürgen Habermas' discourses, while Gunther Teubner's (1989) concept of discourse receives a specific colouring from his adoption of Luhmannian autopoietic systems theory. I shall define the concept of legal discourse with the aid of J.L. Austin's (1911–1960) *speech act theory*. Legal discourse is a series or network of mutually linked legal speech acts.

Speech acts consist of three elements or dimensions: locutionary, illocutionary and perlocutionary. A *locutionary* speech act is the act *of* saying or writing. An *illocutionary* speech act is what I do *by* saying or writing something; illocutionary speech acts include arguing, contesting, promising, baptising, and so on. The *perlocutionary* dimension of speech acts is made up of the effects they have in the extra-communicative world: of what I achieve *through* saying or writing something. The effects may be intentional – when somebody who is told to shut a window does shut it – but their causal chains may also be followed beyond the conscious intentions of the speakers. Locutionary speech acts are characterised by a *sense*, illocutionary speech acts by a (illocutionary) *force*, and perlocutionary speech acts by an *effect*. The distinction between locutionary, illocutionary and perlocutionary speech acts is analytical in nature. A locutionary speech act is also an illocution, and an illocutionary speech act is not possible without a locution. In addition, speech acts usually have perlocutionary effects in extra-linguistic reality.

Speech acts achieve an illocutionary force when they meet the requirements of their *felicity conditions*. These, in turn, are defined by particular social or cultural conventions: a speech act is a promise if it fulfils the culturally-defined felicity conditions of this type of illocutionary speech act. The felicity conditions of illocutionary speech acts may concern, say, the person entitled to make the speech act or the appropriate circumstances for making it. The felicity conditions of speech acts may also be determined by explicit legal norms; at issue, then, are *legal-institutional speech acts*. An example of such a speech act is a declaration of marriage: the formula of the declaration, the persons entitled to make it, and the appropriate circumstances of doing so are all defined by legal norms.[3]

How does legal discourse diverge from other varieties of social discourse? Distinctive to legal discourse is, firstly, its *specific theme*: the existence (validity), interpretation, systematisation and application of legal norms. Legal discourse consists of speech acts that take a position on these normative issues and which, thus, contribute to the ongoing discussion on the contents of the legal order in force. Speech acts attain an illocutionary force as contributions to legal discourse, if and when they are recognised and assessed as such by other contributions. In the following I shall call them *legal speech acts*. Some, but not all, of them are of a legal-*institutional* character; then at least some of their felicity conditions are determined by explicit legal norms. This is the case with, first of all, the laws of the legislator and the decisions of the judges. In order for a speech act to be recognised in legal discourse as a law, it must conform to constitutional provisions on lawmaking procedure. Correspondingly, a speech act can only amount to a court decision if it is acknowledged to meet the criteria set up by procedural law.

However, the felicity conditions of legal speech acts are defined not only by legal norms but also by social conventions of other types. Legal speech acts differ in relation to their level of institutionalisation. The conditions and procedures of legal scholarship are not legally determined. Unlike the laws of the legislator and the decisions of the judges, the discursive interventions of legal scholars do not possess a legal-institutional character. Their illocutionary force and their distinctive weight in ongoing discourse on the contents of the law are based on legal-cultural conventions, such as the prevailing *doctrine of legal sources*. Hence, the status which legal scholars' interventions enjoy in legal discourse varies from one legal culture to another. But nor is the illocutionary force of speech acts of legislators and judges determined solely by legal norms.

Different types of speech act carry different weight in legal discourse. The *internal* hierarchy of legal regulations – the constitution, acts of parliament, decrees and other by-laws – is usually legally confirmed, often by explicit constitutional provisions. In turn, the internal hierarchy of court decisions follows the institutional judicial hierarchy, which is also regulated by law. By contrast, the constitution, or the legal order in general, does not contain provisions on the *respective* weight and hierarchical order of different kinds of legal speech acts, such as laws and other legal regulations, court decisions, and scholarly interventions. This depends on the culturally varying doctrine of legal sources, as shown by the remaining divergences between Continental and common-law legal systems.

We can sum up: the prevailing legal culture ultimately establishes which speech acts are included in legal discourse, who is allowed to participate in this

3 In my exposition of speech act theory, I have relied on Austin (1984) and Searle (1988).

discourse, and what weight their interventions carry. It is on the basis of their shared legal culture that participants recognise each other's speech acts and treat them as contributions to legal discourse.

Speech acts making up legal discourse raise particular *validity claims*, which, then, are assessed in future discourse. I suggest that a conceptual distinction be made between 'illocutionary force' and 'validity', although, as will be argued below, a certain overlap between the two does exist. In expounding their specificities, the founder of speech act theory, J.L. Austin, again provides us with a clue. He points out that although a speech act meets its felicity conditions and obtains an illocutionary force, this does not preclude its criticism by other yardsticks. These vary according to the type of speech act at issue: such as truth/non-truth or right/wrong (Austin 1984, pp. 146–147). Thus, it is only subsequent to a speech act's recognition as an assertion that the truth or non-truth of its locutionary content is judged. Correspondingly, although a legal-institutional speech act succeeds – the legislator's speech act is recognised as a law or a judge's speech act as a court decision – statutes and rulings can still, in future legal discourse, be examined and criticised in terms of their validity.

The validity of legal norms possesses both a formal and a substantive aspect (Tuori 2002a, pp. 262ff.). The *formal validity* of a legal norm overlaps with the felicity conditions of the corresponding speech act of the legislator. The central element of formal validity consists of the requirement that legal norms be established in adherence to the constitutionally-regulated lawmaking procedure. This requirement also defines the main felicity condition of the legislator's speech act. The speech act succeeds and attains illocutionary force when the other participants in legal discourse, such as judges and other law-enforcers, accept its formal validity claim and, by the same token, recognise the legal norm expressed in its locutionary part as valid. If the courts come to the conclusion that the norm (the norm candidate) has not been adopted under the procedure laid down in the constitution, they do not consider it valid, nor do they apply it in their decisions. In this case, the speech acts fails and does not achieve illocutionary force.

The *substantive validity* of legal norms can be approached from the perspective of both their legitimacy – their moral and ethical justifiability – and their expediency or instrumental rationality. What is crucial for the illocutionary force of the legislator's speech act is formal validity. However, the respective legal norm (norm candidate) may stand in such contradiction with substantive validity criteria that the courts leave the norm unapplied. Thus, a formally valid norm's contradiction with fundamental human-rights principles may be considered so flagrant that the courts refuse to apply it. Here we have a new instance of failure of the legislator's speech act. Rights-based constitutional review, as it were, institutionalises substantive validity control and assigns it an immediate legal bearing (see Chapter 8).

However, even when a law or ruling has attained illocutionary force and has been applied by the courts and other law-enforcing authorities, its substantive validity is always open to fresh assessment. To take a conspicuous example, the merits of pivotal rulings of the US Supreme Court – say, *Dredd Scott*, *Lochner* or *Brown* v. *Board of Education* – are constantly re-examined in legal discourse. The reasons supposedly supporting the substantive validity of laws and court decisions can be challenged in subsequent legal speech acts, without this in any way affecting their illocutionary (legal) force. When discussing the moral or ethical justifiability or instrumental rationality of a particular ruling or statute, legal scholarship participates in the (re-)appraisal of the substantive validity of previous legal speech acts. At the same time, with their own interventions legal scholars, too, raise specific validity claims which, then, are subject to testing in future legal discourse, and not only by other scholars, but by judges and the legislator as well.

It is precisely this ongoing reciprocal testing of validity claims that links individual legal speech acts together and that also makes the legal scholar a participant in legal discourse. Legal science lacks the legal-institutional aspect of lawmaking and adjudication; the law does not determine the right to exercise legal science, nor does it regulate its procedures. This entails that the validity claims or felicity conditions of legal scholars' speech acts do not display a corresponding formal aspect. Instead of legal-institutional determinations, the felicity conditions of scholarly interventions, as well as their role in legal discourse, are in their entirety grounded in culturally-varying social conventions, such as the predominant doctrine of legal sources. But this does not deprive legal scholars of their title of participants in legal discourse.

Typical of legal science is a dual normativity: it not only examines legal norms but its results, too, possess a normative character. The contributions of legal science entail explicit, or at least implicit, normative claims, be it a question of interpretive standpoints, doctrinal (legal dogmatical) theories, or what Luhmann has called reflexion theories, that is, theories aiming at a self-description of the legal system as a whole (Luhmann 2004, p. 54). Legal scholarship participates in legal discourse and appraises the validity claims of speech acts by the legislator and judges, as well as other legal scholars. And, correspondingly, with its own contributions it presents normative validity claims whose significance is weighed in future legal discourse. Through their normative consequences, the interpretive standpoints and theories of legal science affect what counts as valid law, thus altering the state of the legal system. This also holds for legal theories as self-descriptions of the legal system: in Luhmann's words, 'the system itself changes if a theory of the system is constructed within the system and the object of the description changes through that description' (Luhmann 2004, p. 458).

In the distinction between theoretical and practical discourses, legal discourse falls into the latter class. *Theoretical* discourses deal with the *truth claims* of speech acts, practical discourses with claims of *normative correctness*. All types of legal speech act raise a claim of normative correctness, but this claim shows type-specific particularities: the validity criteria of the legislator's speech acts are not identical to those of court decisions, and the yardsticks by which the contributions of the legal scholar are assessed also demonstrate some distinctive features.

Lawmaking is a combination of legal and political practices; in Luhmann's terms, the legislator's speech acts establish a structural coupling between the legal and the political system. This leaves its imprint on their validity claims. For the political system, legislation is, above all, a means for achieving political aims, which adds a purposive rational or instrumentalist element to the criteria of substantive validity. In adjudication, the emphasis lies, not in justifying the relevant legal norm as such, but in applying it appropriately to the particular facts of the case at hand (Günther 1993). This, of course, affects the claims of normative correctness which court decisions entail. Finally, scholarly contributions are appraised as products of not only a legal but also a scientific practice. Again, the dual citizenship of legal scholarship plays its part.

Though legal speech acts are primarily assessed by their normative correctness, their validity criteria are not devoid of elements of truth, either. The instrumental rationality of legislation depends on the reliability of factual assumptions about society and societal causal relationships underlying legislative policy decisions. Courts often adhere to a consequentialist argumentation, based on more or less warranted assessments of the probable factual effects of their decisions. The interpretive standpoints of legal scholars, in turn, are related to (hypothetical) fact descriptions, and legal theories and systematisation proposals are underpinned by conscious or unconscious social-theoretical assumptions. But, arguably, in legal discourse truth is subjected to normative correctness.

Legal argumentation is normative argumentation, and this goes even for argumentation in legal science. Legal scholarship's principle objective is not to procure true descriptions or causal explanations of extra-legal social reality. Legal science cannot be declared a loser in a competition with sociology over which academic discipline offers the most adequate social descriptions or explanations. Legal science does not take part in any such competition, nor does it occupy the pole of ideology opposite to that of sociology as science, as Cotterrell, for instance, is prone to contend. In the analysis of legal discourse, we should reject (neo-)Althusserian opposition between ideology and science for the simple reason that it completely loses sight of the normativity of legal argumentation.

The concepts of legal discourse and legal speech acts help us to perceive the differences between legal and social scientific research on law and, correspondingly, between the internal and external perspective. Distinctive to legal science is an internal, participant's point of view. Legal scholars participate in legal discourse, assess the validity of other participants' speech acts, and present with their own speech acts validity claims which are then discussed in subsequent legal discourse. The interventions of social scientists are not legal speech acts; nor do they raise such claims of normative correctness which would be tested in legal discourse. The results of social science can become part of legal discourse only if the participants in this discourse resort to them in their speech acts; for instance, as arguments supporting a certain interpretive standpoint in adjudication or legal dogmatics. Why and how are social scientists excluded from legal discourse? The reason lies in the social conventions that define the illocutionary force of legal speech acts, such as the prevailing doctrine of legal sources. These conventions do not accord social scientists a participant's position in legal discourse. Accordingly, the validity claims of social science emphasise the dimension of truth, instead of normative correctness.

My concept of legal discourse differs from Luhmann's way of defining legal practices as communicative practices and the legal system as a communicative network. In Luhmann's account, what distinguishes legal communication is the binary code of law/non-law. The legal system comprises all communicative acts employing this code irrespective of the institutional position of their subjects. Hence, not only legal professionals but also laymen participate in legal communication. I have proposed that 'legal discourse' be defined through the specific theme and validity claims of legal speech acts. Clearly, this concept, too, can be used in a wide sense, also covering debates within the public at large. However, the important role that differentiation and specialisation play in modern law supports a narrower definition: legal discourse comprises only legal speech acts within practices specialised in producing and reproducing the legal order, such as lawmaking, adjudication and legal scholarship.

Cotterrell has criticised the legal-theoretical internal/external distinction for ignoring the multiplicity of participant positions. If a participant's position is specified through the concept of legal discourse, this multiplicity can be given due attention: it is manifest in the differentiation of legal speech acts and their validity claims. In its background we can depict the divergent functions that different legal practices fulfil in the legal system. However, the variety of participant positions should not be allowed to obscure their points of connection; their networking to a discourse on the contents of the legal order in force. This networking is facilitated by the common *legal-cultural pre-understanding* shared by legal actors occupying different participant positions.

Norms and Facts

The common legal-cultural pre-understanding of legal actors includes the basic distinction – in Luhmann's terms *Leitunterscheidung* – between facts and norms. This distinction is central to legal scholarship, too. However, in legal sociology it seems to evaporate. What for lawyers constitutes norms, and, as such, something distinct from facts, appears for sociologists as facts among other facts; for instance, in the wake of Max Weber as conceptions in the minds of social actors, causally influencing their behaviour. In its descriptive and explanatory accounts, legal sociology may well – and even should – be sensitive to the significance of the facts/norms distinction for legal discourse and the functioning of the legal system. For all that, it does not itself adopt the distinction but treats it as a fact about the law.

Employing the distinction between norm and fact, legal science focuses on the former pole. In spite of the emphasis on the normative side, legal discourse deals not only with norms but also with facts. Notably, however, within the purview of legal discourse and knowledge, facts do not appear independently of norms. In law, facts are dependent on norms and observed through norms. This is a fact of which the institutional theory of law especially has reminded us (MacCormick and Weinberger 1986). In legal discourse and knowledge, facts appear in the guise of *legal-institutional facts*. The subjugation of facts to norms also affects those validity claims raised in legal discourse that concern the depiction of extra-legal social (or psychological) reality. The truth claims of legal speech acts are not identical to the truth claims raised and assessed in sociological discourse.

That law's 'truth' differs from sociology's truth is already perceptible by examining the role of facts in court proceedings. There, the 'truth' of facts is ultimately determined not by criteria employed in empirical sciences but by those provided by procedural and substantive legal norms. Facts are only facts if legally appropriate and sufficient evidence has been presented to support them and if the court acknowledges them as facts for legal purposes. In addition, legal facts are selected facts, with substantive legal norms providing the criteria for pruning. For example, not all that witnesses recount in their statements is considered legally relevant and included in the factual premise of the court's decision. 'Legal truth' is only attributed to facts accorded legal significance by the norm to be applied in the case at hand. In legal proceedings, facts are legal-institutional facts as defined by the institutional theory of law. The peculiarity of legal truth is manifest in the legal institution of *res judicata*. Unlike scientific truth, legal truth cannot, as a rule, be challenged afterwards by new evidence; legal facts retain their status in the face of counter-evidence presented after the proceedings have ended. Exceptions to this rule exist, but these too are legally determined. In the relationship between facts and norms, the latter have the last word.

Law's normativity also influences the facts that legal science deals with. In its interpretive task, legal dogmatics construes hypothetical sets of facts, which function as factual premises in recommendations for statutory interpretation. Such typified facts could perhaps be compared with Weberian ideal types (Weber 1988, pp. 190ff.; Prewo 1979, pp. 85ff.). But their role is entirely different. They are not tools for empirical research but for normative argumentation.

So facts appear in legal discourse as factual premises of court decisions and the interpretive standpoints of doctrinal research. Besides, facts may enter judicial or legal dogmatic reasoning through consequentialist argumentation. Then, facts play a role in formulating not only the factual but also the normative premise: alternative interpretations of statutes or precedents are appraised in the light of their probable factual outcomes. But even in consequentialist argumentation, norms still prevail over facts. Facts are relied on in finding and justifying the correct interpretation of norms – in establishing, not the truth about facts, but the 'truth' about norms. And if it turns out that the court was mistaken in its prediction of subsequent developments in extra-legal reality, this does not, as a rule, strip the decision of its legal validity.

Facts have a role to play in legal theories as well. Dogmatic theories organise general legal concepts and principles of different fields of law, such as contract law, criminal law or constitutional law. As I argue in Chapter 6, the focus of such theories is on legal institutions, understood in the sense indicated by Savigny. In Savigny's conception, legal institutions were related to legal relationships, which possessed both a normative and a factual side, the latter consisting of the factual social relationships (*Lebensverhältnisse*) regulated by legal norms (see Chapter 3). Accordingly, doctrinal theories focusing on legal institutions – say, private law theories of contract or property, or constitutional-law theories of separation of powers – always refer, not only to legal norms, but also to social facts. They are always anchored in a certain conception of extra-legal reality, subject to legal regulation: private-law theories imply a particular view of the economy, constitutional-law theories of the state and the political system, international-law theories of international relations, and so on. However, the main thrust in legal dogmatic theories does not lie in the precise portrayal or adequate explanation of extra-legal social phenomena. Doctrinal theories are argumentative tools, destined to be employed in adjudication and other legal practices. They contribute to the law's coherence and the consistency and predictability of adjudication, and in so doing promote the normative aims of formal justice and equality.

Let us take as an example constitutional theories of separation of powers. In these theories, 'power' refers to legally defined competences and not to factual social or political power. The relations of competence, as determined in the doctrine of separation of powers, do not supply direct information on factual power relations between state organs or the political and social groupings holding sway in them. Separation of powers as a normative problem of constitutional law should not be confused with the factual division of power between political and social actors as an issue of political science or historiography. These problems presuppose different approaches and different manners of argumentation. Constitutional doctrine does not aim to describe or explain the factual functioning of the political system. It does not participate in the discourse of political science, nor does it raise validity claims to be judged by the criteria of this discourse. Its communicative network consists of (constitutional) legal discourse.

We should not, of course, deny the inter-connections between legal and factual division of powers. Constitutional law and the doctrine of separation of powers affect factual power relations. A 'context-sensitive' history of ideas serves to remind us of the socio-political reality underlying constitutional doctrine and discourse; of the power constellations between social classes and groups. These constellations, for their part, account for doctrinal positions, but on the other hand, they themselves have also been influenced by interventions of legal scholars (e.g. Althusser 1959). In Finland in 1917–1919, in the aftermath of independence from Russia and a civil war, debates on the constitutional division of powers in which leading constitutionalists actively participated were very clearly part of the then socio-political power struggle. The Weimar Republic also proffers ample material that evidences links connecting constitutional doctrine to its ideological and political context (see Chapter 4). Constitutional scholars' interventions have perlocutionary ideological and political consequences; indeed, scholars may even consciously strive for them. But the specific normative character of legal doctrine is linked to the illocutionary rather than perlocutionary dimension of scholarly contributions.

As pointed out by Cotterrell, among others, legal ideas have social causes, so that the emergence of dogmatic theories can be explained sociologically; thus, only in certain social conditions, at a certain historical point in time, do modern concepts of property or contract or the legal concept of the state become possible. The modern concept of property could be elaborated only after market relations had extended to cover landed property and the medieval, feudalist doctrine of divided property had lost its societal basis; and the doctrine of the legal personality of the state only after differentiation of economic and political relations and the emergence of the modern, centralised state.

In legal practices, doctrinal theories generally operate unconsciously. But this should not be interpreted as a symptom of their supposedly ideological character. Instead of the binary opposition between ideology and science, it is more apposite to approach dogmatic theories through Anthony Giddens' notions of practical and discursive knowledge, or Michel Foucault's *savoir* and *connaissance*. *Practical knowledge* is tacit knowledge which is indispensable for the conduct of our daily routines but about which we are not immediately aware nor do we need to be. We become conscious of its significance only when confronted with problems. In such a situation we have to convert our practical, tacit knowledge into *discursive* form (Giddens 1979, pp. 24–25).

In legal practices, lawyers inevitably employ doctrinal theories with their principles and concepts but are not necessarily conscious of their importance. *Nulla poena sine lege* is applied in criminal-law and *pacta sunt servanda* in contract-law cases, although they may not even be mentioned in the court's argumentation. Only in hard cases do judges feel the need to transform their knowledge of dogmatic theories from practical into discursive form, to specify and assess their significance. In routine cases, theories operate as practical, tacit knowledge and – we may add – as a central element of lawyers' professional competence.

Doctrinal theories constitute an integral part of the common legal culture shared by legal actors participating in different legal practices. During their education, future lawyers are already internalising the fundamentals of this unifying culture; indeed, it is this internalised legal-cultural pre-understanding that turns them into lawyers. Nevertheless, if the need arises, legal discourse can take a reflexive stance towards its cultural and doctrinal premises. This is exactly what happens when legal scholars elaborate or re-formulate dogmatic theories, or when courts in hard cases ponder the significance and precise contents of legal principles, and, by the same token, contribute to doctrinal renewal. All this attests to the reflexive potential of legal discourse under the conditions of modern law. The specific normativity of legal discourse entails a particular inertia but does not create any irremovable blockage for development of dogmatic theories.

In Cotterrell's view, one indication of the inferiority of legal discourse and knowledge in relation to sociology is their lack of reflexivity. However, the deliberate elaboration of dogmatic theories already tells of reflexivity in legal discourse. This reflexivity is even more conspicuous in the comprehensive reflexion theories reflecting on law's unity.

These theories, too, imply a conception of extra-legal social reality. This conception is not always – perhaps not even in the majority of cases – explicitly spelled out, which warrants terming it a *hidden social theory*. Luhmann has distinguished between two main alternative accounts of law's unity in contemporary legal-theoretical discussion. *Rationalist theories* seek to base law's unity on rationally justifiable principles. *Positivist theories*, in turn, employ a doctrine of legal sources which derives legal validity from explicit decisions by the legislature and the courts (Luhmann 2004, pp. 440–448). The representatives of rationalist theories include such figures as Ronald Dworkin and Jürgen Habermas, while those of the positivist camp include Hans Kelsen (1881–1973) and H.L.A. Hart.

Cotterrell, for his part, has written of *ratio* and *voluntas* as the two poles between which legal discourse shuttles. *Voluntas* represents 'the element of sovereign will, coercive power, or unchallengeable political authority that shapes legal doctrine and is expressed through it ... the co-ordinating and hierarchical characteristics of law as a system of *political* control'. *Ratio*, in turn, is 'the element of reason or principle that structures and presents doctrine in patterns of ideas whose strength to bind and convince the citizen (and the lawyer or official) comes from their logical persuasiveness, normative consistency, or rational coherence' (Cotterrell 1996, p. 317). Theories emphasising *ratio* or *voluntas*, respectively, clearly imply differing conceptions of law's social environment. Again, we might refer to Cotterrell, now to his thesis of *community* and *imperium* 'as images of society that are presupposed in legal doctrine and rhetoric'. The former is 'the image of a cohesive association of politically autonomous people' and the latter 'the image of individual subjects of a superior political authority' (ibid., p. 223).

To sum up, compelling reasons exist for not rejecting the distinction between the internal and the external perspective on law. This distinction should not be treated merely as a legitimising move intended to justify the ideological closure of legal discourse. Legal science is not only a scientific but also a legal practice. As such, legal science partakes in legal discourse, and this imposes on legal science a normativity foreign to the enterprise of sociology. Legal discourse does also deal with extra-legal reality, but views it through normative lenses. The truth in law, and for law, is not identical to the truth in sociology, while the validity claims of legal discourse are not similar to those of sociology. Legal discourse should not be seen as flawed sociology, producing ideological conceptions of society which call for correction and rectification from the side of the science of sociology. Legal science adopts an internal view on law, relies on the constitutive distinction between norms and facts, and raises normative validity claims addressed to subsequent legal discourse. Sociology's position is diverse: it does not participate in legal discourse, it is not bound to adopt the distinction between norms and facts, and its outcomes do not display pretensions of normative validity. Sociology remains an outsider to law and its perspective an external one. As many sociologists – and

Professor Cotterrell is one of them – have emphasised, sociology must include the lawyer's understanding of law in its descriptive and explanatory accounts. But meeting this requirement does not transform sociologists into participants in legal discourse. Their talk remains talk *about* law also when discussing talk *in* law.

What Can Legal Science Learn from Social Science?

Luhmann is acutely aware of legal science's participation in legal discourse and of its ensuing normativity. But his autopoietic systems theory leads him to ignore the other side in legal scholarship's ambivalent position, namely its character as a scientific practice. Legal science shares with other scientific practices certain fundamental commitments concerning, for instance, methodology, argumentation and publicity; these commitments include reflexivity. It also shares with other disciplines the same institutional framework, with universities as the most important loci.

As a legal practice, legal scholarship differs in important respects from adjudication and lawmaking as the other main practices of modern law. Its outcomes receive their binding force only through other legal practices, through their acceptance by judges, lawmakers, or both. Ever since the late eleventh century, the history of legal science is inseparably linked to universities. But although universities have constituted the main institutional locus of legal scholarship, they do not enjoy a similar legally-secured privilege on legal scholarship as do the legislative bodies with regard to lawmaking or courts with regard to adjudication. And although legal scholarship complies with certain methodological rules, these are not legal norms as are the rules regulating lawmaking procedure or legal proceedings in courts. The methodological rules of legal scholarship are not of a legal but of a scientific nature. In fact, the distinctive features of legal scholarship as a legal practice are largely due to the scientific aspect of its dual identity.

In turn, legal scholarship's scientific identity appears to be rather insecure. This, too, is a consequence of its dual citizenship, of its membership not only among scientific practices but also among legal practices. If its peculiarities as a legal practice derive from its also being a scientific practice, the same holds conversely: legal scholarship largely owes its particular features as a scientific practice to its being a legal practice, too. Its character as a legal practice, its participation in legal discourse, accounts for its dual normativity: a normativity that extends both to its research objects and to its results. This specific normativity lies in the background of legal science's almost continuous bad conscience, its qualms about its scientific nature.

If we are to believe Harold J. Berman (1983, pp. 151–164), the legal science fashioned by the scholastic jurists in the late Middle Ages constituted the prototype of modern Western science in general. Be that as it may, the subsequent history of legal scholarship rather speaks of a weak self-identity as a scientific practice and of a corollary need to seek guidance from some other, model science. In different cultures and at different times, this position has been occupied by diverse disciplines. German eighteenth-century rationalistic natural law theorists employed geometric models of argumentation; the German historical school of the following century borrowed from contemporary evolutionary theory and evolutionary linguistics; and the later conceptual jurisprudence (*Begriffsjurisprudenz*) relied from time to time even on the vocabulary of natural science. In the United States, the 'Langdellian' legal science of the late nineteenth and early twentieth centuries assumed influences from several more established academic disciplines, among them geometry, Spencer's evolutionary theory, and contemporary natural sciences. In their programme of scientification of law, the Legal Realists, in turn, drew their main inspiration from social sciences. And, to come closer to our own times, recent decades have witnessed a plethora of law-and- … approaches, each of them trying to prop up the scientific credentials of legal scholarship with the backing of its chosen model discipline.

Legal scholarship's tendency to borrow methodologies from other disciplines has been commented on by, among others, Jack Balkin (1996). He has also argued that legal scholarship's professional focus compensates for its intellectual deficiencies; consequently, law cannot be entirely absorbed by any other discipline. 'Law is continuously invaded but never conquered', concludes Cotterrell's (1996, p. 178) summary of Balkin's analysis. To put it in my own terms, what shelters legal scholarship from conquest is its safe haven as one of the legal practices. Paradoxically enough, the non-scientific side of legal scholarship's dual citizenship shields its independence as a scientific practice!

Normative legal scholarship is not and does not pretend to be sociology, nor should it be judged as a defective version of that discipline. But legal scholarship's inclusion among legal practices does not necessarily make it deaf to sociological insights; it only creates a filter which these insights must traverse before they can find their way into legal discourse. Sociology's talk *about* law has first to be translated into legal science's talk *in* law. Conceding this much, we can still criticise Luhmann's (and Teubner's) thesis that sociology and law as discursive realms are closed to each other. Thanks to legal scholarship's dual identity, what it hears from social sciences is far more than mere noise (cf. Teubner 1989). Legal scholarship can learn much from sociology, political science, or economics, even if these have no means of imposing its lessons, of 'conquering' legal scholarship.

Lessons may be at least threefold in nature: argumentative, critical and reflexive. Consequentialist argumentation gains in cogency if predictions concerning the factual effects of legal decisions are supported by sociological evidence; this is the *argumentative* lesson that social science can offer to legal scholarship. But here, too, the truth of social science is subjected to legal normativity. The methodological aspect of legal culture – in Koskenniemi's (2005, pp. 563ff.) terms, the grammar of legal argumentation – includes the doctrine of legal sources. This doctrine determines the place of consequentialist arguments and social scientific insights in legal argumentation.

I have stressed the normative character of legal theories. But this specific normativity does not deny the legitimacy or fruitfulness of their *critical* assessment from the side of sociology. Sociology can try to expose the conception of society implied by dogmatic theories and appraise it by social scientific standards. It may well be that the 'hidden social theory' of legal dogmatics is no longer grounded in a sociologically adequate description of extra-legal social reality. Given the inherent fossilising tendency of dogmatic theories, such findings should not come as a great surprise.

Doctrinal theories lie at the kernel of lawyers' professional culture, imbuing their tacit legal pre-understanding. However, these theories are not closed to reflexive assessment and explicit development. In Continental legal cultures, in particular, legal scholarship is engaged in consciously elaborating doctrinal theories in order to improve their responsiveness to the legal problems of a rapidly changing society. In this task, legal scholarship should be receptive to sociological criticism of its doctrines' social-theoretical premises.

Hence, social science can assist doctrinal legal research by excavating and explicating its implicit social-theoretical assumptions and judging them in the light of the sociological truth. But is this not exactly what the programme of critique of ideology amounts to? Has my own argument ultimately led me to examine the relationship between legal scholarship and sociology against the (neo-)Marxist distinction between ideology and science? This is not the case. In my account, the sociological critique of legal doctrine does not employ the yardsticks of legal discourse and remains a critique from the outside. Again, we have to be aware of the normative aspect of doctrinal legal theories and of their role in the service of formal justice. The peculiar inertia of legal concepts and doctrinal theories may perform an important task in the functioning of the legal system, and so should not simplistically be attributed to sheer ideological blindness. Too much susceptibility to ever-new sociological insights would deprive dogmatic theories of their potential to secure the consistency of application of law and to promote formal justice. Seen in this light, what Cotterrell has called the closure of legal discourse is a consequence, not of ideological self-deception but of the specific normativity of this discourse. In addition, the reflexive capacity of legal discourse shows this closure to be merely relative and suspensive, but not absolute.

Dogmatic theories display an in-built inertia, deriving from their stabilising task in the functioning of the legal system. However, this inevitable and, at least to a certain extent, normatively desirable immobility should not make dogmatic theories immune to a sociologically-grounded critique of their social-theoretical premises. Even comprehensive legal theories – Luhmann's reflexion theories – should be sensitive to disclosure and critical assessment of their sociological assumptions. The exposé and possible criticism of legal theories' implicit social-theoretical assumptions provides an important meeting-place for legal and social scientific discourse; perhaps this is the very locus of a 'structural coupling' between law and sociology! However, establishing a fertile line of communication requires not only legal scholarship's receptiveness to social scientific criticism but also social science's awareness of the tasks that legal theories fulfil in the legal system and of the specific normativity these tasks entail.

Under the conditions of modern law, the possibility of the law's internal criticism reaches beyond explicit legal material – such as individual statutes and decisions – to its legal-cultural underpinnings. But what is difficult to perceive from the internal perspective of legal actors is the position that law and legal discourse, including legal science, hold in society as a whole. Such a perception seems to require an external, social scientific point of view. Here, social science can enhance legal scholars' awareness of the social presuppositions and consequences of their enterprise and, thus, add to their *reflexive* self-conception.

The fragile self-identity of legal scholars may lead them to think that they are merely on the receiving end in the learning processes between social and legal science. But this is not so: in their research on law, social scientists depend on the assistance of legal scholarship. In order to be able to talk *about* law, sociologists must understand talk *in* law. They must adopt what Neil MacCormick (1981, p. 37) has termed the hermeneutic point of view: although they view the law from the external perspective of an observer, they have to comprehend what it means for a participant to adopt an internal perspective. This is only possible given familiarity with the grammar and vocabulary which the participants employ in their talk *in* law. Legal science can teach social scientists the language of law.

As Weber already noted, legal science also provides legal sociology with epistemological and causal support. Sociological research on law should be guided by the fact that legal facts are institutional facts. In empirical sociological studies, legal phenomena – say, the elements of legal proceedings – can only be identified through legal concepts, i.e. concepts worked out and systematised by legal doctrine. Legal scholarship may even have a causal significance in empirical legal sociological inquiry: it is justified to assume that in legal disputes, parties and their lawyers are guided by prevailing dogmatic interpretations and theories (Tuori 2002a, pp. 298–299).

The Critic's Narrative of Law and Legal Discourse

With its claims to be able to tell the truth about law and legal discourse, social science challenges normative legal scholarship from without, as it were. Normative legal scholarship has faced contenders from within legal science as well. In addition to positivist and rationalist strands, twentieth-century legal science includes a third, *realist* trend. The realist approach tends to deny the law's normativity, its *Sollen*-dimension, by reducing it to empirically observable facts of *Sein*; such as the behaviour of judges and other enforcers of the law. But rejection of the legitimacy of normative legal science does not necessarily presuppose an empiricist legal ontology. It is also possible simply to deny the scientificity of normative legal scholarship participating in legal discourse, and to require that academic legal science maintain an external, observer's perspective and refrain from normative standpoints.

This is the stance of the collective character in contemporary legal science whom I call the *Critic*, already introduced in the Preface, and whom I have clothed in female form. As will be shown in the following chapters, the Critic's narrative has far-reaching historical roots; precursors include Jeremy Bentham (1748–1832), even Thomas Hobbes (1588–1679). A kinship with some of the American Legal Realists of the first half of the twentieth century is also clear. The foremost present-day Critics include scholars standing close to the (former?) Critical Legal Studies movement, such as Martti Koskenniemi, Duncan Kennedy and David Kennedy.

In the Critic's narrative, the law appears, first of all, as an instrumental tool in the service of individual or group interests: legal actors' personal or collective interests; the 'institutional' interests of a legal institution, such as a court; clients' interests; or the interests of social classes and groups. The law's instrumentality permeates and determines legal discourse. Legal actors and participants in legal discourse adopt a strategic posture towards the law and other legal actors. This guides the normative standpoints that legal actors take on interpreting and applying the law or on the balancing of principles and counter-principles: legal actors are inclined to advocate positions favouring the interests they are – consciously or unconsciously – pursuing. Law and legal discourse include consensus and universalism, but these result from strategic action, from the hegemony achieved by a particular standpoint. In legal discourse, the 'raw' preferences of social actors are translated into universalist legal language, so that, by the same token, particular interests are presented as general and 'objective':

> Consensus is, after all, the end-point of a hegemonic process in which some agent or institution has succeeded in making its position seem the universal or "neutral" position ... All law is about lifting idiosyncratic ("subjective") interests and preferences from the realm of the special to that of the general ("objective") in which they lose their particular, political colouring and come to seem natural, necessary or even pragmatic. (Koskenniemi 2005, p. 597)

American Realists approached the law from a practicing lawyer's perspective (Leiter 2007, pp. 71–72). Here, too, the Critic follows in the footsteps of her Realist predecessors: the Critic's narrative focuses on legal disputes, where the parties, aided by their lawyers, try to make their interests prevail. As seen from this angle, legal argumentation appears as strategic action aiming at benefits at the expense of the other party. Consequently, Koskenniemi argues that 'the lawyer comes to a normative problem always from some perspective, to defend a client, an interest, a theory'; therefore, 'the field of legal argument is constructed in an adversarial way: a defence is meaningful only as defence against something' (Koskenniemi 2005, pp. 598–599).

The Critic may also undertake to disclose legal discourse's deep structure. But here, too, the paradigmatic perspective is that of legal disputes and legal counsellors. Koskenniemi calls the infrastructure of legal discourse its *grammar*. This grammar consists of argumentative rules governing the production of arguments which are recognised as valid in legal discourse. In Ferdinand de Saussure's (1868–1943) terms, these rules constitute the *langue*, while the arguments produced in adherence to them the *parole*, of the law (of legal discourse). In Koskenniemi's account, the grammar of international law is based on the 'binary opposition' of (realist) apology and (normative) utopia. What is essential is that grammar does not dictate the substantive content of legal argumentation, of discursive interventions. It only provides the discourse with its basic structure: international-law discourse alternates between the poles of apology and utopia, which, in deconstructionist analysis, can be shown to depend on and to be constantly transformed into each other. Legal discourse displays both strict structural formalism and vague substantive indeterminacy. The deep structure of the discourse, its *langue*, in no way obstructs but, rather, facilitates the discussants' strategic posture, which determines the contents of their *parole* (Koskenniemi 1999a, p. 363). The strategic stance is imposed on legal actors by the law's fundamentally adversarial nature. The reconstruction of legal discourse's deep structure does not proceed from 'the adversarial nature of (international) law … (as) an anthropological or sociological datum about it – even less (as) an essentialist claim about its "nature"'; the law's adversarial nature is 'an internal, constitutive presupposition of legal argument itself'. Antagonism is 'embedded in the *raison d'être* of the law itself and carried within it as the endlessly repeated rejection of its "other" ("discretion", "politics", "power", "violence", "corruption" etc.)' (Koskenniemi 2005, p. 599).

In the Critic's narrative, the strategic approach that ensues from the law's adversarial character affects not only the argumentation of legal counsellors but guides the interventions of other legal actors, too. The narrative tells about a strategic power game over defining the contents of the law; over the universalisation and objectivation of particular interests.

Judges and legal scholars do not – at least not directly – pursue the interests and strategic aims of the parties to individual legal disputes. Nonetheless, beneath the robe of seeming neutrality worn by judges and scholars, the Critic's clinical gaze detects various kinds of interest, which determine the way the law's grammar is employed and its *langue* applied in the *parole* of legal arguments. Judges have their professional interests, which are often connected to the power game between legal institutions: say, the judiciary and the legislature; private- and criminal-law courts and administrative courts; national and transnational courts; or the European Court of Human Rights and the European Court of Justice. For instance, through their arguments from principles and from basic rights, the courts prop up their status in relation to the legislature; when defining their proper jurisdiction, the courts are engaged in internal turf wars; and when the European Court of Justice 'discovers' and develops the basic-rights dimension of EU law, it tries to ward off the threat that national (constitutional) courts and the European Court of Human Rights pose to its interpretive monopoly under EU law.

International law is a favourite field for the Critic's detached analysis. The fragmentation of international law has engendered relatively independent regimes, which, in addition to their normative orders, possess a distinct institutional structure as well. The regimes contest control of their respective, partly overlapping, fields. Each of them defines legal disputes from the perspective of its own normative order and institutional structure: for the regime of international environmental law, the whale trade constitutes a problem of environmental law, while the WTO regime sees in it an issue of international commercial law; the WTO regime treats patents on AIDS as a question of international commercial law, whereas the issue for the human-rights law regime is the right to life, guaranteed by international human-rights instruments (Koskenniemi and Leino 2002).

In the Critic's view, the strategic dimension in judges' activity is not restricted only to pursuing professional and institutional interests. Judges are also influenced by conscious or unconscious ideological and political preferences, which affect, say, the weighing of principles and counter-principles. Principles are shown to be mere rhetorical façades, camouflaging social interests; they turn out to be policies, encrusted by rhetoric (Kennedy 1997, pp. 316ff.; Koskenniemi 1999b).

The Critic submits principles elaborated and articulated by normatively-oriented legal scholarship to an equally merciless dissection. Legal scholars are unable to escape the law's political determination through their rhetoric of principle. Lists of principles, each endowed with its prima facie weight, imply at bottom a preferential ordering of social interests. Legal scholars, just as judges, are also moved by their particular professional interests, which now appear in the (dis)guise of legal scientific discourse. Scholars strive for academic positions, and disciplines compete for resources and influence. Private law and public law argue about the privileged perspective on the law of the 'post-expansionist' welfare state; about, for instance, the respective weight of private and public law considerations in privately produced social services, such as daycare. Squabbles between labour law and social law, the latter still fighting for its disciplinary independence, concern control over interpreting and systematising, say, pension legislation. In addition, the field of legal scholarship is traversed by the frontlines separating theoretical schools and paradigms, each pursuing its particular academic interests. The (hi)story of Western legal scholarship of the last two centuries is replete with examples: historical vs. analytical jurisprudence; conceptualism vs. realism; Law and Economics vs. Critical Legal Studies, and so forth. For the Critic, such antagonisms, far from being something exceptional, only make plain the normal state of legal scholarship. Furthermore, academic battles are waged, not only within the field of legal scholarship, but at its external frontiers, too. Thus, social and legal science offer two alternative fashions of depicting law, each with its distinctive vocabulary and argumentative grammar. They are engaged in a strategic contest over the power to tell the truth about the law.

Social criticism may be of a normative or an unmasking character. In normative criticism, the critic measures the existing state of affairs against a normative yardstick. The yardstick may be considered immanent to the object itself, as was the case in the Frankfurt school's Marxism-inspired critique of ideology: the bourgeois society was said to have engendered the very ideals of freedom and equality and thus provided the criteria for normative criticism turned against itself. In unmasking criticism, the critic is content with unveiling the existing reality and with showing how it has come to be. Such criticism refrains from normative judgements and normative objectives. At most, it purports to prove the contingency and transformability of contemporary social arrangements; in what direction they should be changed, is to be discussed and decided by the social actors themselves.

For many disciples, Foucault's genealogies have epitomised the mode of unmasking criticism. And it is this mode to which the Critic's narrative also clearly adheres: the truth of strategic interests and the power game is excavated from beneath the normative rhetoric of legal discourse, so that the characteristic universalism of legal discourse is shown to be a mere drape covering particular interests, and eventual consensus a hegemony of interests, successful in their strategic aims. The law's *ratio* is revealed to be merely masked *voluntas*. The Critic abstains from normative judgements, from setting up and applying normative criteria; the Critic does not want to replace one form of deceptive universalism with another, equally deceptive one. Criticism of the law's strategic power game does not apply a normative yardstick; the Critic is content with reconstructing the *langue* of legal discourse and disclosing the role that strategic interests play in its *parole*.

The Critic concedes that the fallacy of legal universalism is not necessarily attributable to the cynicism of legal actors. It may well be that legal actors are not aware of the strategic dimension of their activities; that in their self-conception, the role that particular interests play in their interventions has been successfully suppressed. The Critic's narrative may include a theme of self-deception. Judges may believe that their decisions derive solely from the law in force, and its correct and neutral interpretation in light of the facts of the case. Correspondingly, legal scholars may be convinced of the correctness of their interpretive standpoint or the superiority of their articulation of constitutional doctrine – say, the doctrine of separation of powers – over previous alternatives. The Critic may perceive her task as that of a Therapist who makes what is unconscious conscious, frees legal actors from their illusions, and empowers them to adopt a 'healthy' posture towards the law and legal discourse; to detect in law an instrument for attaining extra-legal aims; to recognise the political choices which are unavoidable in legal practices; to discover behind *ratio* the truth of *voluntas*. The aim of the critical narrative about international law has been 'to liberate the profession from false necessities' (Koskenniemi 2005, p. 572). In this aim, too, the Critic can claim a renowned predecessor from the tradition of American Realism: the psychoanalytical approach in Jerome Frank's (1889–1957) *Law and the Modern Mind* (1930).

The Problem of Reductionism

My examination of modern law is premised on the idea that modern law is pervaded by certain basic tensions which largely account for its internal dynamics.

I have already, in the wake of Luhmann and Cotterrell, referred to one of them: that between *voluntas* and *ratio*, which, in the development of modern law and legal doctrine, has assumed various guises. For instance, in recent legal-theoretical debates it has been discussed under the terms of policies and principles.

Three ways are available to treat such tensions of law. The first approach converts them into *dichotomies*, the parties to which remain strictly separated. This is how Kelsen conceived of the relationship between the Ought and the Is, the *Sollen* and the *Sein*: social and psychological facts belong to the world of the Is, legal norms to that of the Ought. Kelsen argued that the world of the Is cannot be examined from the normative perspective of the Ought, nor the world of the Ought from the point of view of the causality reigning in the world of the Is. Kelsen's pure doctrine of law appeared to be particularly vulnerable at the unavoidable interface of the worlds of the Is and the Ought, say, at the point where a legislative act in the world of the Is bears a new inhabitant into the world of the Ought: a new legal norm.

The second way of dealing with the law's internal tensions is *reduction*. Now the chosen strategy is to reduce one side of the tension to the other or to define it in terms of the latter. This has especially been the programme of the Scandinavian Realists in their search for an empiricist definition of the law's normativity. Some theorists proposed defining 'legal norm' through predictable reactions on behalf of law enforcement authorities, whereas Alf Ross (1899–1979) found the empirical referent of 'valid law' in the prevailing ideology among judges, that is, in a social psychological fact (see Chapter 4). Such empiricist reductions have not succeeded: all the definitions include an obstinate normative, non-factual element. Thus, judges and other law-enforcement authorities whose behaviour or social psychology we are supposed to examine when examining the law can only be identified through the legal norms that confer on certain individuals such a legal-institutional character. Judges and other authorities are not biological entities but legal-institutional facts that exist only due to respective constitutive norms.

In my own discussion, I attempt to follow a third alternative: that of *mediation*. No permanent solution is available to the tensions: these are tasks and challenges which the actors of modern law have to tackle over and over again and in ever-new forms. The programme of mediation applies the logic of *both/and*, whereas both dichotomisation and reduction adhere to an *either/or* thinking. Modern law includes both *voluntas* and *ratio*; they are not only perspectives *on* the law but are present *in* the law as its internal tension. Legal research should explore their varying forms and mediations and reject a one-sided voluntaristic or rationalistic approach.

The Critic's narrative is afflicted by a basic reductionism, although it is not easy to convince the Critic of this. It is difficult for the Critic and her critic to find a common language of debate. The Critic tends to fend off every criticism with an appeal to the hegemonistic goals which her interlocutor tries to achieve through the 'politics of descriptions', by employing vocabulary that serves the strategy of the criticism. In spite of these difficulties, I venture to propose speech act theory as the conceptual framework of the discussion.

As with speech acts generally, legal speech acts – such as laws, court decisions and legal scholars' interventions – possess three dimensions: locutionary, illocutionary and perlocutionary. When focusing on the locutionary aspect, at issue are the propositional contents of legal speech acts, whereas the perlocutionary aspect concerns their extra-discursive effects. In the illocutionary dimension, attention turns, firstly, to speech acts' illocutionary force – those legally regulated or culturally defined conditions that make certain speech acts legal speech acts. In addition, as I have argued above, the illocutionary aspect is related to legal speech acts' validity claims which are tested in ongoing legal discourse. The reciprocal testing of validity claims links legal speech acts together into legal discourse. In this sense, it is the illocutionary aspect that is crucial for identifying the distinctiveness of legal discourse.

By contrast, the Critic's narrative is dominated by the perlocutionary dimension, with its focus on speech acts' extra-discursive consequences. For the Critic, an essential feature of legal speech acts is their overt or covert strategic aims, relating to their extra-discursive consequences. The locutionary or illocutionary side gains significance in the Critic's narrative only as a means for achieving perlocutionary effects.

Due to the dominance of the perlocutionary aspect, the Critic's narrative does not allow space for such an independent assessment of legal speech acts' normative credentials which would detach itself from the strategic perspective. The Critic attempts to stay aloof from legal discourse: the Critic does not perceive herself as a participant in this discourse nor her speech acts as interventions therein. In the Critic's understanding of law and science, legal discourse and normative argumentation transpire outside the walls of academic research, somewhere beyond legal *science*. We have tracked down the first manifestation of reductionism in the Critic's narrative: the Critic absolutises the strategic, perlocutionary aspect of legal discourse. Normative argumentation with its emphasis on the illocutionary dimension is expelled from the Critic's narrative and from legal science in general.

Legal speech acts do involve a perlocutionary dimension, and they can be examined from this perspective. But this does not in any way inhibit us from focusing on their specific normative validity claims while bracketing the perlocutionary aspect: examination of legal speech acts from a perlocutionary and an illocutionary point of view are complementary and not mutually exclusive research tasks. Legal scientific interventions have conscious or – perhaps mostly – unconscious perlocutionary aims: both individual scholars and rival schools contend over such prizes as academic positions, chairs, law reviews, or resources. Proposals for a new systematisation of the legal order or for new branches of law and corresponding academic disciplines – communications law, media law, sports law, medical law – can be treated as moves to occupy new niches within the legal and the academic field. But they can also be assessed independently of such strategic, extra-discursive purposes: if it is possible to see legal speech acts' illocutionary dimension as subordinate to their perlocutionary effects, it is also possible to bracket the perlocutionary dimension and focus on illocutionary validity claims. To stress the significance of the perlocutionary aspect is not yet to fall prey to reductionism; what is reductionism is to absolutise the perlocutionary dimension and to examine the illocutionary aspect merely as a servant of strategic aims.

The Critic's reductionism subjects the law's *ratio* to its *voluntas*. The law's *voluntas* is allied with instrumental reason: from the perspective of the *voluntas*, the law is a means to achieve political aims. The Critic's narrative shares the instrumentalist interpretation of law: legal speech acts are strategic moves in an interest-oriented power play, whether they be laws issued by the legislator, decisions given by judges, or interpretive standpoints or systematisation proposals presented by legal scholars. For the Critic, law is politics, and political goals are determined by interests attached to social positions. Such a conception ignores those restraints limiting the law's instrumentalism which derive from legal-cultural structures, from legal traditions. These restraints manifest the law's sedimented *ratio* which primarily functions through the legal-cultural pre-understanding of legal actors and which also maintains the law's coherence. The Critic is inclined to reduce the law to its surface level. The Critic, too, perceives in law a kind of deep structure but this consists only of fundamental argumentative rules. The Critic ignores the law's normative and conceptual infrastructure, which, however, plays as important a role in the legal-cultural pre-understanding of legal actors as the grammar of legal discourse.

The law and legal discourse definitely possess a strategic aspect, and it is no doubt justified to examine them from the adversarial perspective of legal counsellor. But this is not the only possible perspective, nor should it be allowed to monopolise the picture of law and legal discourse. Law and legal discourse involve not only strategic, but also consensual elements, which are linked to the illocutionary dimension, ignored by the Critic. The strategic aspect is conspicuous in the interventions of parties to legal disputes and of the lawyers representing the parties. Nevertheless, even these interventions involve normative arguments and raise normative validity claims, which can be judged independently of strategic goals. If the deep structure of legal discourse is reconstructed from the perspective of the judge, rather than the parties and their lawyers, then interventions in legal proceedings appear in a new light. The parties describe the facts from the point of view of their own interests and propose the case to be resolved by those prima facie applicable legal norms which correspond to this particular fact description and, by the same token, favour their interests. It can be argued that, from the judge's point of view, the lawyers' strategic posture ensures that all relevant facts and norms are taken into account and, hence, serves the appropriateness of the decision. In view of such a reconstruction of the dialectics of legal proceedings, lawyers' strategically motivated speech acts constitute merely a preliminary phase of thesis and anti-thesis which is overtaken by the judge's synthesis (Habermas 1996, pp. 234–237).

What is the reason for the Critic's absolutism, for her narrow emphasis on the law's adversarialism and on the interest-bound nature of legal discourse? One explanation might be found in the background in international law of some of the most prominent Critics, such as Koskenniemi. International law, in line with constitutional law, is intimately linked with politics, which make it particularly conflictual by nature and attach to its argumentation a more obviously strategic label than is usual in other fields of law. In international law, court procedures are still quite underdeveloped, while as a rule the jurisdiction of courts or other dispute-resolving bodies depends on the consent of the parties. We should be cautious against making over-sweeping generalisations from what might be the case in this particular field of law. Indeed, such generalisations subvert the way international law has habitually been treated in legal theory. International law has been conceived as a borderline case because of the still rudimentary stage of its application and enforcement (e.g., Hart 1980, pp. 208ff.). If international law is elevated into a paradigmatic example of all law, then the exception prevails over the rule.

The Critic's narrative leaves no independent space for the law's *ratio*. By the same token, this narrative excludes an immanent normative criticism which would justify its yardsticks through a reconstruction of the law's internal *ratio*; Habermas' reconstruction of modern law's normative deep culture in terms of 'the system of rights' and fundamental *Rechtsstaat* principles (Habermas 1996) may serve here as an example. Immanent criticism, on the other side, can accommodate critical narrative. Let us analyse normative criticism through what might be termed the *relation of critique*: the relation between the normative yardstick and the object to which it is applied. In immanent criticism of the law, reconstruction only specifies the former side, that is, the normative criterion. As regards depiction of the object pole of the relation, the Critic's narrative of the strategic dimensions of law and legal discourse may well be of assistance. Immanent and unmasking criticism are based on divergent conceptions of the character of (socio-)legal criticism. Nonetheless, they are not necessarily mutually exclusive.

In the apparently never-ending debate on the scientific credentials of legal scholarship, variants of the Realist school, in particular, have tended to banish normative legal scholarship from the realm of science. Again, the Critic follows her predecessors' example and rules out from the academy doctrinal research which presents openly normative interpretive standpoints and systematisation proposals. In her own research, the Critic tries to retain the position of an external observer and does not consider her research a contribution to legal discourse. The Critic's reductionism extends to her conception of (legal) science. In line with Cotterrell and Luhmann, the Critic attempts to solve the problems ensuing from the dual citizenship of normative legal scholarship by denying its membership among scientific disciplines. Through this move, one more characteristic tension within modern law is effaced.

The wall the Critic erects between academic research and normative legal discourse may also separate different aspects of the Critic's professional activities.

The Critic may engage in normative argumentation as a practising lawyer, as a counsellor to the government, or as the author of doctrinal articles. However, according to the Critic's self-understanding, she does not do this in her researcher's role, as a Critic; she has now moved over to another language game and adopted another style. The Critic sees that her academic research and her doctrinal or counselling activities are as unrelated to each other as are a Writer's in writing a novel and compiling an income declaration for taxation (Koskenniemi 1999a, p. 360). But this certainly stretches the point. In her claim, the Critic ignores the legal-cultural level which connects her seemingly detached analysis to legal discourse dealing with openly normative standpoints, arguments and validity claims.

The Critic does not recognise the multi-layered nature of legal normativity and is, therefore, unable to thematise what might be called the *imposed normativity* of all legal scholarship. Its significance is not restricted to doctrinal research (legal dogmatics). Legal research adhering to the Critic's programme also draws its pre-understanding, its tacit knowledge, from the law's cultural layers. At the same time, the Critic, too, contributes to their reproduction. This accounts for the imposed normativity which even the Critic's legal research cannot escape. The Critic brackets the normative validity claims of legal speech acts she examines and abstains from presenting such claims. But through this move, the Critic is not able to free herself from the normativity imposed by her inescapable dependence on legal-cultural resources and preconceptions.

The Critic's narrative does not include such a reconstruction of the law's sub-surface layers that recognition of this imposed normativity would require. The Critic's reductionism prevents her from perceiving those unavoidable preconditions and implications of her critical activities which are related to the multi-layered nature of the law's normativity. The Critic sees in law merely speech acts on the surface level and argumentative rules governing them. The Critic herself may be in need of therapy enhancing her self-understanding!

Because of its reductionism, the Critic's narrative is not suited to a framework in the exploration of modern law's tensions, such as that between *voluntas* and *ratio*. But just as the social scientist's external description (*Fremdbeschreibung*) of law and legal discourse increases a legal scholar's self-awareness, the Critic's narrative is a healthy reminder of the strategic aspect in legal discourse. Both the external descriptions provided by social scientists and the critical narrative have their space in the following chapters.

PART I
The Historical and Cultural Dependence of the Law's Ratio

Chapter 2
The Traditions of Law

The Time and Space of Modern Law

For Immanuel Kant (1724–1804), time and space were transcendental and ahistorical preconditions of human experience and cognition. However, they have not been spared the historicisation of Kant's epistemology: conceptions of time and space, the ways of experiencing them, have turned out to be historically contingent, dependent on their cultural and societal environment. They are *cultural patterns*, functioning in the minds of social actors like Émile Durkheim's (1858–1917) social facts.[1]

The evolution of conceptions of time and space is often presented schematically, as subsequent stages. Such schemes, of course, inevitably ignore historical multiplicity and variety, but, still, they serve to relativise our present cultural patterns, which we are often inclined to take for granted. Otthein Rammstedt has distinguished between diverse forms of time consciousness and experience, which follow each other and are tied to the basic structures of society (Rammstedt 1975; see also Rosa 2005, pp. 26–27). In line with many other discussants, Rammstedt has characterised the pre-modern conception of time as cyclical. The course of history was seen to possess a revolving nature: historical phases reverted to their starting-point, and everything began anew. By contrast, in the modern view history is conceived of not as a rotating movement but as a *linear* process. The linear conception of time distinguishes between the past, the present and the future as the temporal horizons towards which social action is oriented. Reinhart Koselleck (1923–2006) argued that in the Western cultural sphere, the space of experience (*Erfahrungsraum*) and the horizon of expectation (*Erwartungshorizont*) were detached from each other during the time span between 1750 and 1850. Christianity had already adopted the linear conception. However, in Christianity the future is predetermined, it has its end-point. Only the dissolution of this predetermination opened the future or, in Koselleck's terms, the horizon of expectation (Koselleck 1984, pp. 349ff.).

Not only conceptions of time but ways of experiencing space, too, undergo change. Some theorists speak of specific time-space regimes, referring to the intertwinement and interaction of temporal and spatial perceptions (Rosa 2005, pp. 61–62). What is crucial in the modern conception of space is the *extension of space* beyond the locale, the interaction between immediately experienced

1 Stephen Kern's *The Culture of Time and Space 1880–1918* is an excellent portrayal of the historically-varying nature of our cultural ways of experiencing time and space.

space and merely imaginable space. This development, the detachment of space and locale, also opens up the possibility to enter into social relations not only with those in one's immediate presence but also with those absent. The social environment of modern individuals, their spatial horizon, reaches out beyond the village and neighbourhood (Schroer 2006, pp. 110–119).

Modern conceptions of time and space also find their expressions in law, as cultural preconceptions that define the way legal actors approach the world. Modern law is predominantly *positive* law, constantly changing and changeable law, where the legislator is the primary agent of change. A corollary of the law's positivity is its potential *instrumentalisation* for the political aims of the legislator. The law's positivisation and instrumentalisation manifest a linear conception of time where the future is seen as open-ended and malleable. The modern conception of politics is based on specific temporal assumptions, which also leave their mark on the law as a political instrument. According to this dynamic conception of politics and history, society is never finished but rather constitutes a continuous political project, always setting up new tasks. Legislation is seen as an instrument in the service of this unending political project. It is not a final act but a device for managing social development and, as such, in need of constant re-definition.

Thus, modern law and legal actors (especially the legislator) adopt the linear, progressive conception of time where the future always differs from the past. In turn, modern law's spatial horizon exceeds the narrow confines of the immediate locality. The law's instrumentalisation is not only linked to changes in time patterns, but also manifests the widening of space: instrumentalised law regulates relations between those absent, serves *systemic* integration, transpiring through objectified economic and administrative mechanisms, instead of *social* integration through the face-to-face interaction of members of society.

However, a word of caution is appropriate when discussing the imprint on modern law of the linear conception of time and the extension of space. Not all areas of law are similarly affected. In his *Theory of Communicative Action*, Jürgen Habermas instructively distinguishes between law as a medium and law as an institution. *Law as a medium* is a servant of the economic and administrative sub-systems and assists these to accomplish their systemic functions. *Law as an institution*, by contrast, is an inhabitant of the life-world (*Lebenswelt*) of the members of society and serves to strengthen its morally-integrated communicative structures (Habermas 1989a, p. 365).[2] Economic and administrative law are typical instances of law as a medium, whilst law as an institution is epitomised by the core areas of criminal and family law. Modern law's policy orientation comes to the fore in those branches that represent law as a medium. But there is more to modern law than just its instrumentalised departments. Law as an institution still addresses face-to-face social intercourse, and lacks the conspicuous purposive and future-related features typical of law as a medium.

2 In *Between Facts and Norms*, he actually – in my mind, over-hastily – withdrew the distinction (Habermas 1996, note 48 on p. 562).

Temporality and spatiality can be approached, not only as cultural patterns of experiencing time and space, but also as *structural qualities of society*: as durations and rhythms, boundaries and cross-boundary connections. Societal modernisation is characterised by *temporal acceleration* (Rosa 2005) and *spatial expansion*, the conquest of ever-wider space (Schroer 2006). Modern society is a functionally differentiated society, and acceleration and expansion as general temporal and spatial characteristics of modernisation assume different manifestations in different sub-systems. The law can be examined as one of these sub-systems.

Societal acceleration affects law, too. The instrumentalist legislator, carrying out the political project of social engineering, maintains constant legal change. But the law's relation to societal acceleration is not unequivocal: the law also includes features tempering change, slowing down the velocity of time. A characteristic of modern law is not only changeability but rather a *dialectic of changeability and stability*.

The law's tasks in the modern political project require law's malleability. Under conditions of societal acceleration, the pace of legislative change must also intensify. But as has been emphasised by, among others, Niklas Luhmann (2004, pp. 142ff.), one of the law's functions – if not *the* function – is to generate stability. In legal doctrine, the prerequisite of stability, of relative unchangeability, has received multiple expressions. In the early versions of the rule of law doctrine and the *Rechtsstaat* theory, the very concept of law included not only the criteria of generality and abstraction, but also that of permanence. Stability is closely linked to *legal certainty*: only relatively permanent norms can create the constancy presupposed by long-term planning in social sub-systems, such as the economy, or – for that matter – in the everyday life of individuals and families. *Protection of legitimate expectations* is one of the major substantive principles of EU law; indeed, many national legal orders have adopted it as well. This principle offers protection, not only against abrupt shifts in the practice of administrative authorities, but also against legislation-induced alterations in the legal environment. However, at issue is not absolute protection, but its extension expresses the fragile balance between stability and changeability.

The respective significance of, and the optimal balance between, changeability and stability is not identical throughout the law. Changeability is needed where the law is employed as a medium of social management: in administrative and tax law, environmental law, and so on. By contrast, the pace of change is slower in fields where the law functions as an institution strengthening the moral structures of the life-world and contributing to social integration, such as family law. Law as a medium and law as an institution manifest different temporalities.

Another way of pinning down the varying relationship between permanence and change in law is to distinguish between framework regulation and interventionist regulation of, say, the economy. A certain constancy in the *framework regulation* of property and contract is indispensable for the economic system. Through *interventionist regulation*, the legislator aims to correct functional disturbances in the economic system and to compensate for their detrimental effects in other social sub-systems or in the daily life of members of society, in their *Lebenswelt*. The lifespan of such regulation is shorter than that of framework regulation.

Constitutional law plays a particular role in balancing the contradictory demands of legal stability and change. The relatively high degree of permanence expected of the constitution is already manifest in the procedure for its amendment; for instance, the requirement of a qualified majority, or acceptance by two subsequent parliamentary compositions, or by referendum. While these requirements aim at securing the legitimacy of the constitution and the political system, they also possess a temporal aspect, linked to constitutional stability. A standard modern constitution includes an organisational part and a Bill of Rights. Demand for stability arises both from the constitution's role as a framework regulation of the political system (the organisational part) and from its intimate ties to fundamental principles of the legal order (the basic-rights part).

Viewing law as a multi-layered phenomenon sheds light even on the dialectic between change and stability. The rapid pace of change is a quality of the law's surface, consisting of explicit, discursively formulated normative material; here, the activity of the legislator maintains continuous movement. The briskness of change is tempered by the deeper layers of the law; they change too, but according to a slower rhythm. The legislator's omnipotence does not extend to the legal culture, which changes only gradually, as a joint effect of legal practices. The particular role of the legislator in the legal and political system, as it were, forces it to embrace the ideology of societal progress. The legal culture that governs the interpretation and application of instrumentally-conceived legislation offers a conservative counterweight to the legislator's radicalism. This aspect of modern law's temporality can be expressed in terms of *voluntas* and *ratio*, too. The *voluntas* of the legislator engenders surface-level turbulence, which is calmed down by the *ratio* sedimented into the law's cultural layers. The law's *voluntas* and *ratio* obey divergent rhythms.

Nonetheless, legal change extends to legislation's legal-cultural underpinnings and even to what can be termed the law's deep culture: its fundamental normative principles and the categories that enable legal thinking, argumentation and regulation in the first place. If in general it is justified to talk about different historical types of law and about, for instance, pre-modern law's transformation into modern law, justification derives from fundamental changes in the law's deep culture. But the pace of deep cultural changes is slow; the pace of deep culture measures the law's *longue durée*. The centuries-long history of the emergence of modern law, beginning with the revival of Roman law during the twelfth and thirteenth centuries, is a history of the gradual formation and stabilisation of its conceptual, normative and methodological infrastructure.

At its surface level, modern law itself defines its time and space. In Hans Kelsen's pure theory of law, time and space are present as dimensions of the validity of legal norms (Kelsen 1989, p. 198ff.). The law's temporal and spatial coordinates are decided by the legislator. Laws are issued to be in force until further notice or for a limited period – indeed, the legislator may even accord them retroactive effect.

The temporality of modern law should be explored as a quality, not only of the legal order and its layers, but also of the *legal practices* producing and reproducing this order. Lawmaking and legal proceedings in courts have their distinctive durations. These are in part legally determined; the procedural rules of parliament, for instance, may define intervals between readings of a bill. However, the pace of legal procedures is also affected by their discursive requirements. The lawmaking of a democratic *Rechtsstaat* takes time, as is made particularly clear by Habermas' ideal model of democratic lawmaking.

This model includes diverse forms of communication. Lawmaking begins with pragmatic discourses focusing on ends–means relations. If the values underpinning the ends of a legislative reform turn out to be obscure or controversial, the process continues with ethico-political discourse, aiming at a value consensus. If interest conflicts prevent a consensus, then consensus-oriented discourse must be replaced by compromise-oriented negotiations. At the next stage, the moral acceptability of values and interest compromises is tested in moral discourse. Finally, juridical discourse is needed to monitor the consistency and coherence of the legal order (Habermas 1996, pp. 157–168). Contemporary society is characterised by increasing complexity, as well as by growing cultural pluralism and the differentiation of particular interests. In these circumstances, finding an optimal regulatory solution, or defining a common value basis and reconciling divergent interests, are increasingly demanding and time-consuming tasks.

In turn, the pace of legal proceedings in courts is governed by procedural requirements manifesting the principle of impartiality: all parties are allowed to present their version of the facts and their interpretation of the relevant norms. The objective of legislative and adjudicative procedures is to ensure that laws and rulings as legal-institutional speech acts meet the criteria of normative correctness. But this also makes them rather ill-suited to the general tendency of societal acceleration, which seems only to gain in strength in the development of modern society.

An integral aspect of the temporality of legal practices consists in how they relate to the time horizons of the past, the present and the future. As will be discussed below in this chapter, legal practices differ in, for instance, their relation to tradition.

Thus, modern law has its time. However, this is not singular but plural time: it varies in different branches and at different levels of the legal order, while legal practices, too, display their distinct temporalities. Modern law occupies its characteristic space as well. Its privileged space has been that of the *nation state*. Modern law and the nation state have in many ways been dependent on each other. The legislator of the nation state has been the central legal actor of modern law, of which legislation is the central source. At the other end of its span of functioning, the law has been applied by nation-state courts and executed by the state's coercive machinery. The nation state, in turn, has needed the law as a means of organising itself and implementing its policies. Modern law's links to the nation state account for its positivity and increasing instrumentality. The *voluntas* of the law has been, first of all, the *voluntas* of the legislator of the nation state.

The emergence of nation states expresses the extension of society's spatial horizon beyond the immediate locality. The nation state both manifests and facilitates entering into social relations beyond the narrow confines of a particular locale. This accomplishment of the nation state is largely due to the law, which regulates the relationships of, not only those present, but also those absent from each other.

The modern nation state is a *territorial state*. State territory belongs, along with state people and state power, to the three characteristics of the standard concept of the state, espoused by, for instance, the German late constitutional school of public law. Nation states are separated by boundaries which also define the territory for each state's sovereignty. The space of the nation state, delineated by state boundaries, is exclusive and excluding: a sovereign state power does not accept another sovereign state power in its territory. The aspiration of the modern nation state is to monopolise all political power in its territory. It abolishes pre-modern political pluralism, which allowed for several power centres to wield their authority at the same time and in the same territory: the king, the Church, the lord of the manor, the town … (Schroer 2006, pp. 189–193).

The sovereignty of state power implies sovereignty of the national legal order. The law's space is as exclusive and excluding as that of the nation state; the national legal order does not accept another rival or overlapping legal order in its territory. And just as the modern nation state puts an end to pre-modern political pluralism, modern law eliminates pre-modern legal pluralism: canon law, feudal law, manorial law, borough law, royal law, mercantile law, and so on (Berman 1983).

The interdependence of modern law and the nation state has, of course, left its trace on modern legal theory. In his pure theory of law, Kelsen went as far as to hold state and law to be identical. In his view, the state is merely a personification of the legal order, while the concept of the state was a similar legal fiction as subject concepts in general. Kelsen had studied under the influence of the German late constitutional school. Georg Jellinek (1851–1911), Kelsen's teacher, had embraced the definition of the 'state' through the three elements of state territory, state people and state power (Jellinek 1914, pp. 394ff.). Kelsen argued that none of these elements can be conceived independently of the legal order. State territory equals the legal order's territorial scope of validity; state people its subjective scope of validity; and state power its efficacy (Kelsen 1989, pp. 286–290). Adding the temporal dimension of the legal order's validity, we arrive at the following definition: 'Thereby the state whose essential elements are population, territory, and power is defined as a relatively centralised legal order, limited in its spatial and temporal sphere of validity, sovereign or subordinated only to international law, and by and large effective' (ibid., p. 290). Following such a definition, the concept of the *Rechtsstaat* loses its independent significance: if the state is identical with the legal order, every state is a *Rechtsstaat*.

Kelsen conceived of the legal order as a hierarchically organised whole, where lower-order norms derive their validity from higher ones: by-laws from laws, laws from the constitution and the constitution from a hypothetical, presupposed *basic norm* (*Grundnorm*). Kelsen's hierarchical legal order, *Stufenbau*, is, above all, the legal order of a nation state: the basic norm crowning the hierarchy commands obedience to the (historically first) constitution of the nation state, while the norms on the lower echelons are issued by state organs empowered by this constitution. It is true, though, that Kelsen's world of legal *Sollen* included international law, too. He advocated a monistic view, where both international and national law are subject to the same basic norm: either that of international law or that of the national legal order. Kelsen's monism does not question the nation-state premises of his construction. International law regulates merely relationships between states. Even if the legal *Stufenbau* is constructed starting from the basic norm of international law, international law only provides the national legal order with its validity basis, leaving the national legislator free to decide on its normative content in compliance with the (procedural) requirements of the nation-state constitution (ibid., pp. 328ff.).

The nation state is also the primary site of law for H.L.A. Hart, the other great twentieth-century exponent of positivist legal theory. He discusses his *rule of recognition*, crowning the hierarchical legal order and replacing Kelsen's basic norm, in the context of the nation state. His main example of a rule of recognition is as follows: law is what the Queen in Parliament decides (Hart 1980, p. 99). Hart's rule of recognition addresses the judges and other law enforcers of the nation state. In his account of law, he reserves a place for international law, too, but his examination is based on the assumption of national legal orders reigning in the space of nation states and limited by their boundaries. He also argues that international law has not yet reached the level of a developed legal system, where primary behavioural rules would be complemented by secondary rules on the production, change, application and recognition of legal rules (ibid., pp. 208ff.).

Kelsen's and Hart's positivist accounts view modern law from the standpoint of the *voluntas* of the nation-state legislator. But even those who have assumed the perspective of the *ratio* and offered an alternative to Kelsen's and Hart's positivism have, more or less self-evidently, identified law with the law of the nation state. Klaus Günther (2001, p. 560) has detected implicit nation-state assumptions in Habermas' reconstruction of modern law's normative deep culture. And, to take another example, Ronald Dworkin's political community, whose law is supposed to be governed by the principle of integrity, seems to be one and the same as the citizenry of a nation state (Dworkin 1986).

Nonetheless, the link to the nation state is not as evident for the law's *ratio* as it is for its *voluntas*. Kelsen's and Hart's positivism remains mainly on the law's surface and focuses on discursively formulated norms, with their main sources in legislation and in judicial precedent. By contrast, examining the law's *ratio* presupposes opening the law's sub-surface levels: reconstructing the normative principles, as well as the conceptual and methodological premises, sedimented into the legal-cultural layers. The space of these layers is wider and their territorial boundaries are more porous than are those of the surface level, tied to the nation state. This is implied by references to legal families or legal-cultural groups, such as Romano-Germanic and Anglo-Saxon legal cultures. And if we accept the notion of the law's deep structure (deep culture), denoting the common core of modern legal cultures, it must be defined in even wider territorial terms. From the very beginning, elaboration of modern law's deep-structural components has been a transnational enterprise, whether the conceptual and methodological studies of the Romanist learned lawyers or the substantive normative discussions of the natural-law thinkers at the dawn of the modern era.

The nation state constitutes modern law's most important – but not its only – spatial determination. We could continue our journey through the spaces of modern law, say, by analysing the specific loci of legal practices and institutions, such as parliament and court buildings. These have their specific spatial constellations – such as the triangle of the plaintiff, the defendant and the judge defining the space of legal proceedings – which convey important symbolic meanings. However, analysing these would exceed my present purposes.

This chapter deals with the law's relations to *tradition*. At issue is the law's temporality, but not only that: the law's traditions have bound it, not only temporally, to its history, its past, but also spatially – to a certain place. In turn, loosening of the law's ties to tradition affects not only the law's temporal qualities but its spatial qualities as well.

The Historicity of the Law's Historicity

As Jarkko Tontti, among others, pointed out in his *Right and Prejudice* (2004, pp. 1–2), one of the main defects of neo-Kantian legal theory lies in its ahistorical approach: law and legal scholarship have been treated as phenomena divorced from history. Kelsen's pure theory of law constitutes the high point of this way of theorising about law. In turn, Kelsenian legal positivism gives rise to and justifies the familiar figure of the omnipotent legislator. The pure theory of law is interested in the law's time and space merely as dimensions in the validity of surface-level legal norms.

But law and legal scholarship are thoroughly historical enterprises. They are bound to the law's past, to its memory, to the conceptual, normative and methodological resources transmitted from the law's history and sedimented into its cultural layers. This dependence on the past holds for all legal practices, not only for adjudication and legal scholarship but also for lawmaking. The idea of the legislator's omnipotence runs into difficulties right here. Without the conceptual, normative and methodological means provided by these levels, the legislator could not issue its statutes, the judges their decisions, or legal scholars their articles. The law's cultural layers constitute the very possibility of the legal practices that produce constant shifts and developments on the law's surface.

It is greatly to the credit of hermeneutical legal philosophy, honourably represented by Tontti with his study, that it has so emphatically stressed the historicity of law and legal scholarship in defiance of the ahistoricism implicit in neo-Kantian legal positivism. Ironically, the blame for ahistoricism can just as well be directed towards at least certain works in the 'tradition' of hermeneutical legal philosophy, influenced, most notably, by Martin Heidegger (1889–1976), Hans-Georg Gadamer (1900–2002) and Paul Ricoeur (1913–2005). The law's dependence on its past also varies in time and place. The historicity of the law's historicity may elude us if we examine it in the framework of Heideggerian ontology and define it as qualities of Being (*Sein*) and Being-there (*Dasein*) which determine transcendental conditions for all human understanding and interpretation, all human acts of consciousness. Such an approach easily leads to a failure to acknowledge any differences in the law's reliance on its history as minor bagatelles on the 'ontic' or 'practical' level. The law's relation to its past, to its 'traditions', must be conceived historically.

We can discern in legal history distinct periods and distinct types of law, without necessarily committing ourselves to disputed evolutionary assumptions. We can further assume that every historical type of law is marked by a characteristic relation to its past; that during different historical periods, the law's temporality varies. Thus, modern law displays a particular way of relating to its past, divergent from the historicity of previous types of law. At present, the law's relationship with its history again appears to be undergoing significant transformations. The modern era, too, should be approached historically, as those espousing the concept of reflexive or late modernity have advocated.

The general hermeneutical premise, with its emphasis on the law's basic, all-embracing, 'primordial' historicity, is in need of specification in another respect, too. It is true that law's inevitable reliance on its 'traditions' holds for all legal practices, for lawmaking as well as adjudication or legal scholarship. But, again, the hermeneutical, Heideggerian-Gadamerian emphasis on the importance of 'tradition' for all legal practices – for all legal cognition, understanding and interpretation – can make us insensitive to essential divergences. Temporal orientation in lawmaking is not necessarily the same as in adjudication or legal scholarship. We again face the danger that the notion of the fundamental historicity of *Sein* and *Dasein*, Being and Being-there, reduces important divergences to negligible contingencies on the 'ontic' level.

Historicity – and this is my third bid for specification – also varies within diverse branches of law. Arguably, orientation towards the future is more prominent in fields where the law is used as a medium than in those exemplifying law as an institution, in Habermas' sense of the terms.

So let us be precise and examine the law's historicity, its relation to its past, historically. Let us also allow for the possibility of variations in the relations that different legal practices – such as lawmaking, adjudication and legal science – maintain with the law's past. And, let us also bear in mind that in different fields of law, its temporality may assume different configurations. In what follows, my principal focus will be on the distinct temporality of the historical type of law we are accustomed to calling modern law. Thus, earlier, pre-modern law will mainly figure as a contrast to throw the distinctive features of modern law into relief. The danger lies in simplification: the pluralism characterising pre-modern law should function as a warning-sign of excessive generalisation. My hope is that the reader, too, keeps this non sequitur in mind.

Two Concepts of Tradition

I would like to propose a distinction between two concepts of tradition: a philosophical one and a sociological-historical one. Of course, connections exist between the two. For example, Habermas (1984 and 1989a) has in a way transformed the philosophical *Lebenswelt* concept into a sociological one; the philosophical notion of the *Lebenswelt* – stemming from Husserlian phenomenology – is closely related to the concept of tradition.

The contents of the *philosophical* concept of tradition are to be sought from the *hermeneutical*, Heideggerian-Gadamerian 'tradition'. Hermeneutical philosophy stresses that all human acts of consciousness – all acts of understanding, interpretation and cognition – are bound to tradition. We humans never approach the object of our cognition or interpretation with a tabula rasa consciousness but always through the conceptual and interpretative means provided by a specific tradition. 'Tradition' in this sense is equivalent to the pre-understanding and prejudices which – as Gadamer emphasises – are indispensable for the process of understanding and interpretation to be launched at all. We draw this pre-understanding from the culture into which we have been 'thrown'; the culture in which we have grown up and internalised our fundamental conceptions of the world. The human artefacts that constitute the object of interpretation are, in a sense, products of the same tradition as the subject, the interpreter. The object, say a piece of literature or art, has become what it is through a culturally-bound history of effect (*Wirkungsgeschichte*) to which all previous interpretations have made their cumulative contribution. We are not able to reach to Plato's dialogues or Shakespeare's *Hamlet* in their 'pristine' condition but only as shaped by earlier interpretations, the preceding *Wirkungsgeschichte*. But as interpreters we have been moulded in our preconceptions by the same cultural history. The subject and the object of interpretation are inevitably intermingled (Gadamer 1993, pp. 265ff.).

These basic hermeneutical insights apply to legal cognition and interpretation, too. We always approach the law, the 'object' of legal cognition and interpretation, through a certain pre-understanding, a tradition in the philosophical sense, employing the conceptual, normative and methodological tools which our legal culture has provided us with. The law itself is a product of the same tradition, the same culture. Thus, we can already argue for the inevitable interconnectedness of the subject and object of legal cognition and interpretation on this philosophical-hermeneutical basis. But we should also be aware of the specifics of law and legal scholarship: the inter-relations between law and legal scholarship display peculiarities absent from, for example, other human and social sciences. These peculiarities are due to the *dual citizenship* of legal scholarship: to its being at one and the same time a scientific and a legal practice. As a legal practice, legal scholarship – most conspicuously doctrinal research (legal dogmatics) – influences through its own results the development of its object in a way that has no exact counterpart in other human or social sciences. The speech acts of legal scholars are interventions in the ongoing legal discourse on the contents of the legal order. At its surface level, the legal order can be conceived of as the always temporary result of a discourse where legal scholars participate as one of the main groups of discussants. It is true that sociology, for instance, also affects society's development through its results and that sociology, too, is part of its own research object: society. However, sociology's impact on society at large is not of a similar immediate nature as is legal science's influence on law.

The philosophical-hermeneutical concept of tradition does not tell us anything about our capability of becoming conscious of our preconceptions and reflecting on them. Gadamer's version of hermeneutics may lead us to think that it is the existential fate of human beings to be imprisoned in their traditions, in the prejudices they have inherited along with their cultural baggage, and that to wage a battle against these would be a doomed enterprise. In fact, Gadamerian hermeneutics has been suspected of in-built conservatism and of questioning the very possibility of a critique of ideology challenging cultural traditions (Habermas 1982, pp. 271ff.). It is true, though, that some hermeneutical philosophers, amongst them Tontti, have stressed our ability to maintain a certain distance from the object of our interpretation – our capacity for 'distanciation' – and, thus, to gain scope for a critical posture towards our traditions. Ricoeur (1970, pp. 32–36) argued that the hermeneutics of faith (*foi*) is not our only alternative but that we are also able to practice a hermeneutics of suspicion (*soupcon*). Tontti (2004, pp. 76ff.) has tried to ground this possibility in the Heideggerian ontological level, in the 'querulous' nature of Being. In the eyes of one critical reader at least, this seems to remain a mere postulate.

It is evident that the extent to which traditions (in the philosophical-hermeneutical sense) are open to criticism varies historically: the possibility of criticism is not determined by any transcendental condition of human understanding and interpretation. Significant historical-sociological differences exist between the 'traditions' of various societies with regard to the leeway of critical reflexion. Therefore, hermeneutical lessons of the cultural presuppositions of human cognition and interpretation must be placed in a historical setting. Just as the law's historicity is historical by nature, its cultural dependence varies culturally. In addition, when analysing criticism in law and legal scholarship, we have to be attentive to the distinctive features of legal cognition, interpretation and pre-understanding.

The philosophical-hermeneutical concept of tradition calls for a complement through its *historical-sociological* counterpart. Here, I use as my guide Anthony Giddens (Giddens 1994, pp. 79ff.). He views traditions as something distinctive to pre-modern or 'traditional' societies. Tradition means commitment, not only to time, to the past, but also to a place.[3] Traditions are predominantly local traditions that define personal and collective identities, and divide people into friends and foes, into insiders and outsiders. Discussion over the barriers separating traditions is difficult, if not impossible. Traditions involve a particular interpretation of the world and the way people should live in this world; they confound the descriptive with the prescriptive.

The truth of traditions is – as Giddens terms it – a 'schematic truth'. It is upheld by specific *guardians* who possess the monopoly over declaring and interpreting the tradition, such as priests and magicians. The guardians may discuss and even argue over the right interpretation of the tradition but a fundamental challenge to it is unthinkable. Finally, an essential feature of traditions consists of rituals that link traditions to social practices and through which adherence to and respect for traditions are renewed and reinforced.

In societal and cultural modernisation, pre-modern traditions are gradually dissolved or at least they alter their character. Let us cite two clear-sighted social observers from the middle of the nineteenth century:

> Constant revolutionising of production, uninterrupted disturbance of all social conditions, everlasting uncertainty and agitation distinguish the bourgeois epoch from all earlier ones. All fixed, fast frozen relations, with their train of ancient and venerable prejudices and opinions, are swept away, all new-formed ones become antiquated before they can ossify. All that is solid melts into the air, all that is holy is profaned, and man is at last compelled to face with sober senses his real condition of life and his relations with his kind.[4]

The relation of modernisation to traditions is by no means unilinear or univocal. Local traditions are dispersed and cultural foundations of local communities destroyed but, at the same time, new traditions are engendered. Eric Hobsbawm (1983) has explored what he calls 'invented' traditions. These are connected to the rise of nationalism, the cultural cement of modern nation states. Nationalism as a 'civic religion' has provided nation states with their (empirical) legitimacy and

---

3 Giddens can be criticised for putting excessive emphasis on the local nature of traditions: not all pre-modern traditions are localised but may display universalist traits. This holds for Christianity and other world religions. But in their universalism, they can perhaps be – in the wake of Max Weber – regarded as augurs of cultural modernisation.

4 The quotation is from Marx and Engel's *Manifesto of the Communist Party*. I have used the version available on the Internet. See www.socialistparty.net/pub/manifestcomm.

created the state people, referred to by the standard three-element concept of the state, as a cultural-sociological whole. By the same token, it has facilitated such ties and emotions of belonging together which give expression to the typically modern expansion of space beyond the immediate locale. Nationalism generates, 'invents', new national traditions and new rituals for their reinforcement, such as Independence Day parades or opening and closing ceremonies of national parliaments. Nationalism also has its own guardians, such as professors of 'national sciences': say, history, literature and linguistics. Because of its intimate links to the nation state, law, in its long history of modernisation, has not been spared nationalist influences. Suffice it to evoke common law's frequent celebration as a manifestation of the particular English national character (Van Caenegem 1973, pp. 87ff.) or the German historical school's view of law as an expression of the *Volksgeist*. Law professors have also played a part as guardians of nationalist traditions.

However, the general tendency during the modern age is towards the dissolution of traditions. Pre-modern traditions stand out against modern *expert systems* which replace the guardians with specialists. The truth of the experts is not a schematic truth but one that lays itself open to scientific testing and contesting. Expert knowledge can always be corrected, and this requires an attitude of systematic suspicion. The group of experts is not closed, as is that of guardians, but open to anyone who is able to demonstrate possession of specific skills and knowledge which laymen lack.

Traditions are locally embedded, whereas expertise, by contrast, is by nature disembedded. It is universal, non-local, and distances itself, not only from time, from the past, but also from place, from embeddedness in a certain location. Unlike traditions, expertise is the same everywhere, in China as well as in Finland. Since the validity of expertise is not spatially bound, no hindrances exist to its removal from one place to another. As expert systems detach the present and the future from the past, they also disconnect social actions and knowledge from their local ties. The replacement of traditions by expertise manifests the modern expansion of space. In sum, the dissolution of traditions reflects fundamental changes both in society's temporality and in its spatiality.

The guardians of a tradition may debate its interpretation, but their disputes are different from those concerning expert knowledge. The natural state of a tradition presupposes deference, not only from the community at large, but also from the guardians. Hence, the critique of a tradition can only be conducted within very narrow limits. For experts, by contrast, criticism, systematic suspicion and mutual disagreement constitute the very motor of their activities.

As Giddens (1994, p. 91) notes, we also speak about 'traditions' within institutions which are based on expertise; within academic science and research, for instance. However, the universalism and scepticism that govern the practice of modern science guarantee that both the supporters and critics of these 'traditions' conceive them to be relatively arbitrary. Pre-modern traditions were sealed off from each other; discussion between them was nearly impossible, and criticism tended to be tantamount to total rejection. By contrast, expert 'traditions' are receptive to reciprocal criticism, which remains within the boundaries of reasonableness. Such criticism is not only possible but even expected.

The general trend during the modern age is towards replacement of traditions by expertise. But again, this movement is not without its ambiguities. For instance, science and scholarship can at times and within specific fields display features which are more characteristic of traditions than expert systems. Schools and paradigms may close up and defer to their prophets and guardians of schematic truth: Marxism, Freudianism, Deconstructionism …

Now, armed with two concepts of tradition, one philosophical-hermeneutical, the other historical-sociological, we can examine the role of traditions in law and legal scholarship.

Common Law between Tradition and Modernity

Modern society is often termed a post-traditional society, and modern, largely positivised law post-traditional law. These denominations have their justification, but they should not obscure the fact that modern law, too, retains a relation to its past, to its history, and that the philosophical-hermeneutical concept of tradition, at least, retains its validity. Legal actors derive the conceptual, normative and methodological resources necessary for their practices from the existing legal-cultural reservoir.

But the 'traditions' of modern society and modern law differ from pre-modern traditions. What under the conditions of 'mature' modern law can be called tradition in the philosophical-hermeneutical sense diverges from pre-modern society's legal tradition. In the course of its modernisation, the law has been gradually transformed from a tradition in the direction of an expert system, although development has been far from unilinear.

Arguably, pre-modern customary law constituted a tradition in Giddens' sense. Customary law had its 'schematic truth', which was guarded by the judges; they declared the law and held the monopoly over its authentic interpretation. The law was upheld and renewed in legal proceedings which displayed strongly ritualistic traits. An important function of ritualistic legal proceedings consisted in strengthening respect for the legal and communal tradition whose guardians the judges were.

Sociologically-motivated historical periodisations and contrasts, such as that between pre-modern and modern law, can be illuminating and have great heuristic value. But we should be aware of the pitfalls involved in their use. This is proved by the intricate and paradox-replete history of the modernisation of English law. This history is instructive in another sense as well: it provides us with an opportunity to deepen our discussion of the role which the tension between *ratio* and *voluntas* has played in modern law and its pre-history, and it informs us about the many guises in which this tension has been vested.

In Anglo-American doctrine, debates between *ratio* and *voluntas* have been dominated by opposition between common-law doctrine and positivist legal thinking. Over the centuries, common law has, of course, undergone many alterations. Emphasis on the law's historicity, on its ties to tradition, has remained, but in contemporary doctrine the relationship between stability and change greatly diverges from the early variants of the doctrine. Common-law thinking has had to open up towards the future; this is shown by, for instance, debates in English constitutional doctrine on the relationship between the rule of law and the sovereignty of Parliament (see Chapter 7).

England experienced a precocious legal modernisation as early as the twelfth century. The basic institutional and normative structures of the common-law system were established during the reign of Henry II. R.C. Van Caenegem (1973, p. 88) has summed up the situation at the end of the century as follows:

> The Common Law of England – so different from the *jus commune* or common learned law of the European universities – is the oldest national law in Europe. It is the oldest body of law that was common to a whole kingdom and administered by a central court with a nation-wide competence in the first instance. In the rest of Europe, the law was either European or local, not national.

Centralisation and nationalisation were accompanied by yet another token of early modernisation: professionalisation through formation of a professional corps of royal judges (Dawson 1968, pp. 34ff.; Van Caenegem 1973, pp. 19ff.). The law of evidence also underwent what can – in the wake of Van Caenegem (ibid., pp. 63ff.) – be described as a shift from an irrational to a rational direction: the jury system, so characteristic of common law, replaced devices like ordeals, judicial battles and compurgation. The proto-modernisation of English law was mainly brought about by the measures of an energetic king: originally, common law was royal law, administered by royal courts. It was common in relation to local customary laws – the *iura propria* of England – which were applied in local courts (Glenn 2007, pp. 25ff.).

In the course of centuries this precociously modernised legal system came to be seen in the eyes of many a critical observer as hopelessly archaic; this is one of the many paradoxes in the history of English common law. Already 'to a continental observer in the early 16th century the Common Law must have looked quaintly antiquated and hopelessly medieval, full of archaic elements, which elsewhere had been swept away like cobwebs by Romanist doctrines; a fossil from the days of Western feudalism' (Van Caenegem 1973, p. 105). Van Caenegem (ibid., pp. 108–109) explains this turn-about with the early timing of common law's establishment: this transpired before the revival of Roman law could have had a profound impact on it, and, afterwards, common law's firmly-rooted structures successfully resisted Romanist influences.

Other paradoxes materialised with the arrival of the politically-animated seventeenth century, a crucial period in the development of common-law doctrine. Common law had surfaced as royal law, as an instrument of the king for consolidating his power base. Now it was consulted to support the domestication of unrestricted royal power. By the same token, defenders of common law, this precocious moderniser, advocated what can be termed traditionalist conceptions against forces representing further modernisation!

In what follows, I am interested in the self-understanding of common law as articulated in the seventeenth and eighteenth centuries by the classics of English legal literature, such as Edward Coke (1555–1634), Matthew Hale (1609–1676) and William Blackstone (1723–1780). This phase of common-law thinking is especially pertinent with regard both to its immediate discursive context and to its socio-political environment. Common-law writers articulated their standpoints in defence against emerging positivist thinking; in seventeenth-century debates, the leading proponent of the positivist stance was Thomas Hobbes, whereas Jeremy Bentham was the main and sharpest critic of common law at the turn of the eighteenth century. In turn, the socio-political backdrop was provided by the further centralisation of political power and the extension of market relations; that is, processes pivotal to societal modernisation. In the seventeenth-century debates, the political edge of interventions by common-law theorists was directed against aspirations for royal absolutism. As is implied by, for instance, C.B. Macpherson's (1962) thesis of possessive individualism, Hobbes' political philosophy can be related, not only to royal absolutism, but to economic modernisation, too. The ties of Bentham's legal positivism to socio-economic modernisation are even more conspicuous. Bentham was well aware that a community built on personal relations and tradition, presumed by common-law thinking, was being replaced by a society of individuals integrated through contract-based social relations.

In this transitional phase, the advocates of common law felt the need to formulate its conception of law, with its traditionalist elements, as clearly as possible. In the following, I shall largely rely on previous analyses of classic common-law ideology, in particular, on those of Gerald J. Postema (1989, 2002 and 2003) and J.G.A. Pocock (1989, pp. 212ff.). My aim is to shed light on the battle between old and new, traditionalist and modern elements, in the development of English law, and to procure material for further discussion on the role of *ratio* and *voluntas* in law. I am not claiming to offer a fresh account of English legal doctrine in the seventeenth and eighteenth centuries; rather, my objective is to create a background and a contrast to 'mature' modern law's cultural specificity and to discuss the tasks which fall on the *ratio* under the conditions of modern law.

Pocock characterises common-law ideology, as established in about 1600 or even earlier, as both traditionalist and empiricist. It was traditionalist in identifying the law with immemorial custom, which was declared and interpreted in countless decisions of common-law courts. It was empiricist in the sense that in new cases, the law as immemorial custom was constantly subjected to the test of experience. In fact, what was immemorial in common law was not its content but its unbroken continuity. The law consisted of a series of responses to demands raised by ever-new situations. Pocock (1989, p. 221) refers to Hale's way of depicting the law as a river: what was important for Hale was the uninterrupted flow of this river, not the exact contents of the water.

The authority of the law, its validity, derived from the continuity of custom, tradition; what was crucial was the conviction of the present authority, the obliging nature, of uninterrupted tradition. The law was historical in character, with its historicity oriented towards the past. Law, such as presented in seventeenth-century common-law doctrine, did not yet reflect the modern differentiation of time horizons: the past dominated the present, and the present conveyed the past to the future.

In such a view of law, the judges were not supposed to make but to declare law: *jus dicere* and not *jus dare*. The role of common-law judges was pivotal, but it was the role of an oracle, as Blackstone famously put it, or of a guardian, as Giddens would say. Common-law ideology distinguished between the law and the formulation a judge gave to it; the judge's formulation was never final or authoritative. This distinction is akin to the conceptual pair of 'sources of origin' and 'sources of (re)cognition', employed by the German historical school of the early nineteenth century in its doctrine of legal sources (see Chapter 3). Common-law practices also included a ritualistic element. As Postema (1989, p. 72) has noted, 'the processes and practices of common law define a kind of public ritual; engaging in practices used "time out of mind" is significant for participants, not because their actions simply reiterate age-old routines, but because these actions, like ritual acts, *re-enact* traditional patterns and give them a sense of continuity with the past'.

Thus, common law was seen to express immemorial custom and tradition, continuity with the past. But what tradition, and whose custom, exactly? Here we confront some of the central ambiguities of common-law thought, which should caution against seeing legal modernisation as a linear, evolutionary process and projecting into it a black-and-white contrast between pre-modern and modern.

Common law emerged in the late twelfth century as royal law, and an integral role in its establishment was played by royal legislation: royal assizes and writs. How, then, could common law in general be said to embody immemorial custom? Part of the answer lies in the distinction between unwritten and written law, *lex non scripta* and *leges scriptae*, which still had a prominent place in the writings of seventeenth-century common lawyers, such as Hale. As Postema (1989, p. 14) has made clear, the distinction was related to the law's validity basis, and not to its mode of documentation. *Lex non scripta* derived its validity from communal practices and immemorial custom, whereas the validity of *leges scriptae* was of a formal nature: it received its authority from its being established by an acknowledged lawmaking body in an acknowledged procedure. It was possible that *lex non scripta* had also been expressed in formal laws, but these did not substitute for communal custom and tradition as its validity basis. Medieval legal thinking reserved a place for written laws. But legislation was supposed to fulfil the same task as court decisions: it only gave linguistic form to a law which already existed embedded in the community's traditional practices. Even the legislator was not supposed to create new law but merely articulate existing law. It was also possible that a transition occurred from *lex scripta* to *lex non scripta*: that a law which first derived its validity from an enactment was later accepted as part of the fabric of customarily validated common law.

Another explanation can be sought in the specific focus of royal legislation through which the centralised, nation-wide common-law system was established. The royal assizes and writs regulated forms of action, legal procedures and remedies available for particular grievances. This conferred upon common law its particular procedural emphasis, some of which it retains even today. As H. Patrick Glenn (2007, p. 29) puts it, 'the history of the common law is dominated by questions of jurisdictions, writs, and remedies'. As regards substantive law, much leeway existed for custom and tradition.

However, we have not yet cleared all the ambiguities surrounding common law's customary nature and its relation to tradition. We still have to discuss common law's relation to two, partially overlapping, distinctions: that between local and 'general' custom, and that between the custom of the people at large (the legal community in the broad sense) and the custom of the corps of professional lawyers (the legal community in the narrow sense).

As Glenn (ibid., pp. 29–30) has expounded, the royal, common-law courts recognised two types of custom: general and local. General custom equalled the (substantive) common-law doctrine which was implicit in judicial practice but which was not necessarily given explicit written form (the notion of *stare decisis* did not develop until the nineteenth century). In fact, this custom was primarily upheld by the closely-knit corps of professional lawyers and transmitted from generation to generation through the craft-like initiation of new members of the corps. But this professional tradition was influenced by, and maintained contact with, the customs of the realm. Thus, 'the rules and principles and standards and concepts to be enforced', such as definitions of felonies, and the concepts of seisin and disseisin, 'took their meaning from custom and usage'; they 'were derived from informal, unwritten, enacted norms and patterns of behavior' (Berman 1983, pp. 480–481).

Common-law courts were not only introduced as centralised royal courts; they also included a local, popular element in the shape of the jury. Through the jury, local customs, held up by communal practices, could influence the substantive law applied in common-law courts: 'the jury's monopoly of decision-making on the substance of a case meant that local custom could continue to prevail (in indiscernible form) until the abolition of the obligatory role of the jury in the nineteenth century' (Glenn 2007, p. 30; see also Postema 2002, p. 163). The royal judges, too, applied local custom, 'to the extent their functions required and to the extent local custom was the object of proof' (Glenn 2007, p. 30).

So common law was pervaded by elements of a customary nature. However, the varied, partly even contradictory character of these elements often makes it difficult to discern what common-law writers exactly refer to when they emphasise common law's customary features (and virtues!). This holds not only for the classical writings of the seventeenth and eighteenth centuries but even contemporary theorists.

The emphasis on common law's customary features must be understood in the setting of increasing legislation, resulting from further centralisation of political power. Common lawyers were responding to the doctrines of, first, *royal prerogative* and, subsequently, *parliamentary sovereignty*. They were also confronting the emergent *positivist theory of law*: custom was closely linked to the *ratio* with which common law was supposed to tame the *voluntas* of posited law. Postema (2003, p. 18) summarises seventeenth-century common lawyers' view of legislation as follows:

> Typically, common lawyers in this era contrasted the reasoned and considered judgments of the courts with the arbitrary and heedless legislation of Parliament. The latter they regarded as the product of a temporary aggregate of wills rather than the product of publicly deliberated common judgment. Because legislators were not constrained by any rational discipline beyond the political pressures of the moment, even the most reasonable of them could not be expected to create laws that fitted coherently into the common law or the common life of the people. Moreover, legislation, commands of a sovereign law-maker, represented an inherently troubling exercise of power in the eyes of common lawyers.

Arguments of this type were destined to have a great future: they resurfaced in the nineteenth-century codification debates, not only in England, but also in Germany and the United States, and they are not wholly foreign to contemporary discussion, either. Some critical reader may perhaps detect traces from them even in this study!

Positivist legal theory, along with the doctrines of royal prerogative and parliamentary sovereignty, stood diametrically opposed to the traditional medieval conception of legislation as a mere articulation of existing law. It was premised on the king's or parliament's power to establish *new* law, which was not seen, or at least not exclusively, as an expression of social order but could be engaged in a deliberate effort of modifying that order. Legislation that derived from the will of individual persons and not from the existing order of the community posed a serious threat to the authority and the coherence of common law (Postema 1989, pp. 14–16).

Postema (ibid., pp. 16ff.) has perceived various strategies with which common-law theory responded to the threat arising from written law. One of them still treated legislation as primarily an expression of common law, *lex non scripta*. If this was not possible, the text of the legislation should be construed as narrowly as possible, in order not to upset the coherence of common law. The implicit premise was that written law could only be accepted as part of English law if it could be reconciled with common law. Hale, for his part, built his argument on the transformation of written law's validity basis, on written law's incorporation into common law. Hale distinguished between written and unwritten law in the accustomed way with reference to their validity basis: written law drew its validity from a legislative decision, taken in compliance with the constitution, and unwritten law from custom and communal practices. But he noted that part of unwritten law had its origin in Acts of Parliament. However, over time and due to their application and interpretation by common-law courts, these laws had been incorporated into common law. Their validity basis had changed; they no longer owed their validity to the procedure of their establishment but to their being part of common law (Hale 1971, pp. 3–6). But, of course, it was possible, too, that no successful incorporation occurred; that common law rejected legislative implants. In such a case, they had but very restricted legal significance; they existed merely 'as isolated rules, temporary surface disturbances on the legal sea having no deep impact' (Postema 1989, p. 25).

As Coke, Hale and Blackstone articulated classical common-law thinking, the doctrine of the rule of law – the Anglo-Saxon counterpart to the *Rechtsstaat* notion – had not yet been formulated; the basic text of modern rule of law doctrine, A.V. Dicey's (1835–1922) *Introduction to the Study of Constitution* was published as late as 1885. I shall discuss this doctrine in Chapter 7. For now it is enough to say that the variants Postema has discerned in common law's reaction to written law's expansion make a re-entry in the debates on the rule of law. With one exception: the medieval notion of legislation as a mere manifestation and recording of customary law had lost its credibility in the latter half of the nineteenth century.

In the view of the seventeenth- and eighteenth-century common lawyers, common law embodied not only custom but also reason: the *voluntas* of written law – and the narrowly conceived reason allied with this *voluntas* – was opposed by the *ratio* of common law. This *ratio* was of a particular character: it was supposed to be *artificial reason* in contrast to the *natural reason* which all human beings, including the sovereign ruler, possessed. Let us try to specify both sides of the contrast, both 'natural' and 'artificial' reason.

In the polemics of the seventeenth century, the term 'natural reason' appears to have had two different connotations, one more backward- and another more forward-looking. The latter, forward-looking conception was articulated by Hobbes in his common-law criticism. However, I shall start with the former, backward-looking understanding of natural reason.

According to Postema (2003, p. 2), one of the earliest uses of the notion of artificial reason was Sir Edward Coke's response to James I's (1566–1625) attempts to encroach upon the jurisdiction of common-law courts. Coke contrasted common law's artificial reason with the natural reason which informed the king's sovereign will. Coke argued that 'the common law itself is nothing else but reason', but specified that this was 'an artificial perfection of reason gotten by long study, observation, and experience, and not every man's natural reason'. Coke pointed out that 'his Majesty was not learned in the laws of his realm of England, and causes which concern the life, or inheritance, or good, or fortunes of his subjects, are not to be decided by natural reason, but by the artificial reason and judgment of law'.

Coke's conception of 'natural reason' still bore connotations drawn from late-medieval, scholastic natural-law thinking – 'the reason of broad, universal principles external to ordinary sources of law, accessible to individual rational minds, by which that law is measured' (Postema 2002, p. 178). In late-medieval doctrine, which had received its great synthesis in Thomas Aquinas' (1225–1274) *Summa Theologiae*, natural laws constituted a part of objective reason: of *lex aeterna* which defined the rational order of the universe. Through their in-born subjective reason, human beings were seen to participate in this objective rational reason: they found inscribed in their subjective reason those principles of the objective rational order which related to human and communal life. Human, subjective reason was subordinated to the objective reason establishing the order of the universe.

Common-law thinking abandoned scholastic natural law's immutable *ratio* which was supposed to direct human legislation and define its substantive limits as an external yardstick. In common-law writings, the *ratio* was both historicised and internalised. Common law's artificial reason was of a *historical* character; it was wisdom accumulated over the centuries in common-law practices. And it was also *immanent* in the law, in the legal tradition, and not an external measure by which the law could be judged. As Pocock (1989, pp. 220–221) notes, according to common-law ideology, laws had been generated in circumstances and for reasons which there could be no knowledge of and which, therefore, could not be assessed or criticised. But the mere survival of a law justified the assumption that not only had it originally been beneficial but it had also subsequently adequately responded to the needs of situations where it had been invoked, and would satisfactorily resolve the problem at hand, too.

In contrast to natural law, common law's *ratio* was not universalist and abstract but particularistic and pragmatic reason. It was inseparable from individual cases whose uninterrupted chain bestowed upon the law its coherence. The reasoning of common-law judges proceeded from case to case; it was not deductive or inductive but rather *analogical* by nature. Hale argued – obviously to counter Hobbes – that a philosopher may well detect logical connections between abstract ideas but these ideas do not provide solutions to practical legal problems (Postema 1989, p. 31). Analogical reasoning served the solution of concrete cases, not abstract theorising.

Common law was implicit in its practices; norms and practices had not yet been differentiated in the way often held typical of modern law. Correspondingly, common law's artificial *ratio* cannot be separated from the 'subjective' reason brought to bear by its practitioners. Common law was seen, first of all, as a *practice*, and its reason matched the reason its practitioners exercised. In contrast to individually employed natural reason, common law's artificial reason was shared reason, to be learned and put into effect in joint practices. Instead of the natural reason all individuals possessed but used separately, to partake of common law's artificial reason required skills that could only be achieved by means of time-consuming studies and extensive practical experience. In this way, the notion of artificial reason also justified the craft-like education of future lawyers, so typical of common law (Postema 2003, pp. 3–11).

Coherence was seen as an integral feature of common law's rationality. But at issue was *local coherence* implicit in analogical reasoning and serving the pragmatic aim of case-solving, but not systematic global coherence achieved through abstract theorising. Let me present the argument through an illuminating, although rather lengthy, citation from Postema (2003, p. 5):

> Indeed, analogical thinking rested on the conviction that past decisions set examples, established patterns for future deliberation and action and must cohere with other solutions of the law. This was a major constraint on their pragmatic problem-solving. Still, common lawyers typically sought *local* coherence. Global theoretical coherence of the law was seldom of concern, unless the case actually demanded it. Artificial reason was simply not much interested in abstract theory, either for its own sake or as a potential fund of resources for solving the practical problems it faced. It was unsystematic in its primary motivations, in the perspective it took on the problems it addressed, and in the solutions that is sought for them … it was content with what, from a more theoretical perspective, might have appeared to be a lack of systematic coherence. Overall coherence of moral or practical vision was less important to common lawyers than workability on the ground. As conceived by its practitioners, common law resisted reduction to a system of axioms, an economical set of first principles from which its constituent maxims, rules, and decisions could (at least in principle) be inferred.

It is true, though, that eighteenth-century authors such as Blackstone, the first occupant of the first chair in English law in Oxford, might argue in terms of a rational science of common law, supposed to articulate its general principles; these might even be called natural-law principles. However, the *ratio* of these principles, too, was practical and historical in character, internal to the tradition; the common-law scholar's natural law was not aprioristic but historical natural law. The principles were to be distilled from individual decisions which manifested common law's inherent reason (Postema 1989, p. 36). Accordingly, Lord Mansfield (1705–1793), whom Neil Duxbury has named 'perhaps the greatest 18th-century defender of the view that the common law is founded upon reason and principle', argued that the common law 'does not consist in particular cases, but in general principles which run through cases and govern the decision of them' (Duxbury 2004, p. 146).

At least as seen through its self-understanding, formulated by seventeenth- and eighteenth-century writers, common law displayed many features of a tradition in the historical-sociological sense. These include the narrow boundaries restricting critical reflection. Reason was inherent in common law as a tradition; no external rational yardstick existed against which common law could be assessed. As Postema (1989, p. 76) notes, criticism was possible only within the tradition. It was possible to question whether certain particular customs or practices were compatible with the tradition, but the tradition itself could not be challenged.[5]

Hobbes, an advocate of the positivist conception of law, rejected the doctrine of artificial reason which could only be deciphered by professional judges as their craft mystery and which was ultimately impervious to reflective reason; he regarded such a doctrine as dangerous to both the human mind and the stability of the state (Pocock 1989, p. 216). Hobbes criticised common-law authors' notion of artificial reason from the direction of both the *voluntas* and the *ratio*. He defined 'law' in general in terms of positive law, as a command of the sovereign: 'it is not wisdom, but Authority that makes a Law' (1971, p. 55). The law's validity did not derive from *ratio* but from *voluntas*: the will of the sovereign. In lawmaking, the sovereign was, though, guided by reason, but this was his natural, subjective reason. The law was and should be a product of natural reason, and as such comprehensible to anybody with the right use of their rational faculty.

Sir Matthew Hale, defending the notion of common law's artificial reason against Hobbes, seems to have still used 'natural reason' in its backward-looking meaning.[6] But that was not the position from which Hobbes attacked common law's artificial reason. In comparison with common law's alleged inherent reason, the natural reason employed by sovereign legislative *voluntas* was of an external character. However, it had very little in common with the Thomist view of the objective rational order of the universe and of the subjective reason partaking of this order. Hobbes defined practical reason in terms of ends-means rationality, as *instrumental reason*: '(those) actions are most reasonable, that conduce most to their ends' (1976, XV, s. 204). When individuals enter into a social contract with each other and establish a political body, they also commit themselves to obeying the sovereign's will, guided by his natural, instrumental reason: through his laws, the sovereign pursues specific aims, most importantly that of preserving the peace. Laws are based on natural reason, defined in instrumental terms, for the simple reason that this is the only kind of practical reason that Hobbes acknowledged.

Common-law authors embraced a traditionalist, communal view of social bonds. By contrast, Hobbes' positivism implied a view of society which Cotterrell (1996, p. 223) has termed *imperium*: 'the image of individual subjects of a superior political authority'. In the *Gemeinschaft–Gesellschaft* distinction coined by Ferdinand Tönnies (1855–1936), it clearly comes close to a *Gesellschaft* of atomistic individuals and contractual social relations. Sovereign power and laws as the sovereign's commands unite individuals no longer present to each other in the way assumed in a *Gemeinschaft* conception. Instrumental ends–means rationality also opened the law's temporality towards the future and facilitated uncoupling

5 In his concept of tradition, MacIntyre (1988, pp. 349ff.) emphasises that the criteria of rationality are always derived from a certain tradition.

6 'Hale contrasted the judge's disciplined reason with the natural reason, not of ordinary persons, but of "casuists, schoolmen, moral philosophers" and political actors trained by them' (Postema 2003, p. 3).

the future from the past. Bentham's detachment from the traditionalist, close-knit community of a *Gemeinschaft* was, if possible, even more conspicuous; he adopted 'the conception of a pluralistic, individualistic society bound by agreement – or the perceived need – to abide by certain rules of the game which organised and co-ordinated otherwise chaotic activity of individuals in pursuit of individually defined goals' (Postema 1989, p. 310).

The Shifting Positions of *Ratio* and *Voluntas*

In Chapter 1, the constitutive tension between *ratio* and *voluntas* was introduced through analyses of Cotterrell and Luhmann. But they are not the first to have approached the history of law and legal discourse in these terms. Cotterrell explicitly connects to one of his precursors: Franz L. Neumann (1900–1954), a German scholar forced to emigrate from Nazi Germany, first to London and later to the United States, who was affiliated to the Frankfurt School of Max Horkheimer (1895–1973) and Theodor W. Adorno (1903–1966).

Neumann views modern law as predominantly positive in character; law has undergone a process of disenchantment (*Entzauberung*), as Neumann, with overt reference to Max Weber, chooses to portray positive law's gradual detachment from natural law (Neumann 1980, p. 85). Starting from the dissolution of Thomist natural-law thinking, Western political and legal philosophy has been pervaded by the antinomy between force and law, might and right, sovereignty and the rule of law (*Rechtsstaatlichkeit*), or *voluntas* and *ratio*. Neumann argues that this antinomy found its completion in Kant's strict separation of law and morals (ibid., p. 168), which – we can add – was later adopted in Kelsen's pure theory of law and other variants of twentieth-century legal positivism.

According to Neumann, the antinomy between *voluntas* and *ratio* led to two different concepts of law: a political one and a rational one. The *political* concept reduces law to mere *voluntas*: it identifies law with the decision of the sovereign, regardless of content or of individual or general focus. This was Hobbes' concept of law, and in subsequent jurisprudence, so Neumann claims, John Austin (1790–1859) was Hobbes' most consequent and uncompromising disciple.

The *rational* concept, by contrast, is substantively determined. It does not see law in every measure of the sovereign, nor does it restrict the law merely to such measures of the sovereign. Law is *ratio* and includes an ethical postulate, such as the requirement of equality. Law can be issued by the sovereign, but this is not conceptually necessary: rational, substantive laws can also exist without relation to the sovereign will and even if the positive laws of the state ignore their postulates (Neumann 1967, pp. 11–19).

Neumann holds both sovereignty and the rule of law constitutive of the modern state. They are also interdependent. In a way reminiscent of Duncan Kennedy's later analysis of liberal law's fundamental contradiction (Kennedy 1976), Neumann suggests that right cannot be realised without might, without the modern state's coercive machinery. But can right and might, *ratio* and *voluntas*, freedom and coercion, be reconciled? This, according to Neumann, has been the fundamental problem for modern political philosophy: 'the history of political thinking in the modern era is the history of this attempt to find a justification for might *and* right, for law *and* force' (ibid., p. 124). Neumann himself seems to be rather ambivalent on this issue. On the one hand, he argues that sovereignty and the rule of law are irreconcilable, because 'supreme power and supreme law cannot be simultaneously realised within a common sphere' (Neumann 1980, p. 16). He relates the antinomy to pre-war German jurisprudential debates and remarks that neither Carl Schmitt's (1888–1985) norm-less will nor Hans Kelsen's will-less norm was able to provide a solution to the dilemma (ibid., p. 19). But, on the other hand, as William E. Scheuerman has shown, he hints at the possibility of reconciling antinomy through democratic lawmaking: a democratic sovereign produces normatively legitimate laws. Sovereignty can also be regulated through rational law: Schmitt's norm-less will and Kelsen's will-less norm can be replaced by a 'normed will' (Scheuerman 1997, pp. 178–179 and 200–205). Here Neumann clearly anticipates Habermas' way of tackling the tension between *voluntas* and *ratio* (see Chapter 7).

Neumann connects the rational concept of law to natural-law thinking, whose developments he follows from the late-medieval Thomist version onwards. But, in fact, the law's identification with reason is of an even more ancient origin and goes back to antiquity. Cicero (106–43 BCE) coined the catchphrase *lex est suprema ratio*, frequently cited in late-medieval and early modern writings. After the revival of Roman law, the jurists called *Corpus juris civilis* written reason, *ratio scripta*. It was the foundation of the *ius commune* and served as a measure of the rationality of *leges propria*: local customs and positive legislation (Van Caenegem 1993, p. 125; Berman 1983, pp. 140–141). Identifying the revived Roman law with the law's *ratio* proves that the latter could have other than natural-law sources, too; it is true, though, that Romanist jurisprudence maintained a certain interconnection with natural-law doctrine. In the seventeenth and eighteenth-century English debates, the classic common-law writers claimed *ratio* for their side. But their *ratio* was of a very different kind than the natural reason of Thomist natural-law thinking.

Lon Fuller (1902–1978) once remarked: 'When it is said that law represents the rule of reason, it is appropriate to ask what kind of reason is meant' (Fuller 1968, p. 5).[7] Indeed, we should be very attentive to the wide variety of meanings assigned to the law's *ratio*. The *ratio scripta* of *ius commune* is not identical to the all-embracing *ratio* of the Thomist system, nor can the latter be equated with the historical and pragmatically-oriented reason of English common law. Within natural-law thinking, a significant shift occurred with the advent of the early modern individualist doctrine. In eighteenth-century Germany, the school of *Vernunftrecht* followed a geometric model (*moro geometrico*) where legal rules were deduced from self-evident axioms; again, the law's *ratio* acquired novel features. In turn,

7 Postema (2003, p. 2) uses Fuller's phrase as a motto for the second part of his article on classic common-law jurisprudence.

German nineteenth-century conceptual jurisprudence (*Begriffsjurisprudenz*) justified legal science's 'productive' tasks by the law's allegedly logically-oriented rationality (see Chapter 3); a rationality which had very little to do with, say, the artificial reason of the seventeenth- and eighteenth-century common-law doctrine. In the light of this historical resumé, it does not come as a surprise that current proponents of rationalist understanding – say, Habermas and Dworkin – are by no means unanimous about what, exactly, the law's particular rationality amounts to.

The debates of common-law writers with Hobbes and Bentham occurred at the dawn of societal modernisation. Their notion of (legal) tradition and its immanent *ratio*, whose competence did not extend to questioning the tradition itself, has not been able to withstand the pressure of cultural modernisation. Yet I would argue that, in many respects, the seventeenth- and eighteenth-century English debates staked out positions from which *ratio* and *voluntas* have in subsequent legal theory judged each other. The *ratio* with which the law's *voluntas* has been contrasted has undergone many conversions. By contrast, the other pole of the tension, that of the *voluntas*, has proved to be more stable. The *voluntas* has been associated with the sovereignty of the nation-state legislator. Portrayals of the *voluntas* include such extremities as Carl Schmitt's unbound sovereign dictator whose existential decisions arise 'from nothing' (*aus Nichts*) (Schmitt-Dorotic 1921). But in general it would be wrong to conceive of the *voluntas* in terms of irrationality or arationality. As was already the case with Hobbes' sovereign, the legislator, too, is informed by a particular rationality: by external, instrumental reason, which treats the law as a means to achieve the goals of the political *voluntas*.

Hobbes' sovereign was, of course, not yet the legislator *qua* social engineer of the welfare state, trying to guide societal development; the sovereign aimed at securing the framework conditions for a society of the *Gesellschaft* type, maintaining social peace and uniting the individual members of society under his commands – the laws. Nor did Bentham's legislator yet, in the manner of the future welfare state, see society as a national project to be realised in time: the tasks of legislation were, as Bentham conceived of them, still confined to framework regulation. He defined these tasks starting from the premises of utilitarian philosophy. His positivism was utilitarian positivism: according to him, legislation's 'greatest utility lies in defining a stable framework of publicly recognised rules which provide a focus for expectations regarding the behaviour of both citizens and officials' (Postema 1989, p. 210). Legislation was to provide a stable framework for social intercourse, not to influence the direction of society's development or to cure its ills, unlike welfare-state interventionist regulation.

Bentham formulated his version of legal positivism in terms of the sovereign's commands. Legal rules shared a common source, which was instrumental to legal clarity and stability. For Bentham, law was 'a (systematically arranged) set of commands backed by threats all of which commands can be traced directly or indirectly to a common source in the legislative acts of a sovereign whose sovereignty rests on the habit of obedience of the bulk of the community' (ibid., p. 218). Austin adopted from Bentham both the utilitarian philosophy and the command theory of law. Through the impact of Austin, these premises continued to dominate English jurisprudence until H.L.A. Hart's arrival on the scene in the middle of the twentieth century (Duxbury 2005).

Let us try to sum up. Can we infer from the English seventeenth- and eighteenth-century debates such tasks for the law's *ratio* as would still be pertinent in our late modernity, even if the specific ways of fulfilling them differed from those suggested by common-law writers in their defence against the attacks of legal positivism?

I think we can. The most important of these tasks, of course, is the *disciplining of the legislator's voluntas*, which is the highly urgent issue behind lively debates on constitutional review (see Chapter 8). But that is not all there is to it. Common-law authors claimed that the law's inherent *ratio* maintained its *coherence*, which was continuously disturbed by the legislator's *voluntas*: through the instrumentalism of its reason and the volatility of its aims. A certain degree of coherence is still vital for the law (see Chapter 5), although the character of the coherence aspired for has not necessarily remained the same throughout modern law's subsequent development. Common law's coherence was of a *diachronic* nature: it linked the law's present and future with its past, in accordance with the dominance of the past as the law's principal time horizon. By its extension, it was local coherence produced by analogical thinking. The idea of comprehensive, synchronic and substantive coherence was rejected as contradictory to common law's traditionalism and pragmatism. As Hale argued against Hobbes, common law was based neither on general principles and consequences drawn from these, nor on scientific laws.

From the perspective of *voluntas*, adopted by Hobbes and Bentham, substantive coherence lost its crucial significance. The law's unity was formal rather than substantive, guaranteed by the law's origin in the sovereign's will. The natural-law elements in Hobbes' thinking vindicated the necessity of the sovereign and his positive legislation but did not determine the law's content: the law as the sovereign's command was obligatory irrespective of its content. The unity Bentham, in turn, was after was formal systemic unity which was produced by analytical concepts and classificatory premises corresponding to a Linnaean notion of science. Bentham advocated a code or set of codes which would be organised by a new conceptual apparatus, indicating a precise location for different types of norms and legal relations. Bentham belonged to the international codification movement of the turn of the eighteenth and nineteenth centuries, although the codification he espoused did not amount to such a recording of existing customary law as was accomplished by, say, Prussia's *Allgemeines Landrecht* or Austria's *Allgemeines Bürgerliches Gesetzbuch*. His codification purported to serve the cause of instrumental reason, to enhance the stability and transparency of the framework of a *Gesellschaft* society.[8] At the same time, Bentham inaugurated a particular strand in the systematisation of law: systematisation through analytical concepts, considered universal in their application. Here, too, Austin was destined to be his most important follower, who, in turn, transmitted Bentham's influence to twentieth-century jurisprudence.

One further task remains through which, at least in retrospect, common law's inherent *ratio* can be seen to have performed as a counterweight to *voluntas*. The instrumental reason of *voluntas* which positive law was purported to assist left no independent space for the *moral or ethical dimensions of practical reason*; indeed, Hobbes and Bentham as early legal positivists did not in general recognise any other but instrumental practical reason. It fell to common law's *ratio* to defend a broader vision of practical reason, not reduced merely to its instrumental aspect but maintaining its relation to the moral and ethical structures of communal life. This came to the fore in, for instance, the emphasis on common law's principled nature. In the eyes of many present-day authors as well, legal principles not only endow the law with its coherence but also keep open the channels which connect it to the moral and ethical spheres of society.

I shall conclude by drawing yet another link from the English seventeenth- and eighteenth-century debates to present-day jurisprudential controversies. Discussants embracing the perspective of *voluntas* often engage in an unmasking criticism of the law's alleged *ratio*; the interlocutor's speech acts are examined in terms of their perlocutionary aims or effects, such as pursuing narrow professional interests. This is reductionism typical of the *voluntas'* point of view: *ratio* is defined in *voluntas'* terms. Hobbes' common-law criticism can be read as an early version of the Critic's narrative: through their doctrine of the law's artificial reason, common-law judges and lawyers tried to elevate their own opinions into law, and, thus, contradicted both royal legislative power and the law's basic purposes (1971, p. 55). In Bentham's attack on common law, the critical theme is even more salient.

Bentham's declared critical aim was to demythologise, 'to pluck the mask of Mystery from the face of Jurisprudence' (1988, p. 21), and to demonstrate the glaring incongruity between common law's theory and practice. In his account, common law's reason or 'historical natural law' was 'the mere opinion of men self-constituted into Legislators' and could not constitute any public standard, independent of the person propounding it. Common law had become a totally incomprehensible jungle of legal fictions, and its artificial language could only be deciphered by legal professionals. Its sins included both rigidness and manipulativeness. The arbitrariness and uncontrollability of judges' decisions made them essentially retroactive; legal certainty lost its basis, and common law could not accomplish the law's function of stabilising the expectations of the members

8 For Bentham, the greatest utility of codification 'lies in defining a stable framework of publicly recognised rules which provide a focus for expectations regarding the behaviour of both citizens and officials' (Postema 1989, p. 210).

of society. Legal fictions were 'lies, devised by judges to serve as instruments of, and cloaks to, injustice'. This injustice was manifest by judicial usurpation of legislative power, and corruption. The aim of the legal profession, Judge & Co, was 'the extracting, on joint account, and for joint benefit, out of the pockets of the people, in the largest quantity possible, the produce of the industry of the people' (Postema 1989, pp. 267ff.).

Contemporary variants of the Critic's narrative may seem quite moderate in tone, compared to the harsh verdict Bentham meted out to the common-law doctrine and practice of his time. But Postema's assessment applies to both Bentham's critical narrative and its contemporary successors: 'Cynical acid sometimes washes away more than mystification' (Postema 2003, p. 2).[9]

The Traditions of Modern Law

Even under the conditions of modern law, legal actors confront legal problems equipped with a pre-understanding, with certain 'prejudices'; traditions in the philosophical-hermeneutical sense form part and parcel of modern law, too. Legal traditions in the philosophical-hermeneutical sense are still very much with us today, whereas traditions in the historical-sociological sense, by contrast, can only be discussed with strong qualifications. On the line leading from traditions to expert systems, the law has moved towards the latter pole. The example of common law, though, serves as an admonition against simplistic evolutionary assumptions of a linear process of modernisation; by no means has the law ever shed all features of a tradition. Legal proceedings, for instance, still display many ritualistic traits; and these can be of considerable significance for the law's (empirical) legitimacy, as Niklas Luhmann's analyses in *Legitimation durch Verfahren* (1983) demonstrate. In common-law countries, in particular, the ideal of a legal practitioner still possesses traits that recall a craftsman working within a tradition rather than a universalist expert (Kronman 2001). And in the legal scholarship of Continental Romano-Germanic legal cultures, a critical gaze may still discern traces of a tradition, guarded by law professors. Nevertheless, in the context of the law, too, the general drift from tradition towards expert system should be conspicuous enough, both in civil- and common-law cultures.

The development of modern law might seem to suggest that legal positivism, represented by Hobbes and Bentham, has gained a clear victory over its interlocutors; that *voluntas* has vanquished *ratio*. The law has become essentially dependent on explicit decisions, and the legislator's *voluntas* has become its most important source. The law has opened up to the future and detached itself from the temporal and spatial delimitations of tradition and custom. Yet – and this is one of the main theses of this study – *ratio* has a role to play even in 'mature'

9 The cynical acid metaphor seems to stem from Felix Cohen's classic article, attacking American legal conceptualism (Cohen 1935, p. 840).

modern law; the tasks that seventeenth- and eighteenth-century writers assigned to common law's artificial reason are still pertinent. This holds not merely for the pre-understanding indispensable for legal actors.

The problem of the limits of *voluntas* has only been aggravated due to the law's enhanced instrumentality. The law's instrumental tasks have greatly expanded from the framework regulation which both Hobbes and Bentham had in mind; they could not, of course, imagine the interventionism of the welfare state. Because of the legislator's 'increased loquacity',[10] the need for a 'critical reflexive' instance in the law[11] is more urgent than perhaps ever before. But this need cannot be satisfied by a tradition, such as the one to which the classic common-law view still gave voice. Nor is the alternative of eternal and immutable natural-law principles any longer available. Coherence, too, is a quality also essential to modern law, required by such fundamental principles as (formal) equality and predictability. The law cannot sever its ties to morals and ethics, either. Law is not only a medium in the service of social engineering; it is also an institution reinforcing the moral structures of the *Lebenswelt*. Furthermore, the law cannot gain its legitimacy without maintaining its ties to morals and ethics.

So the tasks which fell to legal tradition in classic common-law doctrine are still with us. However, they must now be accomplished in a way which stands in harmony with cultural modernisation and increasing reflexivity. The law's *ratio* can no longer be traditional reason, which restricted rather than facilitated critical reflexion.

'Legal culture' is a contested concept of which many conceptions have been suggested (Nelken 1997). In my proposal, legal culture constitutes the law's sub-surface layer which provides legal actors with the necessary normative, conceptual and methodological resources and in this sense creates the very possibility of legal practices, such as lawmaking, adjudication and legal scholarship. My proposal attaches the concept of legal culture to the philosophical-hermeneutical notion of tradition: it is legal culture that provides legal actors with their hermeneutical pre-understanding. Legal culture thus conceived equals the elite culture of legal professionals (the legal community in *sensu stretto*), as distinct from the general legal culture of the population at large (the legal community in *sensu largo*) (Tuori 2002a, p. 161).

During the twelfth century, a critical period in the history of Western law, development of legal culture took divergent courses in England and on the Continent: England built up its specific common-law culture, whereas on the Continent the revival of Roman law, with its institutional foundation in university-based legal scholarship and education, spawned a transnational legal culture and a transnational corps of learned lawyers. Common-law culture evolved into a peculiar combination of backward- and forward-looking, of traditionalist and modern traits; the terms 'semi-traditionalist' or 'semi-modern' seem apposite here. On the

10 The expression stems from Michel Foucault (1981, p. 144).

11 The concept was coined by François Ewald (1986).

other hand, *pace* Berman's claim of twelfth-century Romanist jurisprudence as the prototype of modern Western science, it would be misleading to depict Romano-Germanic legal culture from the very outset in exclusively modernist terms. The portrayal of Roman law as *ratio scripta* implied strict limits to reflexive criticism: the scholastic method assumed the unquestionable truth of the holy scripts and allowed scholars solely the role of commentator, 'glossator', and organiser of inherited texts. The position university professors were assigned to in the legal systems of Northern Italy and, from the sixteenth century onwards, Germany bore traits of guardians of a tradition: if judges were the oracles of common law, learned jurists were the oracles of – especially German – civil law. Traces of the tradition-bound nature of legal criticism and the prominent role of university professors, most saliently exemplified by the procedure of *Aktenversendung*, clung to Romano-Germanic legal culture for centuries. One might argue that in this respect, fundamental changes only occurred in Germany after the heyday of Pandectism had come to an end with the enactment of the *Bürgerliches Gesetzbuch* in 1896.

So as regards both civil- and common-law cultures, care should be taken to avoid oversimplifying the vicissitudes of legal history. But, as a general tendency, legal culture is increasingly deprived of those features reminiscent of the historical-sociological concept of tradition. Modernisation has, though, manifested itself in divergent ways and forms in common-law countries and the civil-law countries of Continental Europe; in addition, significant differences exist between English and US legal development. I shall attempt to draw a tentative picture of the distinctive features of modern legal actors' pre-understanding; the picture will – so I hope – be clarified and deepened in later chapters. My own background explains and – so I hope – justifies my focus on Continental legal culture.

On the Continent, legal scholarship has borne the main responsibility in articulating and elaborating general doctrines of the various branches of law. Legal concepts, principles and theories, along with the prevailing doctrine of legal sources and specific patterns of legal argumentation, constitute an integral part of professional legal culture. In this sense, legal scholarship replaces pre-modern tradition as the source of legal pre-understanding. In a modern legal system, legal actors draw their necessary pre-understanding from a professional legal culture, interpreted, elaborated and articulated by academic legal science. In addition, the systematisation of legal normative material, accomplished by legal scholarship, plays an important role in guaranteeing the law's coherence.

Contemporary legal scholarship is a plural rather than a singular entity. Ever since the turn of the nineteenth century, different 'traditions' have competed with each other: say, conceptualism in its German or US version with realist and analytical schools, or Critical Legal Studies, as well as Law and Economics, with mainstream (liberal) scholarship. But these 'traditions' cannot be equated with the exclusive and critique-proof pre-modern traditions, as portrayed by Giddens. The 'traditions' of legal science are willing to discuss with each other, they are open to mutual criticism and even presuppose it. What Giddens has written about the debates and criticism within modern expert systems holds for discussions between various strands of legal scholarship, too.

The *possibility of criticism* is one of the main features that distinguish 'mature' modern law from previous types of law. Modern law is imbued with a fundamental positivity; it is based on conscious human actions, such as explicit decisions of the legislator and the judges. Through new decisions, new law can be created and existing law repealed. This requires the possibility of challenging and criticising inherited law; such distancing from the past which was still largely inconceivable for the traditionalist thinking of both classic common-law ideology and German pre-unification Romanist doctrine. Criticism is inexorably linked with mature modern law, whereas in pre-modern customary law and even in 'semi-modern' common- and civil-law cultures, it was limited to the narrow confines of tradition.

Traditions are said to perform their hermeneutical role mainly 'behind the back' of social actors, in the form of tacit knowledge (Tontti 2004, p. 31). This also holds for legal-cultural preconceptions through which modern legal actors confront legal problems. Legal culture – say, the general doctrines of the various branches of law or the prevailing doctrine of sources of law – plays its part primarily through the practical consciousness of legal actors, without their being immediately aware of its effect. Continental European law faculties act as transmitters of professional legal culture; future lawyers internalise it during their university studies, and it is actually this that makes them lawyers. It is because of the criminal-law principle of *nulla poena sine lege* that the judge checks in the code for a description of the crime and the latitude within which the sentence is to be meted out. But in the majority of cases this transpires in a quasi-automatic way, without the judge pausing to think about the demands of *nulla poena sine lege*. Judges explicitly thematise the principle and spell out its implications in their decisions only when, in the case at hand, its significance for some reason appears problematic. It may occur, for instance, that counsel for the defence challenges the validity of a *blanco* regulation which leaves the precise definition of the punishable crime to delegated legislation. As tacit knowledge, *nulla poena sine lege* or the principle of *pacta sunt servanda* function in all penal or contract law cases. It is, in fact, the self-evident applicability of these principles that makes routine cases routine; only in hard cases are the principles taken for closer examination.

What is important in a comparison with ideal-typical pre-modern, traditional law is that legal-cultural preconceptions can, when needed, be transformed from practical, tacit knowledge into a discursive form; they can be openly thematised and subjected to criticism. This is what happens when a court faces a hard case or when legal scholars criticise the prevailing doctrine and propose alternatives to it. Under the conditions of modern law, the possibility of criticism is not restricted to explicitly formulated surface-level norms but extends to their legal-cultural underpinnings. The law's cultural foundation is increasingly losing the sanctity it has enjoyed as a tradition. In their susceptibility to reciprocal criticism and their corrigibility, the 'traditions' of modern law are clearly closer to Giddens' expert knowledge than to the traditions of pre-modern society.

Many recent analysts have pointed to *reflexivity* as one of the distinctive features of modern society (see, e.g., Beck et al. 1994). This reflexivity is apparent in modern law, too. Modern law is predominantly positive law, resulting from conscious human action. The positivisation of law manifests the reflexivity of modern culture: the creation of new law through explicit decisions presupposes the openness of existing law to criticism, in the light of, for instance, the social consequences of legal regulations. Thus, Hart's secondary rules, characteristic of a developed legal system, include a rule of change, which implies the availability, even normality, of consciously induced legal alteration (Hart 1980, pp. 91–96).

In the traditionalist view, which still animated classical common-law authors, the law's *ratio* consisted of layered reason, the accumulated wisdom of bygone generations. Such an idea of the law's layered nature is foreign to the instrumental reason to which positivist legal theory and positivist critical narratives have inclined to reduce the law's rationality. However, a notion of *legal sedimentation* is essential for grasping the manner in which modern legal culture fulfils the tasks it has inherited from the tradition of traditional law: such as providing legal actors with their pre-understanding, disciplining the law's *voluntas*, as well as guaranteeing its coherence. Modern legal culture results from a sedimentation to which the different legal practices participating in production and reproduction of the legal order contribute. In the Continental civil-law culture, legal scholars' inputs, such as proposals for doctrinal reform, play an important role in launching the process of sedimentation. Their credentials are appraised in subsequent legal discourse, and sedimentation cannot get started if they are rejected by other legal actors – the legislator, judges, other legal scholars. In case of such rejection, legal scholars' innovations are destined to share the fate of Bentham's code, which with its new conceptual apparatus has remained a curiosity among the footnotes of the history of legal ideas. On the other hand, in modern legal culture a successful sedimentation is not irreversible. It is always possible to undertake a fresh critical assessment of prevailing legal concepts, principles and theories, as well as patterns of interpretation and argumentation. Hence, the idea of sedimentation is wholly compatible with the reflexivity of modern culture.

What I have called the relation of sedimentation also brings modern law's multi-layered nature into harmony with its positivity. Modern law's positivity must, though, be understood differently from positivist legal theory, say, from Hobbes to Kelsen and Hart. Positivity reaches out from the law's surface to its sub-surface layers. Legal culture, too, has its origin in individual legal speech acts, in the surface-level material produced by legal practices. So, arguably, in modern legal culture the law's *ratio* has been positivised. But this *ratio* amounts to something other than the instrumental reason of positivist legal theory or – we can add – the Critic's narrative.

The possibility of criticism is typical of legal scholarship's relation to the prevailing legal culture, just as it is typical of the expert's relation to expert knowledge and culture in general. But it is also important to stress the restrictions which legal criticism cannot escape even under modern conditions and which relativise the ideal-typical contrast between traditionalist and modern legal culture. Although no longer thwarted by the sanctity of tradition, legal criticism by necessity remains partial in character. It always focuses merely on a limited segment of the current culture, and what is not openly thematised and criticised is, as it were, taken for granted. Micro-criticism entails macro-legitimation, as Thomas Wilhelmsson (1992, p. 49) aptly puts it.

Several ways are available to conceptualise the constraints of criticism in modern law. The philosophical-hermeneutical perspective lays emphasis on the reliance on tradition of even critical interpreters. Not only is criticism always partial in its focus; furthermore, critics cannot draw the criteria and means of their criticism from anywhere else than their own culture, i.e. their tradition in the philosophical-hermeneutical sense. The dual citizenship of legal scholarship also points to the inescapable limits of legal criticism. In line with other legal practices, legal science participates in the law's continuous production and reproduction. This holds, even for critical legal science: through their very criticism, critics contribute to the reproduction of law, that is, the very object of their criticism. This constitutes what can be termed the *dilemma of a critical legal scholar* (Tuori 2002a, p. 308).

A sociologist influenced by Pierre Bourdieu (1930–2002) would approach the law as a social field where those holding different types of legal capital compete for the specific stake and price of the field: the power to say what the law is (Bourdieu 1987). The legal field is accessible only to those who agree to the basic rules of the game. If Critics try to challenge these very rules, they will be excluded, and the criticism they exercise is no longer legal criticism. Finally, we can draw a parallel with Habermas' (1984, 1989a) analysis of the modern *Lebenswelt*, the socio-cultural horizon of our everyday life. Members of modern society can contest the validity of their *Lebenswelt* culture, including its normative elements, but only in a piecemeal fashion, never as a whole. Correspondingly, legal actors can always dispute their legal culture, but never in its entirety.

In his study in the hermeneutical tradition, Tontti claims that all legal practices are bound by tradition and, by the same token, contribute to its transmission. This holds for the legislator, too: the past is the primary temporal dimension even for the legislator. In his support, Tontti (2004, p. 111) evokes Georg Wilhelm Hegel's (1770–1831) intervention in the famous codification debate, whose principal protagonists were Anton Thibaut (1772–1840) and Savigny (Hattenhauer 2002; Rückert 1984, pp. 160ff.). Hegel argued against Savigny's anti-codification stance and maintained that legislation only concretised and actualised customary law, but by no means came to a break with tradition (§ 211, Hegel 1952, p. 70). Here, Hegel still gave expression to the originally medieval view, also shared by the classic common-law authors, which did not yet differentiate between the roles of legislator and judge. Neither the legislator nor the judge was supposed so much to create new law as to declare and formulate existing law.

Again, basic philosophical-hermeneutical insights should not be allowed to block out important differences. The goal-rational approach of the modern legislator displays a wholly different temporality than was typical of, say, a seventeenth-century common-law judge bridging the legal past and future through articulating and interpreting immemorial custom's response to the exigencies of the legal problem at hand. Hegel clearly referred to early modern codifications, such as the Prussian *Allgemeines Landrecht* (1794), the Austrian *Allgemeines Bürgerliches Gesetzbuch* (1811) or – we might add – the Swedish Law of 1734. These were not products of the instrumentally-oriented legislator we have grown accustomed to during the era of the regulatory state. Indeed, the early modern codifications could, to a large extent, be conceived of as authentications and reaffirmations of pre-existing (customary) law, and, as such, they did play a prominent role in transmitting the law's past into the future (see, e.g., Watson 1985, pp. 110–111). The goal-rationality of the welfare-state legislator involves a wholly different temporal attitude. Now the emphasis shifts from the continuity of the past in the future to detachment of the future from the past.

In those areas where the law appears as a medium, we can talk of the transmission of 'tradition' at most in the general philosophical-hermeneutical sense. The basic temporal orientation is towards the future. A goal, defined in terms of a desired state of society, is set in the future, and legislation is treated as a means to achieve it. It is in the very figure of the legislator that modern, positive law's specific temporality finds its most conspicuous manifestation. The judge of traditionalist common-law ideology and the goal-rational lawmaker of the welfare state epitomise two fundamentally different approaches to the law's past and future.

But, again, a word of caution is needed. The authority of the goal-rational legislator varies, and specific modern, future-oriented temporality is not equally evident within every field of law. In modern society, the law is resorted to, not only as a medium of conscious social management, but also – to stick to Habermas' terms – as an institution buttressing the moral structures of society. Arguably, law as an institution – say, the core areas of criminal law and family law – retains stronger ties with the past than law as a medium.

A frequent objection to contrasting modern positive law to pre-modern, largely customary law is that customary law has by no means lost its significance in the modern era and that in certain areas we are currently even witnessing its expansion. But what today is called customary law is very different from the customary law of seventeenth- and eighteenth-century common-law ideology or, to take another example from the dawn of modernity, the 'custom of the land' referred to by the Swedish Law of 1734. Immemorial customs or communal practices are no longer paradigmatic of customary law. An illustrative case is offered by the practices engendered by new information and communication technology which have been accorded immediate legal relevance in EU law on data protection. Often enough, such practices have been explicitly codified by the social actors themselves; 'codes of good practice' abound in professions and activities related to modern expert systems. This amounts, paradoxically enough, to nothing short of a positivisation of customary law! Such customary law suggests more an expert system than a tradition.

In pre-modern law, judges usually play a central role in maintaining and transmitting legal tradition. Under modern law, too, the principal temporal dimension for judges is the past. Both the major, legal, and the minor, factual, premise of the judicial syllogism are composed from materials procured by the past. A norm, derived and construed from acknowledged sources of law, is applied to a past event, reconstructed from acknowledged pieces of evidence. But in spite of the remaining dominance of the past time horizon, modern adjudication's temporality should not be equated with the ties which still, according to seventeenth- and eighteenth-century authors, bound the common-law judge with tradition. The law's sedimented *ratio* no longer imposes similar constraints on present-day judges' critical reflection, but leaves their legal-cultural preconceptions receptive to testing in the light of new evidence or fresh normative arguments. Furthermore, future-oriented considerations play their part in judicial argumentation and decision-making: say, teleological standpoints in statutory interpretation, or general and individual prevention in criminal-law sentencing. But, arguably, such goal-rational considerations are of a secondary nature, unfolding their impact only within boundaries drawn by primary orientation towards the past. Of course, not everybody would subscribe to this argument: contrary opinions have been voiced by, for instance, the German interest jurisprudence (*Interessenjurisprudenz*) and free-law school (*Freirechtsschule*), as well as American Legal Realists and their disciples in the Critical Legal Studies and Law and Economics movements.

The Further Acceleration of Time and Expansion of Space

Transformations in the law's temporality and spatiality have not ceased with the loosening of its ties to tradition, epitomising legal modernisation. Typical of our late modern era is the further acceleration of time and the conquest of new space beyond the borders of nation states; the development by now habitually called *globalisation*. However, acceleration of time and expansion of space have not affected all social sub-systems in a similar fashion. The temporal structures of politics and law have turned out to be more resistant than, say, those of the economy. Politics and law have also been more stubbornly attached to the space of the nation state than other sub-systems.

Nonetheless, the law, too, shows signs of slackening its linkage to the nation state; *transnational law* of a new type is on the rise. During the era of nation states, legal systems have been differentiated in accordance with territorial grounds, into national legal systems. The emergence of transnational law has introduced a rival, *functional* criterion of differentiation: the applicability of the *lex mercatoria* of international trade relations or of the *lex sportiva* of international sport, to take two conspicuous examples, is not determined on territorial but on functional grounds. This is one of the manifestations of a new phase in spatial detachment. As a consequence, the legal system of the nation state has been forced to recognise the presence and functioning of other legal systems within its privileged territory. When the sovereignty of the nation state wavers, so does the national legal system's quest for exclusivity. In its pluralism of legal orders and legal systems, legal late modernity, as it were, is reverting to the pre-modern constellation.

Despite the unifying effect of Roman law, the era of nation states brought about national divergences even at the legal-cultural level. We appear to be entering the age of a new kind of legal-cultural transnationalisation. The legal-cultural reservoir from which legal actors draw their pre-understanding displays increasing transnational, even global traits. The territorial differentiation of legal cultures will probably be complemented, if not questioned, by functionally determined particularities: functionally differentiated legal systems – *lex mercatoria*, *lex sportiva* and the like – will most likely generate distinct legal cultures. Here we confront one more sign of the law's movement from tradition towards a disembedded expert system. If the capital has no fatherland, nor has the expertise. This holds increasingly for legal expertise, too.

The transnationalisation of legal culture and its budding functional differentiation pose the question of the law's unity and coherence in a new fashion. Under a pluralism of legal orders and legal systems, unity can no longer be grounded in the formal factors on which positivist legal theory, committed to the perspective of *voluntas*, has focused: the formal hierarchy of the legal order – Kelsen's *Stufenbau* – or the institutional hierarchy of the judiciary. Both of these hierarchies have rested on nation-state premises. These premises are being contested by phenomena attesting to mounting legal pluralism.

Most likely the acceleration of time, too, will affect not only the law's surface level but even its sub-surface layers. Legal culture constitutes the law's memory, but this memory is set to become shorter than before. Below, in Chapter 5, I will examine recent debates on systematisation of the legal order. Proposals for new branches of law and respective general doctrines seek a new balance between stability and change, between predictability and creativity, between legal certainty and flexibility. We can presume that the law's systematisation, its division into distinct fields, will be constantly changing, and that the lifespan of legal doctrines will be shorter than we have been accustomed to.

The late modern acceleration of time and expansion of space alter the framework for manifestations of the tension between the law's *ratio* and *voluntas*. The nation-state legislator no longer holds exclusive sway over the law's *voluntas*, nor does the law's *ratio* find its exclusive reservoir in national legal culture. In the final chapter, I shall resume examination of the ongoing transformation of the law's temporal and spatial coordinates. Meanwhile, I shall continue to explore how the relationship between *voluntas* and *ratio* has been shaped in the course of legal modernisation and how, in particular, legal scholarship has contributed to the defence and articulation of *ratio*'s viewpoint.

Chapter 3
The Heritage of the Historical School: German Nineteenth-Century Legal Scholarship

The Position of the Historical School

In the preceding chapter, I examined the tension between the law's *voluntas* and *ratio* in the light of the seventeenth- and eighteenth-century debates between common-law writers and the early exponents of legal positivism, Thomas Hobbes and Jeremy Bentham. In these debates, the common-law writers epitomised the pole of law's internal, layered *ratio*, whereas Hobbes and Bentham approached law from the perspective of a sovereign legislator's *voluntas*. In classical common-law writings, the law possessed many features typical of a tradition in the historical-sociological sense of the concept. Tradition provided the actors of common law, primarily judges, with the pre-understanding through which they tackled their legal tasks and conceived of legal problems; tradition in the historical-sociological sense functioned as a tradition in the philosophical-hermeneutical sense as well. Common law imposed constraints on the *voluntas* and instrumental reason of the legislator; written law was supposed to be interpreted and applied within the framework of common law. The law's traditionalism secured its primarily diachronic coherence, linking its present and future with its past.

Societal and cultural modernisation opens up the horizon of the future and detaches it from the past; it also loosens up the bounds of the locale. Such changes in temporal and spatial relations leave but little room for traditions in the historical-sociological sense of the concept. The law, too, increasingly acquires traits of an expert system. This gives rise to a problem, namely how a 'mature' modern law can cope with tasks which have previously been accomplished by tradition and its sedimented *ratio* and which have not lost their pertinence in the course of legal modernisation. In Chapter 2, I argued that under the conditions of modern law, legal actors' pre-understanding is procured by modern legal culture, in whose development and articulation academic legal scholarship plays a central role. This holds especially for the Continental Romano-Germanic legal family.

In this chapter, I shall continue to explore the role of legal scholarship in the legal system. I shall again rely on an example provided by an era of rupture, but I shall now move on to Continental-European law and further in time from the debates examined in the preceding chapter. My primary focus will lie on German nineteenth-century legal scholarship: the historical school and the subsequent conceptual legal dogmatics (*Begriffsjurisprudenz*).[1] In the international respect, the nineteenth century was the prime of German legal science: Germany clearly held the lead, and German legal scholars were praised and emulated even in common-law countries, both in England and in the United States. On the Continent, German doctrine provided the model for legal modernisation. This was also the case in Finland and other Nordic countries, which belonged to the sphere of influence of German legal culture. The extent of German impact has motivated Duncan Kennedy (2006b) to speak of a first wave of legal globalisation under the aegis of German cultural leadership.

The great names of the historical school were Friedrich Carl von Savigny and Carl Friedrich Puchta, both of them writing in the first half of the century. Puchta has often been characterised as a transitional figure, bridging the historical school and *Begriffsjurisprudenz*. Both Savigny's and Puchta's dogmatic field was private law. In public law, the new approach was adopted later, in the latter half of the century. The main credits fall to two former private lawyers, Carl Friedrich von Gerber (1823–1891) and Paul Laband (1838–1918), whose work was carried on and complemented by Georg Jellinek. Jellinek's magnum opus, *Allgemeine Staatslehre*, was published, symbolically enough, in 1900. From Jellinek it was but a step to Hans Kelsen, who even on the first pages of his first monograph, *Hauptprobleme der Staatsrechtslehre*, acknowledged his debt to his teacher Jellinek (Kelsen 1911, p. XIII).

Niilo Jääskinen (1983, pp. 3–5) argues that the cluster of basic assumptions defining legal science has remained essentially unchanged since the middle of the nineteenth century. In this account, the historical school set the general terms for subsequent (Continental) private-law scholarship. Indeed, it is the great merit of the historical school to have thematised legal scholarship's role in modern – or early modern – law and procured elements for legal scholarship's reflexive self-understanding. My argument will go further still: German nineteenth-century doctrine provides us with material, not only for a reconstruction of the background assumptions of modern legal science, but even for an analysis of many of the basic tensions that permeate modern law and account for its internal dynamics.

At the outset, some typical non sequiturs concerning the topic need to be mentioned. In the German debates, it is difficult to keep separate what, on the one hand, is typical of the law's modernisation in general and what, on the other hand, derives from the distinct features of early modern German society and culture, or Germany's specific political situation. The law was examined through the particular circumstances prevailing in Germany and the law's modernisation was conceived of as it occurred in these circumstances. Thus, Germany's political fragmentation

1 The term *Begriffsjurisprudenz* was probably invented by critics. It had a conspicuously negative connotation in the writings of such critics as the 'late' Jhering, whom Haferkamp (2004, p. 26) actually credits for introducing the term in his *Scherz und Ernst in der Jurisprudenz* (1884). I shall try to employ it as a neutral label of a specific legal scientific school.

and lack of a unitary legislator certainly for their part account for the elevated position of legal science among legal practices. In turn, the systematic ideal and the methodological presuppositions of legal science were greatly influenced by German idealistic philosophy, say, from Kant to Hegel. But, as will be discussed at the end of this chapter, in common-law countries too, particularly in the United States, the idea(l) of legal systematisation gained ground and legal scholarship acquired new prominence within the legal system.

A second potential confusion concerns the aims of my exposition. My main interest does not lie in the history of legal ideas as such; I am not engaged in a primarily legal-historical study. I am interested in present law, so that reconstruction of the nineteenth-century debates serves analysis of law's present traits. My reconstruction is deliberately selective, and I am aware of the impact of my present concerns on the questions to which I let my nineteenth-century predecessors respond. Indeed, my relation to nineteenth-century doctrine resembles the latter's relation to Roman law. According to Savigny's and Puchta's programme, Roman law was to be studied in order to obtain responses to questions pertaining to contemporary law, not as an enterprise of an independent discipline of legal history, separated from doctrinal research (legal dogmatics). But even without such explicit purposes, an inevitable consequence of a researcher's cultural connectedness is that contemporary concerns influence the approach to historical material and the narrative the researcher spins from this material. In his recent study, Kaius Tuori (2007) shows how the legal-cultural context of Roman-law historians has affected the shifting positions taken on such seemingly perennial and controversial issues as the birth of Roman 'legal science' and its alleged schools; the *ius respondendi* and its interpretation with regard to Roman jurists' independence of vs. dependence on imperial power; and the Hadrianic *edictum perpetuum* as a supposed codification of Roman law. According to Kaius Tuori, none of the scholarly positions can claim uncontested support from the historical sources; they are only intelligible in the light of their authors' cultural contexts and concerns, and their stance in the pivotal controversies of their day, such as the nineteenth-century codification debates.

The Positivity of Law

For Savigny and Puchta, the law was both an historical and a systematic phenomenon, so that the study of existing law required both an historical and a dogmatic (doctrinal) approach. Legal scholarship was supposed to be a positive science; *positive* in the sense of focusing on a historically-determined object, and *science* in the sense of understanding its object as a systematic whole.

In the conception of the historical school, positive law is not yet identical with legislation or posited law in general. The epithet 'positive' derived from German idealist philosophy and alluded generally to historical determination; this was the sense given to it by Hegel, for instance. 'Positive' drew the line against natural law.

German eighteenth-century rationalist natural law (*Vernunftrecht*), with Christian Wolff (1679–1754) as its main proponent, had treated the law as a logical system, where propositions of law were deduced from 'evident' axioms, revealed by reason (Schröder 1979, pp. 132ff.; Björne 1984, pp. 14–15). The historical school renounced this way of thinking: the law's *ratio* could not be conceived of as the time-and-place-independent reason of *Vernunftrecht*.

By contrast, emphasis on the law's positivity did not entail any position on customary law. In Savigny's and Puchta's view, the law's main *source of origin* (*Entstehungsquelle*) consists of the popular spirit (*Volksgeist*), which can manifest itself equally well in customary law, legislation and jurists' law (*Juristenrecht*) or scientific law, as the latter was also called. The historical school distinguished between the law's sources of origin and its *sources of cognition* (*Erkenntnisquellen*). Judicial case-law constitutes the main source of cognition for customary law. This hints at an important difference between modern and pre-modern, 'savage', customary law: a movement to the positivisation even of customary law!

In the course of the nineteenth century, the historical school increasingly acquired features that led critics to dub it *Begriffsjurisprudenz*. The interpretation of law's positivity underwent a change, too, especially after Germany's unification and subsequent adoption of the constitution of the *Reich* in 1871 and the *Bürgerliches Gesetzbuch* as the 'basic law' of private law at the end of the nineteenth century. Legal scientific positivism was reduced to *statutory positivism* (*Gesetzespositivismus*). Laband's post-unification public-law positivism clearly espoused the premises of statutory positivism. But even Puchta came quite close to a notion of positive law as emanating from conscious human action. Puchta's customary law, whose main source of cognition consists of judicial case-law, had distanced itself a long way from traditionalist society's orally-transmitted customary law (Haferkamp 2004, pp. 196ff.). What Puchta termed 'jurists' law' or 'scientific law' had far-reaching roots in Germany in the reception of Roman law and the prominence of learned lawyers, of which the procedure of *Aktenversendung* was the most telling token. But 'scientific law' is also an expression of legal modernisation: professional legal culture, as well as institutionalised legal science as one of the legal practices specialised in the law's production and reproduction, belong to the distinct features of modern law.

In the positivism of the historical school, the law's positivity equalled its historicity. Such positivism did not yet subscribe to the fundamental delimitations which were constitutive for twentieth-century legal-theoretical positivism and on which positivist reflexion theories were premised: separation of the Ought from the Is and of the legal from the moral Ought. Savigny, in particular, still tied the law tightly to its societal and cultural environment. By contrast, in Puchta's notion of law, germs of the demarcations typical of twentieth-century positivism are already detectable.

For the historical school, the law was an historical phenomenon, but as its primary source of origin lay in the *Volksgeist*, in its early stages it could not really have a history of its own. The law constituted an organic part of the life of the people, along with customs and language. According to Savigny, 'these phenomena have no separate existence, they are only the particular forces and activities of a people, in reality inseparably intertwined and appearing as separate qualities only in our examination'. Therefore, 'the law … has no independent existence, rather its essence consists of the very life of people, examined from a specific angle' (2002, p. 65).[2]

Savigny and Puchta were well aware of the societal and cultural differentiation that characterises legal modernisation. Savigny argued that originally all law is 'popular law' (*Volksrecht*). In the development of the nation, the law adopts a 'scientific' direction, loses its original simplicity and escapes from the reach of the people as a whole. The general tendency is that 'as the culture develops, all the activities of the people are increasingly differentiated'. At the same time, specific professional 'estates' (*Stände*) emerge that specialise in particular activities. This is the case in law, too: further development and application of law are transferred to such a professional estate, to learned lawyers (2002, p. 67). This is Savigny's famous *Spezialistendogma*, which was to greatly influence later conceptions of modern law, for instance Max Weber's understanding of the general developmental tendency of law (Schröder 1976). For its part, present-day systems theory has perceived in Savigny's *Spezialistendogma* a notion of functional differentiation (Stichweh 1992, p. 342).

Savigny emphasised that jurists' law (scientific law) must be conceived of as a continuation and peculiar development of 'popular law'. When creating or articulating law, jurists act as natural representatives of the people and their legal consciousness stands for the general legal consciousness of the people. Yet, we can argue that insight into law's differentiation and formation of the estate of jurists paved the way for an understanding of law as an independent system of legal propositions or institutions, disconnected from its societal and cultural moorings. However, legal scholarship only took this step after Savigny: his system did not yet sever the ties to its environment.

Despite his comments on the law's progressing differentiation and initiation of its 'own' history, Savigny still linked the law to (the rest of) society. The link is provided by his notions of legal institution and legal relationship. *Legal institutions* constitute the building blocks of Savigny's system. Through the intermediary of *legal relationships*, they attach the law to social relationships: to factual 'life relationships' (*Lebensverhältnisse*). Legal relationships possess two sides; they combine a substantive and a formal element: 'firstly, substance, that is, the relationship in itself, and, secondly, legal determination of that substance' (1981, I, p. 333). *Legal propositions* (*Rechtssätze*) equal the law in its objective sense. They provide legal relationships with their formal element, that is, the legal determination of their substance. They stand in an intimate connection with life relationships in accordance with which they are generated and for which they offer protection.

2 In this chapter, translations of German citations are my own.

Savigny stressed the *organic* character of legal relationships. 'Organicity' was one of the key concepts for nineteenth-century German legal science, especially for the historical school but also for the subsequent *Begriffsjurisprudenz*. Usage of the concept varied but usually referred to two things: firstly, that the phenomenon at issue consists of *interdependent elements* and, secondly, that it is subject to the *developmental principle* of living nature. The organic character of legal relationships was manifest by the interplay between their formal and substantive aspects and by their lifespan: legal relationships emerged, developed, and were dissolved.

In Savigny's account, legal propositions as the basic elements of objective law interact, both with the factual relations they regulate, and with each other. They constitute interdependent wholes, legal institutions. Savigny emphasised that legal institutions are not 'abstract' combinations of legal propositions. Like legal relationships, they are organic, developing wholes whose elements are connected by reciprocal ties. Legal institutions are composed of legal propositions, that is, the elementary building blocks of objective law. Thus, legal institutions can also be understood as phenomena of objective law. But in the context of legal institutions, too, Savigny maintained the connection between objective law – or legal order, as we might also call it – and society. He portrayed legal institutions as types (*Typus*) or models (*Urbild*) of legal relationships (1981, I, pp. 9 and 291); in turn, legal relationships, as we may recall, consist of factual life relationships as their substantive element and legal propositions as their formal element. Legal propositions can only be organised into such organic wholes as legal institutions because the factual life relationships they regulate are organised organically. Family-law institutions derive their organic features from the interlocking social relationships on which family law confers legal determination: 'We call the totality of all these complementary relationships – marriage, paternal power, kinship – the family and the legal institutions related to it family law' (ibid., p. 342).

Savigny divided legal institutions into two groups: *natural* and *artificial*. The former possess a 'natural-ethical' foundation which the latter lack. Family law, for instance, includes such natural institutions as marriage, paternal power and kinship, which all possess a natural-ethical foundation. Relationships within such natural institutions as the family can never be exhaustively governed by the law. By contrast, artificial legal relationships are in their entirety subjected to law; they are 'pure, mere legal relationships' (1981, I, p. 370).[3]

Savigny's analysis of legal institutions bears interesting resemblances to recent legal-theoretical debates. It is warranted to see him as a precursor of the institutional theory of law, although he could not, of course, resort to the concept of institutional fact, coined only in post-Second World War philosophical discussion.

3 Not surprisingly, Savigny's examination of legal relationships, legal propositions and legal institutions has evoked much debate, and not all commentators would subscribe to the above interpretation. From the abundant discussion, see Kiefner (1979), Rückert (1984, pp. 342–348) and Nörr (1994, pp. 274–280).

Walter Wilhelm (1958, p. 51) argues that the distinction which Savigny drew between legal relationships and legal institutions diverted the law from social reality and from Savigny's own thesis that the law has no independent existence. This would have cleared the ground for the subsequent legal positivist notion of law as a system of objective norms, with no connections to factual life relationships. Wilhelm's claim warrants two qualifications. First, Savigny did treat the law as a system of legal propositions but he tied this abstraction to the history of society and its law; the law's growing autonomy was a part of its social history. The other qualification concerns legal institutions as systematised wholes of legal propositions of objective law. As Savigny depicted it, the law retained its dependence on factual life relationships even after its differentiation enabled the concept of objective law as an order of legal propositions. For Savigny, the legal order could constitute a systematic whole because the social relations it regulates constitute organic unities, composed of interdependent elements and subjected to the natural principle of development. We may concede that in Savigny's exposition, the separation of the social Is and the legal Ought was already initiated. Nonetheless, he explained the growing independence of the legal Ought in socio-historical terms and derived the principles for its systematisation from the social Is.

In its evolution from Savigny towards the Golden Age of *Begriffsjurisprudenz*, German doctrine gradually widened the gulf separating law and society, and finally shut the legal order in its self-contained world of the Ought. In public law, the key figures were Gerber and Laband. Gerber emphasised in both his private- and public-law writings that the law's systematic unity is based on its own specifically legal principles. Nevertheless, his theory of state law still focused on factual social relations and their subjects, conceived of as relations and subjects of *will*. Gerber openly pointed to the historical presuppositions and limits of his construction. He stressed that he was discussing the modern state and its constitution and that his concepts are not valid under medieval, feudal political conditions. In Laband's writings, by contrast, law and legal concepts were cut off from factual social relations and started to lead an independent life. Awareness of the historicity of law and legal concepts faded, and legal scholarship took a decisive step towards the conceptual apriorism of neo-Kantian legal theory.

Let us come back to Savigny and the ties which, in his conception, still attached the law to its social and cultural environment. For him, the separation between the legal Ought and the social Is was not yet absolute. Nor did his positivism share the other delineation fundamental to twentieth-century legal positivism: the isolation of law from morals and ethics. In Savigny's view, the *Volksgeist* constitutes the law's main source of origin even after the law has started to obtain scientific traits and has lost its original simplicity. In the people's common legal conviction, the law is present as inchoate notions (*Anschauungen*) of 'natural-ethical' institutions, such as marriage. It is, then, up to the learned lawyers as spokesmen for this conviction to bestow on these notions a precise shape. As Jääskinen (1983, p. 66) notes, the *Volksgeist* doctrine of Savigny and Puchta performed three tasks. Firstly, it accounted for the dynamics of law, for its historicity. Secondly, with its emphasis on the law's historical character, the doctrine renounced rationalist natural-law thinking and its way of deducing the law's contents from axioms of universal validity. And thirdly, it provided a justification for the law's ethically obligatory force.

Puchta still reserved a central place for the *Volksgeist* doctrine, but subsequently this doctrine lost its position as the historical school converted into *Begriffsjurisprudenz*. A similar fate would befall the Kantian arguments on which Savigny and Puchta relied in their concepts of legal subject and subjective right and which established a link between moral and legal subjectivity. Puchta argued that man is not only a natural but also a spiritual being, a person, with a capacity for freedom and a free will. It is this very capacity that makes a man a legal subject, so that 'freedom' is the basic concept of law. The legal subject is a subject of will, and, correspondingly, subjective right is identical with this subject's freedom of will (Tuori 1987, p. 181). Detached from its Kantian moorings, the *will* theory of law would be long-lived and would also influence legal thinking in, for instance, the United States (Kennedy 2006a).

What place, then, did the nation state hold in the historical school's conception of law? 'Mature' modern law depends on the state at both ends of its span of functioning: state organs both establish law and guarantee its realisation. The historical school, too, treated positive law as state law. According to Savigny, 'all law in general only receives its reality and completion in the state, as the positive law of that state' (1981, I, p. 380). The state is indispensable for the law, but not so much as the law's creator, legislation being only one of the law's sources of origin; above all, the state is needed to secure the law's execution. In turn, the doctrine of the *Volksgeist* intimated that the state was to be a nation state.

Germany's political and institutional fragmentation before 1871 explains legislation's peripheral position as the law's source of origin in the historical school's view. The German state did not yet exist at the institutional level, nor did Germany have a unitary legislator. By contrast, it can be argued that the German nation state was already a reality at the cultural level and it was for that reason that the *Volksgeist* could substitute for unitary legislation as the law's source of origin. The *Volksgeist*, as it were, took the place of institutional political unity. As the historical school attached law to the *Volksgeist*, it enabled legal science to construe a legal system focused on the nation state, although institutional unity was yet to be won. Paradoxically, then, the historical school's positive law was nation-state law without a nation state. The society to which Savigny related positive law and which laid the foundation for the law's systematisation was a nation-state society. Thus, arguably, the historical school and the subsequent *Begriffsjurisprudenz* focused on German national law as did Jeremy Bentham's and John Austin's analytical school on English law or the nineteenth-century exegetic school on French law.[4]

4 On Savigny's view of the relationship between law, state and people, see Rückert (1984, pp. 312ff.).

The law of the historical school was positive law, which the *Volksgeist* tied to the history of the nation and whose internal system grew from the organic character of the life relationships of that nation. Significantly, however, this positivity had a *supra-positive foundation*, independent of national history. In Savigny's account, 'natural-ethical' legal institutions are based on fundamental relations that exemplify human nature and common human life in general, such as the family. Monogamy is a positive legal institution, whereas 'we assign to marriage in general (in whatever form it may appear) a general necessity' (1981, I, p. 346). In turn, property is grounded in human nature's vocation to subjugate non-free nature. But only positive, national law can make property a legal institution. Property can obtain 'real existence' only by being related 'first to the state and through the rules of the positive law of the state to the individual legal subjects in the state, as proprietors' (ibid., p. 380). Correspondingly, Savigny (1981, II, pp. 2ff.) began the conceptual analysis of legal subjectivity from 'the original concept of a person' (*der ursprüngliche Begriff der Person*). Savigny treated 'legal institution' as a two-level concept: the institutions of national law, say monogamist marriage or private property, positivise supra-positive models of legal relationships, such as marriage or property in general.

Savigny derived supra-positive institutions from an anthropologically-tuned conception of human nature and the basic preconditions of human life. The *Volksgeist*, the popular spirit, as a source of positive law expresses and specifies the 'general human spirit': 'What is active in a people is only the general human spirit, which appears therein in an individual way' (1981, I, p. 21). Hence, the contents of 'popular law' are determined by two elements: 'an individual one, distinctive of the people in question, and a general one, based on what is common to human nature' (ibid., p. 52).

Thus, as Wilhelm (1969), in particular, stresses, Savigny's system of positive law relied on supra-positive preconditions.

The Systematic Character of Law and Legal Science

The historical school underlined both the historical and the systematic character of the law. Awareness of the law's ties to social and cultural history faded in subsequent German doctrine. Now the clear emphasis shifted to the law's system, which was disconnected from history.

Both law and legal science were conceived of as systematic phenomena. Systematicity was a central part of the programme aiming at ensuring legal science's scientificity (Schröder 1979, pp. 99ff.; Stichweh 1992). In the contemporaneous conception of science, the idea of a system held a prominent place. Kant characterised science in the preface to his *Metaphysische Anfangsgründe der Naturwissenschaft* as follows: 'Every doctrine which aspires to be a system, i.e. a principled cognitive whole, is a science' (Kant 1983, p. 11). In order to meet the criterion of a science, legal scholarship's doctrinal constructions must also constitute principled cognitive wholes. In addition, German legal science such as Savigny's and Puchta's historical school also emphasised the systematic nature of its object, that is, the law. How did the law's internal system and the systems of legal science, its doctrinal constructions, relate to each other? This is one the trickiest questions in analysing German nineteenth-century conceptions of law and legal science.

The natural-law strand of Christian Wolff had constructed its system in compliance with the *mos geometricus* ideal of science: the contents of the system were deduced from axioms, treated as evident. The relation between the system of law and the system of legal science was not a problem: the propositions which legal science (legal philosophy) derived from axioms were not only scientific but also legal propositions, natural-law norms. The relation between law and legal science might become problematic only in the historical school's positivism, where the law's primary source of origin was seen to lie in the historically-evolving *Volksgeist*.

Michel Foucault (1974) analyses the cultural break where, in the aftermath of the French Revolution, the classical *episteme* receded before the modern one. The new *episteme* was championed by such disciplines as biology, which studied the organic nature of living creatures, and historically-oriented linguistics, which approached languages as organism-like entities. The historical school's conception of the law's internal system reflects the same epistemic rupture: the law's internal system is supposed to derive from its organic character.

In the context of law, too, this organic quality meant two things: the interdependence of the elements making up the whole, and subjection of the whole to historical change. According to Puchta, 'the law as a living organism possesses 1) a simultaneous multiplicity, due to differentiation of its contents into interdependent elements; 2) a successive one, due to the transformation of the whole and the parts' (1850, p. 100). This double multiplicity, synchronic and diachronic or concurrent and successive, gave rise to and justified the historical school's bifurcated research programme, where the dogmatic-systematic and historical approaches complemented each other.

What engendered the law's systematic character? It was not the result of any autonomous intra-legal movement but arose from a cultural and societal seedbed. Law was a product of the *Volksgeist*, just as language, which, according to the linguistics of the day, also demonstrated internal interdependence and historical evolution. Through the *Volksgeist* as its main source of origin, law was bestowed a similar organicity as language.

Savigny's concept of legal institution informs us about the societal and cultural conditions of the law's systematicity. Law's primary system is that of legal institutions; the organic whole of interdependent institutions. Furthermore, legal institutions themselves are organic unities, composed of interdependent parts and undergoing historical change. Legal institutions are grounded in factual life relationships through the intermediary of legal relationships, so that the law's systematic order grows from the systematic order of social life, from society's organic character. Critics claim that Puchta steered the historical school in the direction of *Begriffsjurisprudenz* and separated the legal Ought from its social foundation; indeed, some textual evidence exists to warrant that claim. However, Puchta's writings also abound with passages where he binds the system of (objective) law to the social relations under regulation. This is demonstrated by the following example:

> The legal propositions that constitute the law of a people are gathered together in distinct sets, in accordance with the relationships they regulate; these sets of legal propositions are called legal institutions. Thus, we call property a legal institution in so far as we think of the legal propositions concerning it. The law is composed of legal institutions and these, in turn, of singular legal propositions. (1850, p. 12)

How, by what method, can legal science capture the law's organic nature? How is the system of legal science related to the system of law? The methodological alternatives available in doctrinal systematisation are often compressed into the dichotomy of induction and deduction. In inductive system formation, legal principles and concepts are generalised from individual legal propositions. In the deductive alternative, the direction of reasoning is the opposite: individual legal propositions are deduced from general legal principles or concepts. No agreement has been reached as to how the method(s) employed by nineteenth-century German legal science should be depicted; it is illustrative of the prevailing confusion that Puchta's system formation has been labelled both inductive, deductive and inductive-deductive (Björne 1984, pp. 219–220; Haferkamp 2004, pp. 105–106).

To a great extent, the confusion is due to an anachronism in the very setting of the terms of the question: the legal-scientific thinking of the first half of the nineteenth century has been approached through the concepts of present-day theory of science. However, it is apparent that such interdependencies which according to the historical school, made the law an organic whole, cannot be captured by either inductive generalisation or deductive derivation. When Savigny and Puchta wrote about the cognition of organic relations, they used the notion of *Anschauung*. This notion has strong roots in the German idealistic philosophy of the late eighteenth and the early nineteenth century; for Savigny, influences especially from Fichte and Jacobi seem to have been crucial (Nörr 1994, pp. 253ff.). *Anschauung* is a difficult notion to pin down, and two different basic meanings of the notion appear to exist, both of which are in use in, for instance, Savigny's writings: a passive one, going back to Kant, and an active one, with its roots in Fichte's philosophy. *Anschauung* in the latter sense involves intellectual shaping of the object and could also be called *intellectual Anschauung* (ibid., pp. 271–273). It is this latter sense that Savigny and Puchta attach to '*Anschauung*' when depicting the legal scientific method. What is essential is that *Anschauung* refers to a holistic way of conceiving organic wholes and their internal relations that lies beyond the dichotomy of induction and deduction. (On *Anschauung* see also Rückert 1984, pp. 345–346 and Haferkamp 2004, pp. 289–290.)

The scientific presentation (*Darstellung*) of law as a doctrinal construction (*Lehrordnung*) is something other than the *Anschauung* of the law's inherent systemic relations. Savigny seems to have considered the relations between doctrinal constructions and the law's internal system to be quite uncomplicated: the latter determines the former, and the former are supposed to reflect the latter. The dogmatic-systematic task of legal science consists in 'reduction of the simultaneous multiplicity to its immanent unity', whereas in the historical dimension legal science focuses on 'examination of the successive multiplicity'. Both tasks presuppose discovering the leading principles of law; accordingly, legal science has to identify 'the internal connection and the nature of the kinship of all legal concepts and propositions' (cited in Wilhelm 1958, p. 22).

In his recent study, Peter Haferkamp (2004, pp. 291ff.) claims that Puchta was aware of the tension between the law's organic nature and its scientific presentation. As Haferkamp presents Puchta's view, it is not possible to describe the law as an organic unity; the legal scientist has to portray the law as a system from the particular perspective he has chosen. For Savigny, legal institutions served as the building blocks of both the law's internal system and legal science's doctrinal constructions. Puchta, in turn, considered several alternatives conceivable: the law could be presented as a system of legal propositions, legal institutions, or subjective rights.

The historical school adopted the general scientific requirement of organising knowledge under a unifying basic principle or idea. Legal science, too, aimed at 'a principled cognitive whole'. Puchta argued that the law's historical development adheres to the principle of equality and that the law's great vocation is to subjugate inequalities to equality, without, however, abolishing them. In the systematic-dogmatic regard, the legal scholar is confronted with a difficult task. The law should be presented from the perspective of a certain basic principle; as it were, deductively. However, the scholar should also respect the law's internal structure, its organic character, which restricts his freedom in system formation (Haferkamp 2004, pp. 305–306).

Puchta premised his exposition of the law as a system of subjective rights on the concept of freedom. The law as a subjective right equals freedom of will, so that the nature of the will's objects constitutes the primary organising principle in the presentation of law. On this basis, the law is divided into property law (*Sachenrecht*), the law of obligations (*Obligationsrecht*), family law, and the law of inheritance. In Haferkamp's view, it is here that the 'deductive' part of Puchta's construction actually ends. More precise criteria for classifying rights are to be – so Haferkamp interprets Puchta – developed from the law itself through *Anschauung* (Haferkamp 2004, pp. 404ff.) The standard claim in commentary literature, at least since the 1920s, is that Puchta's ideal was a pyramid of concepts. This is one of the great myths in the history of modern legal science, with little substantive evidence to back it up. If presenting the system from the perspective of a distinct basic idea is called deduction and if deriving precise criteria for classification from the material proffered by legal sources is termed induction, then we can agree with Björne (1984, p. 219) and term Puchta's method inductive-deductive. Yet, here too we should be careful not to attribute the concepts of present-day theory of science anachronistically to nineteenth-century legal thinking.

Savigny's and Puchta's dogmatic field was private law, and although they both stressed the systematic, organic nature of the law as a whole, their systems were expressly systems of private law. In the latter half of the century, systems-thinking was adopted into state law; there it was introduced by Gerber and Laband, both of them with a private-law background. But the view of systematic traits of law and legal science underwent an essential transformation on the way from Savigny to Laband. The system of law lost much of its organic character and cut its link to organic system(s) of social life. Puchta's writings were still animated by a tension between, on the one hand, the 'logical' aspects in law and legal science, and, on the other hand, the law's organic features and the corresponding method of *Anschauung*. Subsequently, the tension was to be dissolved in favour of the 'logical' side.

In Gerber's exposition, the law's systematic unity derives from specific intra-legal principles. Following Puchta, Gerber grounded the system of private law in the free will of human subjects, thus seeing the system as organising the 'free possibilities of the will'. The specific method of system formation is 'legal construction'. The task now facing legal science is to conceive of state law, too, as a unity. Legal science is to proceed from basic concepts to a system where 'individual conceptions are presented as a development of a unitary basic idea' (Gerber 1880, p. VI). In state law, this basic idea is state power (state will), and in line with private law, state-law legal construction should focus on relations of will: 'at issue in the legal construction of the state and its elements, like every construction, is the detection and delimitation of relations of will' (ibid., p. 221). The construction proceeds as follows:

> The will of the state, state power, has its limits. The first task of state law is to affirm these. They entail in particular determining the legal position of the citizen in the state. Then the state needs constitutional organs, by whose action state power becomes effective. Legal propositions exist that lay down how these organs are formed. The functioning of state organs follows legal norms, which regulate its content and form. Arrangements and legal remedies exist to protect state-law relationships. (Ibid., p. 235)

The law's systematic nature is no longer due to its societal and cultural anchoring, nor is the law's doctrinal presentation in need of complementary historical exposition. However, Gerber still considered it necessary to allude to the social and historical backdrop of the law's autonomy: to social modernisation and the dissolution of medieval, feudal, relations (ibid., pp. 9–10, 69 and 217). Laband published his *opus magnum* after the unification of Germany and adoption of the constitution of the German *Reich* and no longer felt any need to procure historical explanations for the ahistoricity of legal science or social explanations for its lack of social perspective. In Laband's programme, legal science focuses on positive law, defined in terms of statutory positivism, with logic as its exclusive method: 'The scientific task of the dogmatics of a distinct positive law consists ... in constructing legal institutions, in reducing individual legal propositions to more general concepts and, on the other hand, in deriving from these concepts the ensuing conclusions' (Laband 1888, p. IX).

Nevertheless, Laband's statutory positivism also relied on supra-positive support. The most general legal concepts, which state-law science borrowed from its 'more mature big sister', private-law doctrine, are not derived from positive legal propositions: 'What is specific to the German constitution, in line with every concrete legal formation, is merely the use and connection of general legal concepts; by contrast, creating a new legal institution which could not in general be subsumed under a higher and more general legal concept is just as impossible as finding a new logical category or the emerging of a new natural force' (ibid., p. X).

Laband's statutory positivism displays the same tension between the positive and supra-positive traits of the doctrinal system as the historical school. The foundation of Savigny's system lay in the general, historically unfolding concept of law, and Puchta construed his system of subjective rights upon the supra-positive concept of freedom. The tension between the positive and the supra-positive, which in Savigny's and Puchta's writings had manifested itself in the relation between the law's historical and systematic features, continued to bother legal scholarship even after *Begriffsjurisprudenz* had effaced the historical dimension from its research programme. Historical development, through positive legislation, put the law's system under constant threat. It produced ever-new normative material, which endangered the law's internal system and whose insertion into doctrinal constructions created difficulties. This danger, of course, grew as the position of legislation strengthened within the sources of law.

The legislator did not necessarily heed systematic considerations, and yet positive law restricted the freedom of doctrinal system formation. In his early works, Rudolf von Jhering (1818–1892) formulated this restrictive impact as two basic demands on juridical construction: *comprehensiveness* and *non-contradictoriness*. Construction should, firstly, cover all the positive-law propositions which fall under the respective legal concepts, and, secondly, it should not contradict these propositions. But a doctrinal system should reflect 'the natural order' (*Natur der Sache*) as well. The problem was that no guarantees exist that positive propositions of law are in harmony with this 'natural order' (Coing 1969, pp. 164ff.).

One way to try to avoid clashes between the system and history (the law's positivity) was to confine doctrinal construction to the fairly stable core areas of the law. Indeed, it is telling that the nineteenth-century system's strivings did not extend to those gradually widening fields that display the mounting instrumentalisation of legislation and which, subsequently, have been called economic law (*Wirtschaftsrecht*) and special administrative law (*spezielles Verwaltungsrecht*) (see Chapter 5). The main focus of legal science's system formation was on the foundations of, first, private law and then, at a later stage, state law, too. Savigny and Puchta already noted that the legislator produced positive legal material which was irrelevant both for the law's internal system and for doctrinal system formation. These observations, together with Savigny's distinction between natural and artificial legal institutions, anticipate twentieth-century debates on the bifurcation of the legal order (see below, pp. 226–228).

Legal Science as a Legal Practice

In accordance with the general early nineteenth-century conception of science, system formation was a precondition for legal scholarship's attaining scientific status. But presentation of the law (legal knowledge) as a system served not only scientific but also practical purposes. System formation was instrumental to creation of scientific or jurists' law (*Juristenrecht*). Legal science was not only receptive but productive as well. It constituted a source of law.

According to Savigny, jurists contributed to generation of law in two ways. When the law grows increasingly complicated and differentiated, only its basic traits can, as general intuitions (*Anschauungen*), be present in the consciousness of the people.[5] The law's further elaboration falls to jurists, the estate of learned lawyers. At issue is 'a peculiar continuation and development of the law'. When articulating the law, jurists merely act as the people's natural representatives: 'just as it (the law) previously lived in the consciousness of the whole people, it now finds its place in the consciousness of the jurists, who today represent the people in this function' (2002, p. 67). However, legal science also accomplishes law-creating tasks of another kind, which are directly connected to the law's scientific systematisation. When legal science discovers and articulates the law's internal unity, it also breathes new life into it. Savigny argued that 'the scientific form of the substance reveals and seeks to complete its inherent unity, thus giving rise to new organic life, which formatively affects the substance itself, so that science as such constantly engenders a new kind of law creation' (1981, I, p. 46).

Jurists' law holds an important place in Puchta's doctrine of the sources of law. The law which jurists elaborate as 'the natural representatives of national legal consciousness' is not yet jurists' law in the proper sense of the term. Jurists merely clarify the contents of the *Volksgeist* or *Volksbewusstsein* ('popular consciousness'), and the law, thus clarified, belongs to the domain of customary law. By contrast, jurists' law results from scientific activity.

According to Puchta's early, 1820s version of the doctrine of legal sources, scientific law is created, not only by legal scholars, but also by judges applying the scientific method in their decision-making (Haferkamp 2004, pp. 185ff.). In

5 Here the notion of *Anschauung* is obviously used in its passive meaning.

his writings of the 1840s, Puchta assumed a narrower definition of scientific law and related it to the law's rational character: 'what ensues with internal necessity from existing legal propositions must also, because of the rationality of the law, be valid as law, as the will of the nation' (cited in Haferkamp 2004, p. 374). Scientific law does not draw its validity from common popular conviction or the legislator's external authority but from the internal authority which is based '1) on the rationality of the existing law, 2) on the truth of the principles derived from it, and 3) on the correctness of the conclusions drawn from these principles' (cited in Wilhelm 1958, p. 77). Significantly, too, Puchta confined the relevance of scientific law to cases of lacunae, where legal science was supposed to replace natural law as a subsidiary source of law.

The passage quoted above may be read as an exposition and justification of the *constructivist method* at which critics of *Begriffsjurisprudenz* directed their heaviest artillery. This method consists of two phases: an 'inductive' one and a 'deductive' one. In the first, 'inductive' phase, legal principles and concepts are generalised from propositions of positive law. Then, in the second, 'deductive' phase, these are used as premises for deriving new legal propositions. Critics have argued over and over again that from inductively-won general principles and concepts, only the same legal propositions can be deduced that have served as the basis of induction (see Chapter 4).

This type of methodological criticism questions scientific law's position as a source of law. But at least with regard to Savigny and Puchta, it appears to miss the point. Firstly, their system formation – detecting and exposing general principles and concepts – did not stick to the logical-inductive model of the current theory of science. What was essential was to capture the law's organic character, its internal interdependencies, and to express these as legal principles and concepts. This required a sense of the whole, intuition (*Anschauung*), rather than simple inductive generalisation.[6] Indeed, this methodological premise of the historical school is closer to Dworkin's principles-based constructivism than to the caricature drawn by the critics of *Begriffsjurisprudenz*.

It is true, though, that when commenting on the legal scientific method, Puchta, in particular, from time to time employed the term 'deduction'. But it is disputable whether with this terminology, he would have been referring to a formal-logical operation in the closed world of the legal Ought. Both Savigny and Puchta underlined the significance of *analogy* as the means of legal problem-solving, especially in cases of lacunae. For Savigny, the privileged standing of analogy as a method of the law's 'organic complementation' ensued from the position of legal institutions as the law's basic systemic elements:

> This law-finding through analogy appears in two stages. First, when a new, hitherto unknown legal relationship emerges for which, therefore, hitherto formed positive law does not contain a legal institution as a model. Here a new

6 Haferkamp (2004, p. 449) also emphasises this point in his Puchta rehabilitation.

> model legal institution will be created, adhering to the law of internal kinship with already known institutions. Secondly, and much more often, when a specific new legal question emerges in the context of an already known legal institution. This will be answered in accordance with the internal kinship of the legal propositions belonging to that institution. (1981, I, p. 291)

Wilhelm's (1958) exposition of the development of German nineteenth-century legal science puts excessive emphasis on those features of the historical school which anticipate the turn to *Begriffsjurisprudenz*. Nonetheless, he fittingly portrays Savigny's analogical method as follows: 'when following these principles, complementing and elaborating positive law appeared as a creative development of the law, as the formation of new legal substance, not as a rigid deduction from ready-made concepts' (Wilhelm 1958, p. 67).

Following Savigny, Puchta also stressed the role of analogy when explaining how scientific law can accomplish its task as a subsidiary legal source. The 'deductive' phase of Puchta's method includes: '1) deriving a legal proposition from the principles under which the case of its nature belongs (legal inference) 2) demonstrating that this conclusion also appears in the existing law under similar circumstances (analogy)' (cited in Haferkamp 2004, p. 430). Haferkamp (ibid., p. 451) claims that Puchta never pretended that legal science could derive new law through formal-logical operations. Neither of the two phases of Puchta's method – concept formation and inference of new propositions of law – can be interpreted in terms of formal logic. The analogical method is based on an assumption of the law's consistency, but, as Savigny noted, this is not primarily a formal-logical but an organic quality.[7]

In the language of present-day legal-theoretical debates, the historical school stressed the law's principle- and value-based *coherence* rather than its formal-logical *consistency*. Legal science as a legal practice contributed to the law's development through system formation and analogy conclusions. This was possible due to the law's organic nature, but not its supposed subjection to universally valid rules of formal logic.

Foray: Conceptualism in a Common-Law Setting

The historical school of Savigny and Puchta, as well as subsequent *Begriffsjurisprudenz*, must be examined against the backdrop of German legal history of the previous 300 years, beginning with reception of Roman law. German nineteenth-century legal science built on the doctrinal accomplishments of its

7 'The use of analogy is always based on the internal consistency of the law; but this consistency is not always a mere logical one, such as the pure relationship of premise and consequence, but also an organic one, which arises from the total conception of the practical nature of legal relationships and their models' (1981, I, p. 292).

predecessors; the standing of legal scholarship in the decades preceding German unification and enactment of the *Bürgerliches Gesetzbuch* constitutes merely the culmination of a long development.

Surprising as it may appear, in the United States during the so-called classical era – from about 1870 to about 1920 – legal development also took a turn which bore many resemblances to what transpired in Germany. In the United States, too, a doctrinal movement emerged that strove for systematisation and produced a version of conceptualism, a US variant of *Begriffsjurisprudenz*. But the United States had no legacy of Roman law or of university-based legal scholarship to which the late-nineteenth-century reformers could connect. On the contrary, the United States had inherited English common law, including its distinct mindset: the 'sceptical view of systematic legal reform', 'instinctive mistrust of abstract speculation' and stress on 'the wisdom of proceeding on a case-by-case basis instead'. The common-law lawyer, though, 'believes that general principles have a role to play in the law but doubts that most serious disputes can be decided by reference to them alone' (Kronman 2001, p. 21). Before the Civil War, university-based legal scholarship and education played but a minor role. The regular route to become a lawyer was through apprenticeship and not university studies; law faculties were few and staffed mainly by practising lawyers; and legal treatises, which began to appear in the 1820s and 1830s, were also compiled by men of practice and not by professional scholars.[8]

The law's 'scientification' stood but awkwardly with traditional common-law thinking as exposed in seventeenth- and eighteenth-century debates. Anthony Kronman, who has written a forceful defence of the traditional view of common law as a craft, has compared the efforts of the American classical-era scholars with Thomas Hobbes' and Jeremy Bentham's attacks on common law in the name of science. Kronman's point is that whereas Hobbes – and in his wake, Bentham and Austin – opposed common-law tradition from the outside, late nineteenth-century American scholars 'invented a method for attacking the common law from within'; the predominance gained by Classical Legal Thought amounted to 'a victory for Hobbesian ideas in the heartland of the common law' (Kronman 2001, p. 185).

What, then, brought about the rather abrupt change in American legal thinking? German influence and the German model played their part. The exceptional level of German scholarship and Savigny's personal stature as the century's leading legal scholar were recognised in the United States, too; the reformers studied German doctrine; some of the most prominent amongst them, such as Harvard professor James Barr Ames (1864–1944), even spent time in Germany; and the exalted status of German professors in the legal system offered a role model to be emulated (Hoeflich 1989 and Reimann 1993; see also Ames 1900). Clearly, though, German influence alone does not explain the breach in legal tradition unleashed by

8 The most prominent of these were the Commentaries by Joseph Story, a Justice of the Supreme Court, and Chancellor James Kent (Simpson 1981, pp. 669–671).

Classical Legal Thought. The key factors are to be sought in the internal legal and socio-economic development of the United States, not in external influences.

The ancient system of writs of action had brought a certain organisation to common law, albeit of a formal-procedural nature. In the United States, as well as in England, the system was abolished during the nineteenth century. This cleared the ground for a systematisation of law on other, substantive grounds. At the same time, appellate courts in different states were pouring out great amounts of new decisions; the profusion of legal raw material called for ordering. Simultaneously, post-bellum America was undergoing economic and social unification through the creation of nation-wide markets. This added to the need for common law's synchronisation (Reimann 1993, pp. 178–179; Wiecek 1998, p. 89; Kronman 2001, pp. 182–184). Here we encounter a similarity to the situation in Germany: legal scholarship was assigned the task of generating legal unity in a politically fragmented country.

By no means was it self-evident that this task would fall to legal science. Another conceivable possibility existed for achieving the desired organisation of the law: codification. Indeed, the United States witnessed its own codification debate, as did the former mother country, England. But the codification of substantive law, which was most determinedly campaigned for in New York State, came to nothing, perhaps owing to the traditional mistrust in legislation, so typical of the common-law mindset, perhaps because of a fear of the politics of unpredictable legislative majorities.[9] In any case, the failure of the codification movement left the field open for legal scholarship.[10]

The post-bellum turn in legal development appeared not only in doctrinal reform but in many other guises as well: the growth and professionalisation of university-based law schools and their novel significance in the legal system as a whole; the monopolisation of legal education by the law schools and their adoption of the Langdellian case method; the rise of treatises, law reviews, and case-books as the primary forms of legal literature; and the professionalisation of the Bar (for a summary, see Friedman 2005, pp. 463–482). Although all these developments were closely intertwined, in the following my main focus will lie on doctrinal transformation.

The classical view came to be linked especially to Harvard Law School and such eminent professors of a new generation as Charles Columbus Langdell (1826–1906), Joseph Henry Beale (1861–1942) and Ames. Langdell has also been credited with introducing case method in law-school teaching, a method which

9 Some of the arguments with which Savigny had opposed codification against Thibaut were recycled in the North American debates; another token of the international influence of Savigny (Reimann 1989).

10 On codification projects in the United States, see Reimann (1989) and Kronman (2001, pp. 182–183). On English debates see Van Caenegem (1993, pp. 45–48) and Allison (2004, pp. 122–123).

has by far outlived the zenith of the classical doctrine (see, for example, Kimball 1999). How, then, did Langdell and the other representatives of the new trend conceive of law and legal scholarship? The emphasis lay on developing law into a science; actually, in the United States the very term 'legal science' is often connected to Langdell's programme of university-based legal scholarship and education. A correspondence with the stress on *Rechtswissenschaft* of Savigny and his followers is evident. But the similarities reach even further. In line with the German historical school, the Langdellian programme, too, included both a doctrinal and a historical dimension, although in practice the doctrinal side clearly dominated: no American equivalence exists to Savigny's *Geschichte des römischen Rechts*. References to history remained mainly lip service to common law's organic, evolutionary development, while the main focus of the new generation of academic scholars lay on doctrinal systematisation, just as it was in contemporary German *Begriffsjurisprudenz*.[11]

Classical orthodoxy's conception of legal scientific method has been characterised as conceptual and formalist.[12] Like their European counterparts, classical scholars saw legal science's principal task in the law's ordering and its exposition as a coherent whole, reduced to its fundamental concepts and principles. In accordance with the constructivism of *Begriffsjurisprudenz*, the method consisted of an 'inductivist' and a 'deductivist' phase. In the first phase, the law's basic concepts and principles were inferred from existing legal material. In the second phase, legal rules were deduced from the concepts and principles, and applied to individual cases. The *conceptualism* consisted in the objective of conceptual ordering, the *formalism* in the belief in formal(-logical) methods of inference. Pursuing the conceptual aim, contract-law rules and doctrines were subsumed under the heading of 'will', while the law of torts was organised through the concepts of 'negligence' and 'fault'. Thus, as Horwitz (1994, p. 13) notes, 'between 1870 and 1900, the architecture of law was once more rearranged, this time around general concepts that submerged the concrete particularity of the previous organising schemes'. German Roman law-

11 Langdell famously wrote that 'law, considered as a science, consists of certain principles or doctrines' and 'the number of fundamental legal doctrines is much less than is commonly supposed' (cited after Grey 1983, p. 13). Some US legal historians have emphasised that a historist strand did exist in late nineteenth-century legal thought, in, for instance, constitutional law (Siegel 2001; Rabban 2003).

12 Thomas Grey defines 'formalism' and 'conceptualism' as follows. '"Formalism" describes legal theories that stress the importance of rationally uncontroversial reasoning in legal decision, whether from highly particular rules or quite abstract principles', whereas '"conceptualism" describes legal theories that place a high value on the creation (or discovery) of a few fundamental principles and concepts at the heart of a system, whether reasoning from them is formal or informal' (Grey 1983, pp. 9–10). Reconstructions of the method of Classical Legal Thought are not lacking. In addition to Grey's seminal article, see Duncan Kennedy's (2006a) and Wiecek's (1998) monographs, as well as Horwitz (1994, pp. 9ff.); Duxbury (1995, pp. 14–25); Kronman (2001, pp. 170ff.).

based and American common law-based legal science shared a central substantive premise, too: the concept of will.

Academic legal scholarship and education had to justify itself on two fronts: before other scientific disciplines, in order to legitimate its presence in the universities, and to legal practitioners, in order to demonstrate, not only the practical relevance of its doctrinal constructions and formalist method, but also the superiority of university education to traditional apprenticeship. Scientific support was sought from several directions: from natural science, evolutionary biology, Spencerian sociology, and geometry. Langdell seems to have been particularly fond of analogies from natural science. He defended law's legitimate place at the university as follows:

> Law is a science, and … all the available materials of that science are contained in printed books. If law be not a science, a university will consult its own dignity in declining to teach it. If it be not a science, it is a species of handicraft, and may best be learned by serving an apprenticeship to one who practices it. If it be a science, it will scarcely be disputed that it is one of the greatest and most difficult of sciences, and that it needs all the light that the most enlightened seat of learning can throw upon it. Again, law can only be learned and taught in a university by means of printed books. (Cited in Speziale 1980, p. 12)

Grey argues that geometry is the most fitting model science for comprehending the Langdellian programme (Grey 1983, pp. 16ff.; see also Hoeflich 1986). However, unlike German eighteenth-century *Vernunftrecht*, at issue is not a geometry starting from self-evident premises but geometry where, in the wake of John Stuart Mill (1806–1873), the premises are understood as generalisations from sense perceptions. In this conception, geometry possesses not only a deductive but also a preceding inductive phase, although the latter is often bypassed in learned expositions.

But if law is a science, comparable to natural sciences, and if the library is its laboratory, as Langdell also wrote, what constitutes its specimens? Or if legal science is conceived of after the model of Mill's geometry, what is the basis of legal induction? It is the cases, judicial precedents, collected in the reports stored on the shelves of law libraries, that provide legal science with its empirical material. Here the common-law context is evident. If the positivism of the German historical school and the subsequent *Begriffsjurisprudenz* turned into statutory positivism, the positivism of classical American legal thinking was very much *case-law positivism*.

Classical legal scholars clung to the traditional view of the organic, piecemeal growth of common law through cases. Through this process, history procured legal science its empirical raw material, its specimen, from which concepts and principles were extracted. But history could also cause surprises and generate threats to the law's conceptual ordering; this was a perception which US legal scholars shared with their German conceptualist colleagues. After all, no guarantees existed that the new specimen – in Germany, new statutes and other regulations, in the United States new cases – produced by history were in harmony with the concepts and principles generalised by legal doctrine. In this sense, decisions could be 'incorrect'. And, as Grey (1983, p. 15) comments, the doctrine of *stare decisis* and precedent entailed that 'in law, unlike science, error, if persisted in, at some point became truth'; 'where that point lay could only be determined according to considerations of acceptability that were never satisfactorily formalised'.

Common law's organic growth was seen to encompass the evolution of its principles; here ended the analogy to geometry. How did this evolution transpire? Here legal scholars played the role of a vehicle of legal progress, reminiscent of the productive tasks that *Rechtswissenschaft* was assigned in German nineteenth-century legal thinking. Progress occurred through discovery of 'a previously unrecognised principle, one that provided a simple and satisfying explanation for existing decisions, and that at the same time reflected the slowly changing needs and conditions of society'. This was clearly an instance of what Savigny and Puchta had called 'scientific law':

> Such a principle, because immanent in decided cases, was already the law, so that its articulation was an act of discovery, not one of illegitimate legislation. On the other hand, once discovered it would produce different, better decisions than had the older, less scientific formulation of doctrine and hence would contribute to the progress of the law. (Grey 1983, p. 31)

As an example of such scientific development of law, Grey (ibid.) points to Louis Brandeis' (1856–1941) and Samuel Warren's (1852–1910) renowned article from 1890, where they extracted 'a right to privacy from a scattering of older cases previously regarded as unrelated'.

The emphasis on law as a science implied a strict separation of law and politics, of legal and political argument and reasoning. This manifests the *formalism* of the classical method: legal rules were supposed to be deduced from concepts and principles through a rational and uncontroversial method, and application of these rules to concrete cases, too, was presented as a matter of similar deductive reasoning. The formalist view entailed a sharp difference between judicial and legislative decision-making. In line with common-law lawyers' traditional posture, the classical scholars viewed legislation with suspicion and relegated it to a peripheral place as a source of law. The legislative process was regarded as a scene of irrational and emotionally-loaded politics and bargaining, and seen to lack the deliberative qualities of judicial proceedings. American Classical Legal Thought adopted common law's defensive stance to legislative *voluntas*, despite its rather un-common-law programme of the law's scientification. Recourse was also taken to time-honoured common-law devices for limiting legislation's disruptive effects on the legal system: legislation should be construed in harmony with common-law principles and, in case of explicit deviations, given a narrow interpretation (Wiecek 1998, pp. 99–101).

Classical Legal Thought drew a clear line between private and public law. Like the German historical school, it focused on the former. Private law was the realm of common law, whereas public law was the locus of the legislature's disturbing interventions. Private law was governed by the common law's internal, principled reason, public law by the legislator's political *voluntas*. Public law was indelibly tainted by politics, so that the exclusion of politics from legal science entailed the exclusion of public law. Grey (1983, p. 34) summarises the views of the classical scholars as follows:

> The classicists did not regard public law, including constitutional law, as amenable to scientific study at all ... Constitutional law was unscientific, because hopelessly vague, as typified by the police power doctrine; whether a statute was 'reasonably related to safety, health or morals' could not be treated formally. To the legal science mentality such open-ended questions were political, not legal, and the courts abandoned any scientific role in trying to answer them.

In Germany, the ideal of systematisation, the constructivist method and the conceptual premises of *Begriffsjurisprudenz* were introduced to public law by the founders of the late constitutional school, primarily Gerber and Laband. In the United States, no corresponding 'scientification' of public law occurred.

In its formalism, classical American scholars tried to maintain legal reasoning distinct, not only from politics, but from openly moral arguments as well. The American conceptualists did not espouse anything like the German historical school's notion of a *Volksgeist* which furnished law with a moral and ethical foundation, nor did they elaborate any counterpart to Savigny's concept of legal institution, which connected law to factual social relationships. In their strict demarcations towards politics and society in general with its moral and ethical spheres, the proponents of the American version of legal science were undoubtedly closer to Pandectist *Begriffsjurisprudenz* than Savigny's *Rechtswissenschaft*.

But of course, despite pretensions of 'pure' science, Classical Legal Thought and its judicial applications had social and policy consequences. These consequences, more than any 'internal' flaws in its doctrinal constructions, account for its future reputation as a particularly reactionary legal ideology. There has been no renaissance or even rehabilitation of Classical Legal Thought, in the same sense that we can speak of a rehabilitation of *Begriffsjurisprudenz* in Germany. Classical Legal Thought is generally considered a bygone phase in American legal history, almost an aberration, which however – luckily enough – passed away without leaving any traces. Its only remaining acknowledged importance seems to be to constitute an object of critique, in which role it has, as it were, inadvertently facilitated innovative strands of American twentieth-century legal thinking. It is illustrative of the general consensus that *The Canon of American Legal Thought*, a recent collection of canonical writings which have shaped and continue to shape American legal thinking, contains no contribution by the classical writers but several attacking them, beginning with Oliver Wendell Holmes' (1841–1935) *The*

Path of the Law (1897). In their introduction, the editors justify the absence of pre-Holmes authors as follows:

> the modes of legal thought that they developed before and directly after the Civil War have largely fallen out of use. Indeed our authors initially developed the ideas about legal reasoning contained in these texts as a revolt against what they understood to be the dominant modes of legal thought in post-Civil War America. Their revolt was largely successful – these are the ideas that have endured, and that continue to be taught in America's law schools and deployed by America's lawyers and judges. Holmes represents the watershed – the emergence of a self-consciously American and modern sensibility for legal professionals. (Kennedy and Fisher 2006, p. 1)

Critical reconstructions have exposed laissez-faire capitalism as the 'hidden social theory' of classical thinking. Its central concept was that of will, while the central function the law was supposed to accomplish was to delimit reciprocally the autonomous spheres of different categories of abstract will subjects. Due to its formalism, it for instance denied any legal relevance of factual market positions for contract law: 'contract' was defined as a meeting of free wills, no matter how constrained that will might be by social or economic realities (Kennedy 2006a). In adjudication, the conceptualist and formalist approach of Classical Legal Thought found its manifestation in the Supreme Court's *Lochner*-era jurisprudence: a series of rulings with which the court quashed legislative acts interfering in the free functioning of the economic market and regulating working conditions in particularly vulnerable industries. The *Lochner* decision itself, which concerned labour conditions in bakeries, became an epitome not only of a distinct era of Supreme-Court jurisprudence but of Classical Legal Thought in general. And when, with the advent of the New Deal, this era fell into what seems to be permanent disrepute, the same fate awaited Classical Legal Thought as a school of legal science.

Nonetheless, in one important sense the present prevalent derision of Classical Legal Thought may be short-sighted and ill-informed. It may be that in fact, many of the concepts and principles elaborated by the classical authors have firmly sedimented into American legal culture and even today exert an important although most often unconscious and unnoticed influence through the practical knowledge of legal actors. If this is so, Grey's (1983, p. 50) hint at 'Langdell's secret triumph' is warranted.[13] And if we turn from doctrinal and methodological aspects to other

13 When arguing for 'Langdell's secret triumph', Grey fittingly describes how sub-surface legal-cultural layers function through legal actors' practical knowledge: 'categorical schemes have a power that is greatest when it is least noticed. They channel the attention of those who use them, structuring experience into the focal and the peripheral. In so doing, they influence judgment much as the agenda for a meeting influences the results of its deliberations. Heedless of this power of categories, modern legal theorists have not

dimensions of the post-bellum rupture in American legal history, the lasting impact of the classical era is undeniable. University law schools and university professors as a legal profession have come to play in the United States a role singular for a basically common-law system; treatises, case-books and law reviews remain the principal forms of legal literature; and university education has become the exclusive route to legal professions, including the Bar. These features have made the law in the United States in some important respects resemble Continental civil-law systems rather than the English common law.

Indeed, it seems appropriate to conclude our foray into the common-law world by casting an eye on what happened in England, the mother country of the common law. Actually, not very much happened, at least when compared with the quite profound transformations in the United States. In England, too, efforts were made to achieve a substantive ordering of distinct branches of common law, and the treatise as the central form of legal literature experienced a boost in the nineteenth century (Simpson 1981, pp. 661–668); Sir Fredrick Pollock (1845–1937) was a key figure here (Duxbury 2004). But no significant expansion of university-based legal scholarship and education occurred until the second half of the twentieth century. Blackstone had been the first professor of English law at Oxford, and his successors at the main English universities until 1950 are easy to list. In the English legal system, law faculties as an institution or law professors as a legal profession never obtained the same prominence as on the Continent or in the United States.[14] English exceptionalism, which so puzzled Max Weber in his account of the law's modernisation, has been of a highly persistent character!

The Tensions of Modern Law

Let us return to the main topic of this chapter and try to summarise the German historical school's view of the law in general and modern law in particular. The law was seen as a historical phenomenon, and acknowledgement of the law's historicity led to a positivist programme. The law should be approached as positive law. In a politically fragmented Germany, the positivism of the historical school could not yet amount to statutory positivism; the positive law to which the historical school referred had also other and even more important sources than legislation. This entailed that the law's positivity was not yet as grave a danger to its coherence, its internal system, as it became when positivism turned into statutory positivism; the

supplanted the classic ordering but have left it to half-survive in the back of lawyers' minds and the front of the law school curriculum, where it can shape our thinking through its unspoken judgements' (Grey 1983, p. 50).

14 '... whereas Americans had accorded law a clear identity within their university system by the end of the nineteenth century, it was not until well into the second half of the twentieth century that law began to acquire much academic credibility within the English system' (Duxbury 2005, p. 4).

legislator's *voluntas* did not yet threaten the law's internal *ratio*. As positivity in the sense of historicity bound the law to the *Volksgeist*, it strengthened rather than disturbed the law's coherence.

The historical school took note of the differentiation, typical of modern law, and expressed it in the *Volksgeist* terminology. When the law grew more complicated, specifying and articulating the *Volksgeist* as the law's primary source fell to the estate of learned lawyers. Yet the historical school claimed that the law still reflected the *Volksgeist* and, through jurists' specific culture, was still connected to general (legal) culture. By the same token, the law retained its link with moral and ethical aspects of social life.

Savigny's notion of legal institutions tied the law to its social environment. Legal relationships possessed a factual side on which legal propositions conferred a legal form. Legal institutions were composed of legal propositions regulating social relations of a distinct type; legal institutions constituted models or basic types of legal relationships. They were organised in accordance with the social relations they regulated.

The historical school underlined the law's positivity but assigned this positivity a supra-positive foundation. Historically-determined, positive law manifested the law in general. It gave shape to the general concept of law, just as the *Volksgeist* gave shape to the general human spirit. In Puchta's *oeuvre*, the law's general, supra-positive foundation was expressed in the general concept of law in which the legal subject was conceived of as a subject of will and subjective right as free will. The supra-positive element is also manifest in the principle of equality, which, according to Puchta, governed the law's history.

The historical school approached existing law not only as a historically-determined entity but also as a system. In the early stages of its development, the law did not yet possess a history or system of its own. It was only the law's differentiation which both gave it a distinct history and created the possibility of examining it as a system organised in accordance with its internal principles. The law's internal system was organic in character. The law derived its organic features from its connection to the *Volksgeist* and to the social relations it regulated. What typified an organic system was the interdependence of its elements and the principle of development to which both the whole and its elements were subjected.

The law's differentiation and autonomy was a precondition for, not only its specific historicity, but its internal system as well. Significantly, unlike many later variants of positivist legal theory, the historical school did not treat autonomy and systematicity as self-evident or quasi-transcendental premises, but acknowledged the historicity of these crucial qualities of modern law. The same holds for Gerber, who transferred to public law the approach the critics started calling *Begriffsjurisprudenz*. Gerber stressed that an approach focusing on the law's internal system would not have been possible under medieval, feudal conditions.

The historical school was acutely aware of the social, extra-legal preconditions for the law's internal system. These preconditions guided the ordering of legal material, starting from the definition of the system's building-blocks. Savigny's system of law was built on legal institutions, which, as models or basic types of legal relationship, were organised in accordance with the social relations (life relationships) they regulated.

The historical school attached autonomous and systematic law to its cultural and societal environment. Germany's political unity existed only as a political programme, but the central role of, in particular, the concept of *Volksgeist* warrants the claim that the historical school examined the law within the framework of the nation-state society and culture. The task falling to legal science was to create a modern, unitary legal order, required by the nation-state society, even before the political-institutional nation-state programme had achieved its objective.

It may be illuminating to compare the historical school's view of the law's organic system with the classical common-law approach to coherence. The coherence of common law was primarily *diachronic* in character and guaranteed by the law's ties to its past; by its traditionalism. By contrast, for the historical school – we might say in spite of its name – the law's coherence is mainly of a *synchronic* nature, unfolding its effects here and now. Coherence is due to the law's internal organic unity, the interdependence of its elements, such as legal propositions and legal institutions, propped up by its link to the *Volksgeist*. As an organic system the law is governed by the principle of development, but this principle does not so much bind the law to its past as express its changing nature.

On the path towards *Begriffsjurisprudenz*, legal science's doctrinal system grew increasingly logical and, at the same time, autonomous, even though the logical relations internal to doctrinal constructions may have been vindicated by the allegedly logical relations prevailing within the law itself. The organic vocabulary was still in use, but it was given new emphases as the conception of the law's system and internal rationality assumed logical undertones.[15] Even after the turn to statutory positivism, the systematic nature of positive, enacted law relied on supra-positive support. This support was the work of the most general legal concepts, a priori with regard to positive law.

The relations between the law's internal and legal science's doctrinal system raised strenuous methodological problems. Should the latter faithfully reflect the former? If this was the case, how could legal science capture and expose the law's internal, organic system? Subsequent observers have argued about the specific nature of the historical school's concept and system formation: was it of an inductive, deductive or, perhaps, inductive-deductive character? However, these alternatives, formulated with the concepts of the present-day formal-logically oriented theory of science, do not actually grab hold of the particular methodological posture which, according to Savigny and Puchta, is needed in examining organic wholes and which they, borrowing from contemporary German idealist philosophy, termed *Anschauung*. Scientific exposition was guided by

15 For 'young' Jhering, the law was 'a logical organism of legal institutions and concepts' ('ein logischer Organismus von Rechtsinstituten und Rechtsbegriffen') (Coing 1969, pp. 159–160).

the Kantian requirement of organising knowledge under a leading principle. A scientific system should consist of the unfolding of a basic idea, as Gerber (1880, p. VI) noted in his programme for a science of state law. The methodological requirement was difficult to meet, and Puchta's system of subjective rights, for instance, bears at least a partial resemblance to a Linnaean classification of *genus* and *specie*.

A central task of legal scholarship was to extract and articulate the law's internal reason and system. It is one of the great merits of the historical school that it paid so much attention to the tasks of legal scholarship in a differentiated legal system. It took note of legal scholarship's dual role and examined it, not only as a scientific practice, but also as a legal practice which participates in the continuous development of the legal order. It was this very dual role that enables legal scholarship to make its contribution to pronouncing and safeguarding the law's *ratio*. Legal science tackles its systematising task not only as a scientific but also as a legal practice, and systematisation serves not only scientific but practical purposes as well. In its practical role, legal scholarship imbues legal practices with the *ratio* it has disclosed as a scientific practice.

The heritage of the historical school is still pertinent to our present legal-theoretical concerns. It opens up a perspective to many of the tensions which have subsequently permeated the self-understanding of modern law and the legal theory formulating this self-understanding. These tensions can be listed as follows:

- Modern law is predominantly positive law but still depends on a supra-positive foundation.
- Modern law is autonomous law but still interacts with the surrounding society and culture.
- Modern law is not only positive but also systematic law, with its positivity posing a constant threat to its systematicity.
- The task of legal scholarship is to expose the law's internal system. In so doing, legal scholarship constitutes, not only a scientific, but also a legal practice which contributes to the law's development.

The legal theory of the last century can be understood as a series of attempts to dissolve these tensions, typical of modern law. However, as I try to argue in this study, it is not possible to dispose of them in the reductionist way: by way of effacing one side of the tension or defining it in terms of the other side. Twentieth-century legal-theoretical positivism has denied positive law's supra-positive foundation. Furthermore, through separation of the Ought from the Is and the legal from the moral Ought, it has endeavoured to cut the law's ties to its societal and cultural environment. Nor has it been willing to recognise legal science as one of the law-producing and -reproducing practices. The vicissitudes of legal theory prove that the suppressed has an irksome tendency to recur as disconcerting symptoms. Perhaps we should adopt another posture towards modern law's basic tensions, such as those listed above, and acknowledge them as its constitutive features?

The law has not, of course, stood still after the heyday of the historical school, and our legal experience at the beginning of the twenty-first century does not, of course, equal the situation in Germany during the first half of the nineteenth century. Yet, I venture to claim that the tensions disclosed through reconstructing the historical school's conception of law and legal science are still with us and can, thus, serve as an overture to an exploration of our present law.

But we must keep in mind that Savigny and Puchta wrote at the dawn of the era of modern law and in a politically fragmented Germany. They were aware of the potentially conflictual relationship between the law's systematic and positive dimensions and, in their own research programme, between dogmatic and historical studies. But they could not yet experience this as a tension between the law's internal *ratio* and the political legislator's *voluntas*, nor did they feel the need to articulate *ratio*'s function as a constraint to instrumentally-oriented *voluntas*. The legislature occupied but a marginal position in pre-unification German law, so that the historical school did not yet identify positive law with the law enacted by the legislature. Legal positivism was only converted into statutory positivism after German unification; and only under pressure of political democracy and budding welfare-state development did legislation's instrumentalisation for political aims begin seriously to threaten the law's systematic character. In common-law thinking, the law's historicity ensured its coherence. In the view of the historical school, too, the law's organic evolution was in basic harmony with the systematic interdependence between its elements; indeed, when Savigny or Puchta stressed the organic character of the law, they referred to both of these features. The law's historicity and positivity only becomes a menace to its coherence when historicity, as it were, changes direction and, instead of tying law to its past, opens it towards the future, and when positivity starts to denote, above all, the law's malleability through explicit legislative decisions.

In German state law, the new terms of the opposition between *ratio* and *voluntas* were manifest in the development of the *Rechtsstaat* theory. In legal sociology, Max Weber, in the early twentieth century, formulated the danger that instrumentalisation posed to the law's systematic quality as the tension between formal and substantive rationality. This formulation has had plenty of adherents in subsequent debates, both in Germany and elsewhere.

Chapter 4
The Critique of Conceptualism: Legal Realism and Analytic Jurisprudence

The Rhetorical Task of Legal Concepts

The development of legal concepts is often presented as a gradual, peaceful process where the emphasis lies in continuity instead of ruptures, in evolution instead of revolutions. Legal concepts are seen as carrying the law from one time to another, extending the law's past into the present and even beyond. Above, I have also stressed the slowness of legal culture's time in comparison with the rapid pace of the law's surface. Legal culture evolves as a result of sedimentation, starting from the surface level, which cannot transpire at a moment's notice.

On the other hand, social, political and legal change, so typical of modern society, engenders an unremitting need of conceptual renewal. The freezing of legal concepts can only be countered by conscious striving for reform, for which the reflexivity of modern culture creates the necessary space. Established doctrine has its supporters, too, with debates between divergent schools, 'traditions', even at times becoming heated. This holds especially for periods of rupture or transition which witness alternative, if not antagonistic, doctrines with their alternative conceptual apparatus. In this chapter my focus will be on a specific case of doctrinal rupture: the criticism of conceptualism, which in the latter half of the nineteenth century had risen to a dominant position in Romano-Germanic legal cultures and, in a common-law version, in the United States as well. The exact timing of the rupture varied. In Germany, anti-conceptualist criticism was already gathering wind during the last half of the nineteenth century, while in the United States the decisive decades were the 1920s and the 1930s. In turn, the heyday of Scandinavian Realism fell into the period between 1930 and 1960. Finland was a latecomer: the analytical school only launched its criticism of *Begriffsjurisprudenz* in the post-war era, with the 1950s and 1960s as its most active decades.

Significant variation occurred as well in the motives and the philosophical background of the critical movements. The American Realists were of a quite practical mindset and, as a rule, not very interested in propping up their critical points with philosophical ballast. In this respect, the difference with Scandinavian colleagues is conspicuous. As latecomers, Finnish analytical scholars, for their part, could already draw from post-war philosophical developments. But in spite of this disparity, anti-conceptualist polemics in different countries and eras also display a considerable number of – indeed, astonishingly many – common themes, such as the accusation of formalism and conceptual metaphysics. Similarities in the arguments exist, too, so that a rough division into *analytical* and *realist* points seems largely to cover the field. The analytical and realist discussions may have taken divergent routes, but often enough they were closely related. This was the case in both American and Scandinavian Realism. The similarities warrant a common discussion of anti-conceptualism in legal theory. I shall start with some observations on German *Interessenjurisprudenz* and the *Freirechtsschule*, turn to American realist and analytical trends, and then via Scandinavian Realism arrive at Finnish post-war debates.

Diverse approaches exist to doctrinal ruptures. In a sociological external description (*Fremdbeschreibung*), the contest between legal scientific schools can be examined in the framework of Pierre Bourdieu's theory of social fields: in the legal field, the schools are engaged in a battle over the power to define the contents of the legal order, to state what the law is (see below, pp. 159–160). A central means of this battle consists of the law's language: concepts as its vocabulary and argumentative rules as its grammar. Bourdieu's theory of social fields comes close to the Critic's narrative of the law as a strategic, interest-bound power game. Another perspective is offered by Thomas Kuhn's (1922–1996) philosophy of science: legal doctrinal ruptures may amount to a change of paradigm, in Kuhn's sense of the term (Kuhn 1967).

Yet another alternative is provided by the conceptual approach to intellectual history. Quentin Skinner and Reinhardt Koselleck are perhaps the most prominent exponents of this approach, which draws our attention to a vital aspect in the functioning of legal concepts which legal scholars often ignore. Legal concepts not only serve mutual communication between legal professionals and play a heuristic role in legal problem-solving. They also pursue a rhetorical objective: by means of legal concepts and following specific rhetorical strategies, rival schools try to boost their support. The role of rhetoric is perhaps most conspicuous in legal proceedings, where the parties (their lawyers) try to convince the judge (or jury) through rhetorical devices. But the rhetoric of concepts is an inseparable aspect of legal argumentation in other contexts as well. Argumentation and rhetoric are reverse sides of the same coin and the emphasis they receive largely depends on the position from which we view legal discourse: the external perspective tends to stress the rhetorical while the internal one the argumentative aspect.

Rhetoric is present in all legal discourse and argumentation, but times of doctrinal rupture have in particular produced material exemplifying its significance. The stakes in the rhetorical game between scholarly strands may be raised by external connections that link legal discourse to the political and ideological controversies of the day. Such connections are typical of fields of law that are 'structurally coupled' with politics: constitutional and international law. One legal scholar most acutely aware of the rhetoric of legal discourse was Carl Schmitt. His doctrinal interest focused on constitutional and international law, and especially in his writings during the Weimar era he commented on the polemical edge of legal concepts. Nor is it a mere coincidence that the Critic's narrative, with its spotlight on the strategic aspects of legal discourse, prefers to appeal to examples provided by international law.

Both sociological analysis of the legal field and examination of legal discourse in terms of rhetoric purport to suspend normative assessment of legal speech acts. But, once more, we have to keep in mind the other alternative: we can also suspend the rhetorical or strategic aspect and concentrate on the merits of the arguments put forth. That will be my line of attack at the end of this chapter, where I shall appraise the grounds of anti-conceptualist criticism. But before turning to a discussion of this criticism, I shall dwell for a moment on the methodology of the history of concepts and Schmitt's overtly polemicist conception of legal concepts.

Texts and Contexts

In an important article, published in 1992 and related to his monograph *Korko, raha ja sopimus* (*Interest, Money and Contract*, Tolonen 1992a), the Finnish legal theorist and historian Hannu Tolonen (1945–2004) discusses the methodology of conceptual history. He argues that in conceptual history – or the history of legal ideas in general – it is never possible wholly to exclude the influence of contemporary concepts or contemporary normative debates: historical reconstructions are always written in the present (Tolonen 1992b, p. 128). Tolonen employs the terms 'historical' and 'rational reconstruction', referring to the relationship between a text's concepts, bound to its time, and the historian's concepts, bound to the historian's time. Furthermore, he ponders the roles of *textual-hermeneutical* and *functional* reconstruction in the history of ideas. The former focuses on the text's internal dimension of meaning and attempts to grasp the text's meaning from within. In turn, in functional reconstruction the text is located in its context, which is seen as determining the text's meaning.

Tolonen contends that in the history of ideas, a contextual approach – functional reconstruction – is justified, even necessary, but only on the text's terms. Functional reconstruction is warranted in so far as the text itself alludes to its functional context; presupposes it, or tries to influence it. Respecting these conditions and limitations, texts dealing with legal concepts related to economic activities, for instance, can and even should be situated in the economic context of their day (Tolonen 1992b, pp. 137–143).

Skinner, who was a major source of inspiration for Tolonen, gives us further guidance as to how the relationship between a text's internal and external dimension should be conceived of and how the contexts of texts should be specified. Skinner has expounded his approach in the framework of speech act theory. He argues that texts should be examined, not only from a *semantic* perspective focusing on the meaning of linguistic expressions, but also – perhaps even primarily – from a *pragmatic* standpoint, concentrating on the use of language. Texts are speech acts, which entails a fundamental demand for contextuality. In order to understand what authors did in writing their texts, the texts must be placed in their contexts. Texts do not merely convey a meaning; they also aim at distinct *illocutionary effects*. The historian of ideas sees a text as a move, an intervention, in a specific argumentative game; and must conceive of it as a speech act and recognise its illocutionary aim: 'any act of communication will always constitute the taking up of some determinate position in relation to some pre-existing conversation or argument' (Skinner 2002a, pp. 114–115).

In Chapter 1, I argued that normative legal scholarship, too, focuses on the illocutionary dimension of legal speech acts. How, then, does Skinner's method of conceptual history, when applied to legal texts, relate to such legal scholarship? The latter participates in legal discourse and adopts to it an internal point of view. Normative legal scholarship does not examine legal speech acts merely with regard to their illocutionary force but assesses speech acts' claims to substantive validity and arguments warranting these claims. By contrast, the historian of concepts refrains from such assessments, being only interested in the illocutionary aspect of speech acts in so far as this is needed for deciphering their argumentative context.

Let us call a text's *immediate context* the argumentative milieu where the text as a speech act finds its location and where it argues, criticises, endorses, attacks, or defends itself. But we should recall that speech acts pursue not only illocutionary but also perlocutionary effects beyond the communicative context. Texts dealing with the economic or political action field not only participate in a particular argumentative game. Additionally, they seek to influence the way economic or political actors think and behave. As Skinner (ibid., p. 149) notes, perlocutionary effects are obvious in the intentions of ideological reformers. The perlocutionary goals and effects of the texts under examination require a wider conception of their context, say, the positioning of economic texts in their economic environment.

Texts' illocutionary and particularly their perlocutionary effects highlight the significance of their rhetorical dimension. According to the classic definition, rhetoric links *pathos* to *logos*; it appeals to the passions and emotions of the audience in order to obtain support for a specific standpoint (Skinner 2002b, p. 268). Rhetorical strategies are important for champions of ideological renewal who want to upset established manners of conceiving and valuing the world. The very term 'rhetorical strategy' intimates Skinner's view of the conflictual nature of debates on society's normative premises. He claims that 'the principles governing our moral and political life have generally been disputed in a manner more reminiscent of the battlefield than the seminar room' (Skinner 2002a, p. 7). Here the edge of Skinner's polemical speech act is without doubt directed at the political philosophy of John Rawls (1921–2000) and Jürgen Habermas, as well as their disciples. In this connection, Skinner notes his kinship with Reinhart Koselleck, another important figure behind the contemporary interest in the history of concepts. Koselleck (1984, p. 113) remarks that semantic battles over the definition of political concepts are typical of times of crisis and that these battles are closely linked to the political power contest.

A Military Science of Concepts

Tolonen, Skinner and Koselleck remind us of the importance of the contexts of texts and teach us how to specify this context by understanding texts as speech acts pursuing illocutionary and perlocutionary effects. They urge us to pay due attention to texts' rhetorical and conflictual dimension, which gains in importance particularly during periods of social or political crisis. When discussing Schmitt's constitutional texts from the Weimar era, these lessons may seem almost self-evident.

The historiography of legal concepts often adopts a textual-hermeneutical approach. It may acknowledge the influence exerted by the historian's concepts – the interpretative framework – but it tends to ignore the context as understood in Skinner's terms. The distinctive traits of constitutional law enhance the significance of texts' rhetorical-polemical aspect and the need to specify their context. Legal concepts in general display a particular normativity, at least in the sense of delimiting heuristically the solutions that can be indicated to legal problems. But the concepts of constitutional law possess another type of normativity, too, related to the constitution's dual location in both the legal and the political system and to its intermediary function between these social sub-systems. The central concepts of constitutional law, such as 'sovereignty', 'democracy' and 'separation of powers', are at one and the same time both legal and political concepts. Hence, how these concepts are defined in legal discourse has implications for political discourse as well. The connections between constitutional-law doctrine and political discourse are particularly conspicuous in times of political crisis.

In addition to the distinct features of constitutional law and the turbulent history of the Weimar Republic, we should also pay attention to Schmitt's specific conception of legal science in general and constitutional-law science in particular. In Schmitt's view, legal science is a servant of the political *voluntas* rather than the *ratio* tempering the former. The following typical, aphoristically concise expression from his *Über die drei Arten der Rechtswissenschaft* (1934) could serve as a motto for his whole *oeuvre*: *Es gibt eine freischwebende Jurisprudenz ebensowenig wie eine freischwebende Intelligenz*[1] (Schmitt 1934, p. 30). Schmitt was well aware of the central role that concepts play in law and legal discourse. For instance, this is manifest in his predilection to begin his writings with succinct conceptual remarks, such as *Souverän ist wer über den Ausnahmezustand entscheidet*[2] (Schmitt 1985, p. 11) or *Der Begriff des Staates setzt den Begriff des Politischen voraus*[3] (Schmitt 1987, p. 20).

1 'A "free-floating" … jurisprudence does not exist, any more than a "free-floating" intelligentsia' (Schmitt 2004b, p. 73).

2 'The sovereign is the one that decides on the exception' (Schmitt 2004c, p. 5).

3 'The concept of the state presupposes the concept of the political' (Schmitt 1996, p. 19).

Schmitt focused on the pragmatic dimension of concepts. His writings abound with observations on the polemical or political nature of concepts. In his essay on the concept of the political, he stresses the polemical sense of political concepts: 'They are focused on a specific conflict and are bound to a concrete situation; the result (which manifests itself in war or revolution) is a friend-enemy grouping, and they turn into empty and ghostlike abstractions when this situation disappears'. Or expressed through examples: 'Words such as state republic, society, class, as well as sovereignty, constitutional state, absolutism, dictatorship, economic planning, neutral or total state, and so on, are incomprehensible if one does not know exactly who is to be affected, combated, refuted, or negated by such a term' (Schmitt 1996, pp. 30–31).

In Schmitt's view, the fundamental concepts of constitutional theory do amount to political concepts. They are political as regards not only their reference but also their polemical character, their engagement in the political and ideological battles of their time. For Schmitt, the relevant context of concepts reaches out beyond their immediate argumentative environment. In his political theory, the basic distinction of politics separates friends from foes. This distinction must be taken seriously in examining his constitutional concepts, too. The field where Schmitt's concepts should be located and which also determines their specific meaning is not the syntactic field of structuralists, but, rather, a battlefield of conceptual allies and enemies. In addition, the field may involve neutral concepts which remain outsiders to fundamental friend/foe distinctions. Analysis of the conceptual battlefield calls for a 'military science of concepts'.

Schmitt's criticism of liberalism includes a criticism of liberal theorists' manner of employing concepts. In Schmitt's account, political liberalism is a doomed attempt to avoid distinguishing friends from foes and the decisions this presupposes. Instead of grasping the friend/foe distinctions that constitute the crux of politics, liberalism waters the political down to economy and morals. The same holds for concepts coined by liberal theorists. In its ethical pathos and material or economic *Sachlichkeit*, liberalism is guilty of de-politicising and de-militarising concepts: in liberal thinking, the political concept of battle is transformed, in the economic field, into 'competition' and, in the intellectual realm, into 'discussion'. In liberalism, the dynamic of perpetual competition and perpetual discussion substitutes for the clear separation of war and peace. Through such conceptual transformations, 'state' and 'politics' are subordinated to economic categories and individualistic morality and thereby deprived of their distinct political meaning (ibid., pp. 71–72).

A Schmittian analysis stresses that conceptual realignments do not result from any self-motion within an autonomous sphere of ideas but from conscious moves by the players, speech acts of constitutional theorists. Distinctions between friends and foes not only classify concepts but also organise the players of the rhetorical, polemical game into opposite schools of constitutional law. In constitutional theory, Schmitt's main adversary was state-law positivism of the late constitutional school. This trend, represented by Gerber, Laband and Jellinek, had obtained a leading position after the unification of Germany and the issuance of the German constitution. In the eyes of their critics, state-law positivists were guilty of value relativism, even value nihilism, and of ignoring the political reality; this was a state-law variant of the criticism of conceptualist formalism. The critics, including Schmitt, developed conceptions that can be termed material or substantive.

Schmitt's *oeuvre* must be placed in its immediate argumentative context. But this is not enough when following the programme of a Schmittian military science of concepts. The schools of constitutional legal scholarship are linked to the political and ideological friend/foe groupings of the day. The Weimar debates show with exceptional clarity how scholarly positions in disputes over constitutional doctrine are related to contemporary political controversies. The front lines within state-law debates quite closely followed political and ideological constellations; the immediate and the wider context of speech acts of constitutional doctrine were intimately intertwined. In Weimar, state-law positivism equalled a stance in favour of the Weimar constitution, based on parliamentary democracy and including an extensive chapter on basic rights. The positivists were close to the centrist parties, which were the main political backbone of the Weimar constitutional system. By contrast, most of their critics were suspicious of the political system established during the revolutionary period of 1918–1919 and did not believe in its longevity. With his speech acts, Schmitt aimed not only at illocutionary goals internal to legal discourse. Schmitt's primary ideological-political purpose, the perlocutionary objective of his scholarly interventions, was to promote the demise of the Weimar constitutional system and to contribute to its replacement by an authoritarian state, relying on plebiscitary legitimacy.[4]

Clearly, the 'military science of concepts' cannot be raised to a universally valid method of the history of concepts, and its ability to shed light on the rhetorical dimension of legal concepts may be limited. Quite possibly, its main field of application lies in the constitutional (and international) law of times of crisis. But it certainly suits exploration of Schmitt's Weimar writings. The conceptual field where Schmitt made his strategic moves should be analysed through relations between friends and foes – allied and adversary concepts – also paying due attention to concepts retaining neutrality with regard to the field's primary contradictions.

The first step in the analysis is to determine the *key concept* through which relations within the field are unfurled. This concept is positioned within the field through its oppositional concept(s), that is, the concept(s) on which its criticism and polemics focus. For instance, if we take the concept of the *Rechtsstaat* as our starting-point, this is localised through its relation to, say, 'police state' or 'welfare state'. But this does not yet suffice. We should also identify the *Rechtstaat*'s conceptual allies, and neutral concepts, too, play their part in the configuration within the conceptual field. We can, for instance, explore how, in the history of

4 Plebiscitary legitimacy is characterised by a direct link between the rulers and their subjects, maintained through, for instance, referendums. In the Third *Reich*, referendums were in frequent use.

Rechtsstaat theory and in the interpretation of diverse theoretical schools, the position of 'democracy' has shifted between that of an allied and that of a neutral concept (Tuori 2002b).

However, a static description of the conceptual field is not enough. We should also explore the moves through which the actors try to alter its configuration and to reorganise it in accordance with their preferences and objectives.

In constitutional law, the normativity that typifies legal concepts in general acquires an additional feature from the intimate links of this branch of law with politics. Constitutional-law concepts relate to the basics of society's political and legal order. They not only describe but also evaluate these basics; they have positive or negative value connotations. In Skinner's (2002a, pp. 148 and 161) terms, they are *evaluative-descriptive* or *persuasive* concepts. 'Democracy' is a model example of such a value-laden constitutional concept. We may ask how the value sense of a concept referring to society's normative grounds is determined. An allusion to the general cultural climate of the era is not a very precise answer, but it presumably points in the right direction.

Keeping in mind the evaluative character of concepts, we can distinguish between three alternative conceptual strategies within the doctrinal battlefield. Firstly, one can try to hijack a positively-laden concept from the adversary. Secondly, when hijack is not possible, one can endeavour at least to neutralise a positively-laden and strategically important concept. Finally, one can attempt to transform a concept's value quality from positive to negative or vice versa. The contest in the field is a contest, not only with concepts, but also over the concepts.

In Schmitt's Weimar writings, 'democracy' is the key concept opening the conceptual field. This was a positively-laden concept which Schmitt must hijack from his main opponent, liberalism and state-law positivism as its epitome in constitutional theory. In his book on parliamentarianism, Schmitt (1988a, p. 30) states explicitly why 'democracy' was so crucial for dominance of the field. The time of dynastic legitimacy propping up monarchy was over; it had been replaced by democratic legitimacy. Schmitt drew the main political-ideological dividing line in Weimar between two legitimacy principles, both swearing in the name of democracy: the legitimacy principle of a parliamentarian legislative state and that of a plebiscitary democracy.

In order to win 'democracy' over to his side, Schmitt had to sever its tie to 'parliamentarianism'. He argued against liberal theorists that democracy and parliamentarianism are by no means 'natural' allies. Parliamentarianism can even become an enemy of democracy, and that was exactly the case in Weimar's 'party state'. In Weimar's political constellation, 'liberalism' and 'parliamentarianism' were not 'democracy's' conceptual allies but rather its adversaries. Reorganising the field through hijacking or neutralising concepts is generally not possible without providing the respective concepts with new definitions. Thus, in order to hijack 'democracy' from the liberal camp, a redefinition was needed. Schmitt defined 'democracy' through two distinctive features: equivalence of the rulers and the ruled, and substantial homogeneity of the people, the political unit. The first feature warrants the claim that 'democracy' and 'dictatorship' are not necessarily conceptual opposites: in the transitional period of a dictatorship, democratic equivalence can exist between the ruler(s) and the ruled, and the will of the people can well be decisive (Schmitt 1988a, p. 28). 'Dictatorship' and 'liberalism' contradict each other; 'dictatorship' and 'democracy' do not (ibid., p. 16). The other defining feature, substantial homogeneity of the people, entails that democracy is not possible without fundamental friend/foe determinations. Democracy presupposes decisions on inclusion and exclusion: 'democracy presupposes … first homogeneity and second – if the need arises – elimination or eradication of heterogeneity' (ibid., p. 9).

Thus, 'democracy' exemplifies Schmitt's attempt to take over the key concept of the field from his opponent, by means of the rhetorical strategy of redefinition. With regard to the *Rechtsstaat*, during the Weimar era Schmitt employed rather the strategy of neutralisation. The *Rechtsstaat* belonged to the central concepts in liberal constitutional theory, and Schmitt could not wholly ignore such a positively-laden notion and leave it to the arsenal of his adversaries. But instead of attempting a hijack, he contented himself with the strategy of neutralisation. We can guess at the reason for this option: from the theoretical premises Schmitt adhered to during the Weimar period, he was not able to provide the concept with a meaning-content that would constitute a convincing alternative to the prevailing liberal interpretation. This only became possible in the Third *Reich*, where Schmitt coined the specification 'national-socialist *Rechtsstaat*' (Schmitt 1935).

An ideological reformer (or revolutionary) may also aspire to dominance of the conceptual field through changing the value sense of a key concept. In Schmitt's Weimar writings, a telling example is provided by the concept of dictatorship, which, for Schmitt, might be worthy of a positive valuation. 'Democracy' and 'dictatorship' are not necessarily conceptual adversaries but can be allies, too (Schmitt 1988a, p. 32).

Finally, control over the conceptual field might be achieved by introducing new conceptual distinctions. One of the principal maxims in the military science of concepts lays down that one should always aspire to the power to define the concepts under which normative controversies are conducted. Indeed, Schmitt's writings during the Weimar period provide a rich reservoir of new conceptual distinctions. Three examples will suffice to prove the point: firstly, the distinction between 'sovereign' and 'commissionary dictatorship', which set the terms for debates on constitutional emergency powers (Schmitt-Dorotic 1921, pp. 136ff.); secondly, the distinction between the 'constitution as a decision' or the 'constitution in the positive sense' and 'constitutional laws', which was designed to blur the legal force of the written constitution and to create conceptual vagueness, facilitating application of Schmitt's ideas to rapidly changing political situations (Schmitt 2008, pp. 75–79); and thirdly, the distinction between a legislative, governmental, administrative and jurisdiction state, each endowed with a specific legitimacy principle (Schmitt 2004a, pp. 3ff.). The last distinction was instrumental to Schmitt's critique of the

Weimar constitution: one of his main points was that the Weimar legislative state had drifted into contradiction with its legitimacy principle.

German Criticism of *Begriffsjurisprudenz*

If conceptualism, in its prime, was an international phenomenon with national varieties, the same goes for criticism of it, which enjoyed its zenith from the turn of the nineteenth century to the 1960s. Duncan Kennedy (2006b) terms it the second globalisation of modern law under the dominance of a social conception of law. The anti-conceptualist movement displayed national particularities with regard to its specific themes, its exact timing, as well as its discursive and wider economic, social and political contexts. But semblances also existed, justifying a transnational and comparative perspective.

The 'hidden social theory' of conceptualism was based on individualism and a clear separation between an autonomously functioning market economy and the state (the political sphere); the latter was supposed to guarantee general framework conditions for the former but not to intervene in its workings. In the economically most developed countries, social and economic problems engendered by industrialisation and urbanisation had become increasingly conspicuous by the end of the nineteenth century. By the same token, social-theoretical assumptions of legal conceptualism lost much of their credibility. As a consequence, voices were raised calling for employment of the law to combat new problems, such as poor labour conditions and industrial accidents, unemployment, or urban misery. At the same time, democratisation opened the political and legislative processes for new political forces and ignited the hope of improving the lot of economically and socially depressed classes and groups by political means. Law was increasingly conceived of as an instrument for achieving politically-defined social and economic goals. This view of law was not possible without a thoroughgoing criticism of the dominant conceptual mode of legal thinking. On the other hand, laissez-faire thinking, implicit in legal conceptualism, still had its supporters. The immediate argumentative context of jurisprudential debates was clearly related to a wider economic, ideological and political environment.

The clash between conceptualism and its critique from the positions of a social view of law was a clash between two legal paradigms, in Habermas' sense of the term (see below, pp. 203–204). It embraced the law's conceptual and doctrinal apparatus; its division into distinct fields; its methodological standards; and its underlying social-theoretical assumptions. The stakes were high, as regards both the power game within the legal field and the perlocutionary effects of legal discourse in other social fields. The debates were openly polemical and provide abundant evidence of the significance of the rhetorical dimension in legal argumentation: anti-conceptualist critics were in practically open competition over the most fitting and memorable expressions of irony and ridicule. In *Scherz und Ernst in der Jurisprudenz*, Rudolf von Jhering, one of the earliest German detractors from conceptualism, told of his dream about a heaven of concepts (Jhering 1884, p. 27); this was a favourite story for many American Realists. Oliver Wendell Holmes, godfather of American Realists, called Christopher Columbus Langdell, the epitome of US conceptualism, 'the greatest living legal theologian' (Holmes 1880, p. 234), and Roscoe Pound (1870–1964), another proto-Realist, coined the expressions 'mechanical jurisprudence' (Pound 1908) and 'slot-machine jurisprudence' (Pound 1921, p. 170).

In the following, I shall undertake a brief geographical and legal-cultural tour of anti-conceptualism, by the same token attempting to pin down the main common points in both its critical and constructive programme, in order to submit them to a concluding critical assessment. After briefly exploring German antecedents I shall turn to American Legal Realism and end my tour with the Scandinavian version of realism and the Finnish analytical strand. The French variant of 'social law', masterfully explored and exposed by François Ewald in his *L'État providence* (1986), has to be left aside, in spite of the important model it offered to the 'second wave of legal globalisation'.

Accusations of ethical and political relativism, hurled during the Weimar era at the late constitutional school of Gerber, Laband and Jellinek, exemplify the criticism of conceptualist formalism. In state law, statutory positivism held sway until the end of the *Kaiser Reich*, but in other fields of law anti-conceptualism is of more remote origin. The main figure in early private-law criticism was Jhering, who had made his famous conversion from the Saul of *Begriffsjurisprudenz* to the Paul of *Interessenjurisprudenz* by the late 1850s and whose *Scherz und Ernst* set the tone for much of the subsequent assault. In fact, the very term *Begriffsjurisprudenz* seems to have been a product of Jhering's ingenuity (Haferkamp 2004, p. 26).

In the wake of Jhering's polemics, German late nineteenth- and early twentieth-century debates already raised two central themes which then resurfaced in the interventions of American and Scandinavian Realists. The first of these is *conceptual abstraction*. *Begriffsjurisprudenz* was alleged to rely on eternal concepts, detached from the needs of practical life; it was guilty of 'Conceptual Platonism' or of a 'Cult of Mummies' – a reference to the Roman-law origin of the Pandectist conceptual system. The basic concepts were understood as a priori, transcendental premises instead of results of inductive derivation, as the modern conception of science would have required. *Begriffsjurisprudenz*'s conception of concepts manifested the fundamental *formalist* sin: ignorance of practical needs, practical interests, and social values (Haferkamp 2004, pp. 39–43).

In the legal worldview of *Begriffsjurisprudenz*, centre stage was occupied by the learned lawyer, the legal scholar. By contrast, critics from the *Interessenjurisprudenz* and *Freirechtslehre* movements emphasised the role of the legislator and the judge. Clearly, this shift in emphasis was largely due to socio-economic and political transformations, to which the critics of conceptualism lent a jurisprudential voice. Industrialisation and urbanisation raised a call for social legislation through the political voice of the labour movement. At the same time,

German unification created a national legislature and a national judiciary; this was destined to enhance the status of legislation and precedents as sources of law. German *Juristenrecht* finally culminated in the *Bürgerliches Gesetzbuch*, the 'legalisation' of the Pandectist system.

Despite the increased activity of the legislator, rapid socio-economic development was bound to produce ever-new problems which had not been directly addressed in legislation. This is one of the factors behind the focus on judicial decision-making in anti-conceptualist legal theory, not only in Germany but in American and Scandinavian Realism as well. Much of the German discussion concentrated on judicial reasoning in situations of lacunae in the law.

This brought to the fore the other main theme in anti-*Begriffsjurisprudenz* literature: the *critique of deductivism*, which complemented the critique of 'conceptual Platonism'. Conceptualist theorists were accused of a rather elementary logical fallacy: new legal norms were supposed to be deducible from abstract concepts, thus enabling putative gaps in the law to be closed. But, as the critics kept repeating, only those same norms can be derived from a legal concept from which it has been inductively inferred in the first place. If a concept has been formed on the basis of Norms 1–n, no logically valid way is available to deduce from it an additional Norm n+1. *Begriffsjurisprudenz* was held guilty, not only of deficient inductivism in the formation of concepts, but also of quasi-productive deductivism in their application. A corollary of the critique of deductivism was a critique of *Juristenrecht* or scientific law as a source of law. Various pejorative tags were attached to the alleged deductivist method of *Begriffsjurisprudenz*, such as *Inversionsmethode*, coined by Philipp Heck (1858–1943).[5]

Anti-deductivism was closely associated with *anti-formalism*. Deductivism was claimed to make judges blind to the social context of law and legal problems: the interests and needs of life (*Lebensbedürfnisse*) that lay behind both legal rules and the issues the judges were called on to resolve. Jhering and his disciples propounded the alternative of an instrumentally-tuned *teleological method* which required examining and, if necessary, balancing the interests involved. This was the majority position among the anti-conceptualist reformers of judicial reasoning, although different views were expressed as to the extent to which judges were constrained by statutory law in their interest assessment and teleological reasoning. The controversies between the *Interessenjurisprudenz* of Heck and the *Freirechtslehre* of Eugen Ehrlich (1862–1922) and Hermann Kantorowicz (1877–1940) largely concentrated on this issue.[6]

---

5 Representative criticisms of *Begriffsjurisprudenz* include Rümelin (1907) and Heck (1909).

6 See the collections of Ehrlich's writings (Ehrlich 1967 and 1986), and the English edition of his *Fundamental Principles of the Sociology of Law* (2001), as well as the collection of Kantorowicz's writings (Kantorowicz 1962). The collective volume *Interessenjurisprudenz* (Ellscheid and Hassemer 1974) includes central texts by Heck and Rümelin.

If the debates in the *Kaiserreich* were mainly about the position of the legislature and judges, the 1920s saw a revival of interest in the role of legal scholarship. The notion of *Begriffspyramide*, which has subsequently become an almost standard characterisation of Puchta's conceptual system, dates from this period; the credit for its attachment to Puchta seems to go to Heck. In their treatment of legal concepts, Puchta and his followers were allegedly guilty of the same deductive *Inversionsmethode* which was claimed to be the *Begriffs*jurisprudential solution to the judicial problem of gaps in law (Haferkamp 2004, pp. 94–96).

The most radical critics of *Begriffsjurisprudenz*, those forming the *Freirechtslehre* camp, voiced claims of a reversal of legal science: of its conversion into research into 'socio-legal' reality. Ehrlich appears to have been one of the first to use the very term *Rechtssoziologie* (sociology of law) (Schröder 1976, p. 44).

Realist Anti-Conceptualism in the United States

American Realism is an intellectual phenomenon hard to pinpoint with an unambiguous definition. It was not a jurisprudential school with clear contours, nor perhaps even an academic movement in the style of the Critical Legal Studies of the last quarter of the twentieth century. As noted in 1931 by Karl Llewellyn (1893–1962), perhaps the brightest and most original of the principal Realists, American Realism involved a general mood among legal intellectuals rather than a homogeneous group of academics. Thus, who 'really' can be counted as a Realist seems to be an inexhaustible topic in the historiography of American legal thinking. Nor does agreement exist on themes that would have linked the Realists together. Some commentators confine the common denominator to the critical aspect – criticism of conceptualism – (e.g. Kronman 2001, p. 186) while others, such as Brian Leiter (2007), argue that this was not all and that practically all Realists subscribed to some joint substantive or methodological postulates as well. In line with the alternative they proposed to the discredited conceptualism, two main types of Realists have been discerned: Scientists and Prudents (Twining 1985, p. 54) or Scientific and Prudential Realists (Kronman 2001, p. 168).

If the party of Realists has proved difficult to delineate, the main proto-Realists, who had already introduced some of the main Realist themes, are easier to identify. Three names stand out: Oliver Wendell Holmes, Roscoe Pound and John Chipman Gray (1839–1915). Holmes taught the Realists that law was not a self-sufficient body of autonomous norms which could be mastered with the tools of logic but an instrument for achieving social goals; that judicial decision-making was not a logical operation in the realm of reason but included discretionary choices where the will of the judge performed a pregnant role; and that the nascent social sciences could provide a helping hand in the policy choices the judges had to address. The standard Realist conception of the law and such basic legal concepts as 'right' and 'duty' also drew its inspiration from Holmes' writings. Not the least reason for the enduring respect for Holmes among the Realists was his typically crisp but at the same time sufficiently enigmatic fashion of expressing himself. For the Realists, Holmes was the epitome of a hero judge who had a profound understanding of the nature and demands of judicial activity. Pound, in turn, was the archetypical legal academic, whose law-school career spanned more than half a century. Pound's early critique of 'mechanical jurisprudence' (Pound 1908), his attempted shift of emphasis from 'law in books' to 'law in action' (Pound 1910), and his denouncement of the idea of an autonomous legal science and advocacy of 'sociological jurisprudence' with its social-engineering view on law (Pound 1911a, 1911b and 1912) showed many Realists the way in both their critical and constructive enterprises. Whilst veneration for Holmes never wavered, Pound's reputation suffered fatal blows from the late 1920s onwards; Pound became the favourite whipping-boy of the Realists, with 'Pound-pounding' their preferred sport. The reasons were many: Pound's controversial behaviour in the Sacco-Vanzetti case, the cause célebré for Llewellyn and many other Realists; Pound's polemical attack on Llewellyn in the 1930–1931 Realism debate; his continuous accusations levelled against the Realists during the 1930s for ignoring the doctrinal and 'ideal' elements in law; and his espousal of the anti-New-Deal critique of the administrative state or 'administrative absolutism' as Pound also put it. Finally, Gray, who was a judge with an academic affiliation, foreshadowed Realists with his court-centred view on the law (Gray 1909).[7]

The proto-Realists Holmes, Pound and Gray were well acquainted with the German critique of conceptualism and the instrumentalist alternative offered by *Interessenjurisprudenz* and *Freirechtslehre* (see, for example, Herget and Wallace 1987). But despite the many parallels to German debates, the story of American Realism is not, of course, primarily about the reception of ideas within a self-sustained realm of doctrinal ideas. In the United States, legal conceptualism was seen as an ally of *Lochner* jurisprudence. The courts, including the US Supreme Court, had stricken down many early attempts at social legislation, with which legislatures had responded to the socio-economic ills brought about by unbridled capitalism. The legal grounds for these decisions were found in the substantively-interpreted due-process clause of the Fourteenth Amendment and the principle of freedom of contract. The critique of legal conceptualism was closely associated with the critique of *Lochner*-era jurisprudence and its underlying socio-economic and political assumptions and objectives. In the political respect, anti-conceptualism was closely allied with Progressive political thought (Grey 1983, pp. 40–41; Horwitz 1994, pp. 145ff.; Fried 2001).

7 An immense secondary literature already exists on the proto-Realists, especially Holmes. See, on Holmes' significance for the Realists – Twining (1985, pp. 15–20), Gordon (1992), Horwitz (1994, pp. 109–144) and Duxbury (1995, pp. 32–50); on Pound's changing reputation in the eyes of the Realists – Twining (1985 pp. 22–24 and 72–81), Duxbury (1995, pp. 54–63) and Hull (1999); and on Gray's role, Twining (1985, pp. 20–22) and Duxbury (1995, pp. 50–54).

In their criticism, American Realists invoked the same accusations that in Germany had been aimed at *Begriffsjurisprudenz*: the abstraction of traditional concepts, and their deductive use in legal argumentation and decision-making. Taken together, these alleged central failures of Classical Legal Thought accounted for its formalism: its aspiration to strict demarcation of autonomous law from politics and ethical values.

To make his point as clear as possible, Felix Cohen (1907–1953) began his 1935 article 'Transcendental nonsense and the functional approach' by paraphrasing the dream Jhering had recounted in his *Scherz und Ernst*:

> Some fifty years ago a great German jurist had a curious dream. He dreamed that he died and was taken to a special heaven reserved for the theoreticians of the law. In this heaven one met, face to face, the many concepts of jurisprudence in their absolute purity, freed from the entangling alliances with human life. Here were the disembodied spirits of good faith and bad faith, property, possession, *laches*, and rights in *rem*. Here were all the logical instruments needed to manipulate and transform these legal concepts and thus to create and to solve the most beautiful of legal problems. Here one found a dialectic-hydraulic-interpretation press, which could press an indefinite number of meanings out of any text or statute, an apparatus for constructing fictions, and a hair-splitting machine that could divide a single hair into 999,999 equal parts and, when operated by the most expert jurists, could split each of these parts into 999,999 equal parts. The boundless opportunities of this heaven of legal concepts were open to all properly qualified jurists, provided only that they drank the Lethean draught which induced forgetfulness of terrestrial human affairs. But for the most accomplished jurists the Lethean draught was entirely superfluous. They had nothing to forget. (Cohen 1935, p. 810)[8]

The question Cohen set out to explore, with leading textbooks and opinions of courts as his material, and 'the Shade of von Jhering' as his guide, was: 'How much of contemporary legal thought moves in the pure ether of von Jhering's heaven of legal concepts'? (ibid.). The answer was: quite a lot. In every field of law, Cohen came across 'thingified' and 'hypostatised' concepts which are treated as 'supernatural entities' and 'which do not have a verifiable existence except to the eyes of faith'. They are employed in 'legal magic', 'word-jugglery' and circular reasoning. The long list of such concepts includes 'property', 'corporation', 'fair value' and 'due process'. For instance, if we assume that a corporation 'travels

8 Even in 1911, Roscoe Pound had drawn on Jhering's metaphor: 'The jurists of whom Jhering made fun, translated to a heaven of juristic conceptions and seated before a machine which brought out of each conception its nine hundred and ninety-nine thousand nine hundred and ninety-nine logical results, have their counterpart in American judges who insist upon a legal theory of equality of rights and liberty of contract in the face of notorious social and economic facts' (Pound 1911b, p. 146).

about from State to State as mortal men travel', 'surely we are qualifying as inmates of von Jhering's heaven of legal concepts when we approach a legal problem in these essentially supernatural terms' (ibid., p. 811).

Even if the concepts of Classical Legal Thought were not seen as exemplifying 'transcendental nonsense' or 'supernatural entities', their abstract character was put under attack. Llewellyn criticised 'lump categories', such as the general concept of contract, which group together a great variety of heterogeneous phenomena. Llewellyn stressed 'the need for re-examining the majestic categories of the romantic period of jurisprudence'. These 'old categories are imposing in their purple, but they are all too big to handle'; 'they hold too many heterogeneous items to be of any use' (Llewellyn 1930, p. 457). He also drew attention to the general ossifying tendency, affecting even concepts originally derived from experience. He argued that 'categories and concepts, once formulated and once they have entered into thought processes, tend to take on an appearance of solidity, reality and inherent value which has no foundation in experience ... although originally formulated on the model of at least some observed data, they tend, once they have entered into the organisation of thinking, both to suggest the presence of corresponding data when these data are not in fact present, and to twist any fresh observation of data into conformity with the terms of the categories' (ibid., pp. 453–454).

In their assault on 'legal fundamentalism', American Realists received backing from analytical jurisprudence, continuing on the trail blazed by Bentham and Austin. The German debates largely lacked the analytical dimension, which in Scandinavian Realism, again, occupied a prominent place. The great name in American analytical jurisprudence was Wesley Newcomb Hohfeld (1879–1918), whom the Realists considered an ally, if not one of their own. Indeed, Hohfeld himself linked his analytical scheme to a larger jurisprudential enterprise. What he called 'Formal or Analytical Jurisprudence' was 'not ... a mere matter of juridical ornament or intellectual delight'; 'on the contrary, it would be difficult to overestimate the economic and social value' of such an undertaking (cited in Horwitz 1994, p. 152). As Horwitz (1994, p. 153) notes, 'Hohfeld clearly regarded his own efforts at analytical jurisprudence as a preliminary step toward understanding how law related to what he called society's "underlying policies and purposes"'.

The Realists quickly perceived the value of Hohfeld's system of jural relations for deconstructing such abstract 'lump categories' as 'property' or 'freedom of contract'; for showing the logical fallacies in conceptual reasoning under attack; and for demonstrating that nothing natural or self-evident existed in, say, property but that it was wholly a creation of law and that its exact contents depended on policy-based legal choices. 'Property' did not refer to a relationship between a man (a legal subject) and a thing but to a complex web of inter-human relations which could be de-constructed through Hohfeld's scheme of opposite and correlative concepts.[9] As Arthur Corbin (1874–1967) argued, '"property" has ceased to describe any *res*, or object of sense, at all, and has become merely a bundle of legal relations – rights, powers, privileges, immunities' (Corbin 1922, p. 429). Hohfeld had also shown that if two legal positions do not relate to each other either as correlatives or opposites, no inferences from one position to another are logically defensible. Thus, a right cannot be logically derived from a privilege. This insight provided the basis for Walter Wheeler Cook's (1873–1943) criticism of the US Supreme Court's decision in *Hitchman Coal*. The court had held that an employee's agreement with his company not to join a union created a right in the company to ban a union organisation drive. Cook argued that the *privilege* of the company to employ non-union labour did not entail that it would also have a *right* to prevent unionisation (see Horwitz 1994, p. 155).

Although the coming Realists promptly learned how to exploit Hohfeld's innovations for their critical purposes, he is a rather strange figure in the American anti-conceptualist scene. His attack on the conceptualism of Classical Legal Thought included an attempt to construct a new, equally ahistorical and universally valid, albeit more sophisticated, conceptual system. And in line with the adherents of Classical Legal Thought, Hohfeld pursued the law's systematisation and unification, although not through abstract substantive concepts but through even more abstract analytical categories. When Hohfeld died in 1917, 'less than a generation later … the method behind Hohfeld's categories was lost and his system of legal classification had become "a sack of dried beans" delighted in only by apolitical pedants' (Horwitz 1994, p. 202). The close link that had connected the emergent Legal Realism to analytical jurisprudence was severed.

The use of Hohfeld's concepts indicates that the Realists were not hostile to concepts per se, but merely to the abstract 'lump categories' of Classical Legal Thought. *Pace* Hohfeld's universalist pretensions, the dominant Realist attitude towards concepts was rather pragmatist: concepts were to be judged by their performance. For such an approach, a Hohfeldian deconstruction of the traditional 'lump concepts' merely set the stage for their redefinition. Concepts were needed to organise experience, but they were to be more specialised and more limited in their scope than their predecessors. And they had to be formed through induction, have their foundation in experience. The Realists were not always very careful in specifying what this experience was but usually they referred to what the courts did: the typical approach of American Realism was very much court-centred (Twining 1985, pp. 136–137; Fischer 1992, pp. 273–274; Horwitz 1994, pp. 199–206).

When attaching concept formation to experience and induction, the Realists sometimes sought backing from contemporary philosophy of science (see Cohen 1935, pp. 824ff.). Yet it would evidently be mistaken to relate the American Realists' 'predictivist' definitions of basic legal conceptions in a straightforward manner to

9 For general assessments of Hohfeld's impact and importance for the Realists, see Singer (1982, pp. 1056–1059); Twining (1985, pp. 34–37); Horwitz (1994, pp. 151–156); Fried (2001, pp. 51–54).

the empiricist epistemological doctrines of the first half of the twentieth century, such as logical positivism. In their redefinitions, the American Realists were not after universally valid, 'philosophical' concepts, which would have been reduced to merely empirical referents. Nor should they be blamed for the inevitable failure of such an empiricist enterprise. The redefinitions adopted a particular perspective and pursued – in a spirit of pragmatism – a particular purpose.

The primary predictivist definitions were coined already by Holmes, and subsequently paraphrased by, for instance, Llewellyn. The citation list of American legal literature is topped by the following proposition from Holmes' 'The path of the law': 'The prophecies of what the courts will do in fact, and nothing more pretentious, are what I mean by the law' (Holmes 1897, p. 702). Correspondingly, 'the primary rights and duties with which jurisprudence busies itself again are nothing but prophecies'; 'a legal duty … is nothing but a prediction that if a man does or omits certain things he will be made to suffer in this or that way by judgment of the court – and so of legal rights' (ibid., pp. 699–700). Similarly Llewellyn (1930, p. 448), with an explicit reference to Holmes, argued that 'statements of "rights" would be statements of likelihood that in a given situation a certain type of court action loomed in the offing'; 'a right … exists to the extent that a likelihood exists that A can induce a court to squeeze, out of B, A's damages'. As to the law itself,

> this doing of something about disputes, this doing of it reasonably, is the business of law. And the people who have the doing in charge, whether they be judges or sheriffs or clerks or lawyers, are officials of the law. *What these official do about disputes is, to my mind, the law itself.* (Llewellyn 1969, p. 12; italics in the original)

It is easy to demonstrate that such redefinitions do not succeed in defining basic legal concepts in purely empirical terms, and that they refer to normatively determined entities like courts and judges. It is also easy to ridicule – as H.L.A. Hart in *The Concept of Law* does – predictivist definitions by pointing out that a judge can hardly be predicting his own behaviour when pondering what the law in the case before him is. In his 'Transcendental nonsense', Cohen anticipated such simplistic criticism. When a judge, in the course of writing his opinion, puts the question 'Is there a contract?', 'he is not attempting to predict his own behavior', but 'is in effect raising the question, in an obscure way, of whether or not liability *should* be attached to certain acts'. This, for Cohen, was 'inescapably an ethical question'. Cohen made it very clear that the specific perspective he advocated for 'functionalist' concept formation was that of 'a successful practical lawyer'. From that perspective, and 'washed in cynical acid, every legal problem can … be interpreted as a question concerning the positive behavior of judges' (Cohen 1935, pp. 839–840). And, as Brian Leiter (2007) convincingly argues, that was also the general perspective from which the proto-Realist Holmes and other Realists, such as Llewellyn, explored law and legal concepts.

In the Realist view of legal reasoning, there was no place for a deductive use of concepts, neither the traditional 'lump concepts' nor Hohfeld's analytical concepts, or predictivist, redefined concepts. For Realists, the main purport of Hohfeld's scheme was to deconstruct the abstract concepts of Classical Legal Thought and to lay bare the points where policy considerations and choices inevitably made their entry. Deductivism was criticised on logical grounds already familiar from the German debates: no new norms can be derived from such concepts as 'freedom of contract' or 'property', but only those on whose basis they have been formed in the first place. But the major grounds for criticism were to be found elsewhere. As a description of what judges in fact do, deductivism was held to be deceptive and illusory: it obscures the many choices that confront judges in selecting the relevant rule, describing the facts of the case, and applying the rule to the facts. Rules and principles are 'in the habit of hunting in pairs', as Walter Wheeler Cook (1928, p. 406) memorably formulated one of the central Realist insights, which the Critic has subsequently made so much coinage of. Principles have counter-principles, and precedents can be found to support contrary rules. So, washed in the Realists' cynical acid, analogical reasoning did not fare much better than deductivism: the judge has always to choose the key of analogy – the relevant feature by which the precedent and the subsequent case were compared – and the significance of a precedent in future cases can always be assessed on either a wide or a narrow reading of it.

So deductivism was considered decidedly misleading in a descriptive respect. It had thrown a veil of objectivity over judges' policy choices, and under this veil outdated libertarian and anti-labour political and ideological premises had been smuggled into the rulings and opinions of the courts, most alarmingly in *Lochner* and other US Supreme Court rulings quashing social and interventionist economic legislation. The Realists' normative programme – here, again, Holmes had shown the way – was to transform judicial reasoning in an openly policy-oriented direction; to make explicit the implicit policy choices which conceptualism had wrapped up in its shroud of deductivist objectivism. As the proto-Realists Holmes and Pound had already demanded, deduction was to be replaced by *overt policy considerations* and *the balancing of interests*.

American Realists held an explicitly instrumentalist view of the law. Not without reason, Felix Cohen (1935, p. 836) termed Thomas Hobbes the grandfather of Legal Realism. But the socio-economic and political context of the Realists' instrumentalism was, of course, very different from that of Hobbes or even Jeremy Bentham. At issue was no longer establishing and securing the legal framework for an emergent market economy and centralised state, but remedying the socio-economic consequences ensuing from the free reign of large-scale capitalism. Nevertheless, in their instrumentalism the Realists shared Hobbes' and Bentham's faith in the power of science to find solutions to social problems. In their emphasis on law as a science, the Realists, especially those who fall under the label 'Scientific Realists', also shared Hobbes' hostility to the common-law tradition and its central idea of 'artificial reason'. Paradoxically enough, in this hostility and their emphasis on scientification of law they stand shoulder-to-shoulder with Christopher Columbus Langdell, the figurehead of American Classical Legal Thought (Kronman 2001, p. 201).

The Realists' instrumentalism led them to embrace legal scholarship's integration with social sciences, which Pound, with his notion of sociological jurisprudence, had already advocated. The social sciences, especially economics, were supposed to assist not only the legislator but judges and legal scholars, too, in assessing policy goals and the legal means to achieve them. The Realists held diverse views about the extent and depth of the required integration and reform of legal science. The Scientists among them were inclined to transform legal scholarship into an empirical social science and to renounce traditional doctrinal research as an incurably unscientific undertaking. Once they had deserted Columbia Law School, their main institutional locus in the 1920s, the Scientists were primarily ensconced at Yale and at Johns Hopkins (Schlegel 1995; Kalman 2001). The Prudents, foremost among whom was the 'mature' Llewellyn, were more moderate in their claims. Llewellyn acknowledged the role of craft in common law, and along with it the significance of tradition and doctrine.[10] Through their doctrinal research, legal scholars could also provide valuable assistance to judges.

In their approach, Legal Realists were court-centred, and in their doctrinal efforts they continued along the same line of appellate-court jurisprudence as their predecessors. However, from the Realists' instrumentalist perspective, the reformist legislator, too, accomplished a legitimate function in the law's development. The Realists did not embrace the traditional common-law mistrust in the legislator but conceded to legislation a prominent role as a means of reformist policy. They also accepted the rise of the administrative state, which was an upshot of New Deal legislation in particular. It would certainly be exaggerated to call Legal Realism New Deal jurisprudence, but it was no mere coincidence that a significant number of recognised Realists went to Washington to work in the newly-established administrative agencies (Horwitz 1994, pp. 151–152). The Realists did not subscribe to the concern that Pound, in increasingly alarmist terms, expressed about the fate of the rule of law under the pressure of 'administrative absolutism' (Pound 1939, 1940 and 1944).

Realist Anti-Conceptualism in Scandinavia

Scandinavian Realism was roughly contemporaneous with its American counterpart. It emerged in Uppsala in the early twentieth century under the influence of the

---

10 Llewellyn's 'mature' view is most extensively expounded in his *Common Law Tradition* (1960). But his 'prudentialist' view had already started to ripen in the 1930s, as can be read from *Jurisprudence*, a collection of Llewellyn's writings, which he managed to edit before his death in 1962 (Llewellyn 2008). On Llewellyn's prudentialism, see also Kronman (2001, pp. 209–225).

philosophy of Axel Hägerström (1868–1939) and enjoyed its Golden Age from the late 1920s to the 1950s. If Realism in America did not constitute a homogeneous school, nor did its Scandinavian counterpart. The discursive as well as the wider socio-economic and political context varied in different Nordic countries. Yet certain common premises, themes and emphases are noticeable enough. Equally evident are parallels with anti-conceptual polemics in the United States and Germany. Because of traditionally intimate cultural links to Germany and the high prestige of German legal science, the Scandinavian theorists were particularly familiar with the German discussion. By contrast, American developments were not as closely followed. Hohfeld, though, was known and Östen Undén (1886–1974) alluded to his scheme as early as in the 1920s (Undén 1928, p. 174). But the inner circle of American Realists, or their proto-Realist predecessors such as Holmes and Pound, did not arouse much interest. This may seem strange, given how near each other were the American and Scandinavian Realists on some key issues.[11]

Of course, differences existed, too. Like their American colleagues, the Scandinavians combined an analytical and a realist approach, and adopted an instrumental stance on law. But for the Scandinavians, conceptual analysis possessed a much greater value and a more independent significance than for the Americans. For the Scandinavian reformers, the main issue appeared to be legal science's scientificity, which also accounted for the importance of conceptual analysis. For the Americans, by contrast, conceptual analysis clearly played a subservient role with regard to practical issues concerning the law's policy connections. This difference in emphasis is related to the divergent philosophical backgrounds of these two strands of Legal Realism. American Realists were inspired, first of all, by the 'non-philosophical' philosophy of American pragmatism, while the Scandinavians drew on the European empiricist epistemological doctrines of the first half of the twentieth century; Finnish post-Second World War legal scholarship here constitutes a special case.

Leading Uppsala legal theorists, such as Vilhelm Lundstedt (1882–1955) and Undén, had learned from Axel Hägerström the empiricist philosophical premises they applied in their conceptual analyses. These ontological and epistemological starting-points acknowledged only an objective reality, independent from human cognition and possessing temporal and spatial coordinates; cognition of this objective reality merely through sense observations; and investigation of objective reality through empirical means as the sole legitimate task of science – philosophy included. All concepts and propositions lacking a connotation in an empiristically-defined objective reality were labelled metaphysical. This, for instance, was the fate of normative value assessments; values were not part of objective reality but merely expressed the emotions of the persons pronouncing them. (On Hägerström, see Bjarup 1982 and Lyles 2006.)

---

11 Analyses of the similarities and dissimilarities of the two Realisms are surprisingly few. See, however, Alexander (2002) and Pihlajamäki (2004).

This was the philosophical arsenal with which the Uppsala School undertook analysis of basic legal concepts, such as 'law in force', 'legal rule', '(subjective) right' and 'duty'. Typically, analysis proceeded through three phases. The first task was to describe how the concepts were in fact used in legal language. This was followed by a critique: demonstrating the metaphysical nature of prevalent definitions. The third, concluding phase consisted of an attempt at redefinition, at a realist reconstruction of the concept that would satisfy the empiricist criteria of the Uppsala School's philosophy of science (Helin 1988, pp. 46–48).[12] Hence, from Hägerström onwards, 'objective law' or 'the law in force' was understood to refer to the empirical fact that the legal authorities in fact observed certain rules. 'Legal rule' or 'legal norm' could also be defined as a relationship between a certain kind of behaviour on the part of the members of society and the subsequent reaction of an authority.

In his writings during the 1950s, Alf Ross, perhaps the internationally best-known of the Scandinavian Realists, subscribed to the philosophy of science of logical empiricism. This led him to redefine or, at least, to specify the tasks of legal philosophy: now the focus shifted to analysis and assessment of legal scientific concepts and propositions in the light of the verification test. If they failed the test and were not verifiable by empirical criteria, they were to be expelled from the realm of science to that of metaphysics. Ross' own definition of 'law in force' attempted to pass the test by reference to the prevailing judicial ideology, understood as an empirical socio-psychological fact (Ross 1958, pp. 29ff.).

The Scandinavian Realists extended their conceptual analyses and the accompanying critique of metaphysics to the basic concepts focusing on the legal position of legal subjects, such as 'right' and 'duty'. Traditional concepts were shown to imply metaphysical entities with no empirical substance. Lundstedt, evoking the anti-conceptual criticism of Jhering and Leon Duguit (1859–1928), among others, blamed legal scholars for employing the terms 'right' and 'duty' 'as if they connoted entities that were independent of the functioning of the legal machinery' (Lundstedt 1956, pp. 78–93). In the 1950s, Ross published a deservedly celebrated article, entitled with more than a hint at verbal incantation, 'Tû-tû'. His point was that the terms 'right' and 'duty' are used as if they referred to an entity located between legal facts and consequences; engendered by the former and giving rise to the latter. But no such entity exists, so that the terms lack an empirical referent (Ross 1956).

On Lundstedt's realist reconstruction, subjective rights are 'relationally protected positions' that owe their existence to the 'regular functioning of legal machinery'. This is true of property rights as well; they cannot be scientifically conceived as relating to some pre-political and pre-legal supernatural, and hence, metaphysical substance. Lundstedt argued that, scientifically understood,

12 In my presentation of Scandinavian Realism, I have greatly benefited from Markku Helin's seminal study *Lainoppi ja metafysiikka* (*Legal Dogmatics and Metaphysics*), which unfortunately is only available in Finnish.

'property right' (or 'ownership') connotes factual possibilities of action, whose exact contents depend on the rules adhered to by the legal machinery (Lundstedt 1956, pp. 93–95).

In line with their American colleagues, the Scandinavians spent much of their critical and (re)constructive energies on analysing ownership and property rights. And also in line with the Americans, they here applied the lessons of a Hohfeld-style analytical jurisprudence. Undén diverged from the mainstream of the Uppsala School by examining legal concepts as legal fictions, which, despite their fictional character, could accomplish a useful function, at least in the law's systematisation. Concepts refer to relationships between legal facts and consequences, so that 'property right', for instance, is a short-cut denomination for the complicated state of affairs that on certain conditions the legal order offers a certain kind of protection to the owner of a thing (Undén 1928). A crucial insight was – as also for American Realists – that the traditional concept of property right lumps together diverse owner positions which in reality do not necessarily go together. Thus Ross, in the wake of Undén, stressed that 'ownership' comprises various 'functions' in various relationships and that these functions need not all belong to the same person (Ross 1958, pp. 170ff.). This implied a condemnation of *Begriffsjurisprudenz*-style deductivism, in which the first step was to determine that A was the owner and then, as the second step, A's position in the legal relationships that ownership comprised was inferred from this determination. The analytical approach was in a way independent of realist epistemological commitments. Its significance was seen in the enrichment of legal heuristics: the analytically redefined and refined, relational conceptual apparatus facilitates the posing of legal questions which the abstract 'substance concepts' of *Begriffsjurisprudenz* blocked. To take an example, transfer of ownership can be conceived of as a temporally differentiated process with distinct functions of ownership following divergent timetables.

The Scandinavian Realists' methodological alternative to discredited conceptual deductivism was quite close to the policy orientation of American Realism. The Scandinavians endorsed the instrumentalist understanding of law which was to govern judges' and legal scholars' reasoning and argumentation. Lundstedt's key notion was 'social utility' (*samhällsnytta*), which was to proffer guidance for legal actors after metaphysical concepts and scholastic, deductivist and circular reasoning had been stripped off (Helin 1988, pp. 108ff.). Lundstedt's 'social utility' is a clear indication of Scandinavian Realism's political and ideological commitments. The links of American Realism to interventionist economic and social regulation and to the New Deal, in particular, are crystal clear. Equally so are Scandinavian Realism's connections to the cause of the nascent Nordic Welfare State and related political developments – the rise of the social democratic parties and their alliances with the centrist agrarian parties. Lundstedt, who also happened to be a social democratic Member of Parliament,[13] argued that scholastic juridical constructions, centred on property rights, had misled even the legislator. Thus, negative attitudes towards expropriation can be due to the claim that expropriation violates the right of ownership. But this it cannot possibly do because rules on expropriation belong to the determinants of the contents of private ownership (Lundstedt 1929, pp. 117–118). Analytical concepts of property and ownership – adopted by both American and Scandinavian Realism – are illustrative examples of the Schmittian rhetorical strategy of redefining key concepts, thereby striving for hegemony within the conceptual field and, by the same token, pursuing specific objectives within the economic, social and political fields as well.

Lundstedt was not a loner in his explicit instrumentalism. After the war, Per-Olof Ekelöf (1906–1990), a 'late' representative of the Uppsala School, made his scholarly name by advocating a teleological interpretative method.[14] And, more generally, the stress on consequentialist arguments (*reella hänsyn*) became a commonplace in Scandinavian legal textbooks.

Despite its conspicuous instrumentalist trait, Scandinavian Realism did not aim to efface the boundary between law and politics, nor did it propound a far-reaching integration of legal with social science. Political questions were regarded as questions of value, and in the Realist epistemology, value standpoints did not possess any truth quality measurable by empirical criteria. Legal scholars could present such standpoints in their interpretative and *de lege ferenda* recommendations, but they were obliged – so the Realists claimed – to separate them clearly from propositions with scientific pretensions. In fact, most of the Realists espoused a fairly conventional view of doctrinal research as the core of legal science. For some scholars, such as the Norwegian Torstein Eckhoff (1916–1993) and Theodor Geiger (1891–1952), a German exile in Denmark, Realism constituted a gateway to legal sociological research. But the majority, Alf Ross amongst them, contented themselves with a realist reconstruction of basic legal concepts so that legal dogmatics could pass the test of scientificity.

The search for verifiable content also explains Ross' espousal of a predictivist reading of propositions about valid legal rules. I have already argued that Hart missed the point in his criticism of the predictivist notions of American Realists on the ground that judges cannot be alleged to predict their own behaviour when establishing the content of law. Hart relied on exactly the same argument in his criticism of Ross, and does not appear to have hit the mark this time, either.[15]

13 Undén, for his part, served as foreign minister in Tage Erlander's post-Second World War social democratic government. Ross' advocacy of social democracy was also well known.

14 Ekelöf has not been translated into English. His main programmatic writing is *Är den juridiska doktrinen en teknik eller en vetenskap*? (*Is Legal Doctrine a Technique or a Science?*) (Ekelöf 1951).

15 Hart's article 'Scandinavian realism' is a review of Ross' *On Law and Justice* (Hart 1959).

Whilst the predictivism of the Americans adopted a legal counsellor's point of view, Ross was interested in an empiricist interpretation of the propositions presented by doctrinal researchers.

A Postscript to Realist Anti-Conceptualism: Finnish Analytical Scholarship

Finnish legal scholarship only joined the anti-conceptual chorus after the Second World War. We may conjecture that this was connected to Finland's sluggish socio-economic and political development in comparison with, for instance, Sweden and Denmark. Finland lagged behind in industrialisation, urbanisation and the intensity of economic exchange; the political preconditions for welfare-state legal interventionism also only ripened after the war. But latecomers may benefit from their position. In their anti-conceptualist polemics, Finnish legal theorists were able to draw from such novel sources of inspiration as Wittgenstein's late philosophy and the Oxford philosophy of language. This, for its part, explains some of the distinctive features of the Finnish debates.

In the writings of the Uppsala School and Ross, conceptual analysis and empiricist epistemological premises often went together. That they could also be separated, however, was shown by Finnish analytical scholarship of the 1950s and 1960s. The leading figure was Simo Zitting, who earned his reputation with his analysis of property rights and the concomitant critique of deductivism. In addition to the Nordic discussion, Zitting was greatly inspired by Hohfeld. In his basic philosophical assumptions, he was closer to the normativism of Hans Kelsen than the empiricism of the Uppsala School or logical positivism. When Finnish scholars, such as Zitting, demanded examination of the 'real' legal position of an owner instead of deductive reasoning from the concepts of ownership or subjective right, the usual reference was to positive legal rules and not to empirical facts: the 'real' legal position was equivalent to the legal position as determined by positive law. Zitting's Kelsenian mindset comes clearly to the fore in his following methodological premise:

> In order to detect the different moments in an owner's legal position, as well as their legal nature and reciprocal relations within a unitary system, we have to operate with pure legal concepts and propositions. The purity of the method and the unitary character of the system are inseparably linked ... Elements which are external from a legal standpoint prevent the gapless interconnectedness of the systems' constituent parts ... Correspondingly, social, economic, and other such interests constitute legally foreign elements. (Zitting 1952, p. 392)

Nevertheless, the Finnish debates did not totally forego realist stimulus. As was the case in other Nordic countries, too, these were confined primarily to realist-tuned redefinitions of basic legal concepts. Kaarle Makkonen's (1923–2000) study from 1965 proffers a late example of a realist reconstruction of the concept of a legal rule (legal norm). In his definition, Makkonen ties the existence of a legal norm to the possibility of invoking, in accordance with certain forms, a reaction – an 'organ reaction' – on the part of the authorities on the basis of certain behaviour by a member of society (Makkonen 1965, pp. 28–29).

Along with Zitting, Makkonen is the other main proponent of Finnish analytical scholarship. His main credits lie in introducing post-war linguistic philosophy into jurisprudential debates and in problematising his predecessors' anti-conceptualism in the light of fresh philosophical insights. In the Finnish context, Makkonen was an intermediary between two phases of jurisprudential thought: *analytical realism* and *analytical hermeneutics*. He wholeheartedly supported the criticism of 'thingifying' conceptual jurisprudence and concurred with Zitting's attack on the traditional concept of ownership for postulating 'a given, irrational substance, as a foundation of all property rights'. Zitting had stressed that 'ownership' connotes a person's legal position in certain correlative relations, determining 'the sphere of a multi-place social relation'. Thus, 'a vaguely used term of ordinary language has been attributed an exact and value free sense, and more or less fuzzy ontological substance has been transformed into a scientifically apt concept, or ... qualities have been shaken off from the knots of a relational net' (Makkonen 1959, pp. 60–61).

Makkonen noted that legal scholarship displays an inherent tendency to conceptual 'mummification'; in his view, epistemological realism was a reaction to conceptual jurisprudence. However, in spite of his own sporadic incursions into the field of realist reconstruction, Makkonen considered analytical realism's demarcation of legal theory's task too narrow. He emphasised that conceptual analysis should focus not only on the language of legal science but on legal language in general, such as its functions in legal practices. If the acceptability of legal concepts is seen to require the passing of the empiricist test of verification, their functions are defined too restrictedly. Concepts also perform other tasks in legal language than simply describing empirical reality. In conceptual analysis, the question should be posed *semantically*: one should ask what it means when we state, for instance, that something constitutes a legal person. If possible, one can strive for an answer that satisfies the demand for 'real' (i.e. empirical) knowledge. But law abounds with terms that cannot possibly meet this demand but whose meaning we should still discuss because they are part and parcel of legal language. More appropriate than 'to expel such terms from the realm of science with the arms of modern philosophy is to try, with the same arms, to clarify their meaning and conditions of use' (ibid., p. 55).

Makkonen argued that an unconditional requirement of empirical semantic reference reduces the meaning of concepts to a mere name relation and epitomises an *extensional* approach. He detected signs of one-sided extensionalism even in the writings of some critics of conceptual jurisprudence, such as Lundstedt. If the expression 'subjective right' cannot be shown to stand in a name relation to any phenomenon of empirical reality, it does not, according to Lundstedt, have any meaning (*Sinn*). Makkonen proposed a different methodological guideline for conceptual analysis:

> If one wants to see in the expression 'subjective right' a name, which has an empirical referent, the issue of the factual conditions of (its) use is obscured or even ignored. And this is precisely the theoretically and practically most pertinent issue, when one tries to understand what talking about subjective right means. The scholar must primarily focus on everyday use of legal language, examine the language as something which happens rather than as a system of signs. (Makkonen 1967, p. 116)

In Makkonen's writings, the semantic issue no longer concerned the *extension* – the empirical semantic reference – of concepts, but their *intension* – their meaning. In fact, his semantic question pointed to the *pragmatic* dimension of language; to Wittgenstein's late writings and the philosophy of ordinary language. In a late-Wittgensteinian spirit, Makkonen stressed that the meaning of legal concepts depends on the contexts in which they are used – on the language game in which they partake. In some connections, concepts may stand in a name relation to an empirical phenomenon, but this is by no means always the case. It is not up to legal philosophy to prune from legal language concepts that do not meet the purist criteria of empiricist philosophy of science; rather, legal philosophy should aim to clarify the meaning of concepts by exploring the contexts in which they are employed. One of Makkonen's favourite Wittgenstein citations was the following:

> We may say: *nothing* has so far been done, when a thing has been named. It has not even *got* a name except in the language-game. This was what Frege meant too, when he said that a word had meaning only as part of a sentence. (Wittgenstein 1966, 49 (p. 24))

Legal Induction

As the above discussion has shown, anti-conceptualist reaction in different countries possessed many semblances, although it displayed divergences, too, owing to particular discursive and wider socio-economic contexts. It is time to try to assess the merits of the criticism, focusing on its common arguments and drawing on the summaries presented by Finnish post-war scholars.

The first critical point concerns the inductive phase of the constructive method; the 'deficient inductivism' which the German critics viewed as the reverse of the primary sin of 'productive deductivism'. Makkonen's study from 1965 includes a representative critique of legal induction (Makkonen 1965, pp. 195ff.). Makkonen took his own realist (re)definition of the concept of legal norm as the basis for his exploration of what legal induction might mean. Legal norms connect legal facts with legal consequences. In legal induction, generalising from individual legal norms, we would reason as follows. From the fact that given norms attach certain legal consequences to certain legal facts forming part of a certain class, we conclude that the same consequences also ensue from other facts belonging to this class.

In his problematisation of legal induction, Makkonen relied on the example provided by Finnish law on judicial review. Before an Act of Parliament expressly granted a general right to appeal in 1950, Finnish legislation contained merely scattered provisions on judicial review of particular administrative decisions. These provisions could be interpreted to warrant diametrically opposite conclusions: either the so-called enumeration principle, confining review to explicitly regulated decisions, or a generalised system of judicial review. The former conclusion would epitomise *e contrario* reasoning, the latter legal induction. But, Makkonen contended, the initial norms or the inductive method itself cannot vindicate the primacy of generalisation over the *e contrario* argument.

Makkonen also addressed the claim that on the basis of their education, professional lawyers can well tell when individual provisions point to a general rule and when they constitute exceptions to it. He argued that such a judgement relies not merely on the initial particular norms but also on a more general knowledge of the legal order: the interpretative choice is made against a wider idea of law than just some individual provisions in positive legislation. Makkonen's final point in disputing the feasibility and legitimacy of legal induction was the familiar concern that had worried the systematisers of law ever since the German historical school of the early nineteenth century: the capriciousness of the legislator. The legislator's will poses a constant threat to the law's systematic reason; this prevents us from equating the law's internal relations with the regularities prevailing in nature:

> The attachment of legal consequences to legal facts depends on value judgments, diverse considerations of expediency and legal policy etc. The legal order does not constitute such a system of invariances which would allow for generalisations through induction. The issuance of a legal norm is an act of will, a volitional decision beyond the criteria of truth. The legislator is capricious. In one case, the confirmation of twenty relations between legal facts and consequences may signify a general rule, in another case an exception to such a rule. If nature does not make leaps, the legislator makes them the more! (Makkonen 1965, p. 203)

It is easy to agree with Makkonen's critique of legal induction. Nevertheless, this type of critique does not necessarily hit the mark. It is doubtful whether the mainstream of German *Begriffsjurisprudenz* or its American counterpart would really have understood the first phase of the constructive method in terms of logically-warranted inductive generalisation. For the historical school, *Anschauung* was a central methodological concept. It connoted a specific manner of conceiving organic connections – interrelations between wholes and their constituents – which the dichotomy of induction and deduction, cherished by subsequent formal-logically oriented philosophy of science, does not really capture. German nineteenth-century *Begriffs*-jurisprudents frequently stressed the law's rationality and logic as its method. Yet it appears that their doctrinal constructions were animated by the idea of the law's organic interdependencies, which formed the basis for legal scholarship's generalisations. Makkonen's critically-intended observation that generalisations from individual norms implicitly presuppose a wider knowledge of the law would not have come as a surprise to the *Begriffs*-jurisprudents.

Indeed, the way German nineteenth-century legal science envisioned the law's systematicity is related to recent theorising on legal principles where the law's unity has been seen to result from principle-based coherence. Individual statutory provisions or precedents provide information on coherence-creating principles. However, principles cannot be drawn merely from such particular legal sources but attention should be paid to a larger normative field, ultimately – following Dworkin's mythical Judge Hercules – the legal order in its entirety.

The historical school was conscious of the legislator's capriciousness. Indeed, the uneasy relation between the law's positivity (historicity) and systematicity was one of the central themes in German nineteenth-century jurisprudence, in the writings of both the historical school and the subsequent *Begriffsjurisprudenz*. This seems to be one of those epitomes of the tension between the law's *voluntas* and *ratio* which cannot be simply effaced but which should be coped with in compliance with the methodological strategy of mediation (see Chapter 1).

The Law's Organic Unity

Another standard argument employed by diverse variants of anti-conceptualism concerns the allegedly logical interpretation of the law's internal relations. Conceptualists were – so the typical accusation goes – engaged in a (quasi-) logical or even (quasi-)mathematical conceptual game; often enough, this is claimed to exemplify their formalist mindset. Aulis Aarnio, a representative of Finnish analytical legal hermeneutics, focused his criticism on two central ideas which he attributed to *Begriffsjurisprudenz*: the doctrine of the law's organic unity, of legal norms in some sense presupposing each other; and the doctrine of universal validity of legal concepts. Aarnio maintained that it was the idea of the law's organic unity that had warranted the task to 'derive from known norms such norms which had not been explicitly spelled out in legislation but which still stand in a necessary relation of dependence with known norms'. But, Aarnio added, it is 'evident that the legal order does not constitute a logical system, where each element, in adherence to the rules of logic, presupposes the other'. No rule of logic has obliged the legislator to adopt provisions on avoidance and recovery in the case of bankruptcy; the legislator has made a value-based decision, purporting to offer creditors protection against the debtor's actions. The doctrinal systems of *Begriffsjurisprudenz* were quasi-logical constructions, and 'appeals to organic connections obscured the fact that system formation involved various kinds of value judgements and choices' (Aarnio 1979, pp. 202–203).

Again, the criticism is correct in claiming that the law cannot be conceived as a logical system whose constituent elements presuppose each other in accordance with the rules of formal logic. But, again, it is questionable whether this is really the way the mainstream conceptualists understood the law. For the historical school, the law's *organic* interdependencies were clearly not of a formal logical nature, nor should too much be read into the at times logically-tuned idiom of the subsequent *Begriffsjurisprudenz*, either.

Differing from Aarnio, present-day discussants would probably not appraise the law's unity by the rules of formal logic but by employing the looser concept of coherence, alluding to the law's principle-based systematicity. Recent interest within legal theory in principles and the coherence they produce has two main sources of inspiration: European theory of legal argumentation, represented by, among others, Robert Alexy, Neil MacCormick and Alexander Peczenik, and Ronald Dworkin's depiction of judicial decision-making in hard cases and his idea of constructive interpretation.

Argumentation-theoretical developments and Dworkinian influences have led to a shift of emphasis even in Continental doctrine. What united *Begriffsjurisprudenz* and its analytical critics, such as Zitting, Makkonen and Aarnio in Finland, was the emphasis on conceptual elements in the general doctrines of different fields of law. Morally-laden legal principles received less attention, if any at all. In the history of legal ideas, this can be related to an anti-natural-law reaction and to the legal positivist aspiration to maintain a clear boundary between law and morals. In this limited sense, Aarnio's claim that the present principle-discourse signifies a return (and regression?) to natural-law thinking is warranted (Aarnio 2002). Post-analytical theorists contend that the coherence in law is not created so much by its conceptual structure but rather by legal principles; law should be understood, not as a logical, but as a value- and morals-induced unity. It is systematicity whose monitoring, in the division of labour between legal practices, falls primarily to legal scholarship and adjudication. Such a conception inevitably raises the issue of democracy: is it justifiable that judges and legal scholars, through interpreting and systematising law, continue, and maybe even 'correct', the work of the democratically-elected legislature? This question is particularly urgent in Continental legal systems, such as the Nordic ones, where the legislature's prevalence has constituted an almost self-evident premise (see Chapter 8).

German nineteenth-century legal science held different views of what the law's organicity actually meant. In Chapter 3, I attached to it two central ideas: reciprocal interdependencies between the elements of a whole; and the developmental principle which both the whole and its elements obey. Evidently, when the historical school turned into *Begriffsjurisprudenz*, organicity received a logical colouring as the historical aspect was increasingly pushed aside. But the original key ideas are still relevant today and serve as a reminder of such qualities of law which analytical acid often washed away: the idea of reciprocal interdependencies draws our attention to the issue of the law's coherence and the developmental principle to its historicity.

Conceptual Apriorism

Ever since Jhering's scathing attacks, the accusation of conceptual apriorism or Platonism belonged to the staple arsenal of anti-conceptualism. It retained its role in the writings of the post-war Finnish analytical scholars, from Zitting's early path-breaking contributions onwards. According to Aarnio's depiction, conceptual jurisprudence was premised, not only on the idea of the law's organic interconnectedness, but also on the view that in addition to constantly changing individual rules, the legal order included something permanent, manifested by legal concepts. Such concepts as 'ownership' were thought to distil the law's 'universal, time-and-place independent core'. Aarnio joined the long line of critics who employed the pyramid metaphor, coined by Philippe Heck in the 1920s. In Aarnio's account, conceptual jurisprudence claimed that through legal concepts, the law's universally valid elements could reliably be presented in a hierarchical, pyramid form (Aarnio 1979, p. 202).

How can a critique of apriorism be reconciled with a critique of deficient induction? The latter critique, after all, assumes that the conceptualists' concept formation possessed an inductive basis in given legal norms, whether these had their source in legislation (European statutory positivism) or in precedent (American conceptualism). And this also corresponds to how Paul Laband, in his classic manifesto, portrayed the constructive method's first phase, 'the reduction of individual legal propositions to more general concepts' (Laband 1888, p. IX).

Clearly, Laband's exposition and its like, which underline the positive-law support of concept formation, do not tell the whole truth about the system of either private- or public-law *Begriffsjurisprudenz*. Fundamental legal categories were conceived independently of individual positive-law regulations. *Begriffsjurisprudenz* was born during the pre-unification era when common German private-law legislation was not yet in existence, so that the conceptual system could not be construed on the basis of statutory law. The great task and calling of private-law *Begriffsjurisprudenz* preceding the *Bürgerliches Gesetzbuch* was to create legal unity in Germany at a time when this could not yet be achieved through legislative codification. By contrast, state-law *Begriffsjurisprudenz* from the very beginning adopted statutory-law premises. The late constitutional school, dominating German state law theory until the Weimar Republic, could build on the 1871 German constitution, although its theoretical and methodological foundation had already been laid by Gerber in his *Grundzüge des öffentlichen Rechts*, which came out in 1865.

Although private- and public-law *Begriffsjurisprudenz* arose at different times and from different backgrounds, state-law conceptualism, just as its private-law models, employed two types of concepts, of which the above Laband-quotation catches only one. Late constitutional state-law doctrine included concepts of both an a priori and a posteriori character. The latter were generalised, in line with Laband's methodological credo, from the provisions of positive legislation. By contrast, a priori concepts – such as 'state', 'state power' or 'state organ' – preceded positive legislation and, in fact, constituted its very possibility. But, what is important to underline in light of the severe and often rather denigrating anti-conceptualist criticism, the apriorism of nineteenth-century legal science did not necessarily equal Kantian transcendentalism or Platonist conceptual idealism.

Puchta's private-law system relied on the Kant-influenced concept of freedom, and the basic idea of Gerber's state-law system, too, consisted of free will power, which in the field of state law belonged to the state as a legal person. Gerber's system, following the private-law model, was construed on an a priori basis; it was not a result of a generalisation from positive-law propositions to which Laband alluded. The doctrine of the legal personality of the state did not so much aim to describe positive-law regulations as to explicate their conceptual preconditions. If my reading is correct, Gerber was already quite close to the premises of neo-Kantian state-law theory, although he did not yet embellish his theoretical and methodological ponderings with references to Kantian epistemology. Neo-Kantian starting-points were only explicitly formulated by Georg Jellinek. He argued that the fundamental question for state-law theory is not what the state's legal character is or what the state is as a legal phenomenon, but how the state should be juridically thought of (*Wie ist der Staat juristisch zu denken?*) (Jellinek 1914, p. 21). This is an epistemological question: the problem is how the state's legal nature should be conceived so as in general to enable legal actors – the scholar, the judge or the legislator – to assess juridically phenomena involving the state.

State-law scholars with a neo-Kantian orientation, again in accordance with their private-law predecessors, were inclined to approach the most general legal categories in an ahistorical manner, to identify them with the time-and-place independent core of the law. Here, anti-conceptualist criticism is warranted. In state law, one line of development leads from statutory positivist *Begriffsjurisprudenz* to Kelsen's pure theory of law. Kelsen attempted to expel from the realm of the Ought (*Sollen*) the last remnants of the social or psychological Is (*Sein*) which his teacher Jellinek had still retained in his doctrine of the state's legal personality and in his will concepts in general. Kelsen also overtly spelled out his transcendentalist epistemological starting-points.

Gerber, by contrast, had still stressed the historical preconditions and delimitations of his basic concepts and restricted their validity to a modern society. If we return to the roots of German state-law *Begriffsjurisprudenz*, we can capture the rational and still pertinent crux in the conceptual apriorism of *Begriffsjurisprudenz* which anti-conceptualist criticism nearly obliterated. This apriorism should not necessarily be understood in ahistorical, transcendental terms but can be confined to a specific historical type of law; the one we are used to calling modern law. Interpreted in this way, what German *Begriffsjurisprudenz* tried to achieve through elaborating the most general legal categories was a reconstruction of the necessary 'sub-surface' conceptual preconditions without which it would not be possible for the legislator to issue statutes, for the courts to pass judgements, or for legal scholars to produce learned articles and monographs. This reading might be extended to conceptualist trends in other legal cultures, such as Classical Legal Thought in the United States.

The law's legal-cultural underpinnings constitute an aspect in its functioning which is too often ignored under the zeal of anti-conceptualist criticism and emphasis on the conventional, pragmatist nature of concept formation.[16] This may also be a blind spot in the seeming consensus in the United States that conceptualism is a slain monster, that 'we are all Realists now'. The conceptual apparatus of Classical Legal Thought may still exert its influence at the law's sub-surface level, through the legal-cultural pre-understanding of legal professionals. The same may hold for Continental *Begriffsjurisprudenz*, which has never experienced such a quasi-total loss of reputation as its American counterpart.

Ironically enough, anti-conceptualist criticism has not been free of universalist undertones of its own. These are due to its analytical roots, reaching in the common-law world down to Bentham and Austin. For Austin, such concepts as 'duty', 'right', 'liberty', 'injury' and 'punishment' belonged to the province of General Jurisprudence, as distinct from the particular jurisprudence of a distinct system of law (Austin 1954, p. 367). Hohfeld, probably the greatest of Austin's successors, was equally explicit in his universalist pretensions: his 'Formal or Analytical Jurisprudence' was to provide 'an accurate and intimate understanding of the fundamental working conceptions of all legal reasoning' (Horwitz 1994, p. 152). Of course, the analysts' basic categories differ from those of the conceptualists: they are supposed to be devoid of normative content, and their purport in legal reasoning is not to facilitate deductive arguments but to heuristically open and clarify legal issues. Still, universalist claims remain. And, as was predictable, the at times near-arrogant self-confidence of the analysts could not buttress their approach against subsequent post-analytical criticism.

Conceptual Deductivism

The critique of conceptual apriorism or, alternatively, deficient inductivism was regularly accompanied by a critique of conceptual deductivism, of 'deductive productivism'. In their criticism of the latter phase on the constructivist method, the anti-conceptualists appealed to both logical and policy grounds. For instance, the traditional concept of ownership was not attacked merely because of its alleged apriorism and its 'lump' character but also because of its deductive use as a source for normative conclusions. Condemnation of deductivism was one of the main common denominators in anti-conceptualist reaction, but the alternatives to

16 Their emphasis on the role that craft and tradition play in common law makes the American Prudent Realists, such as the 'mature' Llewellyn, an exception to the rule.

it which the reformers offered showed some variation. American Legal Realists called for open policy considerations. These played a role in the programme of Scandinavian Realists and Finnish analysts, too, but only within the confines of positive legislation. For the American Realists, the attack on deductivism was part of a more general attack on formalism. By contrast, the 'realism' of Finnish post-war analytical scholars was the realism of positive legislation – actually, statutory positivism! – and their call was for grounding legal decisions in positive law instead of a priori concepts.

The analytical aspect of the anti-conceptualist rupture led to a redefinition of the role of concepts in legal reasoning. Their deductive use was denounced and their primary function was portrayed in *heuristic* terms. The normative premises of legal decisions were to be sought elsewhere than in legal concepts: in positive law and explicit policy considerations. The predominantly heuristic task presupposed the disintegration of 'substance' or 'lump' concepts into relational or functional ones.

In German nineteenth-century debates, the role of 'productive deductivism', of *Juristenrecht* or 'scientific law', was mainly reserved for cases of lacunae in positive law. *Juristenrecht* was purported to be merely a subsidiary source of law, taking over the previous task of natural law in this respect. The auxiliary function of *Juristenrecht* already points to the exaggerated character of anti-deductivist criticism. Understood as a methodology for filling in gaps in positive law, the constructivist approach can be stripped of much of the quasi-logical, even quasi-mathematical trimmings with which some *Begriffs*-jurisprudents furnished it.

The anti-conceptualists have kept on repeating as a seemingly genial insight the rather trivial point that, as a matter of formal logic, only those norms can be deductively unpacked from a concept which been have been packed in it in the first place. But it is highly disputable whether this really catches the heart of the issue. In an article published in 1985, Markku Helin presents a reading that distils from constructivism a rational crux, capable of winning acceptance even today. This alleged methodological core of conceptualism can be expressed in terms of analogical reasoning. Helin takes as his example the definition of general partnership as a legal person. The definition is 'inductively' arrived at, starting from particular statutory provisions which explicitly treat general partnership as a legal person. In the 'deductive' phase, it is reasoned that general partnership should be treated as a legal person even in contexts where this is not expressly laid down by the law. Thus, a conceptual definition – the definition of general partnership as a legal person – provides the basis for deriving legal norms which were not included in the inductive phase of concept formation. However, the reasoning can be translated into the language of analogy. The same grounds that have led the legislator to treat general partnership as a legal person in certain contexts may be equally relevant in other contexts which have not been explicitly addressed in positive legislation, and, hence, vindicate a conclusion from analogy (Helin 1985). Indeed, Savigny and Puchta expressly stressed the significance of analogy as a device for legal problem-solving in situations of lacunae.

But, of course, even after such re-reading, the anti-deductivist critique retains at least some of its pertinence. Analogical method cannot do without choices – with regard to, primarily, the analogy key and relevant policy or other substantive considerations – and these choices should not be concealed behind a quasi-logical conceptual game.

Legal concepts can be arranged according to their varying location on a line leading from norms to facts (see Chapter 6). The general categories of *Begriffsjurisprudenz* are nearer the former than the latter pole: they refer to a cluster of norms and actually come quite close to legal principles. Consequently, the notorious conceptual deductivism can also be examined as reasoning with principles. Individual positive-law norms provide institutional support for an unwritten general principle, which the courts may then resort to as a legal source when confronted with a gap in the law. But the demand to tear down the façade of quasi-objective deductive reasoning and to replace it with open morals- or policy-based normative argumentation remains warranted even on such an understanding of the constructivist method.

Actually, the deductive phase of the constructive method, such as the critics understood it, consists of two sub-phases: deducing legal rules from general concepts, and deducing a legal decision using the deductively-derived rule as the major premise. The American Realists pointed to inevitable judicial choices in both quasi-deductive operations, and in Finland as well a central target of anti-conceptualist polemic was the doctrine of the one right answer, backed up by a syllogistic understanding of judicial decision-making. In effect, the main contribution of Makkonen's study from 1965 lay in the analytically-tuned denouncement of this understanding. Again, it is easy to subscribe to the critics' claim that the deductivist façade obscures the many choices which judges face. Nevertheless, the anti-syllogistic critique could have benefited from a distinction between *logic of discovery* and *logic of justification*; a distinction whose significance John Dewey (1859–1952) in the 1920s tried to convey to American legal scholars (Dewey 1924). The syllogistic model is a very poor device for describing how judges in reality arrive at their conclusions. But this does not necessarily deprive it of its justificatory value. The syllogistic model expresses the demand for generalisability which, arguably, is the minimum condition for the justifiability of legal decisions and which ensues from fundamental normative principles of formal equality and justice. Another way to rescue the one-right-answer doctrine would be to treat it as a regulative idea guiding legal decision-making. This is the approach of Dworkin's Hercules the Judge.

Law's Autonomy

The novel German state-law doctrine was introduced in Finland by Robert F. Hermanson (1846–1928) in an article published in 1878–1879. Hermanson distinguished between a negative and a positive side in its methodology. The *negative* aspect equalled the positivism of *Begriffsjurisprudenz*: the object of legal science was to be cleansed of its extra-legal elements and reduced to positive law. The *positive* side, in turn, consisted of the constructive method. These two aspects are also present in American Classical Legal Thought, although the source of positive law was conceived differently from German post-unification state-law doctrine. In the view of the US conceptualists, too, the law is supposed to constitute a domain separate from politics and morals and possessing a distinct manner of reasoning.

In the American Realist critique, the negative aspect of conceptualism was attacked as fiercely as was the positive one, i.e. the deductivist method. The Realists treated formalism and deductivism as the reverse sides of conceptualism. They denounced the idea of the independence of law and legal reasoning, embraced an instrumentalist view of law, and called for open policy argumentation. In terms of the tension between *voluntas* and *ratio*, the Realists tended to inflate the former pole and neglect the latter. They not only accepted legislative social engineering; they also emphasised judicial discretion and the policy choices it entailed. Although, *pace* Hart, too much should not be made of the Realists' predictivist notions, the law's normativity and the doctrinal constraints of legal decision-making were a blind spot for most Realists. Exceptions existed, though, most notably Llewellyn with his keen eye on the significance of craft and tradition in common law.

For the Scientists among the Realists, rejection of the law's autonomy extended to legal scholarship, which they aspired to develop into a non-independent branch of social sciences. Naïve faith in the new, empiristically-oriented social sciences was another blind spot for the Realists. Many of the projects in which the Scientists engaged at Yale and Johns Hopkins were acknowledged failures, and William Underhill Moore (1879–1949), the most uncompromising of the Scientists, became an object of general ridicule with his meticulous observation of the parking behaviour of New Haven drivers (Schlegel 1995, on Moore, pp. 128ff.).

American Realists were not interested in the law's ontology as a philosophical issue. By contrast, the Scandinavian Realists very much were. They exhausted much of their scholarly energies in efforts to find empirical referents for legal concepts and propositions that would meet the demanding criteria of Hägerström's philosophy of science and, later, logical empiricism. If the endeavour did not succeed, the Realist verdict was to expel the concept or the proposition from the realm of science. This also amounted to a denial of the law's autonomy, an attempt to reduce the law's normativity to empirical facts. Again, Hart might have missed the point in his critique of Ross, but, again, the law's normativity proved to be the Realists' stumbling block.

The problem did not escape Ross. In his criticism of American Realism, he argued that 'court' and 'judge' are legally determined concepts: 'The judge bears no divine mark on his forehead investing him as judge. The quality of being a judge is itself legally conditioned.' Consequently, definitions of the law in terms of the court's or the judges' behaviour are not able to dispense with the other, binding or normative side of what Ross called the dualism of legal concepts (Ross 1946, pp. 61–62). Ross may have been mistaken in his assumption that his American colleagues were engaged in a philosophically-motivated discussion of the general concept of law. But he certainly was right in his observation. Ironically enough, exactly the same observation can be made of Ross' own attempts to dissolve dualism by reducing the law's obligatory element to an empirical socio-psychological fact. Scandinavian Realists' metaphysical monism (Helin 1988, p. 250) left no space for the legal Ought and compelled Ross to halt at the doorway that would have led to the institutional theory of law and to recognition of the interplay of constitutive norms and facts, so typical of the law's functioning.

The Scandinavians shared the instrumentalist premises of the German and American anti-conceptualists and can also be blamed for downplaying the significance of the law's sedimented *ratio*. Unlike their American colleagues, however, they did not aim to efface the boundary between law and politics, nor did they strive for the dissolution of legal into social science, as did the Scientists among American Legal Realists and the German anti-conceptualists of the *Freirechtslehre* wing. After realist reconstruction and analytical reform of the heuristically-conceived conceptual apparatus, Scandinavian Realists set doctrinal research free to continue largely in the same manner as before, provided that scientific and value standpoints were kept clearly apart.

The mainstream of Finnish analytical scholarship constitutes a special case among the anti-conceptualist approaches to the negative side of *Begriffsjurisprudenz*. Analysts like Zitting agreed with their predecessors on the necessity to purge the object of legal science of foreign, system-disturbing extra-legal elements. But they claimed that through their 'thingifying' substance concepts, conceptualists created speculative, metaphysical entities, such as the state or other legal persons conceived of as entities separate from human beings and their interrelations. *Begriffsjurisprudenz* had not succeeded in its cleansing objective; to the contrary, it had assumed new fictive entities, in breach of positivist delineations.

American and Scandinavian Realists held divergent views of legal scholarship, but they did agree on the distance which scholars should maintain to normative legal discourse. If scholars present normative standpoints, they do it in another role. This conception of non-normative legal science is an integral part of the Realist legacy which the present-day Critic has adopted as her own.

Begriffsjurisprudenz was born in nineteenth-century Germany as an heir to the historical school. Savigny had envisaged a two-pronged research programme: legal science was to combine a historical and a dogmatic (doctrinal) approach. *Begriffsjurisprudenz* concentrated on the latter side of this programme, and tended to separate law from history and society. It lost sight of the particular fashion of conceiving of the law's ontology which Savigny had bequeathed to his successors. His notion of legal institutions attaches legal normativity to social facticity by tying legal norms (propositions) to the factual life relationships they regulate. Savigny anticipated interpretation of the interplay between legal norms and social (or psychological) reality through the concept of *(legal-)institutional facts*. Intimations of such an interpretation run as an undercurrent through the legal literature of the twentieth century; it is hinted at by the legal sociologist Weber (1988, pp. 340ff.), and by the legal theorists Kelsen (1989, pp. 3–4) and Ross (1946, pp. 61–62). Finally, Neil MacCormick's and Ota Weinberger's (1986) institutional theory of law transferred it from the periphery to the core of legal theory.

PART II
Legal Scholarship and the Coherence of Law

Chapter 5
The Law's System: From Total to Local Coherence

The Traditional System

Under the systematic ideal of nineteenth-century German legal scholarship, each branch of law was to be ordered through its specific general doctrines (*allgemeine Lehren*). But coherence was to be even more extensive, covering the legal order as a whole. Two principal ways existed to attain this. First, the comprehensive systematic coherence of the law might be seen to derive from the most general legal concepts, which, as Paul Laband (1888, p. VII), for instance, affirmed, were common to both private and public law. They provided positive law with a supra-positive foundation, on which the doctrinal constructions of both private and public law were premised even after the turn to statutory positivism. The other way of conceiving the legal order's overall unity was the classification of normative material: its division into distinct fields, where all legal norms were supposed to find an unequivocal location.

The division adopted in German legal science has proved to be tenacious. In Finland and other Nordic countries, it was adopted by the end of the nineteenth century, and even today it is largely adhered to in legal research and education. In his monograph on the development of the legal system, published in 1979, the Finnish legal historian Lars Björne (1979, p. 6) presented it in the form of Figure 5.1 (see next page).

In its general outline, this classification was established in Finland in the latter half of the nineteenth century, with the immediate influences coming from contemporary German *Begriffsjurisprudenz*. However, the roots of the division reach to the origins of Western legal tradition: to Roman law. In Germany, debates on the law's systematisation had continued for centuries, ever since the reception of Roman law. The basic division between public and private law derived from Justinian's *Institutionen*. Classification of the law's objects into persons (*personae*), things (*res*) and actions (*actiones*) went back to Gaius (130–180), and the further division of things into material (*res corporales*) and immaterial (*res incorporales*) was also found in Roman sources (ibid., p. 15). These divisions were reiterated in the five books of the German nineteenth-century private-law *Begriffsjurisprudenz* – Pandect law (*Pandektenrecht*): the general part, the law of obligations, property law (*Sachenrecht*), family law, and the law of inheritance. The only complement to the system of *Pandektenrecht* needed on the private-law side of this figure was the controversial branch of economic law (*Wirtschaftsrecht*).

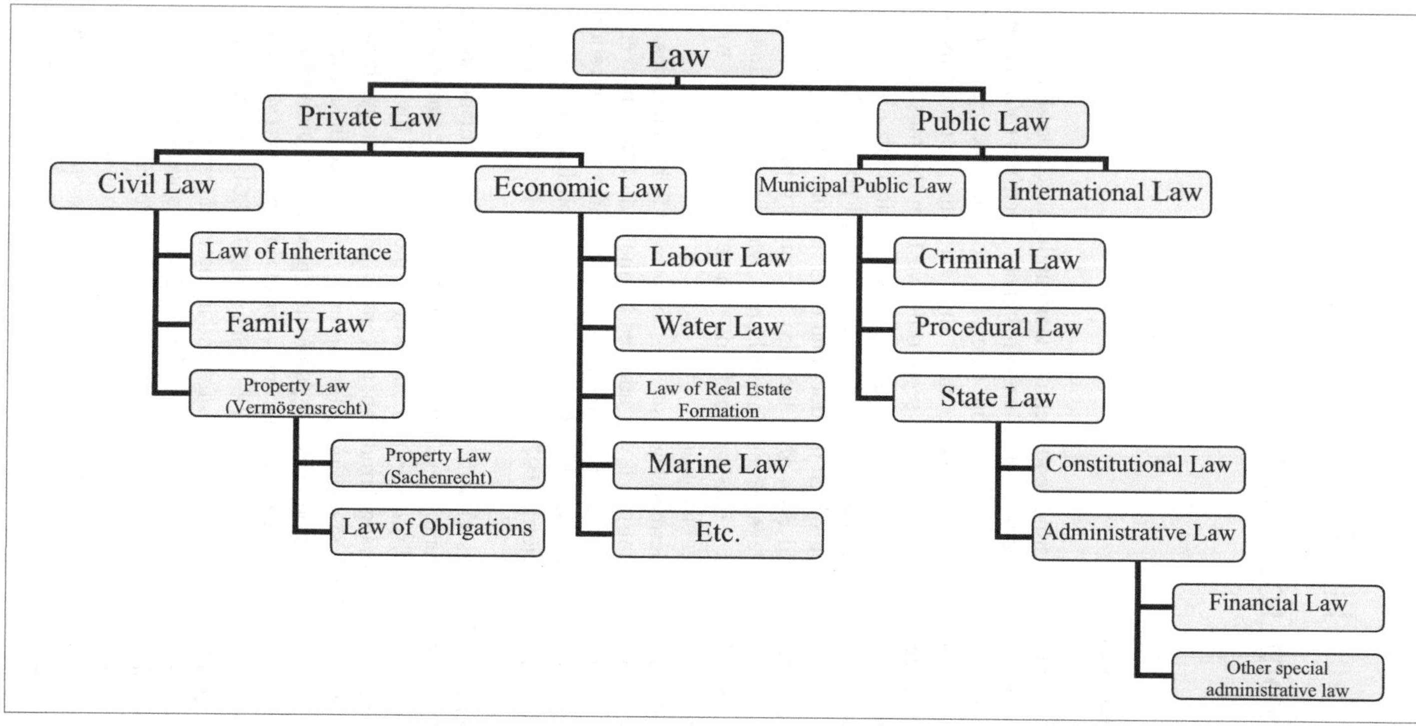

Figure 5.1 The system of law according to Björne (1979, p. 15)

In common-law countries, too, the systematising urge of the nineteenth century manifested itself, not only in the ordering of particular bodies of law, but also in schemes for the law's overall classification or 'arrangement'. And in the Anglo-American debates, too, a distinct strand perceived foundation of the law's unity in universally valid fundamental concepts. Here, John Austin was the great source of inspiration. Austin distinguished between national and particular jurisprudence, on the one hand, and General Jurisprudence of positive law, on the other. This distinction was based on Austin's claim that 'though every system of law has its specific and characteristic differences, there are principles and distinctions common to various systems, and forming analogies or likenesses by which such systems are allied' (Austin 1954, p. 365). General Jurisprudence is 'the science concerned with the exposition of the principles, notions, and distinctions which are common to systems of law'. Austin's conceptual distinctions within the domain of General Jurisprudence were employed by, for instance, Oliver Wendell Holmes in his first published articles, dealing with the problem of classifying the law (Holmes 1870, 1872).

Gerald Postema (2003, p. 5) argues that common law's 'artificial reason' seeks merely local coherence, achieved through principles, and is sceptical of an inclusive systematisation, based on abstract theorising. Correspondingly, in England, which has clung more obstinately to the common-law tradition and embraced a remedial conception of law (Allison 2004, pp. 126–131), interest in comprehensive classification has been much more tepid than in the United States. In turn, the American debates during the classical age were much more practically-oriented than those on the Continent. The main problem was how to bring order into the overwhelming outpouring of legal material from both state and federal courts. The discussion focused on the classification to be used in legal digests and encyclopaedias, or the later more ambitious project of Restatements of the Law, launched by the American Law Institute in the early 1920s. The other perennial issue, of course, was the law school curriculum.

In spite of their more pragmatic emphasis, American debates on the law's divisions were very much influenced by Continental and Roman-law models. The common-law tradition was procedurally oriented and tended to privilege case-to-case reasoning; thus, substantively it did not provide the systematisers with very much to connect to.[1] In consequence, virtually every contribution faithfully reiterated the distinction between public and private law and, within the latter, the Roman-law division based on the law's objects (*persona*, *res* and *actiones*). By the 1930s, the discussion had settled down and a wide consensus on so-called standard classification had been achieved. This classification, which was used, for instance, by the leading American encyclopaedias, followed a distinction into:

1 An exception, which was frequently commented on, mostly in a critical vein, was Blackstone's classification into: 1) Rights of Persons; 2) Rights of Things; 3) Private Wrongs; and 4) Public Wrongs.

1. Persons;
2. Property;
3. Contract;
4. Tort;
5. Crime;
6. Remedies;
7. Government.

The issue that could still arouse classifying passions was defining and systematically locating administrative law, a novel branch of law whose importance the New Deal greatly increased.[2]

Let us return to the divisions familiar from Romano-Germanic legal cultures and manifest in Björne's diagram, too. Björne's study, which appeared only 30 years ago, still reflected a belief in an unequivocal classification of the law and adopted the nineteenth-century system as an almost self-evident premise. Change has been rapid: present-day debates, in Finland as well as elsewhere, have moved far from the compartments of Björne's diagram. Interest in the law's differentiation into specific branches has not vanished or even diminished. On the contrary, we are witnessing a revival of classification debates. The focus, however, has shifted, so that nineteenth-century discussants would have a hard time in orienting themselves in present debates on such putative departments of law as social law, medical and bio-law, sports law, information law, or communications law. Characteristic of recent interventions is that they are no longer concerned with the law's overall systematisation. When labour law, some decades ago, waged its battle for independence, it was, at least on the Continent, still considered important to ponder its place with regard to the basic distinction between private and public law. Present discussants do not seem to be troubled by the location in the law's comprehensive system of the new fields (and disciplines) they are advocating. Instead of *total coherence* of the law, their aim is more modest: to bring about *local coherence* into a particular body of law.

Some recent analysts have doubted the desirability and the possibility of even such a limited, local coherence. Doubts usually grow from observations of the law's increasing pluralism. As has been shown by, for instance, Håkan Gustafsson in his doctoral thesis (2002), the pluralism of late modern law can be examined at various levels and in various dimensions, so that the pluralist argument against legal coherence can also take many guises. One line of argument, familiar from various versions of the Critic's narrative, emphasises the law's policy connections and the great variance of objectives pursued through law. In turn, Thomas Wilhelmsson (2001 and 2004) emphasises the ethical fragmentation of our era, affecting the law, too. He has also questioned the justification of the very principle of coherence. Yet

2 In addition to Holmes' early articles, the other seminal contribution is Pound's article 'Classification of law', published in *Harvard Law Review* in 1924. In addition, see Mallory (1902), Andrews (1910), Terry (1910 and 1917), Kocourek (1934) and Ulrich (1935).

another way of problematising coherence in law relates it to the 'golden age' of modern law: to the sovereignty of nation states and the mono-centric perspective of the nation-state legislator. The sovereignty of the nation-state legislator has been shaken, entailing not only polycentricity of legal sources but also pluralism of legal orders, even legal systems. The fragmented law of the late modern era cannot – so the argument goes – be compressed into the straitjacket of a systematisation dating from a bygone era.

The law's divisions can be approached either from an internal, a normative, or an external perspective. Contributions adopting the internal point of view participate in legal discourse, and either defend the prevailing divisions or criticise them and advocate, for instance, a new relatively independent branch of law. From the external perspective, the focus falls on factors determining development of the law's classifications. In what follows, I shall use both the internal and the external perspective. I shall endorse the normative objective of the law's coherence and the continuous relevance of its divisions. However, I shall also make some observations concerning the extra- and infra-legal factors accounting for the evolution of these divisions.

The Law's Divisions: Law or Legal Science?

Ordering legal raw material, such as statutes or precedents, serves many purposes in the functioning of a legal system. Perhaps the most modest aim is what can be called *encyclopaedic*: to 'store' legal material and to provide legal actors, primarily legal professionals but sometimes even laymen, with simple means of finding the material they need. This aim can be satisfied by, for instance, alphabetical ordering of legal topics and corresponding legal material. Statute books and law reports, as well as legal digests and encyclopaedia, offer abundant examples of the diverse criteria by which the encyclopaedic function can be fulfilled. But classification may have more far-reaching objectives, too. It may expressly serve the legislator in a project of *codification*. The *BGB* is sometimes called the 'little Windscheid', which tells of the importance of the preparatory work of the German nineteenth-century Pandectists. Often enough, classification pursues *pedagogical* objectives, by organising the curriculum of university-based law studies. Law-school curriculum structure leaves its imprint on the structure of the legal consciousness of future legal professionals. Hence, the pedagogical function is closely related to what can be considered legal systematisation's most pivotal effect: its *heuristic* function.

In their heuristic task, the divisions of law function as part of the hermeneutical pre-understanding with which the prevailing legal culture furnishes legal actors. Through these divisions, legal actors identify legal problems and define them, say, as issues of criminal or administrative law. Though legal issues are most often specified and located in a quasi-automatic, unconscious manner, this has important normative consequences. Thus, it indicates the relevance of 'branch-specific' legal principles, such as *nulla poena sine lege* in criminal law or the protection of legitimate expectations in administrative law. Only after we have pinned down the problem at hand within the law's overall system can we tell which rules and principles are pertinent to its solution. Lawyers-to-be largely internalise prevailing, seemingly self-evident divisions during their law studies.

As the heuristic function shows, the law's systematisation through division into distinct fields has aspired to more than a mere ordering of legal raw material. Especially in Continental legal cultures, systematisation, which, in its general outline, was adopted in the nineteenth century, has been a more ambitious project. An integral part of the project has been to articulate and elaborate general doctrines of each of the branches of law. The five 'books' of German Pandect law and, subsequently, the *BGB* reserved a prominent place for general doctrines. One of these books consisted of private law's general doctrines, which in the *BGB* were complemented by the general doctrines of the other books: property law (*Sachenrecht*), the law of obligations, family law and the law of inheritance. In fact, the branches of law only acquired their identity through their general doctrines: their concepts, principles and dogmatic theories.

Contemporary battles for independence, too, seem to set out from the assumption that what is decisive for establishing a new field of law is its own general doctrines. The normative material which such a field is supposed to cover may be delimited through its social object of regulation. However, a definite regulatory object does not yet suffice to constitute a distinct branch of the law. What is further needed are concepts structuring the normative material and its regulatory object, principles condensing its normative contents, and theories combining concepts and principles.

Legal science has played a central role in elaborating the law's overall system. This holds especially for Romano-Germanic legal cultures, but in common-law countries, too, comprehensive classificatory schemes have usually originated in legal scholarship. This raises the following question: do such schemes express the law's internal structure or are they to be understood merely as legal science's way of exposing the law? Are they part of the law or of legal science?

In his study of legal systematisation, Björne drew a distinction between the 'legal order' and the 'legal system'. *Legal order* he defined as the totality of valid legal norms. He emphasised that 'the legal order as a whole is not a strictly logical and gapless entity, because the law in force results from a long development', and because 'individual laws have been enacted at different times and for different purposes without any holistic or systematic thinking' (ibid., p. 3). The legal order is – and here Björne's focus is obviously on modern law – primarily the product of legislative activities. By contrast, elaboration of the *legal system* falls to legal science. The legal system derives from, above all, division of normative material into distinct fields of law. In formation of the legal system, 'one aims, through specific scientific conceptions, at a unitary, usually deductive system or at least at a whole based on comprehensive criteria and indicating for every legal phenomenon its unequivocal place' (ibid., p. 2).

Thus, Björne distinguished between the law in force (the legal order), which was mainly the work of the legislator, and the legal system, which was a creation of legal science. Owing to the capriciousness of the legislator, the legal order lacks a systematic character. Only legal science can inject coherence into the normative material making up the legal order. In his studies, Björne has shown the importance of the models procured by German nineteenth-century legal scholarship for the way its disciples in Finland and other Nordic countries conceived of the law's classification. However, his way of juxtaposing the legal order as a disordered amalgamation of norms and the legal system constructed by legal science appears to deviate from the mainstream of nineteenth-century German discussion.

In the German debates, the historical school, as well as the subsequent *Begriffsjurisprudenz*, conceived of both the law and legal science as systematic entities. Different interpretations were put forth of system-creating grounds, and of the relationship between the law's internal system and legal science's doctrinal system. In Chapter 3, we made acquaintance with Savigny's view according to which the law's internal system derived from the organic nature of legal institutions and their ensembles. This, for its part, resulted from the organic nature of the factual life relationships which constituted the substantive elements of legal relationships. The turn to statutory positivism led to increased emphasis on the system's logical-rational quality but by no means to renunciation of the very notion of the law's internal system.

So the German nineteenth-century discussants seemed to agree that it was the law's internal organisation that basically enabled legal science to portray the law as a system. Nevertheless, no isomorphic relationship existed between the two systems. Legal scholarship had to comply with the general requirements of science and to expound legal knowledge as a principle-organised whole. Yet it retained a certain leeway in choosing the premises of its doctrinal construction (*Lehrordnung*). We may recall that Puchta, for instance, considered it possible to present (private) law as a system of rights, legal propositions or legal institutions. But whatever was chosen as the building block, the scientific demand for a principled whole required that the system be depicted as the unfolding of a basic idea. When the law was exposed as a system of rights, this basic idea was that man was not only a part of nature but also a spiritual being, equipped with capacity for freedom and a free will. Gerber transferred Puchta's system ideal to state law, and endeavoured to construct the system of state law on the basic idea of the free willpower of the state (see above, p. 87).

How should we, then, in the light of German nineteenth-century discussions, respond to the question posed above: do the classificatory schemes form part of the law, of its internal system, or are they merely legal scholarship's device for portraying the law's unity? Or, to use Björne's vocabulary, do they belong to the legal order or (merely) to the legal system created by legal science? The question is, in a sense, misleading. Legal scholarship is one of the legal practices that continuously produce and reproduce the legal order. Through its very results, such as schemes for systematising the law, legal scholarship contributes to development of the legal order. As a rule, the law's divisions are not determined by the legislator nor decided on by the judges but proposed by legal scholars. However, after the scholars' proposals have found general acceptance, divisions, once established, form an integral part of the legal-cultural pre-understanding and unfurl their heuristic effects not only in legal science but also in other legal practices, such as lawmaking and adjudication.

The law's division into distinct branches is both a part of the law and a doctrinal construction of legal scholarship. Björne is right in emphasising legal science's contribution to systematising the legal order and to securing its coherence. Nonetheless, his suggestion to examine this contribution through the concepts of legal order and legal system, as a transformation of the legal order into a legal system, is open to criticism. In my own conceptual framework, the dialectic between disorder and order is approached as a relationship between the levels of the legal order: concrete normative material at the law's surface obtains its systematic quality from principles and concepts located at the sub-surface, legal-cultural levels.[3] Changes in the legal order's divisions are inaugurated by legal scholars' interventions. But, of course, not all proposals for re-systematisation initiate a successful legal-cultural transformation. The fate of many, maybe most, of them is to become only footnotes in legal historiography. This seems, for instance, to have been the typical destiny of the various functionalist proposals of the last century's 'progressive' scholarship, such as the Columbia Law School plan of the 1920s to divide the law into the three major subcategories of political, business and familial relations, complemented by a fourth category of law administration (Twining 1985, p. 48). But one should be cautious of over-hasty conclusions. As is typical of legal culture in general, the pace of change in divisions of the legal order has been protracted. Established divisions may last for centuries, and sedimentation of a re-division may take a long period.

What kind of unity has one striven for through systematising the law, such as dividing it into distinct branches? How, exactly, are the law's compartments supposed to be inter-connected? When the doctrinal system was conceived of as the unravelling of the implications of a single basic idea – as was the case with Puchta's and Gerber's constructions – we can talk in a vague sense of deductive relations between the system's elements. However, this was primarily legal scholarship's way of exposing legal knowledge as a principled whole, and to meet the general criterion of scientificity. It did not necessarily imply the claim that corresponding deductive relations would prevail in the law itself. Furthermore, we should also recall that, according to Puchta, the law could only be exposed

3 I also use the concept of legal system in a sense different from the one given to it by Björne. By 'legal system', I refer to the whole constituted by the law's two aspects: the law as a legal order and the law as specific legal practices, functioning in production and reproduction of the legal order.

as a 'deductive' system after its internal connections had been grasped through *Anschauung*.

In German nineteenth-century legal science, the foundation of the law's internal system was seen either in the organic character of legal institutions and factual life relationships or in the law's logically-tuned internal rationality. But in both alternatives, the system of positive law was seen to rely on supra-positive underpinnings. Savigny argued that the legal institutions of national law, such as monogamist marriage, lent positive shape to supra-positive models, such as marriage in general, and Laband construed his system of positive state law on supra-positive general legal concepts. Neither positive legal regulations nor doctrinal constructions of positive law could do without such concepts. The system expounded by legal science included not only a posteriori concepts derived from positive law but also supra-positive concepts, a priori with regard to positive law.

In current legal theory, a distinction is often made between the consistency and the coherence of a body of law. *Consistency* is about the mutual *logical* non-contradictoriness of legal norms, especially those norms which – in the wake of Ronald Dworkin and Robert Alexy – are called legal rules. Legal culture involves particular standards for resolving conflicts between rules and for securing the legal order's consistency, such as *lex superior*, *lex posterior* and *lex specialis*. *Coherence*, in turn, is about the *substantive* harmony of law. It is a quality of legal principles rather than rules. Arguably, the emphasis in Max Weber's notion of formal rational law, for example, is on consistency, whereas Puchta's and Gerber's systems aimed at a more demanding, substantive coherence.[4]

Puchta's or Gerber's systems did not cover the whole legal order, but just private or state law. With regard to the law's overall structure, the concept of system can be used, not only of such substantive constructions, but also in a less pretentious, classificatory sense. On the latter understanding, the system of the legal order as a whole is not constituted through unfolding the implications of a constitutive legal idea. Rather, the law's divisions adhere to external criteria: its regulatory objects.

Apparently, the majority of the systematising proposals which scholars of different eras and different legal cultures have produced fall between two extremes: classification according to social fields of regulation and systematisation by internal, substantive criteria. In the system introduced at the beginning of this chapter, the diverse departments of law are supposed to acquire internal substantive coherence from their particular general doctrines. But substantive links between departments may be rather thin, and at the level of the legal order as a whole it seems appropriate to speak of a classificatory ordering, based primarily on the external criteria of the law's regulatory objects. It is true, though, that basic legal concepts such as that of will, had a certain substantively unifying effect not only

4 When employing concepts coined in recent debates, it should, of course, be kept in mind that the *Begriffsjurisprudenz* of the latter half of the nineteenth century was not familiar with the present conceptual distinction between legal rules and principles.

within but also between fields of law. All in all, the term *classificatory-substantive* seems appositely to depict systematisations covering the entire legal order.

The law's systematic qualities have often been related to such fundamental normative principles as *legal certainty* and *predictability*, as well as *formal justice* and *equality*. It has been argued that these normative premises of modern law cannot be realised without the law's systematisation through its partition into distinct fields and the general doctrines of these fields.

This argument is frequently put forward in the *internal* discourse of the legal system. However, systematisation of the legal order, as well as the underpinning principles of legal certainty and predictability, can also be viewed from a larger social framework and linked to modern society's basic structures or cultural characteristics. Then the internal legal perspective is replaced by an *external*, sociological or cultural historic perspective. In the horizon of Weber's sociology of law, the legal order's organisation into distinct fields forms part and parcel of the law's modernisation, particularly in Continental Europe. Weber defines modern law's *ratio* in terms of *formal rationality*, with systematicity as one of its main determinants. In Weber's view, formal rationality is a quality of law required by the capitalist market economy and bureaucratic administration, both of them epitomising *societal* modernisation. Furthermore, the law's formal rationalisation partakes of the general tendency towards systematising worldviews, which Weber, especially in his essays on the sociology of religion, considers a central feature of *cultural* modernisation. Hence, Weber connects modern law's formal rational features, including its systematicity, to both societal and cultural modernisation.

Internal and External Determinants of Legal Development

Weber's analysis of formal rational law and its connection to modern society's fundamental structural and cultural traits, serves to introduce a brief discussion of the factors influencing the law's divisions. These factors can be grouped into internal and external ones. Observers stressing the role of the former emphasise the law's autonomy; here, the danger is one of closing the legal system, of legal autarchy. By contrast, scholars focusing on external causes easily end up with an excessively instrumentalist conception, where the law is seen merely as an instrument in realising economic interests or in exercising political and administrative power. Clearly both extremities – autarchy and instrumentalism – should be avoided. The law's systematisation, like legal development in general, is a result of the interaction between external and internal dynamics. The respective emphasis of these dynamics depends, among other things, on the time span under consideration: in the long term, the role of macro-social processes grows, and, conversely, the shorter the time span the greater the importance of internal factors. Nonetheless, in a long-term analysis, too, due attention should be paid to the continuity of the legal tradition. Thus, modern law involves concepts and principles with roots reaching back to ancient Rome.

Weber may help us in specifying the external and internal factors influencing legal development, as well as their interaction. Weber has been called a causal agnostic (Kronman 1983, pp. 125–130). He renounces time-and-place-independent formulae of causal relations and universalist explanations for social change. His remarks on, for instance, the relationship between formal rational law and modern society's 'objectified structures' are akin to a *functional* explanation: modern, systematised law is functionally adequate for a capitalist market economy and bureaucratic administration. As Kronman (1983, p. 35) has noted, Weber also resorts to an *exegetic* explanation. Here society's 'life-orders', such as modern law, capitalist economy and bureaucratic administration, perhaps even institutionalised and doctrinally systematised religion, are all seen to manifest an identical cultural principle: formal rationality.

Weber's functional and exegetic accounts focus on 'mature' modern Western society and its law. In his historical forays, Weber lays more weight on *causal* explanations. Let us briefly examine what role Weber assigns to economic factors in legal modernisation.

Weber ponders the impact of economic factors on the law's rationalisation both at a general level and in the context of particular legal institutions. In his general remarks, Weber recognises the significance of economic factors and interests. He argues that 'certain rationalisations of economic behaviour, based upon such phenomena as a market economy or freedom of contract, and the resulting awareness of underlying, and increasingly complex conflicts of interests to be resolved by legal machinery, have influenced the systematisation of the law or have intensified the institutionalisation of the polity' (Weber 1978, p. 655). He describes the direction in which economic factors influence 'the formation of the specifically modern features of present-day occidental law' as follows: 'To those who had interests in the commodity market, the rationalisation and systematisation of the law in general and … the increasing calculability of the functioning of the legal process in particular, constituted one of the most important conditions for the existence of economic enterprise intended to function with stability and, especially of capitalistic enterprise, which cannot do without legal security' (ibid., p. 883). Here Weber, in a way, reduces to economic interests the expectation of legal certainty which has often been considered to be a central feature of Western legal culture. He also notes that 'the alliance of monarchical and bourgeois interests was … one of the major factors which led towards formal legal rationalisation' (ibid., p. 847).

Nevertheless, Weber is careful to emphasise that economic circumstances have never alone determined the direction of Western legal development. Correspondingly, when exploring the emergence of particular legal institutions, he stresses the indirect nature of the impact of economic factors and the absence of any law-like regularities. He argues that 'purely economic influences merely occur as concrete instances and cannot be formulated in general rules'. For instance, the way in which present branches of law with their basic concepts have become differentiated has, to a great extent, been determined by 'factors of legal technique', and partly also by the structure of the polity, and only indirectly by economic factors (ibid., pp. 654–655). Economic situations do not in general 'automatically give birth to new legal forms; they merely provide the opportunity for the actual spread of a legal technique if it is invented' (ibid., p. 687).

As a contrast to the merely indirect influence of economic factors, Weber points to the immediate relevance of 'intrajuristic' conditions. In his view, the law's development, including its rationalisation, has been most directly shaped by the specific features of the 'upholders of legal thinking', in particular the education they have received. The direction in which the law's formal qualities develop 'is ... conditioned directly by "intrajuristic" circumstances: the particular character of the individuals who by virtue of their profession are in a position to influence the ways in which the law is shaped. Only indirectly is this development influenced ... by general economic and social conditions' (ibid., p. 776). Weber for instance claimed that divergences in English and Continental law are largely due to differences in legal education. In England, legal education has been in the hands of legal practitioners, and, consequently, empirical and craft-like in character. Empirical legal education has halted formal rationalisation of the legal order at the stage of generalisation and casuistry. By contrast, Continental European university-based education has brought it further, to systematisation of the law on substantive grounds.

Weber claims that the immediate impetus to human action lies in material and spiritual interests. Accordingly, the factors which, in Weber's view, have driven forward the law's rationalisation can be condensed into the material and ideal interests of the relevant legal and other social actors. However, Weber stresses that interests never affect social action in a 'pure' form. He continues his comment on the immediate dominance of interests by noting that ideas and worldviews often function as 'gears' (*Weichensteller*), defining the tracks on which the dynamic of interests conducts social action (Weber 1963, p. 252). This complement accounts for the central role of the sociology of religion in Weber's comprehensive research programme for exploring the particularity of modern Western rationality.

Jürgen Habermas is perhaps most prominent among contemporary theorists who have elaborated on the significance Weber attaches to worldviews in social action and development. Habermas views rationalisation of moral and legal conceptions as a pacemaker in social evolution. Cultural modernisation is not a mere 'super-structural' manifestation of economic modernisation but possesses its own autonomy and independent developmental logic, and may even precede societal modernisation. Following Habermas' Weber-influenced interpretation, cultural modernisation is manifest by fragmentation of the unitary medieval worldview into particular 'value spheres', each with its distinct validity criteria – such as truth in science, normative correctness in morals and law, and beauty in art. The value spheres also display an internal dynamism of rationalisation, manifested, *inter alia*, by systematisation. Thus, following Weber's and Habermas' line of argument, legal modernisation forms part and parcel of the cultural modernisation that has created preconditions for societal modernisation, epitomised by the market economy and a bureaucratically organised, centralised state. In turn, cultural modernisation has been driven forward by the spiritual and material interests of 'professional rationalisers', such as university-educated jurists, Savigny's estate of learned lawyers.

When Weber argues for the law's formal rationalisation as a functional prerequisite of the market economy and bureaucratic administration, he mainly alludes to a framework regulation of these societal sub-systems. Formal rational law performs the same stabilising and predictability-enhancing task which Bentham assigned to his code or system of codes (see above, pp. 63–64). Formal rational law, as Weber portrays it, is not interventionist law in the service of the legislator's shifting political aims. On the contrary, Weber fears that the law's instrumentalist use in social management endangers its formal rational qualities, including its systematicity. In his sketchy remarks on further development of modern law, he worries about the law's *materialisation*, which he relates to the increasing intrusion into the law of 'ethical imperatives, utilitarian and other expediential rules, and political maxims' (Weber 1978, p. 657).

Weber sees that the gravest threats to formal legal rationality arise from demands for substantive justice, with their background in modern society's class-related problems. Such demands are voiced by propertyless and socially discriminated-against classes, politically empowered by democracy. These classes do not define the tasks of the law in terms of social stability and predictability but require that it serve social justice, the equalisation of socio-economic living conditions. The *ethos* of social justice focuses on substantive justice in particular cases and conflicts with the formal equality of formal rational law. Weber identifies the central background to the law's mounting instrumentalisation in political democratisation and the emergent welfare state. Indeed, welfare-state law has problematised the law's internal divisions, established in the nineteenth century. By the same token, the tension between the law's positivity and its systematic nature has become more conspicuous than ever before, and legal scholarship's task to bring order into the disorder created by the legislator has become ever more difficult to accomplish.

Let us once more revert to the table of the law's divisions, introduced at the beginning of this chapter. It displays two points of rupture which have facilitated its adaptation to the law's growing instrumentalisation but which have also been conducive to the erosion of its very premises: the departments of economic law (or special private law) and special administrative law. On the one hand, they have enabled addition to the table of new sub-fields to which social and legal development has given rise. But, on the other hand, economic law and special administrative law deviate in one crucial respect from the other branches of law included in the systematisation. They possess no distinct general doctrines, to which the other branches owe their internal coherence and identity. If the status of a relatively independent field of law is tied to identity-creating general doctrines, economic law or special administrative law do not in fact meet this criterion. Thus, economic law constitutes by no means a similar systematic whole, unified by legal concepts and principles, as general private law (civil law) and its sub-fields. Indeed, Björne concedes this when he notes that economic law is a much more heterogeneous field than civil law and that its scope can only be defined negatively: all private law which does not belong to civil law falls under economic law (special private law). Economic law and special administrative law are symptomatic of serious problems that afflict the very idea of a comprehensive system, based on the law's division into separate fields of law and on general doctrines distinct to these fields.

In Björne's diagram, economic law and special administrative law epitomise the interventionist law typical of the welfare state, which employs the law instrumentally, as a means of achieving constantly shifting political goals. Here, the purposive rational, future-oriented perspective of the modern legislator comes most conspicuously to the fore. The felt necessity to introduce two 'deviating' branches of law is a token of the law's bifurcation into two, in some essential respects divergent, parts. Such a split was one of the recurring themes in twentieth-century legal-theoretical and legal sociological debates (see below, p. 20). In Habermas' terms, the law functions in instrumentalist, goal-oriented regulations as a medium, giving expression to Dworkin's policies. To use Cotterrell's terminology, these branches of law manifest *voluntas* rather than *ratio*, and in their context, society appears as an *imperium* rather as a community (see above, pp. 226–228).

In Björne's diagram, economic law and special administrative law are purported to guarantee the comprehensiveness of the system and to subsume welfare-state law under it. But the price for comprehensiveness is partial renunciation of the very premises of the system: general doctrines bringing coherence to distinct fields of law. In present-day doctrinal debates, economic law or special administrative law are but rarely mentioned, and striving for a comprehensive and unequivocal partitioning of the law into specific branches and corresponding scholarly disciplines also seems to be a bygone phase in legal science. But discussion on the law's divisions has not ceased, and new candidates for the status of a relatively independent branch of law are not lacking. Why is this the case?

Changes in the law's divisions are clearly connected to changes in legal regulation. Modern law is positive law, and it is enticing to explain the emergence of new fields of law by expansion of the scope of legal regulation and its extension to previously unregulated areas. Regulation of workplace relationships would have generated labour law; legal ordering of social security and healthcare social law; juridification of the doctor–patient relationship medical law; regulation of the natural and constructed environment environmental law; regulation of new means of information production and communication information law or communications law; and so on. Legal regulation, the activity of the legislator, would account for further internal differentiation of the law. Moreover, new legal regulations also relate to wider-reaching social developments, such as the appearance of the welfare state (labour law and social law), medicalisation (medical law), ecologicalisation (environmental law) and informatisation (information law).

The ultimate impulses launching and guiding legal development, including transformations of the law's divisions, undoubtedly come from outside the legal system. Under the conditions of modern, positive law, the legislator bears the main responsibility for conveying these impulses into the legal system. Nevertheless, the expansion of legal regulation and juridification of new social fields of action only partly explain the emergence of new branches of law. The legislator issues laws but does not decide on the systematisation of normative material. The primary responsibility for the law's systematisation falls to other legal practices; at least in Continental legal cultures, mainly to legal scholarship. Transformations in the system of law cannot be explained without taking adequate note of 'intrajuristic' circumstances on whose significance Weber, in his sociology of law, puts so much emphasis.

Pierre Bourdieu's (1987) tentative analysis of the structure and dynamics of the legal field as a specimen of social field is a proposal for conceiving of these 'intrajuristic' relations. It also provides material for a critical narrative which, in its examination of legal discourse, focuses on the participants' strategic, perlocutionary goals.

Bourdieu approaches the law and legal discourse as a social field where legal professionals as possessors of specific socio-cultural capital compete for the field's particular assets and aim to increase the value of their capital. The possessors of legal (cultural) capital are engaged in a contest over the monopoly of legal interpretation: the power to declare the law and to determine its contents. The players in the legal field are divided into teams according to the specific character of their legal capital: theorists challenge practitioners, private lawyers challenge public lawyers, and so on. The contest may assume various forms, and diverse means may be employed. The fight may be over, say, the horizontal and vertical relationships of competence within the judiciary; the legal education curriculum or allocation of resources among disciplines within law faculties; or composition of boards of lawyers' associations and editorial boards of law reviews. Participation in the contest requires knowledge of the particular rules of the game within the legal field and the capability to comply with them. It is these very rules and their mastery that delimit the legal field from other social fields and confer on it a certain autonomy. In Continental European (and American) legal cultures, future lawyers acquire a common foundation of legal capital and internalise the basic rules of the game even during their university-based legal education.

The autonomy of the legal field is only relative in character. The players in law obtain their clients and, through client relations, their supporters from other social fields, such as business and politics, and the power relations prevailing in these fields affect the score in the legal field. The respective strength of economy and politics cannot but influence the respective potency of private and public law in the legal field. It would be interesting to examine from this point of view how the situation in the legal fields of Western countries changed after the heyday of the welfare state, say, from the 1950s to the turn of the 1970s, as a consequence of financing problems and cutbacks within the public sector, privatisation of public services, and the liberalistic turn in general ideology.

From a Bourdieuan perspective, campaigns for new branches of law – e.g. medical and bio-law, communications law, information law – manifest a race for position in the legal field. Advocates of putative new branches aspiring for independence defy the established disciplines and request their share of, say, resources of legal education or editorial boards and pages of law reviews. These battles for independence exhibit certain typical stages and means, such as establishing an association and a journal. It is telling that established branches of law, being secure in their status, do not in general feel the need for an association or journal of their own. In Finland, no associations exist for civil or procedural law. By contrast, there is a Finnish Association of Social Law, an Association of Sports Law, and an Association of Environmental Law Science. While no Review of Criminal Law exists, a *Review of Environmental Law*, a *Yearbook of Information Law*, and a *Yearbook of Sports and Law* are published. In the early phases of the campaign, a central claim would be over a chair at the law faculty and acknowledged status in the legal curriculum. When a chair has been obtained, it is turned into a bridgehead, allowing consolidation of victories achieved and the prospect of new conquests.

The advocates of a new branch of law have their external patrons. For instance, labour law has been able to rely on trade unions and employers' organisations; social law and environmental law on the relevant state and municipal bureaucracies, as well as on NGOs; and information and communications law on the respective industries. Nonetheless, the outcome of the contest is ultimately determined by what transpires within the legal field and depends on the respective legal actors' ability to exploit their legal capital and competence.

An integral part of this competence consists of argumentative skills, the aptitude to convince other players in the game – other participants in legal discourse – of the weight of one's arguments. A Bourdieuan sociologist observes the legal field from the outside and is inclined to perceive in legal practices merely strategic power games; again, similarities with the Critic's narrative, introduced in Chapter 1, are clear. From the external perspective, normative arguments concerning the law's systematisation are conceived as strategically-motivated moves in these games. By contrast, the internal, participant's perspective on legal discourse presupposes an assessment of the validity of arguments. Now, danger threatens from another direction. The participants easily close their eyes in face of the strategic aspects of legal practices, including their own. Without the sobering effect of sociological insights, the participants are prone to see in associations and journals propounding new fields of law merely new fora for legal discourse, new opportunities for legal argumentation. They certainly do fulfil this function, too, but the clinical gaze of an outside observer may reveal aspects of legal practices that tend to remain hidden to active players in the field.

From a Comprehensive System to Local Coherence

The law's division into specific branches – and the corresponding differentiation of legal science – has served the unity of the law in two ways. Firstly, it has provided the context for elaborating general doctrines, which have been essential for the law's substantive coherence. But, secondly, in addition to the internal coherence of the diverse branches of law, legal divisions, such as those included in the diagram on page 000, have aimed at systematisation covering the legal order as a whole.

In normative debates on the law's divisions, both negative and positive arguments are put forward. Negative arguments are introduced as a criticism of traditional divisions, at times even to warrant renouncing the very aim of comprehensive systematisation. Negative arguments may point to legal anomalies: to legal problems that do not allow for their compartmentalisation within the traditional divisions. General legal concepts provide the fields of law with their identity, but they also separate these fields from each other. Therefore, in certain situations, they may pose obstacles to identifying and defining legal problems rather than accomplishing their heuristic function. Police officers' right to self-defence provides a Continental example of a legal issue situated in the grey zone between established fields of law: it is related to the criminal-law doctrine of general grounds of justification and excuse, to the administrative-law doctrine of competence, as well as to the constitutional-law doctrine of limitations to basic rights (Tuori 2004a). One response to the alleged heuristic deficiency of traditional divisions has been a call for *problem-centred legal dogmatics*. Thus, to take a Finnish example, the study of Anna Mäki-Petäjä-Leinonen (2003) on the legal status of mental patients moves in and between many branches of the traditional divisions: constitutional law, administrative law, criminal law, the law of obligations, family law, and the law of inheritance.

The debate on the jack-in-the-box effect of EU law has also proffered arguments for criticism of traditional divisions. According to Thomas Wilhelmsson's analysis, in cases pending in domestic courts, EU law behaves like a jack-in-the-box, popping up unexpectedly and causing continuous surprises. These have their background in EU law's not complying with the legal divisions to which we are accustomed in the context of domestic law. Consequently, the effects of EU law are not filtered through and tempered by general doctrines premised on these divisions (Wilhelmsson 1997; Tuori 2002a, pp. 205–209). But nor does EU law constitute a new department of law which could simply be added to the traditional table. It constitutes a distinct legal order, which confronts the domestic legal order in individual cases in national courts. This encounter does not always transpire without problems, and problems are often due to the very fact that EU law cannot be relegated to the compartments into which domestic normative material is grouped.

If negative arguments question existing divisions or the classifying project as a whole, positive arguments prop up proposals for reforming the system and introducing new fields of law. Proponents try to prove that a certain set of norms, delimited through its social object of regulation, is unified by particular legal concepts, principles and theories and, thus, is worthy of the status of a relatively independent field of law. As I have already pointed out, recent interventions have not usually been concerned with systematisation covering the whole legal order. No longer at issue is the unity of the entire legal order, its *total coherence*, but, in so far as coherence in general remains a relevant goal, merely *local coherence*.

It may even be argued that the local coherence sought in contemporary debates stands in contradiction with the aspiration for total coherence. The putative new branches of law typically combine normative material which, within the traditional divisions, would fall into several compartments. Labour law was one of the first new fields to shake up the traditional system and to bring its battle for independence to a successful conclusion. As has repeatedly been noted, labour law includes elements of both a private- and public-law nature. In Finland, the prevailing view has been to locate labour law in private law, stressing, however, that labour law possesses public-law traits as well. In environmental law, too, both private- and public-law features have been detected. In one account (Määttä 2000, p. 334), environmental law has emerged and developed through the addition of particular environmental considerations to property-law and administrative-law approaches. In Finland, private-law traits have been considered dominant, and at the Helsinki Law Faculty, environmental law, like labour law, belongs to the department of private law. A Bourdieuan sociologist – or, why not, a legal analyst following the Critic's programme – would probably see this as a manifestation of the power score between the teams of private and public law.

In Björne's diagram, labour law and environmental law were treated as sub-fields of economic law. If the power relations between private and public law had turned out differently, new bodies of law could have found a convenient place on the public law side, too: in special administrative law. As argued above, economic law and special administrative law shook the premises of the system, but they also made continuity possible. The traditional divisions were meant to classify the legal order of the sovereign nation state, although they in part relied on the legal tradition predating the rise of nation states. The welfare state has been a political project of the nation state, and the regulations Björne included in economic law and special administrative law were still attached to the monocentric perspective of the nation-state legislator. Present pretenders to the status of an independent field of law throw a more profound challenge to the traditional system. They are no longer tied to the nation-state legislator but attest to the polycentrism of legal sources and the pluralism of legal orders, perhaps even legal systems. They also blur the sharp boundary between legal and other social norms which, in Weber's view, was indispensable for the law's formal rationality. Environmental law, medical and bio-law, information law, or sports law introduce breaches into the system based on the fundamental distinction between private and public law and gather together norms which, in traditional divisions, are dispersed across several fields. But this is not all. Besides norms issued by the domestic legislator, they include EU norms, as well as other norms of international or transnational origin. Thus, the fragmentation of international law into relatively independent normative and institutional regimes (see Chapter 9) also forms part of the backdrop to proposals for new divisions. Finally, *soft law* material, such as recommendations or codes of good practice adopted by international and national organisations, also plays an important role in the self-conception of would-be new branches of law.

The law's comprehensive systematisation through its division into distinct fields has apparently lost its previous significance in presenting the law's unity. The all-inclusive substantive–classificatory system already seems to belong to legal history. Recent proposals for new fields and their general doctrines have pursued the more modest aim of local coherence. Instead of serving the law's overall unity, the new fields appear to pose a threat to it: they cannot be unequivocally inserted into the traditional system, and they renounce its nation-state premises. But do the law's internal divisions still possess any significance for local coherence, either? And, furthermore, is locally-defined coherence in general a desirable or attainable quality of the legal order?

In face of increasing legal fragmentation and pluralism, we may ask whether the law's comprehensive unity is conceivable at all. It may be recalled that Niklas Luhmann (2004, pp. 54ff.) distinguishes between two types of legal theories. *Legal dogmatic* theories more or less correspond to what I have called general doctrines and serve, in Luhmann's account, the consistency of adjudication. *Reflexion theories*, in turn, purport to portray the law as a unity from the internal perspective of the legal system. Luhmann related the function of reflexion theories not so much to the law's consistency but more to maintenance of its identity. Reflexion theories are self-descriptions of the system; in and through them the legal system reflects on itself and its identity. The law's partitioning into different branches has provided the framework for general doctrines and legal dogmatic theories as their integral element. But, furthermore, it has also proffered a way for presenting the law as a unity.

However, it has not been the only manner of conceiving modern law's unity. We are already familiar with some other reflexion theories embraced in nineteenth-century debates: Savigny's depiction of the law as an organic whole of legal institutions whose unity derived from the organic character of factual social relations and the *Volksgeist* permeating these; and the founding of positive law's unity on supra-positive conceptual premises, an approach shared by both German *Begriffsjurisprudenz* and Anglo-American disciples of John Austin.

In the twentieth-century debates, two main variants of reflexion theories can be discerned. The first of these is legal positivism, as propounded by Kelsen and Hart, which construes the law's unity on a hierarchically-structured continuity of legal validity. Valid legal norms are conceived of as a hierarchical *Stufenbau* where lower norms derive their validity from higher ones, until the level of the (historically first) constitution is reached. Kelsen crowned his hierarchical normative system with the hypothetical, presumed basic norm and Hart with a rule of recognition, a rule in the sense of both an empirical fact and an obliging norm.

In Dworkin's and Habermas' alternative, the focus is on the law's substantive, principle-based coherence. Dworkin (1986) argues that the principle of integrity obliges judges to adopt a constructive method of interpretation; to construe the law as a coherent set of principles that provide the best possible justification for past legal-institutional decisions. In Habermas' reconstruction, in turn, modern law's coherence derives from certain fundamental normative principles, such as those related to human rights and the democratic *Rechtsstaat* (Habermas 1996).

The legal instrumentalism of the welfare state questioned the possibility of systematising the law through comprehensive and unequivocal substantive–classificatory divisions. The law's increasing fragmentation at national, transnational and international levels, so typical of our contemporary late modern legal experience, has but augmented obstacles to an all-inclusive systematisation. Loosening of the law's ties to the nation state has eroded the foundations of both the Savigny-like manner of anchoring the law's unity in nation-state society and culture, and the Kelsenian norm hierarchy, following the institutional-organisational structure of the nation state. Late modern historicist consciousness does not allow for supporting the law's unity on transcendental, time- and place-independent conceptual or normative premises, either. The only remaining alternative appears to be a loose or 'thin' substantive coherence where unifying principles are both historicised and detached from their ties to the nation state and national (legal) culture. But, it may be asked, has late modern fragmentation destroyed the socio-cultural presuppositions for this alternative, too? I will suspend pondering this issue for the moment and return to it in the final chapter.

Why Coherence?

Why should we require coherence of the law? We can approach this question, first, from the perspective of legal argumentation – justification of legal speech acts. Coherence is a basic presupposition of the rationality of argumentation. The requirement of coherence concerns arguments sustaining both factual claims and normative standpoints, and, thus, is relevant for both theoretical and practical discourses. A factual claim or a normative standpoint has not been rationally vindicated if the grounds warranting it do not match up. At issue is not only logical non-contradictoriness (consistency) but what can – in somewhat looser terms – be called internal harmony or, simply, making sense (MacCormick 2005, pp. 189ff.).

In judicial proceedings, justification of a ruling requires coherence of the arguments supporting both the normative and the factual premise. With regard to the factual premise, the requirement can be specified as that of *narrative coherence*. The course of events, as the court reconstructs it from the evidence presented, must be internally coherent with respect to both causal links and the actors' motives. In turn, the normative premise must meet the demand for *normative coherence*. Klaus Günther (1989) has argued for this demand by analysing situations where prima facie applicable norms point to contradictory conclusions. The contradictions must be resolved so that none of the prima facie applicable norms lose their validity. Therefore, justification of the decision norm presupposes mutually coherent interpretation of all relevant norms. Through their justification, these norms and their interpretations are connected to other norms that are not directly relevant to the case at hand. Hence, the demand for coherence extends to a wider set of norms than just those of immediate pertinence.

Günther examines normative coherence as a presupposition for the rationality of individual legal decisions. But normative coherence can, and should, be approached from a wider perspective, too. The courts' decision-making is subject to the requirement of *formal justice* (formal equality): to the requirement of treating like cases alike and unlike cases unalike. Formal justice defined through formal equality is intimately linked with the principles of *legal certainty* and *predictability*: these are guaranteed by treating like cases alike.

How does a body of legal norms attain coherence? Legal norms are coherent if they give expression to the same general principle or to a set of matching principles. To relate to the idea of the law's multi-layered nature, surface-level legal norms acquire their coherence from general legal principles located at the law's sub-surface, cultural levels. Formal justice presupposes that norms applied in individual cases can be conceived as manifestations of more extensive legal principles and that these principles make up a coherent normative whole. The law's coherence is largely a product of the co-operative efforts of courts and legal scholars. Legal scholarship's task is to create prima facie coherence and, in this fashion, to assist the courts to meet the specific demand for the coherence of adjudication. Legal scholarship accomplishes its task, above all, by elaborating general doctrines of the various branches of law. The law's division into distinct branches is obviously not needed in presenting the unity of the law as a whole. But it is still needed as a framework for general doctrines creating local coherence.

In Weber's view, the law's formal rationality guarantees legal certainty and predictability, which are functional prerequisites for a market economy and bureaucratic administration. But legal certainty and predictability can be detached from an external, sociological analysis and included in the normative fundamentals of modern law. But, of course, they have to be set in the context of other, perhaps even contending principles. Formal justice has its counter-principle: substantive, case-by-case justice, or fairness, as it may also be called. Indeed, hard cases are often enough hard precisely because of the necessity to weigh against each other formal and substantive considerations, legal certainty and fairness, formal and substantive justice.

Legal science, in particular doctrinal research (legal dogmatics), plays an important role in generating the coherence indispensable to formal justice. It may be that in recent literature dealing with the tasks of legal dogmatics, this aspect has sometimes received too much emphasis. One might even talk of a return to what in American debates is called the classical age. As a counterbalance, the other important normative premise of adjudication should also be given its due:

fairness or substantive justice, which presupposes sensitivity to the specific traits of individual cases. Legal scholarship still has an important task in ensuring legal certainty and predictability. However, its instruments should also facilitate attention to the particular features of each case, and leave due space for fairness and substantive justice. This has been the message in interventions which have called for creativity in legal problem-solving and flexibility in the doctrinal means serving this creativity.

In contemporary Continental doctrinal research, the purpose of legal systematisation has altered: the objective is no longer a substantive–classificatory system of norms but a looser, principle-based coherence. Theoretical legal dogmatics, summarising the normative premises of a particular field of law, organises the relevant legal principles in order of preference, but this order is merely of a prima facie nature. As has been repeatedly stressed in recent legal-theoretical debates, the respective weight of principles must be defined separately in each hard case, in light of its singular features; in such a weighing, general principles are converted from legal-cultural principles into surface-level norms, constituting the basis for construction of the norm applied in the decision; the *decision norm*, which functions as the major premise of the adjudicative syllogism. Thus, principle-oriented legal doctrines are able to contribute to the local coherence that formal justice presupposes while also allowing for the susceptibility to the specific traits of the case that substantive justice requires.

Predictability and legal certainty cannot be attained without a certain unity in legal culture. Lawyers must speak a common legal language and use legal concepts in a shared sense in order to understand each other and in order for legal discourse to be possible at all. But this is not all: owing to their common legal culture, lawyers define and locate legal problems in an approximately identical manner and hold an approximately similar conception of the normative and argumentative material relevant for resolving these problems. In a stable legal culture, a significant part, probably the majority, of cases are routine cases; and they are routine cases because lawyers, on the basis of their common professional pre-understanding, agree on both the definitions of and the solutions to legal problems. Routine cases hold a key position with regard to legal certainty and predictability: if all cases were hard cases, legal certainty would be under great pressure. But the other extreme is to be avoided as well: if all cases were conceived of as routine cases, creative problem-solving would be squeezed out and the space needed by fairness and substantive justice sealed.

Legal certainty and predictability do not require comprehensive systematisation where all the norms of the legal order would occupy an unequivocal place or where elements would be connected by 'deductive' relations. By contrast, local, principle-based coherence, supported by heuristically-functioning concepts, is still a pertinent goal for legal scholarship. Proposals for new fields of law and their general doctrines volunteer for the service of this goal. When discussing such proposals, we should also discuss the criteria by which we delimit the bodies of law within which new general doctrines should bring about local coherence. If the central argument for coherence relates to the rationality and formal justice of adjudication, we should evidently start by grouping together typical situations of norm application. The demand for coherence is particularly pertinent with regard to norms that appear to be prima facie applicable in the same cases. The problems to which a legal solution is sought in courts arise in society external to the legal system. The legal system does not engender these problems; it only reformulates them in the language of the law. The influence of typical situations of application on the classification of legal norms constitutes one perspective on the relationship between social development and the systematisation of law.

General doctrines, specific to distinct fields of law, are an indispensable instrument for ensuring the local coherence that formal justice requires. But we should be aware of the constant danger that the conception of society, implicit in these doctrines, does not keep up with extra-legal social and technological development; that these doctrines are no longer capable of carrying out their heuristic task in legal problem-solving; and that the legal system no longer possesses language through which it could turn social problems into legal issues and, thus, enable their legal treatment. This danger can only be averted by ongoing debates on general doctrines that proposals for new fields of law also serve to keep alive.

So, contemporary debates aim merely at local and not at total coherence. Legal norms can be classified on divergent grounds, and fields of law may be overlapping and superimposed; the same sets of norms can be included in several fields formed by different criteria. It is typical of new fields of law that they comprise norms which, in traditional systematisation, may be dispersed into different departments. This was already the case with economic law (special private law), which was in breach with the basic distinction between private and public law. But the emergence of new, 'horizontal' fields does not necessarily transform the traditional system into legal history. Systematisation may follow different criteria and carry out diverse tasks in the legal system; the traditional system, too, may still respond to vital needs in, say, legal education.

The Possibility of Coherence

Coherence is still a normatively justified goal, not only in adjudication, but in legal science, too. But is it, in our late modern era, a realistic goal? According to Weber, the law's systematic nature relies on its autonomy: its independence from other social norm systems, such as morals and ethics, as well as from political considerations of expediency. He feared that if moral, ethical or political standpoints invade the law and shake its autonomy, the law loses its systematic character and its formal rationality (Weber 1978, p. 657).

Many subsequent observers of legal development have shared Weber's conception of the legal order's diversification which is fatal to its internal system. One line of argument stresses the law's growing instrumentalisation: the law is increasingly employed in the service of specific policy purposes. As these purposes vary and as legal regulations have been issued at different times and at different political conjunctures, it is futile to search for coherence in law. Legal scholarship as a scientific practice should bow to the inevitable pluralism of policy considerations and renounce the goal of even local coherence.

This argument for non-attainability of coherence can be challenged by a Dworkinian counterargument, premised on the distinction between *principles* and *policies*. Legal norms not only execute policies: goals and programmes concerning the desired state of society. Policies are countered by principles, which, instead of political goals, connect to morals and justify individual rights. Loose local coherence, pursued through the general doctrines of specific fields of law, does not resort to policies but to principles, and the variety, even contradictoriness, of policy considerations does not suffice to prove the implausibility of coherence.

The weight of this counterargument presupposes that Dworkin's principles can in general be separated from policies. Indeed, not all contemporary discussants consider this possible. In the Critic's view, principles are reducible to policies; and even the very distinction between principles and policies is policy-based. The Critic shares the view of Richard Posner, a leading figure of the Law and Economics school, of principles as rhetorically embellished policies (Posner 2007). An integral part of the Critic's criticism of Dworkin is a criticism of the 'rhetoric of rights'; underlying this rhetoric, too, the Critic detects utilitarian policy considerations. Let us try to assess the Critic's arguments.

Firstly, the Critic may resort to an argument familiar from debates in political philosophy between the communitarians and the liberals: the collective good enjoys primacy over individual rights. Correspondingly, Dworkin's principles are in fact grounded in policies. Thus, freedom of expression is based on a certain collective good; it purports 'to support the collective system of political decision-making and public information that prevails in society' (Koskenniemi 1999b, p. 105). I am inclined to accept this argument, but only in part. Basic rights and their underpinning principles are culturally possible only in a society whose strong values involve respect for these principles. But this is not the same as to say that Dworkin's principles can be reduced to policies. The *strong values*, as analysed by Charles Taylor (1985), do not equal the utilitarian, interest-based goals to which the Critic – and, clearly, Dworkin too – alludes with the notion of policy.

According to another argument, the vocabulary of basic rights and principles is merely a rhetorical choice by which judges or scholars pursue specific strategic policy goals; at issue is a politics of description, a strategically determined reorganisation of the normative field. The Critic cherishes the example of EC law's basic-rights dimension, suddenly 'found' by the European Court of Justice. With its basic-rights rhetoric, the court attempted to meet the challenge posed by the constitutional courts of some Member States and to safeguard its monopoly on the interpretation of EC law (Koskenniemi 1999b, pp. 106–107). Here, too, the Critic focuses on the perlocutionary aspect of legal speech acts: their strategic aims and extra-discursive consequences. Legal speech acts do possess this dimension and therefore can be examined from the perspective of a strategic power game between legal actors. Nevertheless, this does not impede us from taking seriously the substantive validity claims of speech acts: arguments invoking basic rights or other principles can be assessed independently from their conceivable perlocutionary policy goals. The same holds for legal scholars' proposals for coherence-creating general doctrines, involving a prima facie ordering of principles. In order to prove principles' subjugation to policies, it is not enough to show that the relationship between principles and counter-principles can be assessed in different ways and that scholarly debates can be approached as a strategic contest over the power of juri-diction: the power of stating the law. The Critic treats normative coherence as a variant of narrative coherence where the course of the narrative is determined by the chosen premise: by the principles that are allowed to bring about coherence in the legal order. But even here a policy analysis from a perlocutionary perspective does not cancel out an examination of principle arguments with regard to their illocutionary validity claims.

The Critic is also prone to refer to frequent conflicts between principles and counter-principles, and the necessity of weighing and balancing them. In the Critic's view, weighing and balancing is inevitably influenced by judges' policy-based choices. Furthermore, the Critic may note that its controllability cannot be enhanced by adopting the Dworkinian distinction between principles (in the narrow sense of the term) and policies and by letting the former triumph over the latter, in adherence to Dworkin's taking-rights-seriously thesis. What is to be considered a principle and what a policy is by no means self-evident; this is a matter of interpretation – so the Critic argues – and hinges on a policy-based choice.

A corresponding argument may be put forward in connection with limitation clauses (saving clauses), included in both international human-rights treaties and constitutional provisions on basic rights. Thus, the European Convention on Human Rights allows for limitations to other than so-called absolute rights on certain 'acceptable' grounds and adhering to the demands for necessity and proportionality (see below, pp. 191–192). Balancing between a human or basic right and the ground for its limitation is akin to determining the respective weight of a principle and a counter-principle in an individual case (Kennedy 1997, pp. 316ff.; Koskenniemi 1999b, pp. 107–111).

Again, I am ready to concede the partial validity of the Critic's argument: in spite of the efforts of legal theorists such as Robert Alexy (Alexy 2002a, 2002b), a *decisionist residue* seems inevitably to afflict the case-by-case weighing and balancing of principles. Nonetheless, again the Critic's argument one-sidedly privileges the perlocutionary aspect of legal speech acts and detaches them from the continuity of legal discourse. What I have termed the decisionist residue is controlled by subsequent legal speech acts, by subsequent legal discourse, where the validity claims of a judge's speech act are appraised. Furthermore, the argument emphasising the necessity of weighing and balancing leaves aside essential aspects in the functioning of legal principles. In adjudication, principles operate not only as discursively-formulated norms, as decision principles which have to be balanced with counter-principles in hard cases; they also function as general legal-cultural principles through the tacit pre-understanding of legal actors (see Chapter 6). Arguably, it is this very aspect that is most crucial in the way basic-rights principles, for instance, generate coherence in the legal order and restrict the influence of policy considerations. Such tacit knowledge is involved, say, when judges use general legal principles to interpret a policy-oriented statute.

When expressing doubts about the attainability of even local coherence, Wilhelmsson (2004) alludes to the diversity of the law's policy goals. However, for him an even more significant argument appears to be the *ethical fragmentation* permeating late modern culture; in his view, this fragmentation makes principle-based coherence not just undesirable, but even unachievable. If the policy argument can be fenced off with the Dworkinian distinction, is not this subsequent move by Wilhelmsson fatal, does it not hit the very dimension of (Dworkinian) principles?

Value pluralism, ethical fragmentation, is not a phenomenon engendered only by late modernity; it has accompanied modern culture ever since the break-up of the unitary medieval worldview in early modern Europe under the impact of voyages of discovery and wars of religion. It is a challenge which modern law has had to confront in defining its legitimacy foundation: from whence can the law draw its legitimacy when recourse can no longer be had to a unitary value basis, systematised in, for instance, late medieval Thomist natural-law doctrine?

I have discussed this question elsewhere (Tuori 2002a, pp. 243ff.), so that no need arises to reiterate my argument here. What is more important to underline in this context is that in analysing the law's underpinning principles, one should take seriously not only the distinction between principles and policies but also another division within the scope of practical reason: that between ethics and morals. *Ethics* is about strong values, conceptions of the good life, as well as personal and collective identity definitions; in ethics, questions are posed from the perspective of an I or a We. In *moral* disputes, equal attention must be paid to the standpoints of all concerned. Moral norms and judgements address real or potential conflicts in everyday human life; at issue is not what kind of life we wish to live and how we define our central values and identity, but how we should live together with other human beings who do not necessarily share our conceptions of the good life (Habermas 1989b and 1991).

Wilhelmsson is certainly right in arguing that the development of modern society has further reinforced ethical fragmentation – the differentiation of identity-defining values and conceptions of the good – which already began with the disintegration of medieval unitary culture. But it is imperative to note that in the distinction between ethics and morals, it is primarily the sphere of ethics that is affected. It may be that in the sphere of moral conceptions and norms, development has taken another path. It may be that instead of fragmentation, agreement on basic moral norms has actually expanded. Consensus, reached at the national and international level, has been codified in constitutional basic-rights provisions and international human-rights treaties, where fundamental moral norms have been translated into the language of the law. But expanded consensus has been accompanied by transformation of moral norms into increasingly abstract and general principles, as a result, emphasis in moral problems has shifted from justifiability of norms to their context-sensitive application. This is how Habermas, for example, interprets development of post-conventional morality (Habermas 1996, pp. 113–118).

Basic and human rights, as well as related general legal principles of particular fields of law, are not so much focused on defining individual or collective values as on resolving conflicts between individuals or groups. This also holds good for such basic and human rights as freedom of religion and conscience or freedom of expression. These rights do not purport to define identity-creating values from, as it were, above but to enable autonomous individual and collective choices. It behoves the normative premises of modern law to recede from the sphere of ethics, thus leaving ethics open for individual and collective value definitions. The task of the law only begins when divergent value orientations cause controversies between individuals or groups. But then we have already left the ethical I- or We-perspective behind us and entered the domain of moral reason.

I have identified reductionism as the fundamental problem in the Critic's narrative. Denial of the distinction between principles and policies is a further manifestation of this reductionism. Once again, the Critic endeavours to dissolve the tension between the law's *ratio* and *voluntas* by reducing the former to the latter. The Critic recognises only one aspect of practical reason: instrumental reason allied with *voluntas*. In the axiological dimension of values and goals, the Critic detects merely the utilitarian, interest-based purposes which instrumentalistically-abridged practical reason is made to serve. Identity-creating strong values, immune to strategically-determined compromise formation, fall outside the Critic's critical gaze. For the Critic, the very distinction between morals and ethics is a strategic choice, governed by instrumental reason.

On one fundamental issue I agree with the Critic: coherence is a perspective-dependent quality. The demand for coherence assumes a different shape from the perspectives of the judge or the scholar. From the viewpoint of the legislator, in turn, the policy goals of the legislative project at stake easily gain priority over coherence. We can generalise: the internal, participant's point of view lays emphasis on coherence, presupposed by such fundamental normative principles as formal justice and equality, and predictability. By contrast, the external perspective emphasises policy goals and the law's fragmentation. The Critic adopts the latter perspective, explores legal discourse from the standpoint of its perlocutionary dimension, stresses the instrumentalist aspect of practical reason, and ends up by subjecting principles to policies.

One further pluralist argument remains which may be advanced to question the very attainability of coherence. Traditional systematisation, introducing the discussion in this chapter, has assumed the monocentric perspective of the nation-state legislator. It cannot capture the polycentricity of legal sources and the pluralism of legal orders and systems colouring our contemporary legal scene. The normative material from which legal decision norms are constructed may derive from diverse sources, so that it can no longer be organised through a doctrine of legal sources premised on the sovereignty of the nation-state legislator. I shall discuss the tendencies of legal polycentricity and pluralism in the concluding chapter; for now, I will confine myself to some tentative remarks on the current significance of the law's divisions.

The sheer variety of legal sources and legal orders eliminates the prospect of total coherence, the possibility of arranging legal normative material into a comprehensive substantive–classificatory system. Thus, as has often been noted, EU law defies such traditional basic distinctions as private and public law or municipal and international law. By contrast, this variety does not necessarily constitute an obstacle to local coherence, generated by general doctrines of the diverse fields of law. Indeed, proposals for new fields and new general doctrines attempt to produce local coherence in a conjuncture coloured by significant transformations in the law's spatiality and temporality: the pluralism of legal sources and legal orders, as well as acceleration of the law's pace, affecting even the level of legal culture.

Chapter 6
Concepts, Principles and Theories

General Doctrines in the Functioning of the Legal System

At present, the main significance of the law's divisions lies in providing the context for doctrinal development. The diverse branches of the law gain their identity from their general doctrines rather than from surface-level normative material. Thus, in Continental Europe, starting from the latter half of the nineteenth century, administrative law constituted itself by constructing its specific doctrines. And in the present debates, candidates for new fields of law attempt to warrant their claims through their doctrinal maturity.

What I call general doctrines are composed of general legal *concepts* and *principles*, as well as legal *theories* as combinations of concepts and principles. For example, the general concepts of German-oriented administrative law include 'administrative act' (*Verwaltungsakt*) and 'competence', while its general principles include proportionality and protection of legitimate expectations. In criminal law, we can point to general concepts of, say, crime and punishment and the general principle of legality (*nulla poena sine lege*). The professional legal culture of lawyers involves methodological elements, too, such as *patterns of argumentation*, typical of the branch of law in question, and *the doctrine of legal sources*, which can also display branch-specific particularities. However, these essential aspects of legal culture remain beyond the scope of the following discussion of general legal doctrines.

General doctrines lie at the heart of professional legal culture through which lawyers approach the law and legal problems. Here, general doctrines fulfil their *heuristic* task. Future legal actors internalise the basics of the prevailing legal culture during their university studies. The main objective of university education is not to inculcate into students as much discursive knowledge of surface-level legal material as possible but, rather, to familiarise them with the conceptual, normative and methodological elements of professional legal culture. This is the *pedagogical* task of general doctrines.

In everyday legal practices, general doctrines function mainly through legal actors' tacit knowledge. Judges apply the principle of *nulla poena sine lege* in every criminal case, although they do not generally mention it in their rulings or even have it in mind during decision-making. Only in hard cases is their attention turned to the relevance and exact bearing of principles or other elements of general doctrines. But decisions in hard cases, as well as scholarly proposals for doctrinal reform, intimate that the law's cultural layers can, if needed, be subjected to conscious assessment and elaboration. We are only able to reconstruct legal culture from its traces in surface-level material, such as rulings of courts and writings of legal scholars. And as is the case with the law's sub-surface layers in general, doctrinal elements are inserted into the prevailing legal culture as a result of a process of *sedimentation* originating from the surface level. Legal-cultural renewal always starts from single insights of legal scholars, judges, or even legislators. But not all heterodoxies introduced at the law's surface level launch a successful sedimentation. The law's history is written in the victors' terms; lost causes are legion.

The legislator is capricious, and the law's positivity poses a constant threat to law's systematicity. Instrumental reason in the service of the legislator's *voluntas* is inclined to ignore considerations of coherence exceeding the legislative project at hand. However, as I argued in the previous chapter, coherence is of continuing significance to positivised law, too, owing to the pertinence of such fundamental normative principles as formal justice and equality, legal certainty, and predictability. But coherence is a fragile quality which must be continuously generated anew. Due to the typically policy-oriented perspective of the legislator, this task falls primarily to legal scholars and judges.

Different strands in legal scholarship have held different views of the respective weight of legal concepts and principles, as well as of their division of labour in, for instance, the systematisation of the law. German *Begriffsjurisprudenz* relied on legal concepts in systematising both private and public law, and analytical legal scholars have shared this focus on the conceptual side of general doctrines. Thus, for Carlos Alchourròn and Eugenio Bulygin (1971), two renowned analysts, legal systematisation equals the conceptual re-ordering of legal material. The common-law mindset has traditionally laid more stress on principles than concepts, although the common-law world has also experienced the specific American classical-age version of conceptualism and the analytical strand from John Austin to Wesley Newcomb Hohfeld. In recent decades, the emphasis has clearly shifted from concepts to principles within the Romano-Germanic legal-cultural area, too. The law's unity is increasingly conceived of as principle-based coherence. This is clearly connected to the elevated status of basic rights and their extension to private (horizontal) relationships.

I will start my discussion of general doctrines from concepts and proceed through principles to legal theories.

Legal Concepts in the Language of Law

Legal discourse consists of the speech acts of diverse legal actors, working within different legal practices. This discourse, cutting across the boundaries of legal practices, is only possible because of legal actors' shared legal culture. A central element of this professional culture consists of a particular legal language.

In Niklas Luhmann's sociological *Fremdbeschreibung* of the legal system, legal communication is demarcated from other social communication through its particular code of law and non-law (*Recht*/*Unrecht*). In what follows, I understand legal language as more richly determined than merely as such a binary code. Legal language relies on ordinary language, but the expressions of ordinary language may be given a specific legal sense – examples are provided by 'contract' and 'intent' – and it may also include expressions unknown to ordinary language – such as 'collateral security'. Participation in legal discourse requires mastery of both its vocabulary and grammar; they both belong to the common cultural reservoir facilitating lawyers' communication with each other.

Legal concepts function as the law's vocabulary. In conceptual analysis, a distinction should be drawn between the *term* (the expression) and its *conceptual meaning*. Thus, it is possible that the conceptual meaning changes while the term remains the same; that the term 'contract', for instance, comes to mean different things than before. Indeed, the law's conceptual transformation largely consists of redefining legal terms, such as 'contract' or 'property' or 'right'. It is also possible that the conceptual meaning remains the same but the term changes. The terminological transformation from 'poor relief' to 'social aid' has not necessarily affected the conceptual content.

Everyday social intercourse is facilitated by the fact that people who speak the same language attribute to the same expressions an approximately similar meaning, so that in the everyday pragmatics of language the expression and its meaning go together. This is the case in legal language, too: participants in legal discourse assign to legal terms approximately the same conceptual content. When a lawyer speaks of *res judicata*, other lawyers recognise what kind of legal phenomenon she is referring to, due to their common legal-cultural pre-understanding. Legal concepts as the law's vocabulary can only accomplish their discourse-enabling function because in lawyers' cultural pre-understanding, legal terms are associated with particular conceptual content. The term and its conceptual meaning are only detached from each other when a concept is subjected to reflexive assessment, when, for instance, an analytically-oriented legal scholar critically appraises her conceptualist predecessors' concept of property.

Language is an instrument of both inclusion and exclusion; it not only unites but also separates. It creates the basis for communication between those fluent in it, but, by the same token, it generates misunderstandings and communication gaps between speakers and non-speakers. All this holds for legal language, too. In legal discourse, social problems are translated into the language of law. When expressed through legal concepts, the problems of people's everyday life, related to, say, child custody or neighbour relations, easily escape beyond their recognition and control. Some legal sociologists have talked here of the lawyers' dispossessing laymen of their problems (Christie 1977).

Observers adopting an external perspective on legal discourse are especially attentive to the exclusionary effects of legal language. Sociologists may consider legal language a means in legal professionals' 'strategy of distinction', their turf-guarding and self-enhancement. Various versions of the Critic's narrative have also connected the exclusionary effects of the law's language to lawyers' particularistic, guild-like interests. Back at the end of the eighteenth and the beginning of the nineteenth century, Bentham linked the artificial, cryptic language of common law to *Judge&Co*'s sinister goals, 'the extracting, on joint account, and for joint benefit, out of the pockets of the people, in the largest quantity possible, the produce of the industry of the people' (see above, pp. 30–31).

We usually only realise the significance of language when communication misfires; that is, when we do not find a common language with our interlocutor. In legal discourse, too, the necessity of common language is revealed when communication within or between legal practices does not work. For example, this may occur when the legislator uses terminology which does not belong to the established legal vocabulary. Legal regulations may resort to social-scientific terms with no specified legal meaning, or EU directives may be implemented in a Member State as translations diverging from the conventions of national legal language. The consequence may be that courts and administrative authorities do not grasp the message the legislator has tried to convey.

Communication also fails when judges and law-drafters reject a legal scholar's proposal for conceptual renewal. The failure may, though, be only temporary. In the long run, the proposal may trigger off a successful process of sedimentation which, over time, will reform the law's language and knit new legal-cultural ties between terms and their conceptual content. The contest between diverse legal scientific schools over the power to state the law involves a contest over the law's language. Carl Schmitt was acutely aware of this: '*Caesar dominus et supra grammaticam*: The emperor is also the master of the grammar' (Schmitt 1988b, p. 179). What I have called the military science of concepts (Chapter 4), clearly manifests Schmitt's sensitivity to legal language's rhetorical and strategic dimensions.

At a certain moment, legal actors may be faced with a choice between alternative vocabularies; the conceptual field may be in a state of flux, as is the case during eras of legal-cultural ruptures or during establishment of a new legal order, such as EU (EC) law. This is an important observation for the Critic's narrative. The Critic focuses on strategic considerations governing choice. Let me again refer to the Critic's argument that adoption by the European Court of Justice of a new, basic-rights vocabulary was a strategic decision intended to prop up the court's monopoly over EC law's interpretation and ward off challenges coming from national constitutional courts (Koskenniemi 1999b, pp. 106–107).

As regards this particular example, the Critic undoubtedly hits the mark in analysis of the strategic background to speech acts of the European Court of Justice. But again, the Critic's narrative transmits but a one-sided picture of legal discourse. The range of available vocabularies is never unbounded but limited to the alternatives implicit in a legal culture. Furthermore, choice does not extend to legal vocabulary in its entirety. It is confined to those segments of a legal culture that are undergoing doctrinal crisis, which are in a state of ferment, and in which the ties between terms and their conceptual content have loosened and lost their self-evident nature. Choices are made, consciously or unconsciously, but for the most part, the prevailing legal culture remains the unquestioned, given horizon of legal practices and legal discourse. And, finally, here too the perlocutionary dimension proffers but one perspective on legal speech acts. Thus, the basic-rights decisions of the European Court of Justice can also be assessed from an illocutionary point of view, with regard to their normative credentials.

Use of language requires proficiency in use not only of its vocabulary but its *grammar*, too. If legal concepts constitute the vocabulary of legal language, how should we conceive of its grammar? Koskenniemi (2005) suggests that the grammar of international law be understood as its distinct pattern of argumentation: argumentation shuttling between the poles of apology and utopia or realism and normativism. Grammar determines what is accepted in international law as a valid argument. Grammar (*langue*) is rigid but leaves ample leeway for argumentation (*parole*). International-law discourse combines rigid formalism with substantive indeterminacy. Through their strategic choices, legal actors determine how grammar is employed and by which argumentative moves substantive indeterminacy is exploited and removed.

Along with the doctrine of legal sources, patterns of argumentation distinct to legal discourse belong to the methodical rules of the game whose mastery entitles one to play in the legal field. Koskenniemi's metaphor of grammar illuminates the role of methodical rules in the game of law. Nonetheless, in the reconstruction of legal culture's methodical aspect, his model of 'binary opposition' is not the only available alternative, nor does the idea of reconstructing legal grammar necessarily compel us to assume his strategic-perlocutionary approach to legal argumentation. Thus, recent analytically-oriented argumentation theory, represented by, for instance, Aulis Aarnio, Robert Alexy and Aleksander Peczenik (1937–2005), offers another example of an application of the *langue*/*parole* distinction. *Langue* refers to the analytical conceptual framework, *parole* to argumentation within the conceptual space opened up (and, by the same token, closed) by this framework. But argumentation theorists have moved in a different direction from Koskenniemi: they do not purport to disclose argumentation's strategic-perlocutionary aims but to invigorate its normative cogency.

Varieties of Legal Concepts

General legal concepts may have different references and they may fulfil different tasks in legal practices. With regard to their relations to facts and norms, legal concepts can be roughly grouped into three classes:

1. Concepts summarising the law's normative contents.
2. Concepts referring to interaction between legal norms and their regulatory objects.
3. Concepts relating to legal norms' regulatory objects.

(1) Examples of concepts falling within the first group include 'negligence' and 'strict liability', which refer to the normative grounds of tort liability. The concept of *res judicata*, familiar in both procedural and administrative law, pertains to the legal effects of court and administrative decisions. Such concepts, whose contents can be presented as legal norms, relegate the social regulatory object of legal norms (the factual side of adjudication) to the background.

In the constructive method of *Begriffsjurisprudenz*, the contents of legal concepts were understood as bundles of norms. This was the case with concepts of both an a priori and a posteriori character. The former consisted of the most general legal concepts – such as 'property' – which were independent of positive regulations and, in a way, preceded them. By contrast, a posteriori concepts were formed and employed in compliance with the constructive method: they were inferred from individual propositions of positive law and then – especially in cases of lacunae – used as premises for deriving new legally relevant norms which positive law did not explicitly lay down but which, nonetheless, it was held to presuppose. We are already familiar with the standard analytical criticism, according to which no new norms can (logically) be inferred from legal concepts: concepts include merely the same norms from which they were formed in the first place. One can easily concede that *Begriffsjurisprudenz*'s or, for that matter, American classical-era conceptualism's quasi-logical conceptual game with its 'inductive' and 'deductive' phases no longer convinces us after more than a century of analytical and realist criticism. Nevertheless, as I have argued in Chapter 4, if we keep in mind that the constructivists of *Begriffsjurisprudenz* conceived of the contents of legal concepts in normative terms – concepts were seen to refer to clusters of norms – we detect interesting similarities with current debates on the role of legal principles. The concepts of our first group can in fact also be approached as principles. Indeed, in German nineteenth-century legal science, the terms 'legal concept' and 'legal principle' were often used as synonyms (Haferkamp 2004, p. 255). The same seems to hold for American conceptualism, too.

(2) Concepts belonging to the second group bridge the gulf between legal normativity and social facticity. Their references consist of combinations of legal norms and social (or psychic) facts: *legal-institutional facts.* 'Marriage' refers to a synthesis of particular social relations – in Savigny's terms, factual life relationships – and legal norms regulating these relations.

(3) The concepts of the third group purport to structure the regulatory object of legal norms, while relegating the normative contents of the legal order into the background. I take my example from a Finnish treatise, Pöyhönen's *Uusi varallisuusoikeus* (*New Doctrine of Property Law*), which epitomises the post-analytical phase in Finnish legal scholarship. Characteristic of this phase is a conscious endeavour to relate general doctrines to their social context, and a shift of emphasis in the coherence-creating and argumentative task from concepts to principles. The primary role of legal concepts is seen in their heuristic function

in legal problem-solving; they are supposed to facilitate principle-oriented argumentation, attentive to the particular facts of individual cases. The central conceptual proposals of Pöyhönen's new doctrine include 'operational context', 'total arrangement', 'interested party' and 'risk position'. These concepts are based on an understanding of the process-character of contractual relations and transactions. They do not purport to classify the normative contents of property law, nor do they refer to legal institutions, to legal institutional facts. They are intended to serve in articulating factual situations calling for a legal judgement, and to assist judges and other legal actors in identifying the legally relevant features of social relationships and processes (Pöyhönen 2000).

How, then, should we locate the concepts elaborated in analytical legal scholarship? At first glance, it seems tempting to place them in the third group, in line with Pöyhönen's conceptual proposals. Let us take as our example 'employment relationship', which, in Finnish doctrine, has been considered the fundamental concept of labour law. The defining features of an employment relationship, such as the employer's direction and supervision, are extra-legal, social facts, and it appears that the concept as such does not imply anything about the legal norms applicable to the facts.

Analytically-oriented labour-law scholars considered 'employment relationship' a 'relational concept'. According to the programme of the analytical private-law school, 'relational concepts' were supposed to replace the 'substantive concepts' of *Begriffsjurisprudenz*. They can be understood as proposals for articulating social relationships regulated by law. On this reading, their references would consist not of normative but of factual phenomena. Thus, the concept of property, propounded by Simo Zitting, founder of the Finnish post-war analytical school, has been characterised by Kaarle Makkonen, another leading figure of the school, as referring to a 'multi-place social relationship', to a 'net of relationships' (see above, p. 130).

However, in the legal positivistic self-understanding of post-war analytical private-law scholarship, 'relational concepts' organised the closed normative world of the legal Ought. Indeed, we should distinguish between two levels in the analysts' conceptual apparatus: that of social relationships – Zitting's 'multi-place relationships' – and that of norms. Like their *Begriffsjurisprudenz* predecessors, the analysts aimed at a conceptual grouping of legal norms, but by different criteria. The level of social relationships laid the grounds for a new type of classification of legal norms, which, in turn, were supposed to be read from positive sources of law, primarily legislation. The 'multi-place relationships' were relationships regulated by legal norms, and, in light of this interpretation, the post-war analysts' way to an institutional theory of law would not have been long. All that would have been needed was the thematising of connections between the two conceptual levels, that of social relationships and that of norms.

To a large extent, the law's functioning is a matter of the interplay between legal normativity and social facticity. In legal concepts, the mutual weight of the factual and the normative aspect varies, but the normative side is never wholly obliterated, and legal concepts are never exclusively about facts. Arguably, the basic type of legal concepts consists of concepts connoting legal-institutional facts and, as it were, openly connecting the worlds of the Is and the Ought. Robert Alexy has called them *genuine legal concepts*; his examples include 'contract', 'administrative act' and 'self-defence'. In his account, the contents of these concepts are indicated by legal norms that determine the conclusion of a contract, the validity of an administrative act, and the justifiability of an act of self-defence. Proposals for redefining such concepts also amount to proposals for altering the respective norms, and – we can add – vice versa. When a factual state of affairs is brought under such a concept, it is thereby also included in the respective norm's scope of application (Alexy 1989, pp. 257–259).

Concepts operate at all levels of the law. Legal concepts constitute an integral part of professional culture which provides legal pre-understanding with its content. We may even talk of the law's conceptual deep culture, consisting of the most fundamental legal categories that delineate and structure the space of legal communication. Finally, legal concepts have a distinct role to play at the law's surface level, too.

We always have to infer the contents of legal culture from its surface-level imprints. No shortcut is available to legal culture, but it must be reconstructed from the traces it has left on the law's surface, such as scholarly writings articulating legal doctrine, and court decisions applying this doctrine. When speaking of surface-level concepts, I do not have in mind such legal-cultural traces but explicit conceptual definitions included, in particular, in legal enactments and usually specifying the regulation's scope of application. These definitions are the legislator's messages to the courts and the administrative authorities responsible for applying and executing enactments. They are designed to ensure that the regulatory language will be understood in the way the legislator intends and that realising the legislator's goals is not hindered by gaps in communication. Let us call these concepts *regulative-technical.*

Regulative-technical concepts and their stipulative definitions have become increasingly common. In Finland, it is at present a standard legislative technique for a law's general provisions to define the concepts it employs. For example, Art. 2 of the Finnish Communication Market Act from 2003 (393/2003) includes definitions of altogether 27 concepts employed in the Act. Long lists of conceptual definitions are typical of EU law, too, and for good reasons. Executing and applying EU law falls to Member State administrative and judicial authorities, which are accustomed to interpreting legal norms in the context of their national legislation and legal culture. But EU norms can only achieve their goals if EU-law concepts are assigned a similar meaning in all Member States, and this the EU legislator aims to secure through explicit definitions. A telling example of EU law's legislative technique is Art. 1 of the EC Regulation on Social Security (1408/71). It includes definitions of concepts such as 'employed person', 'self-employed person', 'frontier and seasonal worker', 'member of the family', 'survivor', 'stay', 'residence', 'legislation', 'competent authority' and 'insurance period'. These legal definitions not only specify the enactment's scope of application but also function as constitutive norms in creating legal-institutional facts. Within the domain of social-security regulation, family members are legal-institutional facts: constitutive facts consist of the respective persons as biological-social beings and constitutive norms of legal norms which are applied to these persons as laid down by the regulation.

The segment of the law where a concept is applied can be called its *area of relevance*. A regulatory-technical concept's area of relevance is narrow, confined usually to the enactment where it is defined. Legal-cultural concepts possess a broader area of relevance, extending to the entire branch of law in question. Finally, the area of relevance of fundamental deep-structural categories covers the whole (national) legal order, and extends even further, crossing the boundaries between territorially or functionally differentiated normative orders.

General legal concepts are inter-connected, and the meaning assigned to one concept affects the way the other concepts in the field of law are understood. In the doctrine of constitutional law, 'legislative power' and 'executive power' cannot be defined independently of each other, and the contents of both these concepts are influenced by the meaning attributed to '*Rechtsstaat*'. Legal concepts receive their meanings in a conceptual field, and, hence, should not be examined separately, severed from their conceptual connections.

Many ways exist to conceive of relationships between legal concepts. In *Begriffsjurisprudenz*, relationships might be understood in a Linnaean classificatory or in a 'deductive' sense. In the former alternative, legal phenomena constituting the concepts' references are organised into classes and sub-classes (*genus – species*), so that phenomena covered by hierarchically lower concepts constitute sub-classes of references of the higher ones. This way of conceptualising the world was typical of the *episteme* which Michel Foucault (1974) terms classic. In turn, in the latter alternative, lower-level concepts are 'deduced' from those located at the conceptual hierarchy's higher levels. Conceptual systems can also combine features of both a Linnaean classification and loosely deductive relations. For instance, this was the case with Puchta's system of private law (see above, pp. 86–87). Correspondingly, Kennedy (2006a, p. 187) has discerned two main types of concept in the conceptual apparatus of American Classical Legal Thought: operative concepts such as 'property' or 'police power', with the power of logical implication, and, at the other extreme, mere 'conventional pigeonholes'.

Arguably, the dominant view in present-day doctrinal research is to treat legal concepts as *cluster concepts*. Legal concepts constitute clusters, with their internal cross-references and inter-relationships; we could also speak of *conceptual networks*. The meaning contents of concepts belonging to the same cluster are interdependent. In traditional general doctrines of German-oriented administrative law, such concepts as 'competence', 'administrative organ' and 'administrative act' formed part of the same cluster. The concepts of Pöyhönen's new property law – 'operational context', 'total arrangement', 'interested party' and 'risk position' – also constitute an interdependent cluster.

Cluster concepts cannot be organised in the kind of deductive or classifying hierarchy which *Begriffsjurisprudenz* or its American conceptualist counterpart were aiming at. Speaking of networking of legal concepts or of their cluster-like nature may seem vague and imprecise. But such vagueness may be an advantage: reciprocal dependencies cannot be compressed into one and the same pattern. 'Networking' draws our attention to the inter-connections between concepts but allows for various ways of understanding them.

This way of portraying legal concepts rejects the deductive model which – at least in the view of critics – tainted the conceptual trees of *Begriffsjurisprudenz*. But even in our post-conceptualist era, it may be perfectly legitimate to conceive of links between legal concepts as logical relationships, too. Hohfeld's proposal for organising the concepts of 'basic legal modalities' as opposite and corollary pairs (Hohfeld 1913 and 1916) has been an important source of inspiration for twentieth-century analytical legal scholarship, not only in the United States, but even in Europe, including Finland. But such logical inter-connections are a borderline case; usually, the means of formal logic do not suffice for organising the conceptual field.

Typically, the conceptual field of a body of law is organised around a particular *focal concept*, which indicates the starting point from which the inter-relationships of the conceptual network can be unravelled. Examples of putative focal concepts include 'administrative act' in administrative law; 'crime' in criminal law; 'contract' in the law of obligations; 'property' in property law; 'employment relationship' or 'employment contract' in labour law; 'democratic *Rechtsstaat*' in constitutional law; and so on. The role of focal concepts may vary from one branch of law to another; indeed, in some branches it might be more appropriate to speak of them in the plural rather than in the singular. Such a variation is, of course, related to how tight a whole the general doctrines constitute. Doctrinal change is often manifest by a change of focal concept; this is bound to have normative consequences, too. Thus, family law's normative contents appear in a new light if its conceptual architecture is based on 'partnership' instead of 'marriage'. At some point in time, rivalry may exist for the focal role, and alternative general doctrines, built on, say, 'partnership' and 'marriage' in family law, may differ precisely in their view of the concept expected to perform this role.

Concepts in Legal Heuristics

Hermeneutical philosophy has drawn attention to the world-disclosing (*welterschliessende*) task of language. The world only appears to us through our language; our language mediates and filters our experience of the world. Language is not only a means of communication or rhetoric; it is also a means of experiencing the world. Expansion of the boundaries of our language also expands our world, and transformations of our language also transform our experience of the world (Gadamer 1993, pp. 438ff.). All this holds for legal language, too. Legal language makes the 'legal world' appear to us; we can only grasp legal phenomena through legal language. Accordingly, when our legal language changes, our legal world changes, too. Legal language not only constitutes the foundation for communication between legal actors, for legal discourse. Common language also guarantees an approximately equivalent legal experience, a shared way of identifying and conceiving of legal phenomena and problems.

Concepts perform a dual function in legal problem-solving: *heuristic* and *argumentative*. In their heuristic task, they facilitate formulation of legal questions, while in their argumentative task they provide guidance in answering these questions. Judges, practicing lawyers and legal scholars engaged in doctrinal research identify legal issues through legal concepts; an administrative lawyer may define the issue confronting her as, for instance, the *res judicata* effect of an administrative decision.

Problems which the legal system treats as legal problems have not arisen in this system. They have originated in conflicts in society outside the law, in, say, the economy or the everyday life-world. They only assume legal guise after being expressed in legal language, after being translated from ordinary language or the specialised languages of social sub-systems into the legal idiom. Such a translation is not distinctive merely to judicial proceedings but is an indispensable element of other legal practices as well. Legal dogmatics relates its interpretative standpoints to real or hypothetical social problem situations (type-situations). In turn, law-drafting is launched by the perception of a social problem, which must first be formulated in legal language before a solution can be envisioned by legislative means.

Legal concepts play a crucial role in translating social problems into legal issues. Through legal concepts, lawyers and judges take possession of problems, and formulate them in the same language in which legal norms, as the reservoir of solutions to them, have been expressed. When social issues are legally re-defined through legal concepts, they are, by the same token, localised and related to the normative solutions proffered by the law. Legal definition of the issue also demarcates the body of law where its solution will be sought. Its naming in terms of administrative law implies the claim that it is this body of law which is of primary relevance for its settlement.

Legal concepts provide the legal system with the stability needed for promoting formal equality and legal predictability. They form part of legal culture, which, with regard to the law's tumultuous surface, represents a conservative layer within the law. It stores up the law's memory, maintains the law's connection to its past, and is transformed at a rather protracted pace. Due to its slower motion, legal culture functions as a counterweight to the abruptness of surface-level alterations and generates the stability necessary for legal certainty.

We cannot pose legal questions without legal concepts which, therefore, play an indispensable enabling or constitutive role. But as concepts create heuristic possibilities, they also restrict their range. Legal heuristics involves an exclusionary aspect, too: legal concepts allow for merely certain ways of formulating legal problems. We can ask just those questions which our conceptual apparatus permits us to ask. Here, the characteristic inertia of legal culture may display its negative effects. It is not only conceivable but even probable that legal concepts do not keep up with the transformations of external society. When legal concepts lag behind social development, legal language no longer provides us with the vocabulary we need for translating social into legal problems. Disturbances in the heuristic function may be the price we have to pay for concepts' stabilising achievement.

Legal concepts possess a natural ossifying inclination. They may be cut off from their original legal and social environment, so that legal doctrine transfers them to contexts where they are unsuited for the heuristic task. No guarantees exist that the pace of law coincides with the pace of the society it regulates. If the discrepancy grows too large, the law is no longer able to react to social problems calling for a legal solution, and legal language can no longer perform its translating task. However, thanks to the reflexivity of modern legal culture, the gulf opened up between legal concepts and social development can in principle be closed off: legal concepts are susceptible to critical assessment and deliberate renewal. But conceptual adaptation takes time, and reformed concepts cannot immediately win a place in the prevailing legal culture and the pre-understanding of legal professionals. Moreover, assistance is always but of a temporary nature; the gulf between law and society is bound to open up anew. I shall use the development of Finnish legal culture as proof of this inevitable fate of conceptual reform.

Post-war analytical scholars attacked the outdatedness of previous concepts, deriving from the Golden Age of *Begriffsjurisprudenz*; their incapability of articulating legally the conflicts arising in a novel economic situation. The greatly increased economic exchange in post-war Finnish society imposed a demand for a more refined legal vocabulary, and the analytical upheaval responded to this need (Aarnio 1979, pp. 13–14). However, over time, the analytically-reformed concepts have not been spared an analogous criticism appealing to a crucially transformed economic and social environment. Post-analytical critics have alluded to welfare-state development (Wilhelmsson 1992), as well as such contemporary tendencies as ecologisation, informatisation and globalisation, which again call for conceptual renewal (Pöyhönen 2000).

Aarnio has argued that conceptual reforms that allow for new ways of posing legal questions demonstrate the progress of legal science. Analytical private-law doctrine increased legal science's problem-solving capacity, and, hence, was more advanced than the preceding conceptualism. When the unitary concept of ownership was dissolved into the proprietor's legal positions in different relations, transfer of property became conceivable as a gradual process, instead of being understood as a necessarily one-time event (Aarnio 1997, pp. 268ff.). Evidently, this is how legal heuristics works. Thomas Kuhn's idea of the anomalies of the previous scientific paradigm functioning as catalysts for change (Kuhn 1967) seems also to apply to conceptual reforms in law and legal scholarship. The need for reform arises from anomalies in prevailing doctrine; from social problems of a new type on which established concepts no longer confer a satisfactory legal formulation.

If the post-analytical critique hits the mark, analytical doctrine has been confronted with its own anomalies. It is far too early to tell which of the post-analysts' proposals, such as the concepts of Pöyhönen's new property law, will be sedimented into Finnish legal culture. What we can tell, though, is that post-analytical criticism disputes the analysts' straightforward belief in progress. A new set of concepts can be regarded as progress if it is able to show the way out of the previous doctrine's anomalies. But since these concepts, over time, will also lag behind social development and cannot avoid their own anomalies, it is more than probable that in a future change of paradigm they, too, will have to recede. The talk of linear, cumulative progress turns out to be problematic. It may well be that general doctrines do 'progress' in some respect, whereas in some other respect they display 'regression'. It may be that in focusing on the heuristic task of legal concepts, the analytical school ignored some important and still pertinent lessons which could be learned from *Begriffsjurisprudenz*. This is what I have argued in my assessment of anti-conceptualist criticism in Chapter 4.

Except for the most fundamental categories constituting the law's conceptual deep structure, legal concepts are organised in line with the law's division into distinct branches; each branch of law possesses its specific concepts, which are vital for its very identity. But because of the different temporality of the law and the society it regulates, it may well be that problems awaiting legal translation do not respect but cut across the boundaries separating branches of law. In recent decades, public administration has in all Western countries been subject to extensive privatisation. Administrative tasks have been assigned to private-law organisations, and the administrative management of society has taken recourse to private-law means, such as contracts. Traditional general doctrines of administrative law, premised on hierarchical power relations between the parties, are no longer able to catch all legally relevant problems in public administration's external or internal relationships. New concepts opening channels between public and private law are needed. 'Administrative contract' might be taken as an illustrative example of such a conceptual renewal.

Grey zones exist between established fields of law, and the corollary danger also exists of legal doctrine ignoring issues falling in such a no-man's-land. From the Continental context, I have already mentioned one such issue: police officers' right to self-defence, with its links to administrative law, criminal law and constitutional law.

Late modern social and legal development seems to shake the foundations of the traditional system by generating problems which are difficult to locate and master with concepts differentiated under established divisions of the law. In adjudication, borderlines have been blurred between different types of proceedings, and conflicts of competence between courts with different jurisdictions are ever more frequent; in Continental Europe, between, say, administrative-law courts and general courts. The privatisation of administration manifests the typical late modern expansion of market mechanisms. This development has extended the relevance of competition-law considerations: competition law traverses almost the whole legal order, including domains traditionally reserved for administrative law.

Late modern society is also coloured by internationalisation or – to use a perhaps more fitting expression – *de-nationalisation*, which displays both a European and a global dimension. It gnaws at the foundations of the law's traditional system and the conceptual apparatus differentiated along its divisions. EU law not only changes the contents of municipal legal orders. Perhaps even more important is that EU law does not succumb to classification following the divisions adopted in municipal law.

What conclusions, then, should we draw from late modern social and legal development and the legal anomalies it seems to create? Legal concepts lagging behind social development do not achieve their heuristic task but turn into 'epistemological obstacles', to use an expression coined by Gaston Bachelard (1884–1962), the French philosopher of science (Bachelard 1980). Should we wholly renounce specific legal concepts or at least give up arranging them into clusters, into general doctrines of distinct fields of law? Such conclusions are over-hasty. Legal concepts are still needed in translating social problems into legal language, nor has the role of legal concepts in creating stability and promoting formal justice and predictability lost its pertinence, either.

But what late modern social and legal development certainly requires is a re-appraisal of the law's conceptual apparatus. Legal concepts should facilitate and not obstruct contacts between departments of law. Administrative and private law have been separated by general concepts such as 'administrative act' and 'contract'; 'administrative contract' unlocks administrative law's general doctrines in the direction of private law. The ongoing debates on new fields of law – such as social law, medical and bio-law or communications law – also manifest a striving for crossing the law's traditional internal divisions and, by the same token, for combining national and transnational approaches.

We should be especially attentive to the conceptual consequences of social and legal de-nationalisation. Concepts which have been elaborated with a view to the national legal order are not directly transferable to EU law. The European Court of Justice has asserted EU law's autonomy in the conceptual respect, too. In EU law, legal terms may be assigned conceptual contents diverging from their meanings in municipal law.[1] A good example is the EU law concept of worker, which is to have a similar content in all Member States for the sake of uniform interpretation of

1 EU (EC) law's conceptual autonomy has been confirmed for instance in *CILFIT* v. *Minister of Health* (283/81, ECR 1982, p. 3415), where the Court stated that 'it must also be borne in mind, even where the different language versions are entirely in accord with one another, that community law uses terminology which is peculiar to it. Furthermore, it must be emphasized that legal concepts do not necessarily have the same meaning in community law and in the law of the various member states'. On the relations between concepts of the EU law and national law, see Lenaerts (2003).

EU law. If a certain EU law term is clearly allowed to be filled with the divergent conceptual contents given to it by Member States, room for such divergence must be explicit. Even in such cases, the Court can set limits to divergence.[2] In all other cases, the task of ultimately defining the meaning of a concept remains with the Court. It usually prefers an autonomous EU law meaning, which can differ from or be the same as its content in some or all Member States' domestic law. Furthermore, interaction between EU law and domestic law may necessitate re-assessment of national legal concepts, too.

Here my example derives from constitutional law. We are experiencing an exceptionally lively discussion – though, unfortunately, largely confined to the transnational scholarly and legal elite – on the politico-institutional and legal characteristics of the EU. This discussion has been prompted by such developments as drafting and adoption of the Charter of Fundamental Rights, enlargement of the Union, and the failed constitutional project. As many clear-sighted participants have noted, the discussion is dogged by certain conceptual difficulties and paradoxes. The legal and political concepts available to us have received their present established meanings in the context of modern nation states, although they may originally date from the pre-modern period. 'State', 'sovereignty', 'constitution', 'democracy' and '*demos*', 'separation of powers', 'civil society' and 'public sphere', as well as 'citizenship', all suggest the nation state as the governing structure. But the EU cannot be equated with a modern nation state, although our unexamined and even obstinate patterns of thinking often lead us in a quasi-automatic way to describe and assess it with conceptual and normative tools tailored to this particular type of polity. Among scholars, no agreement exists on a positive characterisation of the EU. What, by contrast, is generally accepted is its negative portrayal as a non-state: the EU is not a federation that shares its sovereignty with its Member States, nor is it a confederation of sovereign states.

Nonetheless, the concepts and theoretical frameworks coined in the nation-state context are often enough the only available starting-point for analysing the politico-legal peculiarities of the EU. Hence, we are compelled to proceed through a critical application and, at the same time, modification of an inherited conceptual apparatus. We cannot simply abandon concepts attached to modern nation states; rather, the task is to assign them a meaning suited to examining the transnational polity of the EU and its transnational legal order. They must be detached from their 'nation-state logic', so that they can capture the interaction between the transnational and the national, so typical of the EU.[3] This interaction rejects an either-or pattern and adheres rather to a both-and logic (Beck and Grande 2004).

2 For instance, the EU law concept of public policy can vary from one Member State to another, but only within limits set by the Court. See, for example, Schermers and Waelbroeck (2001, pp. 13–14).

3 Dario Castiglione is one of those who have commented on the need to rethink standard normative vocabulary in order to make it suit 'the multiple civic identities and levels of governance that characterise the EU'. Castiglione (2001, p. 79).

Thus, in elaborating the concept of citizenship, due attention should be paid to the reciprocal ties between EU citizenship and citizenship of Member States (Tuori 2004b).

But we should also recognise that the need for conceptual reforms, responding to the intertwining of the transnational and the national, concerns not only EU law but municipal constitutional law as well. Concepts such as, say, 'sovereignty', 'citizenship', 'separation of powers' and 'basic rights' have to be re-examined with a view to capturing the consequences of Europeanisation for the nation-state constitution.

Varieties of Legal Principles

It can be difficult to keep legal principles and legal concepts apart; indeed, no reason exists even to strive for strict separation. Whether we talk of a concept or of a principle may depend, first, on our specific perspective on the law. In the sociology of law, 'legal certainty' may be used as a concept referring to the legal system's task of stabilising the environment of other social action systems, such as the economy. From within the legal system, 'legal certainty' appears as a normative principle purported to govern legal practices.

In legal literature, too, the terms 'legal concept' and 'legal principle' are at times used as synonyms. This, of course, is a consequence of the particular normativity of legal concepts, most conspicuous in concepts referring to norm clusters. To take an example, 'strict liability' may as well be termed a legal principle as a legal concept. And, indeed, both German *Begriffsjurisprudenz* and American conceptualism employed both concept- and principle-talk. Even Puchta, who has often been regarded as one of the founding fathers of *Begriffsjurisprudenz*, might define legal science's tasks in terms of, not concepts, but principles: 'Scientific activity lessens the law's reliance on the external authority of immediate popular conviction or legislative power for its principles and conceives of these as a system, as a whole of interdependent propositions' (cited in Coing 1969, p. 150).

Different strands and eras in legal scholarship have had their own predilections with regard to the at least partly alternative terms of legal concepts and legal principles. Natural-law authors preferred principle-talk; German and American conceptualism shifted the emphasis to legal concepts, as did the analytical school, too. At present, we seem again to be living in an era of principles. Thus, the role of principles in the law's systematisation has grown at the expense of concepts. Post-analytical legal science prefers to organise normative material through principles rather than concepts, and after analytical critique of the excesses of conceptualism, concepts have been left with a primarily heuristic task in legal practices. Doctrinal theories accomplish their systematising objective by summarising the normative contents of the field of law in principles and by arranging these in a prima facie order of preference.

The discussion on principles has been afflicted by the polysemy of the very term 'principle'. The term is used of diverse kinds of phenomena, and principle-discourse has been conducted in different legal contexts. Certainly, room does exist for improvement in the conceptual clarity of the discussion.

I have previously (Tuori 2000, pp. 175 and 196) argued that the norm quality of legal principles prevents us from characterising them as sources of law: since legal principles are legal norms which must find support in acknowledged legal sources, they cannot themselves be considered as such sources. This argument needs adjustment. The norm and the source quality of legal principles do not necessarily exclude each other: legal principles as legal norms are not exactly the same thing as legal principles taken as sources of law. In the legal-theoretical debates introduced by Dworkin (1978) and Alexy (2002a), legal principles have been treated as the other type of legal norms alongside legal rules. But this is only one of the many senses of 'principle' in legal discourse. The following list should indicate the plethora of meanings:

- legal principles as norms applicable in legal decision-making (*decision principles*);
- legal principles as arguments employed in interpreting written sources of law, such as legislation (*interpretation principles*);
- legal principles as summaries of the normative contents of a branch of law or the legal order as a whole (*general legal principles*);
- legal principles as legal sources supporting legal norms (*source principles*); and
- legal principles as normative premises for legislative solutions (*legislative background principles*).

If in general we can speak of a basic meaning of 'principle', my candidate would be that of general legal principles. General legal principles complement legal concepts as the other main element in general doctrines of distinct branches of law. And it is general legal principles, sedimented into the law's sub-surface cultural layers, that bring about the coherence needed to secure legal certainty. They constitute an integral part of lawyers' shared cultural pre-understanding. However, they also receive discursive expressions in surface-level normative material, such as court decisions in hard cases or scholarly writings articulating and elaborating on general doctrines of various fields of law.

Of course, the different types of legal principles are not independent from each other. Indeed, their interdependencies account for assigning varying conceptual contents to the same term. An example is provided by the administrative-law principle of fairness (or equity in its broad, non-technical sense). In legal decision-making, it may function alternatively as a directly applicable decision principle or as an interpretation principle guiding statutory construction. It may also be included in general principles of administrative law. Furthermore, in certain contexts it may constitute a legal source that justifies a norm applicable to the situation at hand.

Analysis of the law's levels and their reciprocal connections may shed light on the relationships prevailing between the various types of principles. In the debates inspired by Dworkin and Alexy, principles have been approached as discursively-formulated legal norms, applicable in legal decision-making. Such decision principles are phenomena at the law's surface level. By contrast, source principles or general legal principles summarising the normative contents of a body of law are not surface-level norms but inhabitants of sub-surface layers. The inter-connections between principles situated on different levels can be analysed as, for instance, relations of specification, justification and sedimentation. Surface-level norms manifesting the principle of fairness *specify* the corresponding source principle which also provides them with *justification*. On the other hand, the source principle of fairness has *sedimented* into the legal culture in a process launched by individual surface-level events, such as court decisions manifesting this principle.

It is true that sub-surface principles must be inferred from their discursive surface-level expressions. However, this is not to be understood as an operation of inductive logic; analytical critique has convincingly shown the pitfalls of legal induction (see Chapter 4). Rather, at issue is something like *Anschauung* which, according to the German historical school, is needed for the comprehension of organic normative wholes. Nor can reconstruction of the law's sub-surface layers rely on such formal (validity) criteria as are used in delimiting the surface-level legal order. Their contents must be derived from the presuppositions and implications of surface-level normative material. Hence, to call for a Hartian rule of recognition for identifying the law's legal-cultural elements (Siltala 2000) is to call for a chimera. These elements must be reconstructed starting from the discursive traces they leave on the surface level, but they should not be equated with these traces.

Thus, 'legal principles' appear in different guises, with different types of principles pursuing different tasks within the legal system. In what follows, I shall discuss the tasks which principles perform in legal decision-making. Their significance in disciplining the *voluntas* of the modern legislator will be discussed in later chapters.

Legal Principles in Legal Decision-Making

The debate on legal rules and principles has focused on conflicts between prima facie applicable norms. In this debate, principles have not so much appeared as legal-cultural general principles but, rather, as surface-level norms: as *decision principles*. In the view propounded by Dworkin and Alexy, *legal rules* adhere to an either-or logic: they are either applied or not, and if two rules stand in contradiction, only one of them can be valid and applicable. By contrast, *legal principles* follow a both-and logic. Conflict between two principles is resolved through weighing, so that neither of them loses its validity or applicability. The losing principle is also applied, but only within limits set by the weightier principle. In its systematising and coherence-creating task, doctrinal research (legal dogmatics) not only identifies general legal principles but also puts forth proposals for their prima facie order of preference. But ultimately, conflicts between decision principles must be resolved case-by-case, in the light of the particular facts of the case at hand.

How, then, can we tell whether a particular norm is of rule or principle quality? If the norm has been expressed in legislation, the wording of the provision may provide a sufficient clue. However, this is not always the case, but often enough determination of a norm's character requires other than linguistic arguments. I shall draw my examples from constitutional basic-rights provisions. In Finland, the nature of basic-rights norms may become an issue not only in courts but also in *ex ante* constitutional control exercised by the Constitutional Law Committee of Parliament. If the basic-right norm under consideration is a rule – and the corresponding right an absolute one – it does not allow for limitations. By contrast, rights other than absolute basic rights may be limited through an ordinary law, if the conditions established by the Constitutional Law Committee in its report in 1994 are met (PeVM 25/1994). These conditions are largely similar to the general limitation requirements adopted in German constitutional doctrine or the case-law of the European Court of Human Rights. They include the inviolability of the core of each basic right. From the perspective of *ex ante* constitutional control of the Constitutional Law Committee, norms concerning rights other than absolute basic rights are partly rules and partly principles. They are rules when protecting the basic right's core area and principles when regulating the area where limitations are allowed. By contrast, constitutional provisions protecting absolute rights merely express rules.

But how do we know when we are confronted with an absolute basic right and a constitutional provision of an exclusive rule character? According to Veli-Pekka Viljanen (2001, p. 56), the answer can be drawn from the wording of provisions. Rules are expressed in the form of absolute prohibitions, as is the provision in the Finnish Constitution on the prohibition of torture and other inhuman treatment (PL 7.2 §). Viljanen mentions Art. 9(4) as a provision giving rise to an absolute basic right. This provision lays down that 'a foreigner shall not be deported, extradited or returned to another country, if in consequence he or she is in danger of a death sentence, torture or other treatment violating human dignity'. But he does not mention para. 1 of the same article which states that 'Finnish citizens and foreigners legally resident in Finland have the right to freely move within the country and to choose their place of residence'. Why? No explicit clause of limitation attaches to either of these provisions. The prevailing interpretation that para. 4 establishes an absolute right but para. 1 does not must be vindicated by arguments other than the wording of these provisions.

International human-rights treaties proffer arguments facilitating identification of absolute basic rights and the rule character of corresponding norms. In the European Convention on Human Rights, articles on rights which may be limited include a specific *limitation* clause (saving clause). Furthermore, absolute rights may not be *derogated* from in a state of emergency, either. Rights excluded from derogation are listed in Art. 15 of the European Convention and in Art. 4 of the UN Covenant on Civil and Political Rights.[4] In Finland, these prohibitions of derogation receive direct constitutional significance through Art. 23 of the Constitution. In an emergency, only necessary 'provisional exceptions to basic rights and liberties that are compatible with Finland's international obligations concerning human rights' are permitted.[5]

In human-rights treaties, provisions on rights protected against derogation do not include a limitation clause either; these rights are absolute from the point of view of both derogation and limitation. In the context of the Finnish Constitution, human-rights treaties are relevant in assessing the prohibition against not only derogation but also limitation. One general condition for limiting basic rights is their harmony with Finland's human-rights obligations. For example, if a limitation to the right of privacy enshrined in Art. 10(1) of the Constitution did not meet the criteria laid down in Art. 8(2) of the European Convention and as specified by the case-law of the European Court of Human Rights, it would not fulfil national constitutional requirements, either. And if international human-rights treaties do not allow for limitations to a certain right at all, limitations are prohibited constitutionally as well.

It may be even more difficult to delineate the inviolable core area of basic rights than it is to identify absolute rights. The wording of basic-rights provisions does not offer assistance here: the same provision expresses either a rule or a principle, depending on whether it is a question of the right's protected core area or the surrounding periphery where limitations are legally possible. The following guideline for defining the 'core area' appears warranted: it is the area where encroachments would leave the right empty and prevent it from accomplishing the task falling to it within the whole of the basic-rights system.

4 Absolute protection covers, first, prohibition of discrimination. According to Art. 4(1) of the UN Covenant, measures undertaken in an emergency may 'not involve discrimination solely on the ground of race, colour, sex, language, religion, or social origin'. In addition, both the UN Covenant and the European Convention, in its Art. 15(1), prohibit derogations from the following treaty obligations: respect for life; the prohibition of torture or cruel, inhuman or degrading treatment or punishment; the prohibition of slavery and servitude; and the prohibition of retroactive criminal law. Furthermore, in Art. 4(2) of the UN Covenant the Signatory States may not derogate from their obligation to recognise everyone everywhere as a person before the law or to respect everyone's right to freedom of thought, conscience and religion.

5 See the Constitutional Law Committee's reasoning in PeVL 48/2002 vp: 'The Committee draws attention to the fact that the criminal-law principle of legality belongs to inviolable human rights, derogation from which is prohibited by Art. 15 of the ECHR and Art. 4 of the UN Covenant, even during war or other state of emergency. Thus, Art. 23, too, includes a corresponding prohibition on derogation from the criminal-law principle of legality.'

Discussion on identifying legal rules and principles touches on doctrine of the sources of law. Critics have blamed H.L.A. Hart's *rule of recognition* for merely being able to identify legal rules. As Hannu Tolonen argues, in identifying legal principles two types of criteria are employed: the substantive significance of putative principles and the requirement of institutional support (Tolonen 1991, pp. 275–277). Legal principles unlock the law in the direction of moral principles and ethical values, but the requirement of institutional support entails that a morally justifiable principle can only form part of the legal order if it is backed up by an institutional legal source, such as legislation or its *travaux préparatoires*, or case-law. In the Finnish legal order, basic-rights principles derive their institutional support from the Constitution. However, in general principles typically may also derive their institutional support from elsewhere than explicit statutory provisions.

Legal sources are engendered by legal practices. Rules and principles differ as to their typical sources, so that shifts in emphasis between these two types of norm imply corresponding shifts in the position of different legal practices and the institutions responsible for these. Divergences in the application of rules and principles as well have a potential impact on the relationship among lawmaking, adjudication and legal scholarship. As applying principles necessarily involves case-by-case weighing, it has a tendency to strengthen the status of the courts at the expense of the legislator. This is an important background factor to the alleged development towards a jurisdiction state which has worried many present observers (see Chapter 8).

Decision principles form part of the normative basis from which judges derive the decision norm for the case before them – the major premise of the judicial syllogism. But principles accomplish important tasks even in the stages preceding formation of a decision norm. Then they appear in the guise of source and interpretation principles.

Legal principles may provide source support for surface-level norms, which, in turn, may be either rules or principles in character. The role of *source principles* falls to general legal principles sedimented into the law's sub-surface layers. Legal principles' peculiar wavering between the law's levels manifests the recursive nature of the legal system. As legal principles result from a process of sedimentation originating from discursively-formulated legal material, they depend on the surface level. For instance, when Tolonen stresses the necessity of institutional support as a condition for a principle's legal validity he is focusing on the decision principles applicable in the courts. But the demand for institutional support extends to legal-cultural principles too; now it manifests the relation of sedimentation, which confers on principles their legal nature.

When legal-cultural principles are resorted to as sources of law, they for their part influence surface-level legal development. Decision norms may obtain source support from principles which themselves are the results of a process of sedimentation with its origin at the law's surface. But, it might be asked, are we not going round in circles if we maintain both that general principles are distillations of surface-level normative material and that they also function as legal sources propping up such material?

My answer is: not necessarily. The initial and the final point of the recursive process are not identical. Sedimentation starts from the normative material which legislative and judicial bodies produce through their decisions. By contrast, norms which receive source support from general legal principles have not been explicitly formulated in such surface-level material. Again, we can take as our example the principle of fairness, which some Finnish administrative-law scholars have regarded as a general principle of administrative law. They have argued for their view by appealing to provisions on fairness-based exemptions from taxes or public charges and to precedents of the Supreme Administrative Court in which the duty to reimburse undue social benefits has been modified on considerations of fairness.

Hence, the accusation of going round in circles turns out to be unwarranted. But a new suspicion may arise: when stressing the law's recursive character, have I not drifted close to the conceptualist constructive method with its 'inductive' and 'deductive' phases? The only difference would be that the intermediary role of concepts would have been transferred to principles: principles are first formed through legal induction and then, at the second stage, used as a premise for deducing new legal norms.

The primary counterargument here is that transitions from surface-level normative material to sub-surface principles and from the latter back to surface-level norms are not formal logical operations. They presuppose a substantive practical argumentation which cannot be squeezed into schemes of formal logic. Furthermore, general legal principles possess a 'horizontal' porosity. The relation of sedimentation connects principles to surface-level material and secures them the institutional support that their legal nature requires. But legal principles also interact 'horizontally' with the moral principles and ethical values prevailing in society. It is this porosity of legal-cultural layers which entails that their contours cannot be exactly drawn by means of formal criteria of validity.

Use of general legal principles as a legal source activates what can be called the *relation of specification* between the law's levels: surface-level law provides a concrete manifestation for legal-cultural principles (Tuori 2002a, pp. 212–216). It may be that the notion of relation of specification and the idea of surface-level expressions of sub-surface layers again arouses suspicions. This is easily interpreted in a Hegelian framework where the world is organised through concepts like 'essence' and 'phenomenon' or 'concept' and 'reality', or – in a Marxist version – 'base' and 'super-structure'. Does not 'relation of specification' exemplify Hegelian 'emanation' thinking where the surface-level legal order emerges in a quasi-spontaneous way from the deeper layers?

This is not the case. Relations between the law's levels are not realised automatically, through a kind of self-movement within the normative world, but through legal practices, such as lawmaking, adjudication and legal scholarship. By the same token, these practices also channel the law's external connections:

for example, to morals and ethics, politics, and the economy. I do not claim that analysis of the law's internal dynamics in terms of the interaction between its levels could provide us with an exhaustive account of how the law functions and changes. Legal change is always ultimately determined by factors external to the legal system, but – this is my argument – the influence of these factors is refracted through the 'intrajuristic' conditions on which Max Weber laid so much emphasis (see above, pp. 154–156).

Legal principles function not only as 'independent' legal sources but as arguments in the interpretation of other sources as well. *Interpretation principles* are resorted to in order to warrant the construction of a norm proposition from written sources of law. One and the same principle can in certain situations figure as a decision principle and in others as an interpretation principle. In the absence of written provisions on applicable criteria, the need principle of social law (to each according to their needs) may constitute a decision principle in allocating social benefits, such as places in a home for elderly people. But in cases where explicit provisions exist, the same principle may be used as an argument in statutory interpretation.

Basic-rights principles display a similar dual character. They are legal norms obliging the courts and can function as decision principles, especially in the absence of other, complementary legislation. In general, though, courts have recourse to basic-rights principles not as decision principles but as interpretation principles. In some legal systems, such as the Finnish, the courts may even be legally obliged to do so. In the *travaux préparatoires* of the Finnish Constitution, the Constitutional Law Committee stressed the duty of courts and administrative authorities to interpret legislation consistently with basic rights (PeVM 25/1994 vp). This obligation is anchored in Art. 22 of the Constitution, which lays down public authorities' duty to ensure realisation of human and basic rights: the duty of protection (*Schutzpflicht*). The New Zealand Bill of Rights of 1990 and the UK Human Rights Act 1998 include explicit provisions on a corresponding interpretive duty (see Chapter 8).

General legal principles enjoy enhanced significance as legal sources within two branches of law: EU law and international law. This is due to the cross-boundary nature of these branches and the ensuing distinctive features of their norm formation. The European or international legislator does not possess a position anywhere near that of the national legislator within the municipal legal system, especially in the Romano-Germanic legal sphere.

In EU law, the status of general legal principles as a source of law derives primarily from the case-law of the European Court of Justice. The Court has also borne the main responsibility for their articulation, although the founding treaties also include some references to general legal principles. According to Art. 340(2) of the Treaty on the Functioning of the European Union (TFEU), 'in the case of non-contractual liability, the Community shall, in accordance with the general principles common to the laws of the Member States, make good any damage caused by its institutions or by its servants in the performance of their duties'. In turn, Art. 6(1) of the Treaty on the European Union lays down that 'the Union is founded on the principles of liberty, democracy, respect for human rights and fundamental freedoms, and the rule of law, principles which are common to the Member States', and, according to Art. 6(2), 'the Union shall respect fundamental rights, as guaranteed by the European Convention for the Protection of Human Rights and Fundamental Freedoms ... and as they result from the constitutional traditions common to the Member States, as general principles of Community law'. As these references imply, the common legal tradition of Member States constitutes the main foundation of, and justification for, EU law's general legal principles (Tridimas 2005, pp. 5ff.; Reichel 2006, pp. 28ff.). As a source of general legal principles, the European Court of Justice has also appealed to 'the structures and ideas underpinning the treaties' (Reichel 2006, p. 28).

The role of general principles as a source of international law is acknowledged in Art. 38(1) of the Statute of the International Court of Justice. Para. c) lays down that the Court must, when deciding disputes submitted to it, also apply 'the general principles of law recognised by civilised nations'. General principles are regularly resorted to even in other international tribunals and dispute-resolving bodies (Cheng 1987; Koskenniemi 1985).

In EU law and international law, legal principles are primarily treated as source principles, but they appear in other guises as well. In Tridimas' account (2005, pp. 29–35), legal principles guide the interpretation of written EU law; they can be invoked as grounds for contesting a particular measure's legality under Arts 263 or 267 TFEU; and they can also support a claim for damages. Hence, general principles in EU law function not only as source principles but also as interpretation and decision principles, as well as general principles procuring normative criteria for justifying and criticising explicit legal material.

This seems to be the case in international law, too. In the concluding part of his study on the application of general legal principles in international law, Bin Cheng (1987, p. 390) has pointed to three tasks falling on them:

> First, they constitute the source of various rules of law, which are merely the expression of these principles. Secondly, they form the guiding principles of the juridical order, according to which the interpretation and application of the rules of law are orientated. Thirdly, they apply directly to the facts of the case wherever there is no formulated rule governing the matter.

Legal Theories

The polysemy we noted in connection with 'legal concepts' and 'legal principles' extends to the use of the term 'theory' in legal literature (Dreier 1981). Proposals for a particular interpretation of legislative texts or for the definition of a legal concept are at times called theories. For instance, in criminal law scholars have debated diverse 'theories' of negligence and intent. In the context of analysing general doctrines of distinct fields of law, it seems warranted to reserve the term 'theory' for combinations of legal concepts and principles. Legal theories assemble cluster concepts, articulate conceptual networks, and organise legal principles of a body of law into a prima facie order of preference. For instance, constitutional- and administrative-law theories include the theory of separation of powers, the *Rechtsstaat* theory, the theory of the legal personality of the state, and the theory of basic rights. In Niklas Luhmann's (2004) distinction between legal dogmatic theories and reflexion theories, my examples fall within the former group. We may recall Luhmann's argument that dogmatic theories purport to secure the law's conceptual consistency; serve the internal legal principle of equality which requires that like cases be treated alike and unlike cases unalike; and contribute to the legal system's primary function of stabilising mutual expectations of behaviour.

I will use as my example the constitutional-law doctrine of separation of powers. In line with other doctrinal theories, this comprises a set of interrelated legal concepts and principles. It involves such basic concepts as 'legislative power', 'executive power' and 'judicial power', which have to be defined before the doctrine has any meaning. Furthermore, it includes legal principles governing relations between these powers and the organisation of their institutional sites; principles such as democracy, legal protection or independence of the judiciary.

One possibility to specify the position of legal theories within the law is to attach them to *legal institutions* and, in so doing, to join the tradition initiated by Savigny. Legal theories would be theories of legal institutions; to our public-law examples we could add private-law theories of, say, property, contract, tort, marriage and inheritance. In his notion of legal institution, Savigny still linked legal normativity to social facticity (see above, pp. 79–80). It was only subsequent positivist legal theory that severed this link and opened the seemingly insuperable gulf between the Ought (*Sollen*) and the Is (*Sein*). The concept of legal institution provides us with the opportunity to re-knit ties with the origins of modern legal scholarship and to articulate anew the relations that connect law to society. Legal institutions, such as marriage or contract – or, rather, the particular instances of these institutions, such as particular marriages or contracts – are *legal-institutional facts* (MacCormick and Weinberger 1986). Through the concept of legal institution, Savigny and the present-day institutional theory of law shake hands.

Analysis of doctrinal theories through the notion of legal institution leads us to examine what Pöyhönen (1981) calls the *factual commitments* of legal theories. Legal theories include an at least implicit conception of the social relationships that constitute the factual side of legal institutions. Property- or contract-law theories rely on a conscious or unconscious view of the economic field of action, its steering mechanisms and developmental tendencies, while, correspondingly, the constitutional theory of separation of powers implies particular background assumptions about the political system and its role and function in society. The factual commitments of legal theories are not always spelled out, and doctrinal scholars may even be unaware of them. Often enough these commitments have to be reconstructed from the presuppositions and implications of legal theories; this is why I have proposed the expression '*hidden social theory*'. The factual commitments of legal theories do not make them descriptive or explanatory theories. These remain essentially normative theories, means of normative argumentation, as I argue in Chapter 1 when plumbing the differences between normative legal scholarship and social science.

In particular in an era of legal-cultural ruptures, divergent legal theories contend with each other, expounding rival interpretations of legal institutions. Alternative theories of separation of powers draw the boundaries between legislative, executive and judicial power differently, and lay different emphasis on principles of legal protection and democracy. Correspondingly, substantive and formal theories of the *Rechtsstaat* diverge in their understanding of the concepts of state and law and of the principles guiding the relationship between these two. Rival theories of basic rights involve divergent definitions of the very concept of basic right and diversely determine the prima facie relations among basic-rights principles. In the Critic's narrative, the contest between theories is explained by a strategic struggle over academic positions and, possibly, by theorists' political-ideological predilections. Again, the Critic focuses on legal speech acts' perlocutionary aspect. By contrast, the law's internal point of view stresses the significance of continuous legal discourse, where contributions advocating rival theories reciprocally assess each other's predominantly normative validity claims. Only future legal practices, future legal discourse, can tell which theory turns out to be most convincingly warranted and which interventions launch a successful process of legal-cultural sedimentation.

In his contract-law study, Pöyhönen presents three contract models as three rival legal theories of contract: the will model, the reliance model, and the welfare-state model. Each model adopts a different view of the leading principle in contract law. In the will model, the contract obligation is based on freedom of will, so that freedom of contract enjoys the role of leading principle. The reliance model aims at furthering economic prosperity, and the interest of exchange occupies the place of the leading principle. The contract model of the welfare state is supported by what Pöyhönen terms the idea of just social practice, which raises fairness to the position of the leading principle. Pöyhönen points to a further important aspect of legal theories: the role which the theory's *deep justification* plays in the prima facie ordering of legal principles (Pöyhönen 1988).

The significance of deep justification is apparent in constitutional doctrine, too. Thus, the principal justification provided for separation of powers determines the respective weight of the relevant principles. At least the following types of justification are conceivable:

- the efficacy argument;
- the power-theoretical argument;

- the legal protection argument; and
- the democracy argument.[6]

The *efficacy* argument is premised on the understanding of separation of powers as essentially an issue of an expedient and efficient division of labour: it is rational to establish specialised bodies for diverse state functions and tailor their composition and procedure accordingly. The efficacy argument has only rarely appeared as the sole justification for separation of powers, but it has certainly played at least an auxiliary role in discussing, say, the respective powers of the representative legislative body and the executive machinery.

The *power-theoretical* argument is familiar from American debates. Classic formulations of the *checks-and-balances* argument can be found in the Federalist Papers, especially in those composed by James Madison (1751–1836). One of the most often quoted is from the Federalist Paper No. 51:

> But the great security against a gradual concentration of the several powers in the same department consists in giving those who administer each department the necessary constitutional means and personal motives to resist encroachments of the others. The provision for defence must in this, as in all other cases, be made commensurate to the danger of attack. Ambition must be made to counteract ambition. The interest of the man must be connected with the constitutional rights of the place. It may be a reflection on human nature that such devices should be necessary to control the abuses of government. But what is government itself but the greatest of all reflections on human nature. (The Federalist Papers 1961, pp. 321–322)

The Federalists argued that distribution of tasks between constitutional bodies and the reciprocal control these exercise prevent concentration of power in the hands of a particular institution and the political or social groupings dominating it. Furthermore, the federal structure was expected to work in the same direction. The checks-and-balances argument manifests a kind of fundamental mistrust in the authority of the state: the main objective of separation of powers is to protect the liberty of citizens and civil society against intrusions by state machinery. Hence, power-theoretical deep justification could also be called the *liberty* argument. This argument is by no means a particularity of American constitutional doctrine, but has been influential elsewhere, too. In Finland, it played a prominent role in the debates leading up to the 1919 Constitution.[7]

---

6 Palmer Olsen's list of 'teleological' background factors of separation of powers is partly similar to but partly divergent from that presented above (Palmer Olsen 2005, pp. 253ff.).

7 The committee drafting the 1919 Constitution argued that separation of powers 'offers an indispensable guarantee for the freedom of citizens and the regular functioning of society. The experience of both absolute monarchies and countries with a republican

Considerations of *legal protection* are important in particular with regard to the independence of the courts, but they can also have relevance in, say, relations between the legislative and the executive power. If the legal protection argument relates primarily to the judiciary, *democracy* warrants the position of, above all, the representative body. Popular sovereignty, the Rousseauan-Kantian idea of society's self-regulation, presupposes assignment of legislative power to a representative body which is conceived of as the institutional culmination of legislative debates conducted within the public sphere of civil society. Habermas (1996) proffers a discourse-theoretical formulation of the democracy argument and of the demand for lawmaking in a representative body surrounded by a public sphere.

In our doctrinal example, analysis of deep justification is complicated by the fact that the same considerations may be used both to warrant separation of powers and to vindicate exceptions to it. In harmony with separation of powers, the principle of democracy presupposes that legislative power be reserved to the representative body. But if this body, in the name of democracy, is given extensive control over the executive and the judiciary, this can lead to a contradiction with separation of powers. Correspondingly, considerations of efficacy may entail conclusions which cannot easily be reconciled with separation of powers. Thus, one may argue that legislation or adjudication must be speeded up and that this requires compromising some of the time-consuming procedural requirements of democratic lawmaking or fair trial. These arguments are particularly enticing in our late modern condition of further social acceleration: we are constantly confronted with the danger that owing to the duration of legislative and judicial procedures, the pace of the legal system lags behind the pace of other social sub-systems.

We have gradually specified the concept of legal theory. Legal theories focus on a legal institution, consisting of legal norms and the social relationships they regulate. The constitutive elements of legal theories include:

- legal concepts referring to the legal-institutional facts of the field of the theory;
- relevant legal principles, which the theory organises in a prima facie order of preference;
- hidden social theory, the conception of social relationships under regulation which the legal theory implies (the theory's factual commitments); and
- deep justification which the theory indicates for the legal institution at issue and which guides the prima facie ordering of legal principles, as well as definition of legal concepts.

régime has demonstrated that a one-sided concentration of state power has led to oppression and also otherwise in many respects harmfully affected political life' (Komiteanmietintö 1917, 7, p. 27).

Legal theories possess their own temporality; their own dynamics and dialectic of change and stability. Pöyhönen's concepts of dogma and construction may be of assistance in conceiving of this dialectic.

Dogmas consist of a theory's fundamental, largely uncontested normative premises. Dogmas appear as strict rules, exceptions to which are only allowed through other rules and even then only on particularly weighty grounds: 'When adhering to the reliance model, exceptions to the dogma of, say, good faith (*bona fides*) can only be made in the direction of freedom of will, if violation of freedom of will would otherwise be particularly grave' (Pöyhönen 1988, p. 83). Dogmas are anchored in the deep justification of the contract model at issue (ibid.). In the doctrine of separation of powers, a dogma could be, say, a prohibition denying legislative and executive bodies the right to interfere in a case pending in court.

Dogmas constitute a stabilising, conservative force in the life of legal theories and restrain their alteration. By contrast, *constructions* are dynamic factors facilitating a theory's internal change. Through constructions, a theory is extended to situations which otherwise would remain outside its focus. In the will model of contract, the assumption of tacit consent functions as a construction: 'Through such a construction, standard contract terms are re-enclosed within the contract model including the dogma of consensus of wills' (ibid., p. 85). A similar construction is resorted to in the medical-law doctrine of informed consent: measures encroaching upon the physical integrity of a patient unable to express her will because of, say, unconsciousness are justified by her assumed or tacit consent. The doctrine of separation of powers may also involve constructions that allow it to be applied to state activities which would be difficult to classify with the basic concepts of legislative, executive and judicial power: for instance, decision-making on state budget or international relations. Constructions come close to what some legal theorists have meant by 'legal fictions'.

Pöyhönen (1988, p. 86) argues that constructions increase a theory's problem-solving capacity and indicate solutions to its (seeming) anomalies. However, it may be difficult to reconcile constructions with a theory's normative premises (its dogmas). Therefore, constructions also expose theories to criticism, revealing their weak sides (Nuotio 1998, p. 45). The assistance which constructions procure to a theory's difficulties may also prove to be only temporary. The need for a legal-cultural renewal will then be apparent.

Today, the general doctrines of a distinct branch of law comprise loosely inter-connected concepts, principles and theories; they no longer aspire to systematic 'development of a basic idea' which Carl Friedrich von Gerber (1880, s. VI) required of the theory of state law. Nonetheless, general doctrines have retained the systematising and *coherence-creating* task which, in the tension between the law's *ratio* and *voluntas*, falls to the former. But the coherence which doctrinal research aims at no longer matches the scientific ideal of German nineteenth-century discussion. *Networking* has replaced (quasi-)deductive relations.

Legal theories should never be examined in isolation: a theory's location in the network of general doctrines influences its basic concepts and the respective weight of its principles. Let us, once more, take as our example the theory of separation of powers. This theory, too, must be set in the context of other constitutional-law theories. The position of the representative body depends not merely on the theory of separation of powers but also on the constitutional theory of democracy. If democracy is equated with majority power, it is detached from the constitution's basic-rights part. If, in turn, 'democracy' is defined on discourse-theoretical premises, protection of basic rights is seen as inherent in democracy. In turn, the principle of independence of the judiciary is further specified by the right to fair trial, enshrined in both national constitutions and international human-rights instruments. According to Art. 21(1) of the Finnish Constitution, the normative requirements of fair trial involve everyone's right to 'have a decision pertaining to his or her rights or obligations reviewed by a court of law or other independent organ for the administration of justice'.

A bill which the Finnish government submitted to Parliament (HE/ 83/2005) in June 2005 highlights the intertwinement of considerations concerning separation of powers and basic rights. The government proposed a law which would have pre-empted the legal effects of a decision which the Labour Court had taken in a labour dispute between the union of border guards and the state. The law would have defined the scope of 'emergency work' as exempt from strike more extensively than the court's ruling. The law would have affected a concrete court decision and, consequently, violated a central normative premise (dogma) of the doctrine of separation of powers, namely, independence of the judiciary. As the law would have regulated a single labour conflict, it would have been a *lex singularis* with the ensuing problems in respect to the principle (and basic right) of equality. Most probably it would also have been in breach of the principle of fair trial, enshrined in Art. 21 of the Constitution (and Art. 6 of the ECHR). Fair trial involves a requirement for the parties' equality (*equality of arms*). The law – which, in the end, was not adopted – would have meant that the state as a party to the labour conflict and to the corresponding labour-law dispute would have resorted to a legal remedy which was not at the other party's disposal.

The networking typical of legal theories entails that changes in a particular theory also affect other, related theories. But legal theories differ as to their 'radiating' effects: some legal institutions and corresponding theories are more important for the identity of the respective body of law than others. In the above, I have talked of focal concepts providing the key to the conceptual network of a field of law. A corresponding approach is called for in examining legal institutions and theories. Within each branch of law, some legal institution obtains the position of a *core institution*, so that the network of general doctrines is organised around the theories, concepts and principles focusing on it. In constitutional law, such a centre could be occupied by the theory of the democratic *Rechtsstaat*; in administrative law, by the theory of the legal personality of the state; in criminal law, by the theory of punishment; and in private law, by the theories of property and contract. Rival strands of legal scholarship may assign such identity-constituting significance to different institutions, thus holding divergent views on the core institution of the body of law in question; in administrative law, candidates for this central role include, say, the legal personality of the state and judicial review. It is by determining the core institution that general doctrines are organised into networked – or to revert to the terminology of nineteenth-century German legal scholarship – 'organic' wholes.

Legal theories, concepts and principles are essential for the identity of a field of law but, in addition, they play a key role in establishing contacts with other fields as well. Diverse branches of law may possess *kin institutions*, such as *res judicata* in procedural and administrative law, or *kin concepts*, such as 'negligence' in criminal and tort law. It is vital to be aware of such cross-boundary doctrinal contacts and correspondences. But the requirement of context-sensitiveness is equally vital: kin institutions and concepts should be examined in their specific normative and doctrinal environment. Straightforward equations should be avoided: the administrative- and procedural-law institutions of *res judicata* are not necessarily identical in their normative content, nor are the criteria of negligence necessarily exactly similar in tort and criminal law. Finnish analytical critics of *Begriffsjurisprudenz* stressed in a late-Wittgensteinian spirit that the contents of concepts vary according to their particular context. This guideline has not lost its pertinence.

The assumption of a *deep culture* in law suggests that diverse fields of law share a common conceptual or normative foundation; this facilitates doctrinal connections between them. We may recall that the nineteenth-century German legal scholars, both the exponents of the historical school and their *Begriffsjurisprudenz* successors, constructed their systems of positive law on an extra-positive foundation (see above, pp. 83 and 88). Although good reasons exist for rejecting the view of the universal, transcendental character of this foundation, we can still espouse Paul Laband's (1888, pp. X–XI) claim that some basic categories, such as 'legal subject' or 'subjective law', operate in diverse departments of the law. A 'weak coherence' of a cross-boundary nature is also brought about by basic and human rights that lie behind many branch-specific general legal principles, providing them with a deep-cultural justification.

Finally, the concept of *legal paradigms* provides a perspective on a weak comprehensive coherence exceeding the confines of a particular department of law. The chapters in Habermas' *Between Facts and Norms* that deal with the system of rights and the principles of the *Rechtsstaat* can be read as his proposal for reconstructing modern law's normative deep culture. In Habermas' account, legal paradigms interpret and specify the basic rights and principles of the *Rechtsstaat* in given historical circumstances and relying on specific social-theoretical conceptions. With his concept of legal paradigm, Habermas points to yet another unifying factor: shared social-theoretical background assumptions.

Acceptance of Habermas' concept does not, of course, oblige us to embrace his reconstruction of the main paradigms of modern law: the paradigm of liberal (bourgeois) formal law, the legal paradigm of the welfare state, and, lastly, what he calls the procedural legal paradigm. As Habermas depicts it, in the inherent social theory of the *liberal paradigm*, the members of society appear primarily as autonomous actors in the marketplace. Through their spontaneous operation, market mechanisms are expected to guarantee even the factual conditions for the exercise of rights and, consequently, social justice. In the *legal paradigm of the welfare state*, society is conceived of as an ever-more complex whole, composed of mutually differentiated domains of action. In this conception, individuals figure – so Habermas argues – only as contingent recipients of systemic effects. On the other hand, administrative power is expected to be able to bind and remedy the effects of systemic (economic) mechanisms on the private sphere of individuals. In the legal paradigm of the welfare state, the autonomous actor of the marketplace is replaced by the client of welfare-state bureaucracies. The procedural legal paradigm, advocated by Habermas, relies on a communicative theory of society. It approaches the political system organised in compliance with the principles of the *Rechtsstaat* as one of society's many action systems. The function of this system is to secure societal integration and to fill up integration deficits left behind by other social sub-systems. In this function it is assisted by legitimate law (Habermas 1996, pp. 388ff.).

PART III
Ratio and *Voluntas* in Constitutional Law

Chapter 7
The Rule of Law and the *Rechtsstaat*

The Constitution in Modern Law

In many respects, the constitution occupies a special position within modern law. It is through the constitution that modern law defines its space as that of the nation state. The constitution and the modern nation state belong together. In its modern sense, as the law of the laws of society, the constitution is one of the main legal and political achievements of the American and the French revolutions. Furthermore, the constitution manifests not only the privileged space of modern law but also the dialectic between stability and malleability which is one of its main temporal qualities. The constitution is supposed to bring stability to the legal (and political) system. This objective accounts, for its part, for the specific procedure for constitutional amendments, with qualified majorities, acceptance by two parliamentary compositions, or a referendum, or both. The constitution not only possesses a higher status than other norms but is also supposed to be the most enduring element of the surface-level legal order.

On the other hand, the constitution also reaffirms legally the principle of malleability of the legal order. The *positivity* of modern law would not be possible without a constitution to regulate production of new legal norms, or, in other words, to lay down what human actions can bring about such norms. It was here that Hans Kelsen, perhaps the greatest theorist of positive law, saw the function of the constitution: the constitution regulates the issuance of new legal norms, defines the structure of the legal *Stufenbau*, and formulates the validity criteria of positive law. Kelsen's substantive concept of the constitution alluded to this very task: according to him, the constitution in the substantive sense of the term connotes 'a positive norm or positive norms which regulate the creation of general legal norms' (Kelsen 1989, p. 222). The constitution contains the central meta-norms of positive law: its official doctrine of legal sources and standards for resolving norm conflicts, such as the *lex superior* rule. In H.L.A. Hart's terms, the constitution defines the *rule of recognition* of the legal order.

So through its provisions on the use of legislative power, the constitution creates the very possibility of modern law's positivity. By the same token, it establishes access to the law for the legislator's *voluntas* and its political aims. We need not subscribe to Niklas Luhmann's radical systems-theoretical premises in order to accept his view of the constitution as an *intermediary between law and politics*. The constitution belongs to two of modern society's sub-systems: both to the legal and the political system. Hence, the functions of the constitution can be examined from both legal and political perspectives. Furthermore, the constitution fulfils the important function of linking the two sub-systems together: it channels the influences of the legal into the political system and those of the political into the legal system. In Luhmann's terms, the constitution establishes a structural coupling (*strukturelle Kopplung*) between the two sub-systems (Luhmann 2004, pp. 404ff.). Legislative acts are operations in both the legal and political system: in lawmaking, the political system is allowed to influence the legal one. From Luhmann's systems-theoretical perspective, it is here that the foundation is laid for the positivity and instrumentality which manifest the law's *voluntas*.

However, the constitution's relation to the law's *voluntas* is not unambiguous. The constitution also constrains the *voluntas* and accomplishes tasks which I have attached to the law's *ratio*. The tension between the law's *voluntas* and *ratio* traverses the constitution. The tasks falling on the constitution are not confined to founding modern law's positivity but include providing a solution to the problem of the law's limits. This is a perennial problem for the law: the law is a coercive order, and not all coercion in the name of law is justifiable. Under the conditions of modern, positive law, the traditional way of posing and resolving this problem in terms of natural law is no longer available. Particularly through their provisions on fundamental rights and constitutional review, modern constitutions appear to procure a solution which respects modern law's positivity and which need not have recourse to universal natural-law principles.

The tension between *voluntas* and *ratio* assumes different guises in different legal cultures. The concept of the constitution has many meanings. At least since Kelsen, constitutional theory has drawn a distinction between the formal and substantive constitution. The *formal* sense of the term refers to a written legal document called the Constitution, whereas the constitution in the *substantive* sense consists of norms fulfilling certain specific functions in the legal system, whatever these functions may be, according to the constitutional theorist in question. These norms may, but need not, be codified in a single statute (a constitution in the formal sense). So, the United Kingdom has a constitution in the substantive but not in the formal sense. This cannot but affect the shape of the tension between *voluntas* and *ratio*.

I would like to introduce yet another conceptual distinction. The constitution is not only about explicit, written norms, often enough gathered together in a single legal act called the Constitution. It is also about *constitutional culture*: constitutional theories, concepts and principles, and ways of dealing with these, i.e. patterns of constitutional argumentation. In line with legal culture in general, constitutional culture plays both an enabling and a restricting role in legal practices. As an integral part of (constitutional) lawyers' pre-understanding, constitutional culture contributes to the very possibility of the legal practices where the constitution is applied and interpreted. But, by the same token, the concepts, principles and theories of constitutional culture impose substantive limits on legally conceivable applications and interpretations.

In accordance with the constitution's dual location, constitutional culture can – and should – be examined not only in legal but also in political terms. In their activities, the actors of the political system – Members of Parliament, Government Ministers, opposition politicians – are guided by a specific political culture through which they tackle their practical political tasks. This political culture includes constitutional ingredients, elements of constitutional culture. The legal culture of constitutional lawyers and the political culture of political actors of course interact and share common themes and emphases. But they may display significant divergences, too. The borders may well be fluid but they do exist; a politician does not usually approach constitutional issues in the same way as a justice of a constitutional court or a scholar of constitutional law. What for a constitutional lawyer appears as an end in itself – say, basic rights and their protection – may be judged by politicians in instrumental terms, as a means of, or an impediment to, attaining their policy goals. We should caution against over-generalisations, but it seems warranted to claim that a constitutional lawyer is inclined to adopt the standpoint of *ratio* and a politician the standpoint of *voluntas*.

Constitutional culture should not be examined only from the standpoint of legal and political elites. In particular, when exploring the constitution's political functions, analysis of merely the elite culture does not suffice. One function clearly depends on the existence or at least the subsequent formation of a supportive *general constitutional culture* among the public at large: the constitution's *legitimating* task. If a receptive general constitutional culture does not exist, the constitution cannot contribute to the legitimacy of the polity. In this general constitutional culture, the borderline between the two dimensions of constitutional culture is effaced: no clear distinction between legal and political aspects can be drawn.

We could continue our analysis by discussing the formation of constitutional culture. However, that would distract us from the main topic of this chapter. Suffice it to say that just as legal culture as an elite culture emerges and evolves as a joint effect of legal practices, likewise constitutional practices or, as they may also be termed, *citizenship practices* are crucial for the formation of general constitutional culture. In these practices – in political debates and associational activities, in elections – citizens contribute to the democratic political processes of opinion and will formation.

In what follows, I am interested in legal constitutional culture, that is, in constitutional doctrine. Of course, constitutional doctrine cannot be severed from its moorings in general legal and political culture. Recently, much has been said and written of the increasing convergence of common-law and Continental European Romano-Germanic legal cultures. The convergence thesis seems over-hasty and exaggerated, despite some clear signs of mutual rapprochement, such as the growing importance of statutory law in common-law countries or the mounting weight of principle arguments in Continental European jurisdictions. Nevertheless, significant and interesting differences remain, pertaining also to how constitutional doctrine deals with the fundamental tension between *voluntas* and *ratio*. The common-law doctrine of *the rule of law* – taken in conjunction with the doctrine of *parliamentary sovereignty* – and the Continental European doctrine of the *Rechtsstaat* can be conceived of as forms in which this tension is processed.

The similarities but also the differences between these doctrines constitute an interesting but hitherto largely neglected topic for comparative constitutional law (see, however, MacCormick 1984 and Heuschling 2002).

I will start from common-law culture. My focus will be on English instead of US constitutional doctrine. The reason for my choice is not only the English origin of the rule of law notion but also the fact that the United States, with its constitutional Bill of Rights, stands in some crucial respects closer to Continental European legal systems than the English one. In English doctrine, the tension between *ratio* and *voluntas* is most manifest in the delicate relationship between two main constitutional principles: *the rule of law* and *the sovereignty of Parliament*.

The Many Meanings of the Rule of Law

In the seventeenth- and eighteenth-century debates between classic common-law thinking and legal positivism, represented by Thomas Hobbes and Jeremy Bentham, the *ratio* sedimented into common law was supposed to tame the legislator's *voluntas* and the instrumental reason allied with it (see Chapter 2). Common law has retained this role even in contemporary debates, although the tension is no longer expressed in terms of common law's 'artificial reason' and the Sovereign's subjective, natural reason. The continuity is conspicuous: the law of the rule of law consists primarily of common law. But discontinuity is evident, too: common law is no longer seen to manifest a traditional, communal *ratio*. The problem which the rule of law doctrine is expected to resolve attests to the influence of societal and cultural modernisation: *the protection of individual rights against arbitrary power*. Such an individual-centred perspective was foreign to the common-law thinking of the seventeenth and eighteenth centuries. The rule of law doctrine, with its focus on the rights of the individual, was only formulated at the end of the nineteenth century. A.V. Dicey's *Introduction to the Study of the Law of the Constitution*, which gradually became the authoritative doctrinal text, was published in 1885. English society had undergone many changes since the seventeenth and eighteenth century, and the changes lay in the direction in which the 'hidden social theory' of Hobbes' and Bentham's legal positivism – their *Gesellschaft* conception – had pointed.

As many observers have noted, the rule of law is a slippery notion whose constituents are difficult to pin down. This is perhaps inevitable; possibly, this very elusiveness allows it to play its role in processing the tension between *voluntas* and *ratio*. But it has also led some exasperated discussants to doubt the very feasibility of such a vague notion in legal argumentation. The rule of law has been variously described as 'the name commonly given to the state of affairs in which a legal system is legally in good shape'; as 'one of those self-congratulatory devices that grace the public utterances of Anglo-American politicians'; as meaning – when used by both parties to a case – little more than 'Hooray for our side'; and as analogous to the notion of the good in the sense that 'everyone is for it, but have contrasting convictions about what it is'.[1]

The notion of the rule of law shares this basic ambiguity with its Continental European counterpart, the *Rechtsstaat*. Åke Frändberg has compared the *Rechtsstaat* with such other value-laden concepts as 'liberty', 'legal certainty' and 'democracy'. The danger inherent in the use of such notions is that they are pumped up with almost everything experienced as positive and, thus, turned into 'rhetorical balloons' (Frändberg 1996, pp. 22–23).

No unanimity exists even on the basic issue which the rule of law addresses. Some authors tend to identify the rule of law with legality in general; with the idea of a law-governed society as opposed to anarchy. Joseph Raz, in an influential article first published in 1977, is somewhat more specific. In his view, 'the basic intuition from which the doctrine of the rule of law derives … (is that) the law must be capable of guiding the behaviour of its subjects' (Raz 1979, p. 214). However, perhaps the majority of commentators, at least those standing in or influenced by the English rule of law doctrine with Dicey as the great founding father, have adopted the following definition of the problem: how to prevent the exercise of arbitrary power by government and to safeguard individual rights? This fundamental problem constitutes the basis for parallels to be drawn between the rule of law doctrine and the Continental European *Rechtsstaat* theory.

The ambiguity of the notion extends to its far-from-clear location on the line leading from normative to descriptive statements: it has been employed both to describe existing features of the legal system and to express normative requirements. In the normative dimension, two basic alternative significations exist. Firstly, the notion of the rule of law may point to certain virtues, certain qualities, which an ideal legal system should possess and against which the existing legal system can be appraised and criticised. In this case, the notion does not necessarily claim anything about the contents of present law, or back up rights or other claims justiciable in court. This is the sense in which Raz uses the notion in his article. For him, 'the rule of law is a political ideal which a legal system may lack or may possess to a greater or lesser degree'. He also emphasises that the rule of law is only one of the virtues which a legal system may possess and by which it should be appraised. In Raz's view, the requirements of the rule of law are predominantly of a formal nature: 'it is not to be confused with democracy, justice, equality (before the law or otherwise), human rights of any kind, or respect for persons or for the dignity of man' (Raz 1979, p. 211).

The rule of law has also been treated, not only as an ideal of a good legal system, but as a legal principle of existing law, as well. As such a principle, it can be employed either directly, as an 'independent' norm giving rise to justiciable claims, or indirectly, as an interpretative standpoint guiding statutory construction in particular cases.

1 The quotations are from Lord Bingham's lecture on the rule of law. See http://cpl.law.cam.ac.uk/Media.

To sum up, we have the following possibilities:

1. the rule of law as a descriptive notion;
2. the rule of law as a normative notion:

    - referring to the qualities of an ideal legal system;
    - determining the contents of the law in force:

        - as an independent legal principle directly giving rise to justiciable claims; or
        - as an interpretative standpoint to be employed in statutory construction.

I wish to emphasise the analytical nature of these distinctions. In practice, the borderlines are not clear-cut. Description often has evaluative undertones, and the transition from an ideal for the legal system to a principle of existing law may be rather fluid. Shifts from one meaning to another can be difficult to detect, even within the same text. This, of course, complicates scrutiny of the discussion, especially for an observer coming from a foreign legal culture.

The rule of law is a central constitutional notion in all legal systems of the common-law tradition. However, its significance and role vary from one legal system to another, turning on, for instance, the existence or non-existence of a formal constitution. Thus, in the UK, the lack of a unified formal constitution has assigned tasks to the rule of law doctrine which it does not necessarily have, say, in the United States with its written constitution, inclusive of a Bill of Rights.

Dicey's Three Meanings of the Rule of Law

The main credit for establishing the notion of the rule of law as an integral element of the English constitutional doctrine falls to Dicey. His exposition in *Introduction to the Study of the Law of the Constitution* still constitutes the almost self-evident starting point for contemporary discussion. Fortunately for subsequent commentators, Dicey wrote vaguely and ambiguously enough to allow for what appears to be an endless debate, not only on the meaning and the role of the rule of law, but also on what, exactly, Dicey's intentions were. I shall also begin with an analysis of this foundational text.

Dicey includes three main elements in the rule of law. Firstly, he links it to *the prevention of arbitrary power*. When speaking of the rule of law

> we mean, in the first place, that no man is punishable or can be lawfully made to suffer in body or goods except for a distinct breach of law established in the ordinary legal manner before the ordinary courts of the land. In this sense the rule of law is contrasted with every system of government based on the exercise

> by persons in authority of wide, arbitrary, or discretionary powers of constraint. (Dicey 1959, p. 188)

Another formulation of the first principle brings forth even more clearly the contradiction between the rule of law and arbitrary power. The rule of law

> means, in the first place, the absolute supremacy or predominance of regular law as opposed to arbitrary power, and excludes the existence of arbitrariness, of prerogative, or even of wide discretionary authority, on the part of the government. Englishmen are ruled by the law, and by the law alone; a man may with us be punished for a breach of law, but he can be punished for nothing else. (ibid., p. 202)

The second meaning relates the rule of law to *equality*:

> We mean in the second place, when we speak of the 'rule of law' as a characteristic of our country, not only that with us no man is above the law, but (what is a different thing) that here every man, whatever be his rank or condition, is subject to the ordinary law of the realm and amenable to the jurisdiction of the ordinary tribunals.

We have to be careful when trying to pinpoint Dicey's second meaning. His principle of equality does not amount to anything like a general prohibition of discrimination on unacceptable grounds, such as those enumerated in Art. 14 of the European Convention on Human Rights. For Dicey, equality before the law provides that all citizens (including officials) are subject to ordinary law and the jurisdiction of ordinary courts, and that no administrative courts exist, as in France, to hear complaints of unlawful conduct by officials (see also Bradley 2006, p. 98). Dicey devotes one chapter of his book to demonstrating the incompatibility of *droit administratif*[2] with the English notion of the rule of law. This specific meaning of equality becomes clear enough in the following formulation: the rule of law

> means, again, equality before the law, or the equal subjection of all classes to the ordinary law of the land administered by the ordinary law courts; the 'rule of law' in this sense excludes the idea of any exemption of officials from the duty of obedience to the law which governs other citizens or from the jurisdiction of the ordinary tribunals. (Dicey 1959, pp. 202–203)

The third meaning alludes to the specific *inductive* way of protecting individual rights in England:

---

2 To emphasise the incongruity between the rule of law and administrative law, Dicey consequently left the French term untranslated.

> There remains yet a third and a different sense in which the 'rule of law' … may be described as a special attribute of English constitution. We may say that the constitution is pervaded by the rule of law on the ground that the general principles of the constitution (as for example the right to personal liberty, or the right of public meeting) are with us the result of judicial decisions determining the rights of private persons in particular cases brought before the courts; whereas under many foreign constitutions the security (such as it is) given to the rights of individuals appears to result from the general principles of the constitution. (ibid., pp. 195–196)

Even a concise exposition of Dicey's views gives rise to several questions of interpretation. First, we may speculate on how Dicey's conception should be located within the analytical alternatives presented above. Dicey's depiction of the three meanings of the notion seems to intimate that what he is doing is describing the English legal system and comparing it with examples from Continental European constitutional law. But he clearly uses the 'rule of law' as an evaluative-descriptive notion: the 'rule of law' is a notion charged with positive value. Dicey's evaluative-descriptive speech act has a polemical edge, directed against Continental legal systems which – according to his judgement – do not provide safeguards against arbitrary power; which do not guarantee equality before the law; and where individual rights depend on formal and abstract declarations.

A normative undertone is present in Dicey's account, but – employing my analytical distinctions – this relates primarily to the general virtues of the legal system; Dicey does not seem to treat the rule of law as an independent legal principle that would back up justiciable legal claims or guide statutory interpretation. Such normative conclusions are of more recent origin in constitutional doctrine.

What, then, forges the three meanings of the rule of law into a coherent whole? How, in particular, is the third meaning linked to the other two? For many commentators, the third limb seems to sit rather awkwardly with the first two, and in the elaboration of Dicey's views it is often more or less left aside. But, in fact, it can be regarded as the key element that accounts for the coherence of Dicey's conception.

The third meaning intimates that in England, the law that safeguards individual rights and constitutes a bulwark against arbitrary power is the ordinary law of the land, that is, the law enforced by the ordinary courts. Thus, 'the right to personal freedom, or in other words to protection from arbitrary arrest, forms part of the constitution because it is secured by the ordinary law of the land' (ibid., p. 198). This law is predominantly common law, reinforced and elaborated through individual judicial decisions in individual cases. The English constitution is based on ordinary law; it flows from individual judicial decisions and not from the abstract principles of a written constitution or a Bill of Rights. In England, 'individual rights are the basis, not the result, of the law of the constitution' (ibid., p. 207). The English constitution and the individual rights that constitute its basis do not result from deduction but from induction. To make his point clear, Dicey compares the Belgian and the English constitution with each other:

> the relation of the rights of individuals to the principles of the constitution is not quite the same in countries like Belgium, where the constitution is the result of a legislative act, as it is in England, where the constitution itself is based upon legal decisions. In Belgium the rights of individuals to personal liberty flow from and are secured by the constitution. In England the right to individual liberty is part of the constitution, because it is secured by the decisions of the courts … If it be allowable to apply the formulas of logic to questions of law, the difference … between the constitution of Belgium and the English constitution may be described by the statement that in Belgium individual rights are deductions from the principles of the constitution, whilst in England the so-called principles of the constitution are inductions or generalisations based upon particular decisions pronounced by the courts as to the rights of given individuals. (ibid., pp. 197–198)

The inductive nature of the English constitution entails two specific benefits in comparison with the deductive mode of Continental constitutional law. Firstly, in England rights are inseparable from corresponding remedies: *ubi jus ibi remedium*. Again, contrasting foreign (Continental European) constitutional law is brought in to prove the point:

> Foreign constitutionalists have, while occupied in defining rights, given insufficient attention to the absolute necessity for the provision of adequate remedies by which the rights they proclaimed might be enforced … there runs through the English constitution that inseparable connection between the means of enforcing a right and the right to be enforced which is the strength of judicial legislation … the Englishmen whose labours gradually framed the complicated set of laws and institutions which we call the Constitution, fixed their minds far more intently on providing remedies for the enforcement of particular rights or … for averting definite wrongs, than upon any declaration of the Rights of Man or of Englishman. (ibid., pp. 198–199)

Hence, the connection between ordinary law and the constitution accounts for the inseparable connection between rights and remedies. But this is not the only reason why the English 'inductive' constitution provides more effective protection for individual rights than its 'deductive' Continental counterparts. Perhaps even more significant is that rights secured by the ordinary law and enforced by ordinary courts, cannot be suspended in the way rights based on the abstract principles of a written constitution can:

> The general rights guaranteed by the constitution may be, and in foreign countries constantly are, suspended … where the right to individual freedom is deduced from the principles of the constitution, the idea readily occurs that the

> right is capable of being suspended or taken away. Where, on the other hand, the right to individual freedom is part of the constitution because it is inherent in the ordinary law of the land, the right is one which can hardly be destroyed without a thorough revolution in the institutions and manners of the nation ... The constitution being based on the rule of law, the suspension of the constitution, as far as such a thing can be conceived possible, would mean with us nothing less than a revolution. (ibid., pp. 200–202)

The reliance of the English constitution on ordinary law, enforced by ordinary courts, enables it to offer effective safeguards against arbitrary power, as required by the rule of law's first meaning. The predominance of ordinary law also explains the equality that pervades English law and that confers on the rule of law its second meaning. Equality before the law means that all classes, including officials, are subject to ordinary law and the jurisdiction of ordinary courts; that there is no specific *droit administratif* applied to civil servants and falling outside the jurisdiction of ordinary courts. Rights against intrusion by government originate from the same ordinary law that protects citizens from intrusions by other citizens:

> in England the rights of citizens as against each other are (speaking generally) the same as the rights of citizens against any servant of the Crown. This is the significance of the assertion that in this country the law of the constitution is part of the ordinary law of the land. The fact that a Secretary of State cannot at his discretion and for reasons of state arrest, imprison, or punish any man, except, of course, where special powers are conferred upon him by statute ... is simply a result of the principle that a Secretary of State is governed in his official as in his private conduct by the ordinary law of the land. (ibid., p. 285)

The history of the *Rechtsstaat* doctrine has often been written in terms of the shifting dominance of *substantive* and *formal* conceptions. Interestingly enough, a corresponding distinction between formal and substantive understandings has been adopted in the rule of law discussion and in the analysis of Dicey's views as well. As is to be expected, no agreement has been reached on whether Dicey employs the rule of law as a purely formal notion or whether he includes substantive elements in it.

Which features of a legal system are termed formal and which substantive is, of course, itself a matter of interpretation. Here I will rely on the definitions suggested by Paul Craig, one of the defenders of a formal understanding of Dicey's conception. According to Craig, 'formal conceptions of the rule of law address the manner in which the law was promulgated (was it by a properly authorised person, in a properly authorised manner etc.); the clarity of the ensuing form (was it sufficiently clear to guide an individual's conduct so as to enable a person to plan his or her life); and the temporal dimension of the enacted norm (was it prospective or retrospective etc.)'. By contrast, 'those who espouse substantive conceptions ...

accept that the rule of law has the formal attributes mentioned above, but they wish to take the concerns further' by arguing that 'certain substantive rights are said to be based on, or derived from, the rule of law' (Craig 1997, p. 467).

The exegesis of Dicey's text in terms of formal and substantive conceptions of the rule of law may be deemed a rather futile enterprise. Suffice it to say here that I am inclined to join the formal interpretation camp. In his account of the rule of law, Dicey was not so much interested in the contents of the ordinary law which ordinary courts enforced and which proffered a bulwark against the arbitrary power of the government. It was the very 'inductive' method of English constitutional law that mattered for Dicey, not the substance of historically evolved and evolving rights.

Dicey's fame reached the United States, too, and in discussing the growth of administrative justice, Roscoe Pound, for instance, referred to him (Pound 1924, p. 339). Yet, emphasis on the 'inductive' constitutional reasoning makes Dicey a thoroughly English writer: the US approach leans more to the 'deductivist' side.

The Rise of Administrative Law

Much has changed in the English legal system since Dicey published his evaluative-descriptive exposition of the rule of law. Dicey wrote in a comparative spirit and expounded the particularities of the English constitution against a backdrop of its Continental counterparts. French *droit administratif* provided him with the main contrast for accentuating the blessings of the English way. As the title of one chapter of his treatise (Chapter XII: 'Rule of law compared with *droit Administratif*') already reveals, he treated the English rule of law and the French *droit administratif* largely as opposites.

In Dicey's view 'there can be with us nothing really corresponding to the "administrative law" (*droit administratif*) or the "administrative tribunals" ... of France'. The citation marks are telling: in English, the expression 'administrative law' makes little sense. This is because 'the notion which lies at the bottom of the "administrative law" known to foreign countries ... is utterly unknown to the law of England, and indeed is fundamentally inconsistent with our traditions and customs' (Dicey 1959, p. 203). The very words '"administrative law" ... were unknown to English judges and counsel, and were in themselves hardly intelligible without further explanation'. This is not for linguistic reasons, but 'the want of the name arises at bottom from our non-recognition of the thing itself' (ibid., p. 330).

One of the paradoxes of subsequent doctrinal development is that administrative law – far from being an external opposite – has come to occupy a central place within the rule of law doctrine. In contemporary accounts, the principles and remedies of administrative law exhaust much of the contents of the rule of law. According to Jeffrey Jowell, a leading contemporary discussant, 'the rule of law ... is enforced through our Administrative Law', and 'in large part, Administrative Law is the implementation of the constitutional principle of the Rule of Law'

(Jowell 2007, p. 18). The rule of law has become the connecting link between constitutional and administrative law.

How can we explain this paradox, the rise of administrative law and its transformation from an external opposite to an integral ingredient of the rule of law? Evidently, the main background factor is the expansion of administrative discretion which has accompanied the rise of the welfare state and the growing involvement of government in economic and social regulation.

Dicey held a rather ambivalent position towards discretionary administrative powers. When elaborating on the first meaning of the rule of law, he was inclined to equate discretion with arbitrariness or at least the danger of arbitrariness: 'wherever there is discretion there is room for arbitrariness ... discretionary authority on the part of the government must mean insecurity for legal freedom on the part of its subjects' (Dicey 1959, p. 188). Nonetheless, he also seemed to acknowledge the indispensability of discretion, at least in certain circumstances. When trying to demonstrate the compatibility and even complementarity of the rule of law and parliamentary sovereignty, Dicey pointed to the necessity of discretionary powers granted to the government by Parliament:

> The rigidity of the law constantly hampers (and sometimes with great injury to the public) the action of the executive, and from the hard-and-fast rules of strict law, as interpreted by the judges, the government can escape only by obtaining from Parliament the discretionary authority which is denied to the Crown by the law of the land ... Under the complex conditions of modern life no government can in times of disorder, or of war, keep the peace at home, or perform its duties towards foreign powers, without occasional use of arbitrary authority. (ibid., p. 411)

In the development of modern society, discretionary powers have proved vital not only in exceptional situations but in the economic and social administration of society in 'normal' times as well. Dicey's main recipe against arbitrary power was to circumscribe the discretion granted to the government by statute law and to let legal relations between officials and citizens be determined by ordinary private or criminal law. In the further development of society, this recipe proved to be more and more illusory: discretionary powers established by statute law could not be disciplined through ordinary private and criminal law (cf. Bradley 2006, p. 97).

Despite the delaying influence of Dicey's views (Allison 2004, p. 23; Bradley 2006, p. 98), safeguards against arbitrary governmental powers were sought in specific administrative-law tools which could – so it was hoped – dissolve the equation between discretion and arbitrariness. *Judicial review of administrative decisions* occupies a prominent place among these tools; according to Jowell, 'the practical implementation of the Rule of Law takes place primarily through judicial review of the actions of public officials'. The principal grounds for such review are threefold. The first of them is 'legality': 'the courts ensure that the official decisions do not stray beyond the "four corners" of a statute by failing to take into account "relevant" considerations (that is, considerations which the law requires), or by taking into account "irrelevant" considerations (that is, considerations outside the object and purpose that Parliament intended the statute to pursue)'. Secondly, judicial review may rely on procedural grounds, on 'procedural propriety'. The basically common-law principle of procedural fairness (or due process or 'natural justice') 'requires decision makers to be unbiased and to grant a fair hearing to claimants before depriving them of a right or significant interest'. In recent years, the requirement of a fair hearing has been extended to situations where a 'legitimate expectation' has been invoked. According to Jowell, 'the notion of legitimate expectation is itself rooted in that aspect of the Rule of Law which requires legal certainty'. It is of significance especially when administrative decision-making touches on the legal position of an individual citizen: 'under the ground of procedural impropriety, the courts may, even where the statute is silent, supply the "omission of the legislature" in order to insist that the decision-maker grant a fair hearing to the applicant before depriving him or her of a right, interest or legitimate expectation'. The third ground for judicial review, irrationality, is again of substantive nature. This ground involves criteria which in German law, for instance, are included in proportionality. This is a principle of central stature in German constitutional and administrative law as well as the primary source of inspiration for the corresponding principle of EU law (Jowell 2007, pp. 18–19).

At this point a brief look at developments in the United States might be instructive. There, too, the rise of administrative law belongs to the characteristic features of the twentieth-century legal system. Administrative law as a distinct branch of law hardly existed before the 1930s. Thus, unlike in Germany, late nineteenth-century conceptualism did not extend to elaboration of general doctrines of administrative law. Although the US conceptualists embraced an anti-common-law idea of legal science, they shared common lawyers' traditional mistrust of public-law legislation. In constitutional law, the doctrine of *police powers* drew the borderline between legitimate and illegitimate regulation; this was one of the main boundaries which the *Lochner*-era courts understood themselves to be called on to monitor. It was only in the 1930s, in the wake of New Deal legislation and the upsurge of freestanding administrative agencies, that administrative law emerged as a distinct field of law, furnished with its own doctrines. The crucial issue was – as it was to be in the UK as well – the reach of judicial review of administrative decisions and action. The debate was often quite heated, and John Landis, a central proponent of this novel branch of law, was certainly not the only one who had a sense of battle between the judiciary and the administration; between judges and the specialists working in administrative agencies or between legalists and reformers. The ferocity of the battle was augmented by the high extra-legal stakes: at issue was also the fate of the New Deal policy of the Roosevelt administration. Within legal discourse, the debate on 'administrative absolutism' was one of the side-fronts in the conflict between the conceptual traditionalists and the pro-New Deal Realists.[3]

Elaboration of administrative-law principles and remedies has led to a narrowing of the gap between English and Continental law which Dicey was so prone to emphasise. The grounds for judicial review in the UK have much in common, not only with the requirements of the German principle of proportionality, but also with the French doctrine of *détournement du pouvoir*, which, in turn, has greatly influenced the administrative law of the Nordic countries, including Finland. The rapprochement has institutional aspects as well: specific tribunals dealing with administrative law cases have been established in the UK.[4] These are not exactly courts in the sense of the administrative courts of, say, France and Germany, but they still reflect acceptance of the view that administrative law may require institutional judicial solutions distinct from ordinary private and criminal law. The fact that in 2000 a section of the High Court in London was renamed the Administrative Court (Bradley 2006, p. 98) is at least of symbolic significance. By the same token, appraisal of Continental models has undergone radical change. It is difficult to imagine that Dicey could have subscribed to the contemporary judgement according to which 'administrative courts in many countries, not least in France, protect the individual against unlawful acts by public bodies' (ibid.).

Of course, the rapprochement between British and Continental doctrine is due not only to the alteration of English law. French administrative law no longer corresponds (if it ever did correspond!) to the *droit administratif* with which Dicey contrasted the English rule of law. In Dicey's view, *droit administratif* is designed to protect officials from the legal consequences of their actions rather than to offer safeguards for citizens against illegal or otherwise arbitrary administrative action. According to his analysis, *droit administratif* is based on 'two leading ideas alien to the conceptions of modern Englishmen'. The first of these is that 'the government, and every servant of the government, possesses, as representatives of the nation, a whole body of special rights, privileges, or prerogatives as against private citizens, and that the extent of these rights, privileges, or prerogatives is to be determined on principles different from the considerations which fix the legal rights and duties of

3 On the doctrine of police powers, see Cook (1907), Powell (1919) and Legarre (2007). On the emergence of administrative law as a distinct field of law and a distinct discipline, see the special issue of the *Yale Law Journal*, Vol. 47, Number 4 (1938), edited by Felix Frankfurter, and Daniel B. Rodriguez's article on Louis Jaffe (1997), one of the central figures of the new discipline. John Landis was another crucial name in the development of administrative-law doctrine. He made his comment on the sense of battle in the issue edited by Frankfurter (Landis 1938, p. 519). In the battle between traditionalists and Realists, Pound joined the former camp with his criticism of 'administrative absolutism'.

4 'As edition after edition of Dicey's *Law of the Constitution* reiterated that the rule of law requires judicial intervention by ordinary courts, administrative tribunals were proliferating to deal with the disputes arising from the expanding social services of the developing welfare state' (Allison 2004, p. 158).

one citizen towards another' (Dicey 1959, pp. 336–337). The second general idea relates to the 'so-called "separation of powers"', which is seen as preventing 'the government, the legislature, and the courts from encroaching upon one another's province'. This also means that 'the government and its officials ought … to be independent of and to a great extent free from the jurisdiction of the ordinary courts' (ibid., pp. 336–338).

The increase in discretionary powers and the ensuing elaboration of administrative law has problematised not only Dicey's first but also his second meaning of the rule of law. The growth of administrative law as a separate branch of law entails that legal relations between the government and citizens are ever more determined by a body of rules distinct from ordinary private and criminal law. If equality before the law is taken to mean that relations between officials and citizens are subject to the same rules as those between two citizens, then the principle of equality has lost much of its pertinence. The development has also eroded the premise on which Dicey based his third limb of the rule of law: his faith in the superiority of the traditional English 'inductive' method over the deductive method of Continental constitutional law. I shall come back to these consequences later in this chapter.

The growth in significance of administrative law is one of the trends which have narrowed the differences between the rule of law and the Continental European *Rechtsstaat* theory. The first German formulations of *Rechtsstaat* theory date from the so-called *Vormärz*: the period preceding the tumultuous events of the year 1848. Before Germany's unification, state-law discussion was dominated by the so-called early constitutional school. It treated the '*Rechtsstaat*' as a substantive concept; the law which was supposed to discipline the arbitrary power of *voluntas* consisted of an extra-positive, substantive norm order. Unification elevated statutory positivism into a leading position in German state law and, consequently, the '*Rechtsstaat*' was transformed into a formal concept. Within state law, administrative law constituted itself as an independent branch and adopted the '*Rechtsstaat*' as one of its central concepts. The *legality of administration* became a leading principle of the *Rechtsstaat*, and the remaining offensive content of the *Rechtsstaat* concept focused primarily on administrative law.

Thus, in an article published on the eve of the First World War, Richard Thoma (1874–1957) argued that the legality of administration constitutes the basis for a modern concept of *Rechtsstaat*, although it does not wholly exhaust its meaning. Thoma formulated the goals on the road to a *Rechtsstaat* as follows:

> Building up administrative law regulation in the sense of a more exact border-line between power and liberty in addition to serving policy goals (*sachlicher Zwecke*), constructing administrative organisation with a view to safeguarding this border-line in addition to its functional capacity … these are the goals of the development which we call specifically *rechtsstaatlich* and which we are still addressing.

Thoma distinguished between four phases in the development of the *Rechtsstaat*. Firstly, law-giving is subjected to the co-decision of a representative body, while at the same time fundamental rights draw a boundary between sovereignty and liberty. In the second stage, control of the administration is complemented with the criminal- and tort-law liability of civil servants. The central aim in the third phase is to create a system of administrative courts which would both facilitate judicial review of administrative decisions and ensure availability of the expertise required by administrative-law cases. In the fourth stage, the goal is to ward off arbitrary decision-making through more detailed substantive administrative-law regulations (Thoma 1978).

In present-day English doctrine, the rule of law provides the connecting link between constitutional and administrative law. The *Rechtsstaat* concept holds a similar position in Continental European public law. The elevated status of administrative law in both rule of law and *Rechtsstaat* theory demonstrates the ambivalent role of this field of law: the tension between *ratio* and *voluntas* pervades administrative law, too. On the one hand, administrative law is employed as the primary means for realising the political aims of the legislative *voluntas*. On the other hand, general principles of administrative law and the remedies it offers private persons provide protection against the excesses of this *voluntas*, thus accomplishing tasks which I have related to the law's *ratio*. The dual role of administrative law corresponds to the distinction between general and special administrative law, common at least in Continental doctrine. Administrative law can be approached from two almost diametrically opposite perspectives: from that of power, *voluntas*, and from that of private citizens, the objects of power.

Let us return to the rule of law doctrine. Administrative-law tools for disciplining the exercise of discretionary powers are predominantly of a formal nature, although substantive criteria curbing the use of discretion play a certain role in judicial review as well. The mainly formal character of the rule of law is often emphasised in more legal-theoretically oriented interventions, too. This holds even for T.R.S. Allan, who has drawn quite far-reaching normative inferences from his rule of law conception. His starting point is the rule of law as 'primarily an ideal of procedural fairness, governing the manner in which laws and policies should be applied to particular persons'[5] (Allan 2001, p. 1). Allan has conflated Dicey's three meanings of the rule of law into two: the principles of due process and equality. These principles are comparable to Dicey's two first meanings, although when elaborating on them Allan distracts from Dicey's conception. In line with many other contemporary authors, Allan tends to downplay Dicey's third meaning, which accentuates the peculiarities of the English constitution. In Allan's case,

5 It is, however, important to read the final part of the sentence quoted above. Allan adds that the rule of law 'also has important implications for the permissible content of such laws and policies'. I shall return to Allan's view of these implications.

this is at least partially due to his pronounced legal-theoretical level of analysis: his focus is wider than just English constitutional law.

The problem with formal accounts, of course, is that normative requirements of the rule of law are reduced merely to the way the law is applied; they do not concern the applicable law itself. Dicey's formalist tendency hinged on two articles of faith: firstly, the controlling power of the common law, i.e. ordinary private and criminal law, and secondly, the compatibility of parliamentary sovereignty with the rule of law. What worried Dicey was legally unrestricted government power, i.e. government power such as it was claimed in England by Sir Francis Bacon (1561–1621) and other advocates of *royal prerogative* in the sixteenth and seventeenth centuries. In Dicey's account, 'the doctrine propounded under various metaphors by Bacon, that the prerogative was something beyond and above the ordinary law like the foreign [i.e. French! – KT] doctrine that in matters of high policy (*acte de gouvernement*) the administration has a discretionary authority which cannot be controlled by the court' (Dicey 1959, p. 371). This doctrine did not prevail in the stormy history of the seventeenth century, but was superseded by the rule of law which subjected government power to legal control. According to Dicey's other article of faith, parliamentary sovereignty in turn does not constitute a threat to the rule of law but rather complements and even enhances it.

Formalist accounts, reducing the rule of law to a procedural principle, easily lead to mere legalism; to a mere requirement of legal forms which can be filled with any content whatsoever. Even accounts in the tradition of Lon Fuller, which extend the formal requirements of the rule of law from the application of laws to the laws themselves, are not free from the danger of legalism. Indeed, this kind of legalism may be wholly intentional. This is clearly the case with Raz, who emphasises that the rule of law is only one of the virtues of the legal system. In his view, the legalism of formalist conceptions of the rule of law is a problem only if the rule of law is – erroneously – seen to encompass all the qualities of an ideal legal system.

Raz's list of components of the rule of law is premised on the basic intuition from which, according to him, the doctrine derives: the law's capability to guide the behaviour of its subjects. The list bears great resemblance to the factors that Fuller (1969) included in the 'internal morality of law':

1. All laws should be prospective, open and clear.
2. The making of particular laws (particular legal orders) should be guided by open, stable, clear, and general rules.
3. The independence of the judiciary must be guaranteed.
4. The principles of natural justice must be observed.
5. The courts should have reviewing powers over the implementation of the other principles.
6. The courts should be easily accessible. (Raz 1979, pp. 214–215)

The Rule of What Law?

The initial problem that the doctrines of the rule of law and the *Rechtsstaat* set out to solve was similar: how to discipline extra-legal government power. The threat against individual rights was perceived to come from the executive branch. For Dicey, the doctrinal opposite pole of the rule of law consisted of the doctrine of royal prerogative, unbound by the law. In the German late nineteenth-century conceptual field, '*police state*' came to be the main adversary concept of the *Rechtsstaat*.

In recent decades, many scholars have been interested in the early concept of police; the 'police' has been held to be one of the key concepts in analysis of the emergence and evolution of the early modern state. The present narrow concept of the police, which relates to the maintenance of law and order, is a relative newcomer in the history of concepts and, actually, first appeared approximately simultaneously with the concept of the *Rechtsstaat*. The wide sense which the concept of the police had in sixteenth- and seventeenth-century Europe covered all public activities aiming at the welfare of the population. The 'police state' was a kind of quasi-welfare state. However, the welfare of the population was not an end in itself but served the primary objective of increasing the power and the strength of the state. Michel Foucault (1980) attaches this broad notion of the police to the idea of *raison d'état*; to that specific political rationality that made its breakthrough in Europe beginning with the late sixteenth century. From the perspective of later opposition between the 'police state' and the '*Rechtsstaat*', special attention should be paid to the fashion in which the relationship between police tasks and the law was conceived. Police tasks did not constitute an area beyond regulation, but, on the contrary, were subject to often very detailed instructions issued by the monarch or the royal bureaucracy. Significantly, however, these instructions were not regarded as legal enactments. They were norms whose legitimisation lay in their purpose, in furthering the happiness and the welfare of the people (Maier 1986). Police tasks lay in the kernel of that area of 'legitimate fiat' where the monarch was free to act on instrumental considerations of expediency.

Both in Germany and in France, from the latter half of the eighteenth century onwards, the traditional notion of the police was increasingly criticised from the standpoint of liberal legal discourse. In France, the new conception of the law was codified in the Declaration of the Rights of Man and Citizen and other constitutional documents of the revolutionary era. In German police literature, in turn, the broad notion of the police, based on the purpose of welfare, gradually gave way to a narrower definition, and thus development began towards opposition between the police state and the *Rechtsstaat*. Instead of the positive aim of furthering the welfare of the population, the tasks of the police were increasingly defined negatively, as fending off dangers threatening the 'happiness' of citizens. This also entailed that the objective of welfare promotion could no longer legitimise a legally unrestricted police power. The 'police state' began to connote the old way of thinking which contradicted the premises of the *Rechtsstaat* and where an essential part of state activity was seen to lie beyond the reach of legal regulation, both as regards its competence basis and its means. Consequently, the 'police state' acquired a negative value sense (Maier 1986, pp. 200–206).[6]

The rule of law and *Rechtsstaat* doctrines not only addressed the same problem of disciplining arbitrary government power. The solution they offered to this problem was largely similar as well: executive power was to be subjected to the control of law, and residual legally uncontrolled prerogatives were to be absent. A new phase in doctrinal development was initiated with the insight that the very solution could be the source of new problems; that the threat to individual rights could arise from the law itself, and that the locus of danger might lie not only in the executive but in the legislative branch, too. In Germany, the time was ripe for this insight when, after German unification and enactment of the German Constitution in 1871, the previous mainly substantive understanding of the *Rechtsstaat* gave way to a formal one. In the view of the now dominant late constitutionalist school, the law consists of positive norms established in the procedure laid down by the constitution. The idea of supra-positive law independent of the state was abandoned. In line with the early constitutionalist conception of the *Rechtsstaat*, late constitutional theory presupposed the state to be bound by the law. But as the law was no longer seen as an order independent of the state but was equated with norms issued by the state itself, it could no longer – unlike in early constitutionalist theory – be raised above the state. The relationship between law and state was reversed: now the state determined the law.

This gave rise to a new problem: if the law is created by the state, how can the state itself be bound by the law, its own creation? Georg Jellinek (1914, pp. 386ff.) responded to this question with his doctrine of the *self-limitation of the state*, following the model of the self-legislating moral subject of Immanuel Kant: the state restricts its own activities through the legal order which it itself establishes. This neo-Kantian doctrine can hardly be considered a satisfactory solution to the paradox of the *Rechtsstaat*; at best, it merely reformulates the problem. It is no surprise, then, that Kelsen, who tried to eradicate from late constitutional doctrine what he considered to be a metaphysical residue, emptied the concept of the *Rechtsstaat* of its very last substantive normative implications by equating the state with the legal order (Kelsen 1989, pp. 312–313).

Within the rule of law doctrine, the new problem, which can be termed 'legal totalitarianism' or 'totalitarianism in legal (dis)guise', led to increasing attention to the concept of law. Dicey devoted relatively little notice to this basic notion, but even here his foundational text contains the premises on which future discussion could build. He defines the concept of law through the jurisdiction of (ordinary) courts: laws are 'rules which (whether written or unwritten, whether enacted by statute or derived from the mass of custom, tradition or judge-made maxims known

6 It may be regarded as a curiosity of doctrinal history that the neutral broad concept of police lived on in the US constitutional doctrine of police powers well into the twentieth century.

as the common law) are enforced by the courts'. Correspondingly, constitutional law also consists of rules recognised by the courts (Dicey 1959, pp. 23–24). In his definition, Dicey does not distinguish between statute law and common law. His concept of law includes rules of both origins, provided that they are acknowledged by the courts. Nevertheless, implicit in Dicey's understanding of the rule of law is a more restricted understanding of the law that is supposed to subjugate arbitrary power and to safeguard individual rights. As Dicey's third meaning of the rule of law clearly indicates, this law consists primarily of ordinary private and criminal law as enforced by ordinary courts and which is mainly of common-law origin. However, because of his belief that the British Parliament can do no wrong, Dicey did not see the relationship between statute law and ordinary common law as a major problem. In this sense, he remained faithful to the unitary concept of law presented at the beginning of his treatise.

As we have already noted (see above, p. 158), one of the undercurrents in twentieth-century legal theory is the insight of a bifurcation of the sets of norms called law. This insight has informed contemporary authors such as Ronald Dworkin in his analysis of principles and policies (Dworkin 1978) or Jürgen Habermas in his account of law as an institution and as a medium (Habermas 1989a, p. 365), as well as such an early theorist as the Soviet Marxist legal philosopher Jevgenij Pashukanis in his discussion of legal rules and technical norms (Paschukanis 1969). Roscoe Pound (1939), in his attack on 'administrative absolutism', evokes the contrast between *coordinating* and *subordinating* law, a distinction he borrowed from Gustav Radbruch (1878–1949). Mention should also be made of Fuller's distinction between law as a form of managerial control and law based on an idea of reciprocity (Fuller 1969, pp. 207–213). Possibly, Fuller's distinction owes much to F.A. Hayek. And it is Hayek who, in the rule of law doctrine, deserves the main credit for openly problematising the concept of law and introducing the theme of bifurcation. If two self-evident points of reference exist in the contemporary rule-of-law discussion, one is Dicey and the other is Hayek. Hayek's influence is quite remarkable, given his scholarly field and cultural background: he was an economist of Austrian origin.

Underlying Hayek's dichotomy of norms is a division of social orders into two: into spontaneous self-generating orders, on the one hand, and into organisations, orders that are deliberately created for a certain purpose, on the other (Hayek 1982, p. 36). A paradigm case of what Hayek considers a spontaneous order is the market economy system. Indeed, Hayek does not even examine any other spontaneous orders; his liberalism is very much economic liberalism.

Hayek terms the norms that guide spontaneous orders *rules of just conduct*. In turn, the norms that regulate organisational orders are *rules of organisation*. Originally, only norms of the first group were called law. Rules of organisation were subsumed under the same concept only after political development that began with the period of absolute monarchy had concentrated the power to issue both types of rules to the same body, the legislature. Hayek himself would prefer to use the term 'law' to refer merely to the rules of just conduct. He argues that expanding the concept to include rules of organisation has led to a hollowing out of the contents of the rule of law principle and to its transformation into a mere demand for legalism (Hayek 1982, pp. 72ff.).

The essential difference between the two types of rules lies in their different goal orientation. The rules of just conduct are not directed at any specific goals. They only make it possible for individuals to seek goals that they themselves have set and to follow plans that they themselves have composed. If it is possible in general to use the concept of goals in connection with such rules, their only goal would be to establish the general framework for a spontaneous order. Demands for abstraction, generality and permanence, which are characteristic features of the rules of just conduct, flow from this independence from particular goals.

By contrast, rules of organisation are oriented towards deliberately set goals. They are not confined to securing free spheres of action for individuals but determine tasks for individuals to fulfil. These tasks depend on organisational goals and the position of each individual within the organisational order. Since rules of organisation relate to particular goals, they cannot, unlike the rules of just conduct, meet the criteria of abstraction, generality and permanence (Hayek 1982, pp. 98ff.).

In general, Hayek's dichotomy of rules follows the borderline that separates private and criminal law from public law (administrative law). The norms of private and criminal law are typically rules of just conduct, whereas public law is primarily composed of rules of organisation. Hayek (ibid., p. 131) claims that development from the late nineteenth-century onwards has led to an expansion in the public law rules of organisation. As a thoroughgoing economic liberal, his worry is that the system of rules of just conduct will gradually change into a system of rules of organisation. Public-law regulation is often justified by appeals to social justice but for Hayek, the concept of social justice is empty of content. He contends that the notion 'justice' can only be attached to the behaviour of an individual and not to the state of society. He warns that ever-new public law rules of organisation, issued in the name of social justice, may result in the establishment of a totalitarian planning and command society that destroys the freedom of the individual (ibid., p. 62).

Hayek's description of spontaneous social orders and of rules of just conduct ensuring the general framework of these orders is, of course, controversial, as is his critique of the concept of social justice. But we do not have to agree with Hayek on every point in order to recognise the threat of totalitarianism which ensues from the positivisation of the law.

Hayek's polemical account of the law splitting into two branches, one of them threatening and the other protecting individual liberty, is a variation on the theme of tension between *voluntas* and *ratio*, permeating (modern) law and legal discourse. In *ratio*'s camp, Hayek's rules of just conduct enjoy the company of Pound's coordinating law, Fuller's law based on the idea of reciprocity, Habermas' law as an institution, and Dworkin's principles. In the other camp, that of *voluntas*, we find, in addition to Hayek's rules of organisation, Pound's subordinating law,

Fuller's law as a form of managerial control, Habermas' law as a medium, and Dworkin's policies. The problem common to all these authors is how to let the *ratio* control the *voluntas*. In debates within the rule of law doctrine, it is Hayek who has most often been called on to formulate the issue. His way of posing the problem of the rule of law was motivated by his basic conservative mistrust of all regulatory, welfare-statist economic and social measures. For authors who do not share this mistrust, the question is even more complicated: the controlling influence of the *ratio* has to be secured but, at the same time, the legislator's policy-oriented *voluntas* must be allowed the leeway it deserves, especially under the conditions of political democracy.

Such an approach is evident in Allan's discussion of the doctrine of the rule of law. He concedes that Hayek is 'right to distinguish between the general "law", whose supremacy the separation of powers is intended to preserve, and those rules or measures whose purpose is the attainment of specific social or governmental goals'. But he criticises Hayek for too narrow an understanding of 'general law'. In Allan's view, 'general law' also includes 'the various precepts of administrative due process that together enable such objectives to be attained within the limits of the rule of law' (Allan 2001, pp. 125–126).

As the above citation suggests, Allan accords central place to the principle of separation of powers in his conception of the rule of law, and, related to this principle, raises *generality* to a normative requirement of (statute) law. The demand for laws' generality is also warranted by the principle of *equality*, which Allan regards as the other main rule of law principle complementing due process. Generality as an absolute normative condition of statute law supports Allan's view that the rule of law involves a prohibition of acts of attainder and other forms of *ad hominem* legislation. But this is not the only restriction on the discretion of the legislator which Allan infers from the rule of law.

Allan emphasises that 'the principles of procedural due process and equality impose constitutional limits on the kind of enactment that can qualify as "law"' (ibid., p. 202). He proposes a broad interpretation of these principles which covers procedural safeguards of administrative law and a general prohibition of unwarranted discrimination, in addition to the Dworkinian idea of equal citizenship. In Allan's view, the ideal of equality, implicit in common law, means that 'each person's treatment must be capable of justification in terms of general rules and principles that express a coherent conception of justice, open to public scrutiny and rational criticism'. This leads him to conclude that the rule of law involves the right to speech, facilitating such public scrutiny and rational criticism (ibid., p. 249).

Allan reaches the same conclusion by another route, too, through an argument starting from the other rule of law principle: the due process of law. This principle obliges government to 'defend every coercive act on the basis of its contribution to the common good'. Allan claims that this obligation does not deprive the rule of law of its mainly procedural character, because the nature of the common good is left open for public debate and governmental choice. On the other hand, such a procedural interpretation of the common good entails that 'freedoms of thought, speech and conscience are to be understood as themselves constituents of the rule of law, in so far as they pertain to the justification of government action: to the extent that these basic freedoms facilitate political debate and public criticism of official bodies'. In Allan's account, these freedoms are warranted not only by the constitutional doctrine of the rule of law but 'derive their constitutional status from a conception of law that is intrinsic to all forms of government built on liberal premises' (ibid., p. 75).

It is evident that any solution to the problem of 'totalitarianism through law' must include limitations on the discretion of the legislature; it is the ambivalent relation of statute law to the law of the rule of law that generates the very problem. But it is also evident that every solution that proposes such limitations is afflicted by a new problem: how can restrictions on legislative power be justified in face of *parliamentary sovereignty*, i.e. the other primary principle of English constitutional law?

In recent decades, the uneasy relationship between parliamentary sovereignty and the rule of law has become manifest in debates on the grounds of *judicial review*. Judicial review of not only parliamentary statutes but administrative decisions and actions as well does not mesh easily with the sovereignty of Parliament. If Parliament has, by way of legislation, expressly granted administrative bodies broad powers, how can restrictions on these powers, imposed by the courts, be justified? Two alternative justifications have been suggested, one appealing to parliamentary sovereignty and the other to the rule of law as a principle of common law. The *ultra vires* doctrine resorts to Parliament's intent: when Parliament grants administrative powers, its implicit intent is that these powers be exercised within the boundaries of the procedural and substantive principles applicable in judicial review. The doctrine has been criticised on two main grounds. First, some administrative bodies have been established on common-law grounds, without any involvement of Parliament at all. Secondly, even with regard to statutory administrative bodies, the doctrine has been claimed to be wholly fictional: the principles and remedies of judicial review have been developed by common-law courts, and ordinary Members of Parliament hardly have any knowledge at all of the intricacies of administrative-law doctrine. Critics of the *ultra vires* justification argue that judicial review is based on the principle of the rule of law, and this principle, in turn, forms part of continuously evolving common law. Supporters of the *ultra vires* doctrine have responded by pointing to the threat of courts' usurping the powers, not only of administrative authorities, but also of Parliament that bestowed on these authorities their discretionary competence.

Intermediary positions have been sought as well. Some in the *ultra vires* camp concede that judicial review has been elaborated by the courts and that Parliament, when granting discretionary administrative powers, cannot credibly be claimed to have even implicitly intended judicial-review principles and remedies to be applicable in all their details. The moderate *ultra vires* view restricts implicit parliamentary intent to the general outlines of judicial review and the authorisation of the courts to work out its details. Furthermore, the prevailing standpoint in both camps seems to be that through clear and explicit provisions – so-called ouster clauses – Parliament can exclude administrative discretion from judicial review. Nonetheless, rulings have occurred through which courts have declared themselves competent for judicial review despite an explicit ouster clause. These cases create difficulties in particular for the *ultra vires* side, with its starting point in the supremacy of Parliament.[7]

In the eyes of an outsider to the English debate, this is of interest mainly as a symptom of the constant tension between the two traditional English constitutional principles: the rule of law and the sovereignty of Parliament. In other respects, it is easy to agree with Allan's judgment:

> The most remarkable feature of the present English debate about the basis of judicial review is that almost all participants appear to agree about almost every significant issue of substance. Adherents to the conception of ultra vires based on legislative intent readily accept that the relevant principles are judge-made, finding the relevant connection with Parliament in the grant of the necessary 'imprimatur' to the judges; and those who insist on the common-law basis of judicial review, rejecting reliance on fictions or fig-leaves, agree that parliamentary sovereignty remains inviolate – at least for the purposes of the debate. The truth of the complaint that any relevant legislative intent is only tacit and general is frankly acknowledged; but tacit approval of judicial creativity could, it is fairly pointed out, always be withdrawn if legislative sovereignty truly remains unqualified. In these circumstances, it is often hard to understand, or share, the passion and excitement which the debate seems to generate. (Allan 2000, p. 414)

Competing Sovereignties

In legal literature, the relationship between the rule of law and parliamentary sovereignty is usually treated in a more or less identical pattern: at the outset, a problem is noted but, subsequently, it is declared to be of a mere prima facie nature and explained away in a rather casual fashion.

This pattern, too, was initiated by Dicey. He stresses the absolute character of parliamentary sovereignty, which he defines as follows: 'The Queen in Parliament has, under the English constitution, the right to make or unmake any law whatever; and further … no person or body is recognised by the law of England as having a right to override or set aside the legislation of Parliament'. He distinguishes between a positive and negative side in the principle and links both of them expressly to the role of the courts: 'Any Act of Parliament, or any part of an Act

7 Christopher Forsyth has edited a representative collection of articles expounding the divergent views on the justification of judicial review (Forsyth 2000).

of Parliament, which makes a new law, or repeals or modifies an existing law, will be obeyed by the courts' (positive side); and 'there is no person or body of persons who can, under the English constitution, make rules which override or derogate from an Act of Parliament, or which (to express the same thing in other words) will be enforced by the courts in contravention of an act of Parliament' (negative side) (Dicey 1959, pp. 39–40).

Dicey is careful to stress that parliamentary sovereignty also covers particular and local Acts. He notes that 'the statute-book teems with Acts under which Parliament gives privileges or rights to particular persons or imposes particular duties or liabilities upon other persons', and that Acts called Local and Private Acts 'are just as much Acts of Parliament as any Statute of the Realm' (ibid., p. 49). In the distinction between formal and substantive concepts of law, familiar from German state-law doctrine, Dicey's conception undoubtedly falls under the former. His conception includes no substantive requirements on statute law, not even that of generality. This is related to the fact that the principle of separation of powers has no place in Dicey's exposition of English constitutional law. He mentions this principle only once in his main work, and then in a critical vein. In his account, this principle in France backed up non-interference of the judiciary in administrative matters and protected the independence of the administration, which he considered to be a central feature – and a central problem! – of the French *droit administratif* (ibid., 337–338).

For Dicey, parliamentary sovereignty and the rule of law are both integral principles of English constitutional law. But he was in no doubt about which one of them is superior. The doctrine of the legislative supremacy of Parliament is 'the very keystone of the law of constitution' (ibid., p. 35). The concept of sovereignty implies 'a supreme legislative body which can make or unmake every law; and which, therefore, cannot be bound by any law' (ibid., p. 72). Judicial legislation is the main source of ordinary law which is the law of the rule of law. But Dicey stresses that judicial legislation is not inconsistent with the supremacy of Parliament. There is no contradiction, because 'English judges do not claim or exercise any power to repeal a Statute, whilst Acts of Parliament may override and constantly do override the law of the judges'. This means that 'judicial legislation is, in short, subordinate legislation, carried on with the assent and subject to the supervision of Parliament' (ibid., pp. 60–61). Dicey also firmly rejects the idea that judges could invalidate Acts of Parliament on moral grounds: 'There is no legal basis for the theory that judges, as exponents of morality, may overrule Acts of Parliament' (ibid., p. 62).

But is not the absolute sovereignty of Parliament fatal to the rule of law? Because no substantive limits to this sovereignty exist and since it is not subject even to the requirement of generality, nothing seems to prevent Parliament from adopting Acts that violate individual rights safeguarded by the ordinary law of the rule of law. The rule of law appears to be left at the mercy of Parliament. Yet Dicey refused to see in parliamentary sovereignty any threat to the rule of law. He conceded that 'the sovereignty of Parliament and the supremacy of the law of the land – the two principles which pervade the whole of the English constitution – may appear to stand in opposition to each other, or to be at best only counterbalancing forces'. Nevertheless, in his view this impression is delusive. In reality, 'the sovereignty of Parliament, as contrasted with other forms of sovereign power, favours the supremacy of the law, whilst the predominance or rigid legality throughout our institutions evokes the exercise, and thus increases the authority, of Parliamentary sovereignty' (ibid., p. 406).

How does the sovereignty of Parliament favour the rule of law? Dicey's first argument appeals to the composition of Parliament: Parliament can only express its will through the combined action of its three constituent parts – the Queen, the House of Lords and the Commons – and this will 'must, therefore, take the shape of formal and deliberate legislation'. His second point actually relies on separation of powers – on the independence of the executive power from Parliament – although he was careful not to expressly evoke this dubious principle. Dicey claims that 'the English Parliament as such has never, except at periods of revolution, exercised direct executive power or appointed the officials of the executive government' (ibid., p. 408). Thus, Dicey concludes, several factors have indirectly supported the rule of law, and, as a result:

> Parliament, though sovereign, unlike a sovereign monarch who is not only a legislator but a ruler, that is, head of the executive government, has never hitherto been able to use the powers of the government as a means of interfering with the regular course of law; and what is even more important, Parliament has looked with disfavour and jealousy on all exemptions of officials from the ordinary liabilities of citizens or from the jurisdiction of the ordinary courts; Parliamentary Sovereignty has been fatal to the growth of "administrative law". (ibid., p. 409)

At least from today's perspective, Dicey's arguments are not very convincing. They hinge on factors of the British political system which have proved to be historically contingent and lost their pertinence. Parliamentary legislation is firmly in the hands of the majority in the House of Commons, while the modifying effect of the other components of the legislature – the House of Lords and the Queen – retains little relevance. Nor can we any longer subscribe to Dicey's claim about the independence of the executive from Parliament. The majority of the House of Commons not only exercises de facto legislative power but also determines who will be the Prime Minister and lead the main executive body. It is evident that the claim that 'the sovereignty of Parliament as developed in England supports the supremacy of the law' cannot be defended on the grounds Dicey counted on. Indeed, in contemporary accounts these factors have largely fallen into oblivion.

However, one point remains which Dicey found to speak in favour of the compatibility between parliamentary sovereignty and the rule of law. And this point, concerning judicial interpretation and statute construction, is still a standard argument.

According to Dicey's argument, 'the fact that the most arbitrary powers of the English executive must always be exercised under Act of Parliament places the government, even when armed with the widest authority, under the supervision, so to speak, of the courts'. Therefore 'powers, however extraordinary, which are conferred or sanctioned by statute, are never really unlimited, for they are confined by the words of the Act itself, and, what is more, by the interpretation put upon the statute by the judges'. Although 'Parliament is supreme legislator … from the moment Parliament has uttered its will as lawgiver, that will becomes subject to the interpretation put upon it by the judges of the land'. The judges, in turn, are influenced by 'the general spirit of the common law' and disposed to construe exceptions to common-law principles narrowly (ibid., pp. 413–414).

The Scandinavian doctrine of sources of law stresses the significance of *travaux préparatoires*. Arguably, this is largely due to a Parliament-centred conception of democracy. Correspondingly, one could imagine that the principle of parliamentary sovereignty would oblige the judges to construe statutes in conformity with the actual intentions of the legislature, such as they appear in *travaux préparatoires*. But such a conclusion was foreign to Dicey, as it is also foreign to contemporary authors who try to demonstrate the compatibility of two seemingly contradictory constitutional premises by referring to judicial interpretation through which common-law principles are made to prevail.

The rule of law's role as an interpretative principle holds a prominent position in Allan's version of the doctrine. Use of executive power is subject to control through judicial review, and 'since the rule of law supports an interpretation of statutes consistent with the principles of justice embodied in the general law, grants of executive power for specific purposes must be construed accordingly' (Allan 2001, p. 45). Parliamentary sovereignty extends only to enactment of general rules. Application of these rules to particular cases and their concomitant interpretation falls within the powers of the courts. Allan requires of the courts deference to the results of democratic legislative processes, but this deference does not affect the courts' independence in applying and interpreting legislation in particular cases. Allan also claims – and here he appears to be expressing the prevailing doctrinal view – that in construing statutes in conformity with the principles of common law, the courts are respecting Parliament's will. However, this will is not identical with the actual intent of the legislature, as reflected in *travaux préparatoires*. Rather, it is a fixed or *assumed will*. The underlying assumption is that Parliament, through the Act it has adopted, does not intend to violate the principles of common law, including those related to the rule of law. This assumption can be defeated – so the doctrine goes – but only by a statute's express and clear wording to the contrary.

Allan stresses that 'although the British constitution apparently confers the widest amplitude of legislative power, it is none the less a cardinal feature of the rule of law that the meaning of an enactment – and therefore its concrete effect in any particular case – is always a matter of judicial interpretation'. And, furthermore, 'since any such interpretation must be sensitive to the general principles that … constitute the rule of law, they possess an inherent immunity to radical legislative infringement with the integrity of the legal order'. In this way, the principles of procedural due process and equality impose constitutional limits on the kind of enactment that can count as 'law'. In Allan's view, these principles, along with civil and political rights fundamental to constitutional democracy, find 'adequate protection in the exercise of judicial sovereignty, as regards the application of law to particular cases'. This leads him to question the idea of absolute legislative power, which, he argues, is 'ultimately plausible only on the assumption that enactments can (or should) be "literally" applied, without interpretation' (ibid., pp. 201–202).

Allan claims that Parliament's legislative sovereignty is complemented and, by the same token, modified by the courts' judicial sovereignty in applying the law and in construing statutes. The same proof of equilibrium between parliamentary sovereignty and the rule of law is proffered by Bradley (2006, pp. 98–99), who also quotes Lord Bridge's ruling in *X v. Morgan-Grampian Ltd* (1991) AC 1:

> The maintenance of the rule of law is in every way as important in a free society as the democratic franchise. In our society the rule of law rests upon twin foundations: the sovereignty of the Queen in Parliament in making the law and the sovereignty of the Queen's courts in interpreting and applying the law.

The doctrine of *bi-polar sovereignty* (Sedley 1995) has drifted quite far from Dicey's reading of the two fundamental principles of the English constitution and their mutual relationship. In Dicey's conception, Parliament is, legally speaking, sovereign over the rule of law, too, although, owing to the specific characteristics of the British Parliament, to no detriment of the latter but rather to its benefit. In the above formulation, the rule of law and parliamentary sovereignty are no longer separate principles but the rule of law is now elevated to a master principle which subsumes parliamentary sovereignty. Correspondingly, in Allan's exposition the rule of law holds sway over parliamentary sovereignty: 'the rule of law ... is truly absolute, constituting the basis of the legal order within which legislative sovereignty must be located and defined' (Allan 2001, p. 201).

Yet an ambivalence, even uneasiness, remains in Allan's argument. On the one hand, he underlines the role of judicial interpretation in maintaining supremacy of the rule of law. But, on the other hand, it is evident that the courts' obligation to construe statutes consistently with common-law principles does not suffice to guarantee that the rule of law will prevail. Implicit in the doctrine of bi-polar sovereignty is the prohibition of singular, *ad hominem*, statutes: if parliamentary sovereignty comprises such statutes, the courts are in danger of losing their sovereignty in applying and interpreting law in particular cases. It is also evident that limits exist to the courts' ability to enforce the common-law principles of the rule of law by way of statutory interpretation. Indeed, this is conceded in the doctrine's requirement that there be explicit and unambiguous wording whenever the legislature wants to derogate from these principles. If this requirement is met, the courts are not allowed – so the doctrine (still?) goes – to let the fixed or assumed will of Parliament prevail over its de facto intent.

So it seems difficult to uphold the two-sovereignties doctrine or to otherwise maintain the rule of law without granting the courts some degree of judicial review in relation, not just to administrative action, but also to parliamentary legislation. But it is a sign of the tenacity of the Diceyan notion of parliamentary sovereignty that British courts have been highly reluctant to exercise such review. Jowell notes that 'in the United Kingdom the principle of Parliamentary Sovereignty has always been able to override the Rule of Law'. Yet he appears to intimate that a fundamental change may be in the offing. He also argues that supremacy of parliamentary sovereignty over the rule of law has not been based 'on the authority of commentators such as Dicey and repeated assertions by the courts over time', and poses the following question: 'In the absence of any formal constitutional source, is it theoretically open to the Rule of Law to replace the Sovereignty of Parliament as our primary constitutional principle?' He is able to invoke a recent case where three Law Lords in their *obiter dicta* 'questioned the relation of Parliamentary sovereignty to the rule of law as had never been done before'. Jowell's conclusion hints at a major reversal in English constitutional doctrine:

> It may take some time, provocative legislation and considerable judicial courage for the courts to assert the primacy of the Rule of Law over Parliamentary sovereignty, but it is no longer self-evident or generally accepted, that a legislature in a modern democracy should be able with impunity to violate the strictures of the Rule of Law. (Jowell 2007, p. 23)

The tension between parliamentary sovereignty and the rule of law is not a novelty for English constitutional doctrine but was already commented on by Dicey. In recent times, parliamentary sovereignty has been confronted by a new challenger in the shape of a very un-Diceyan doctrine: the doctrine of constitutional rights as distinct from the rule of law.

The End of the English *Sonderweg*?

Jowell is not the only British discussant who has recognised the dilemma created by the collapse of Diceyan trust in the harmonious relationship between parliamentary sovereignty and the rule of law. Anti-terrorist legislative measures have aroused concerns about the British constitution's ability to provide effective protection for human rights. These worries have been powerfully presented by, for instance, A.W. Bradley, who has drawn attention to the fact that 'in a system in which Parliament is supreme and in which the Cabinet is supported by a majority in the Commons, executive decisions may readily be clothed with legality'. Accordingly, 'in the United Kingdom, Parliament as the supreme legislator may grant the executive powers which drastically affect the liberty of the individual, as it did in 2001 when it authorised the indefinite detention without trial of foreign nationals suspected of terrorist involvement' (Bradley 2006, p. 101).

Bradley locates the roots of the problem in the absence of constitutional guarantees for individual rights (ibid.). This analysis of the British constitution effectively questions Dicey's third meaning of the rule of law. Dicey pointed to the inductive nature of the English constitution, which results from judicial decisions in particular cases and which contrasts (favourably!) with the continental deductive method premised on a written constitution or Bill of Rights. Those common-law countries, such as the United States, which have adopted a written constitution have already dispensed with this limb of Dicey's conception of the rule of law. Will this be the constitutional future in the UK as well? Has the traditional English method of managing the tension between *ratio* and *voluntas* and fencing off the danger of totalitarianism through law proved to be beyond repair?

This question has received additional resonance from what has been called the *internationalisation of the rule of law*. The UK is a party to several international human rights instruments, among them the European Convention on Human Rights. Within Dicey's dichotomy, these instruments imply the Continental European deductive approach. The traditional English way of protecting individual rights sits rather awkwardly with the UK's international-law obligations. The Human Rights Act 1998, which regulates the Convention's legal significance in domestic UK law, is perhaps not a wholly satisfactory solution to this dilemma. The Act tries to accommodate the Convention with the traditional doctrine of parliamentary sovereignty through the same device which, on the standard view, is supposed to ensure common-law principles' effectiveness despite Parliament's legislative supremacy: judicial interpretation.

Section 3 of the Act provides that 'so far as it is possible to do so, primary legislation and subordinate legislation must be read and given effect in a way which is compatible with the Convention rights'. This does not, as is expressly stated in the same Section, 'affect the validity, continuing operation or enforcement of any incompatible primary legislation'. However, if the court is 'satisfied that the provision is incompatible with a Convention right, it may make a declaration of that incompatibility' (Section 4); again, it is explicitly laid down that such a declaration 'does not affect the validity, continuing operation or enforcement of the provision in respect of which it is given'. In that case, the responsible Minister is empowered to order 'such amendments to the legislation as he considers necessary to remove the incompatibility'. The same holds in a situation where the European Court of Human Rights finds a legislative provision incompatible with an obligation of the United Kingdom arising from the Convention (Section 10). But in neither case does the Act impose on the Minister a legal obligation to use the power and to take measures to remove the incompatibility.

Section 6 of the Act provides another proof of deference to the traditional doctrine of parliamentary sovereignty that circumscribes the Convention's effects in domestic law. This section makes it unlawful for public authorities 'to act in a way which is incompatible with a Convention right'; in this section, 'public authorities' covers courts, too. However, the rule does not apply, if, 'as the result of one or more provisions of primary legislation, the authority could not have acted differently'.

So it seems that the Human Rights Act does not confer on courts a competence of judicial review which would comprise power to invalidate or bypass a provision of an Act of Parliament in a particular case because of its incompatibility with the Convention. As proved by subsequent legislative measures, worries concerning protection of human rights did not really find an adequate response in the enactment of the Human Rights Act 1998. Still, although the Act appears to reassert parliamentary sovereignty's sway over the courts, it may be a harbinger of constitutional change which will undermine the traditional doctrine's self-evident authority.

Two alternative interpretations have been advocated as to how the existing system of judicial review is related to protection of human or fundamental rights. According to one interpretation, the latter are subsumed under the former. Mark Elliott (2000, p. 278) argues that 'the Convention rights, as they apply to the administrative decision-making process, must be rationalised as interpretive constructs which shape internal contours of enabling provisions, thereby ensuring that the courts, in effecting judicial review on rights-based grounds, enforce the limits of discretionary powers which enabling legislation – properly interpreted – sets, rather than cutting down the scope of such powers'. Jowell, by contrast, is inclined to recognise in fundamental rights – 'individual democratic rights' – new constitutional principles which the rule of law does not necessarily encompass. He contends that 'the scope of the Rule of Law is broad, but not broad enough to serve as a principle upholding a number of other requirements of a democracy'. Thus, 'it does not … address the full range of freedoms protected by bills of rights in other countries or in international instruments of human rights, or those now protected by our recently enacted Human Rights Act 1998' (Jowell 2007, p. 22). Jowell's New Constitutional Hypothesis includes the possibility that in the future, courts in the UK might strike down parliamentary legislation as in breach with not only the rule of law but even other 'constitutional fundamentals', such as 'individual democratic rights' (Jowell 2006).

Paradoxes of the *Rechtsstaat* Theory

What, then, about the theory of the *Rechtsstaat*? Has it been able to indicate a solution to the paradox of the *Rechtsstaat*, to break out of the circle into which it had been driven after the turn to statutory positivism? If the law as positive law is seen to originate in state power, how can it be expected to function as a limitation to this very power?

The theory of the *Rechtsstaat* is a product of Continental European legal culture. Typical of this legal culture is a unified written constitution with a specific chapter on basic rights; in Dicey's distinction, Continental European legal culture adheres to the deductive model. The tension between *voluntas* and *ratio* permeates the constitution. Through its provisions on lawmaking, the constitution provides political *voluntas* with access into the law, but it also imposes restrictions on this *voluntas*. Constitutional provisions on basic rights and constitutional review appear to offer a solution to the paradox of the *Rechtsstaat*. Basic rights determine the limits of legal regulation, circumscribe the leeway of the legislator's *voluntas*, and these limits are monitored by legal practices and institutions specialised in constitutional review: a constitutional court, ordinary courts empowered to examine the constitutionality of laws or a separate body exercising *ex ante* control of legislation, such as the French *Conseil constitutionnel* or the Constitutional Law Committee of the Finnish Parliament. This solution is in keeping with modern law's positivity. It does not rely on extra-positive, immutable natural-law principles but a statute of positive law, the constitution in the formal sense of the concept. The *voluntas* of the legislator is controlled as a *self-limitation of positive law*.

However, this solution engenders a new problem, which Dicey, in his criticism of the Continental European constitutional model, already detected. Positivity as a distinctive feature of modern law entails that fundamental rights, too, must be understood as being based on positive norms, such as constitutional provisions; otherwise, the legal practices of modern law would not recognise them as legally relevant at all. Unlike in the natural-law thinking of the early modern age, fundamental rights can no longer be grounded in universal moral principles, independent of time and place. But if norms establishing fundamental rights must be conceived of as norms of positive law, are they not also exposed to the risk of amendment and even annulment, as indeed is central to the notion of positivity? If this is the case, how can they accomplish their task of guaranteeing the self-limitation of modern law? We may recall that Dicey criticised Continental European legal thinking for the ease with which rights enshrined in the constitution or a separate Bill of Rights can, in his view, be suspended.

Mere appeal to a formal constitution will not suffice to resolve the paradoxes of the *Rechtsstaat*. We must evoke the other meaning of 'constitution' which links it to the idea of the law's multi-layered nature: the constitution as constitutional culture. Basic-rights norms can only accomplish their tasks in the law's self-limitation if they are present at the law's sub-surface levels, too; if they have sedimented into an integral element of the legal culture which shapes the pre-understanding of legal actors, such as judges. Basic-rights principles, then, function not only as surface-level norms (decision principles), but also as legal-cultural general principles of law. As such, they might be compared with the 'general spirit of common law', which, according to the rule of law doctrine, is supposed to guide judges in interpreting and applying statutory law and account for common law's tempering effect as a counterweight to parliamentary sovereignty.

In the ideal-typical 'mature' modern legal system, the law's self-limitation is primarily achieved through the tacit knowledge of legal actors; for example, when judges construe policy-oriented statutes in the light of morally- or ethically-laden legal principles. Conceived of in this manner, the law's self-limitation is a daily phenomenon, accomplished through routine legal practices. Constitutions contain provisions on institutional practices which have expressly specialised in the task of the law's self-limitation. Although these practices are the most conspicuous aspect in the law's auto-censorship, in a well-functioning modern legal system their role is little more than complementary. The major responsibility in the law's self-limitation falls to routine legal practices, where the sedimented *ratio* of modern legal culture constrains the legislator's *voluntas* as the pre-understanding of legal actors. Of course, even in such a legal system, it may happen that, for instance, the legislature passes a statute violating a human-rights principle and that we encounter at the law's surface level formally valid norms that stand in contradiction to sub-surface legal principles. If such a case should arise in our idealised 'mature' modern legal system, the floor would now belong to the specific institutional arrangements which have been created to ensure the functioning of the law's self-limitation. These arrangements are the topic of the next chapter.

Chapter 8
Gouvernement des Juges?

Judicialisation and Constitutionalisation

New distinctions, restructuring the conceptual field, played a prominent part in Carl Schmitt's military science of concepts. His conceptual innovations include *Jurisdiktionsstaat*, 'jurisdiction state'. Schmitt initiated *Legalität und Legitimität*, published in 1932 to contribute to the final politico-ideological battle over the fate of the Weimar Republic and its constitution, with a novel classification of state forms. The traditional classification, with its roots in Aristotle (384–322 BC), had grouped state forms (or political regimes) into monarchy, aristocracy (oligarchy), and democracy. Schmitt claimed that this classification was but of scarce assistance in analysing the contemporary parliamentary legislative state or the legality and legal positivism associated with it. Fresh constitutional concepts were called for, concepts that pay due attention to the political constellation of the day. Schmitt proposed a new classification in accordance with the shifting focus and dominant understanding of state power. In the medieval polity, state power was conceived of in terms of adjudication; the state was a jurisdiction state. The absolutist state, emerging from the sixteenth century onwards, relied primarily on the military and the bureaucracy; it was typically a *governmental state* (*Regierungssstaat*). German nineteenth-century constitutional development was based on the duality of state and society and led to a dualist state: the state was simultaneously a governmental and a *legislative state* (*Legislativstaat*). When the position of Parliament strengthened, the latter aspect increasingly gained prevalence (Schmitt 2004a, pp. 3ff.) In his Weimar writings, Schmitt already discerned signs of a new phase: an *administrative state* (*Verwaltungsstaat*) whose activities are dictated by seemingly compelling economic and social law-like regularities (ibid.).

An integral part of Schmitt's argument is the link he establishes between state form and its characteristic *principle of legitimacy*. Here, the immediate argumentative context of Schmitt's speech act includes not only the constitutional discourse of Weimar's final years but also Max Weber's writings on legitimacy. Schmitt argues that legislative, governmental, administrative and jurisdiction state are all endowed with a specific legitimacy principle. The obsoleteness of the Weimar legislative state and its constitution was proven by its flagrant contradiction with its legitimacy principle. The legalism of the Weimar parliamentary legislative state amounted to nothing more than a mere formal shell, without any connection to its legitimacy principle, which Schmitt, in his *Die geistesgeschichtliche Lage des heutigen Parlamentarismus*, published in 1923 (English edition Schmitt 1988a), had analysed through the concepts of publicity, discourse, truth and justice.

Writing in the early 1930s, Schmitt treated the jurisdiction state as mainly a historical phenomenon. Yet, he still identified resemblances to it in contemporary Anglo-Saxon legal and political thinking. And even today, in the conventional account, one of the main differences between common-law and Continental European legal cultures relates to the role of the courts in the functioning of the legal system and in development of the legal order. Many differences exist between the United States and the UK – including the tenacious English principle of parliamentary supremacy – but, when compared with Continental Europe, they are united by the central locus of the courts. Only somebody raised and socialised in a common-law culture could write as eloquently as Ronald Dworkin of courts as the capitals of law's empire and judges as its princes (Dworkin 1986, p. 407). But the differences between common-law and Continental systems may be narrowing: courts have acquired a new prominence in Continental European legal systems as well. Indeed, the enhanced status of the courts seems to be a global phenomenon, levelling down differences which have previously set legal cultures apart. And, not surprisingly, a critical debate on the advance of a jurisdiction state has flared up in many countries and in many and divergent legal-cultural contexts; criticism of judicialisation is a global phenomenon, too.

In Europe, current judicialisation is related to two more general tendencies which have coloured recent legal development: Europeanisation and constitutionalisation.

The *Europeanisation* of law has proceeded at a very fast pace. By Europeanisation, I refer to both branches of European law: both EU law and Council of Europe rule-work, centred around the European Convention on Human Rights. In the legal-cultural regard, EU law is a peculiar amalgamation of Anglo-American and Continental-European influences. The Luxembourg Court's pivotal position in articulating and further developing EU law bears resemblances to a common-law system. Thus, the general principles of EU law largely derive from the court's case-law. This holds, first, for general determinations of the character of EU law and its relation to municipal legal orders, such as its status as an independent legal order, its direct applicability in Member-State courts, its direct and indirect effect, and its supremacy over conflicting domestic law. Here, the failed Constitutional Treaty would only have confirmed the existing legal situation. Even the Charter of Fundamental Rights, included in the Constitutional Treaty and to which the Lisbon Treaty has expressly assigned legal effects, to a great extent merely codifies norms which the European Court of Justice has already treated as general legal principles. In its case-law, the Court has also formulated such substantive principles as proportionality, legal certainty, and protection of legitimate expectations. If the active role of the Court points to Anglo-American common-law culture, the main inspiration for substantive principles stems from the Romano-Germanic legal family.

EU law is a strange normative entity. As the Luxembourg Court has characterised it, it is both an independent legal order and part of the Member States' national legal orders. Its impact on national legal orders is not confined merely to the surface level of explicit legal material but reaches down to the legal-cultural underpinnings, such as legal concepts, principles and theories of diverse branches of law. Furthermore, EU law has influenced national legal systems in the institutional respect as well.

The European Court of Justice holds a prominent position in the development of EU law, epitomising judicialisation at the EU level. By the same token, the interplay between the Luxembourg Court and the national judiciary, primarily within the framework of the preliminary-ruling procedure, has reinforced the latter's role within national legal systems: the courts contribute to the development of EU law, bypassing the intermediary of the legislature. The independence of national courts from the national legislature is further boosted by their obligation to interpret domestic law consistently with EU law and, above all, the principle of supremacy which obliges them to ignore all national law conflicting with EU law, including national law with *lex posteriori* or constitutional status. This principle has been hard to swallow in particular in Member States where legislative supremacy has enjoyed an almost sacrosanct status, such as the UK with its doctrine of parliamentary sovereignty and France with the Rousseauian notion of legislation embodying the General Will (Craig 1998; Plotner 1998).

In the Nordic countries, resistance has not been equally tough, although here too the legislature, not the judges, has traditionally been considered to occupy the throne of law's empire. In Finland, for instance, no evidence exists of defiance on the part of the Finnish courts against such basics of EU law as its direct and indirect effect or supremacy. The courts' subjection to the legislature has been manifest in the high legal source value of not only legislation but *travaux préparatoires* as well. In EU law, *travaux préparatoires* do not enjoy a corresponding status, the case-law of the European Court of Justice being a much more important legal source. EU law will probably affect the Nordic doctrine of legal sources by raising the rank of precedents and lowering that of *travaux préparatoires*. At least in the long run, it is not very plausible that the courts would apply a significantly divergent doctrine of legal sources in EU-law and domestic-law cases.

The European Convention on Human Rights constitutes the core of the other branch of European law. While the Convention entered into force in 1950, even in some of the original Signatory States its domestic applicability was explicitly affirmed only in the 1990s. As is typical of international human-rights treaties in general, the provisions of the Convention are quite vague and leave much leeway for specification through the Court's jurisprudence. Consequently, the Court has played a crucial role not only in monitoring the Convention but also in elaborating its precise normative contents. Insofar as the Convention is applied in national courts – either directly or by way of interpreting domestic law – an interplay occurs between a transnational court and national courts, influencing development of both transnational and national law without intervention by the national legislature.

This interplay can be illustrated through the Finnish case. The prevalent view is that Finland's international-law obligation pertains to the Convention as specified by the case-law of the Strasbourg Court. The Convention has been incorporated into the domestic legal order through an Act of Parliament, and in domestic law, too, it possesses the contents which the Strasbourg Court has assigned to it. Hence, a transnational court is constantly re-defining the normative substance of Finland's national legal order. Furthermore, according to the prevailing doctrine Convention rights define the base line of the protection offered by corresponding constitutional provisions. Therefore, the jurisprudence of the Strasbourg Court has an immediate impact on national constitutional law as well. Consequently, the Constitutional Law Committee of Parliament in its *ex ante* constitutional review routinely invokes the case-law of the Strasbourg Court. In some of its recent precedents, the Supreme Court has also referred to Strasbourg jurisprudence, for instance when weighing and balancing the right to privacy and the freedom of the press as interpretive principles in applying the criminal-law provision on violation of privacy. The Supreme Administrative Court, too, has in several rulings invoked the Convention and Strasbourg case-law when specifying the bearing of constitutional basic-rights provisions.[1]

So the case-law of the Strasbourg Court directly affects the law applied by national courts, without intervening decisions by the legislature. European human-rights law, analogically to EU law, increases national courts' independence from the legislature. Quite probably, it will also leave its imprint on the doctrine of legal sources, at least in the Nordic countries. National courts' obligation to interpret domestic law consistently with human rights supports the primacy of the Strasbourg Court's jurisprudence over *travaux préparatoires*, whose traditionally strong position has expressed legislative supremacy and the Nordic Parliament-centred conception of democracy. In many respects, human-rights law's mechanism of influence resembles that of EU law. However, national courts play a more passive role in human-rights law than in EU law; given European human-rights law's mere base line effect, they may be active enough in determining the level of domestic constitutional protection, but with regard to transnational legal development they tend to be simply recipients.

Europeanisation is intimately linked to the other general development which has added to the authority of the courts even in Continental Europe: *constitutionalisation* of the legal order and the legal system as a whole. Constitutionalisation of the *legal order* is epitomised by the increasing significance of basic-rights arguments in all fields of law, including criminal law and such core areas of private law as property and contract law. The diffusion of basic-rights considerations beyond their traditional domain of public law has strengthened the role of principles in legal argumentation and decision-making. Basic- and human-rights norms not only establish individual or group rights but also function as *legal principles* with a wide range of application, not only in *vertical* relations between individuals and

1 See from the case-law of the Supreme Court KKO 2005:82, 2005:132 and 2006:20 and from that of the Supreme Administrative Court for instance KHO 2002:91; 2003:24; 2004:21; 2006:77.

public authorities but in *horizontal* relations between private subjects as well. Many established principles of diverse fields of law have obtained supplementary support from national constitutional provisions and international human-rights treaties. In Continental European legal systems, rule orientation has at least partly retreated, while principle orientation, often regarded as typical of common-law culture, has gained ground. This cultural transformation has repercussions in relations between different legal practices and the institutions responsible for them.

Arguably, the novel emphasis on legal principles strengthens the status of adjudication and legal science at the expense of lawmaking. Principles may be expressly confirmed in legislation, as are basic-rights principles in the constitution, but often enough they derive from other legal sources, such as precedents or legal-cultural principles as articulated by legal scholars. And even when a legal principle finds institutional support in the constitution or a human-rights treaty, norm-formation transpires outside the regular democratic legislative process. The expanded role of principles in legal decision-making augments the weight of judges' and legal scholars' interventions in ongoing discourse on the contents of the legal order.

Moreover, legal principles in general possess a weaker steering power than rules. Typical of principles is both-and applicability: conflicting principles must be weighed against each other, with the respective weight of principles and counter-principles depending on the facts of the case. Weighing occurs on a case-by-case basis and requires the judge's discretion. In doctrinal theories, the principles of a field of law are arranged in a prima facie order of preference. Legal scholarship assists judges in their discretion but cannot substitute for the reasoning presupposed by weighing principles in the light of the facts. Thus, the particularities that legal principles display in both their formation and application and that set them apart from legal rules tend to boost the status of the courts in the legal system. In addition, recalling the role of scholars in articulating and elaborating principles, principle orientation has the tendency of augmenting the significance of legal science as well.

Constitutionalisation of the *legal order* may proceed even in the absence of a system of *constitutional review*. However, the establishment of constitutional review adds an institutional aspect to normative development and leads to constitutionalisation of the *legal system*. Indeed, constitutional review has been an integral element in the *new constitutionalism* which has swept around the globe in the post-Second World War era, and with renewed momentum since 1989.[2] This is the era of what Duncan Kennedy (2006b) has termed the third wave of legal globalisation. The first wave, in the age of Classical Legal Thought, was dominated by German scholarship, while during the second wave, transpiring under the auspices of a social conception of law, the leadership passed to French

2 The term 'new constitutionalism' is used by, for example, Manfredi (1993), Stone Sweet (2000) and Hirschl (2007). Ackerman (1997) speaks of 'world constitutionalism'.

legal culture. In Kennedy's account, the third wave has in turn advanced under US cultural hegemony.

In the inter-war years, constitutional review remained primarily a US peculiarity which did not take root in Europe. Constitutional development seemed to have led to two fundamentally different models: the European legislative model and the US judicial supremacy model. It is true, though, that the first constitutional courts were established in Austria and Czechoslovakia in 1920, under the influence of the writings of Hans Kelsen. However, these courts played merely the limited role of what Kelsen called a *negative legislator*. They focused on constitutional conflicts between institutional actors and did not exercise rights-based review of legislation, which, in Kelsen's view, implies natural-law thinking and would inevitably transform the constitutional court into a *positive legislator*; into a third legislative chamber (Kelsen 1929, pp. 53–57 and 68–70).

After the Second World War the tide turned, with constitutional review becoming the rule even in Europe. In the institutional respect, the majority of European states have opted for a constitutional court. With the single exception of Estonia, this has been the choice of countries breaking away from a totalitarian past: Germany, Italy and Austria in the wake of the Second World War; Spain, Portugal and Greece after the collapse of their authoritarian regimes in the 1970s; and the post-socialist countries of Central and Eastern Europe after 1989. But the new constitutionalism has also encompassed European countries which have not been confronted with a similar constitutional *Vergangenheitsbewältigung*,[3] such as the Nordic democracies of Sweden and Finland,[4] or the UK with the enactment of the Human Rights Act 1998. The most recent manifestation of new constitutionalism is the establishment of concrete *ex post* review of legislation in France, where, ever since the Revolution, legislative supremacy has been ideologically propped up by the Rousseauian notion of legislation as the untouchable expression of the General Will.[5] At present, Switzerland and the Netherlands are the only remaining European countries with no *ex post* constitutional review of legislation.

In Europe, new constitutionalism displays an important *transnational* aspect. The European Court of Human Rights exercises transnational rights-based review of actions by the authorities of Signatory States. It not only complements national review mechanisms but has also provided an inducement to their development. Thus, even critics of constitutional review might prefer national over transnational

3 'Reckoning with the past'.

4 Sweden included in its constitution of 1974 provisions both on abstract *ex ante* control and concrete *ex post* control by the courts. *Ex ante* control is exercised by the *Lagrådet*, a body consisting of judges of the Supreme Courts and the Supreme Administrative Court (*Regeringsrätten*). Sweden also incorporated the European Convention on Human Rights into domestic law in 1994. Finland incorporated the Convention in 1990, enacted a new constitutional Bill of Rights in 1995, and established *ex post* judicial control in 2000.

5 Michel Troper's (1995) argument against *ex post* judicial review is built on a particular combination of Kelsen and Rousseau. On the recent introduction of *ex post* review see Fabbrini (2008).

control, and considerations of national sovereignty are likely to have played their part, not only in incorporation of the European Convention into the domestic legal order, but also in the adoption or strengthening of institutionalised constitutional review in those Western European countries which have traditionally clung to the doctrine of legislative supremacy, such as the UK or France. The EC-law system of *preliminary rulings* where national courts refer the issue of EC law's relevance and interpretation to the European Court of Justice was designed after the German and Italian model of concrete constitutional review, with the Luxembourg Court in the role of the guardian of 'higher' law. An integral element in the further constitutionalisation of EC law was the Court's adoption of the direct effect and supremacy of EC law over conflicting domestic law. Upholding this principle falls not only to the Luxembourg Court but also to national courts, which, in case of contradiction, are supposed to give preference to EU law. These powers of reviewing acts of the legislature in the light of EU law have presumably levelled the ground for introducing a national system of *ex post* constitutional review in such (former?) bastions of legislative supremacy as the UK and France.

But neither has the spread of new constitutionalism been confined merely to Europe. For example, Canada, New Zealand and South Africa attest to its global reach, so that when discussing globalisation in the context of law, new constitutionalism should be quite high on the agenda. One recent critical observer has described the development as follows:

> Around the globe, in more than eighty countries and in several supranational entities, constitutional reform has transferred an unprecedented amount of power from representative institutions to judiciaries. From the Eastern Bloc to Canada, from Latin America to South Africa, from Britain to Israel. Most of these countries have recently adopted a constitution or constitutional revision that contains a bill of rights and establishes some form of active judicial review. An adversial American-style rights discourse has become a dominant form of political discourse in these countries. The belief that judicially affirmed rights are a force of social change removed from the constraints of political power has attained near-sacred status in public discussion. National high courts and supranational tribunals have become increasingly important, even crucial, political decision-making bodies. (Hirschl 2007, p. 1)

The post-Second World War expansion of constitutional review has often been taken to mean the triumph of the US model of judicial supremacy over the (former) European notion of legislative supremacy. However, such a reading simplifies the issues and ignores the rich variety of institutional forms as well as normative and doctrinal choices displayed by recent global experience of constitutional design. It would be a mistake to equate new constitutionalism straightforwardly with American constitutionalism or to define constitutional options merely in terms of the two extremes of judicial and legislative supremacy.

Different approaches to constitutionalisation and the accompanying judicialisation are possible. The primary perspectival choice concerns the respective emphasis on normative and explanatory viewpoints: we can either engage in a normative discussion of the merits and drawbacks of constitutionalisation and judicialisation or try to provide explanations for these developments. Here, too, the Critic is prone to search for the strategic aims of the central legal and political actors, and now she can find company among political scientists, such as Alec Stone Sweet, who have published actor-centred accounts of the constitutionalisation of EU law and of judicial empowerment in general. Hirschl, the above-cited critical observer, has presented a sweeping thesis of the explanatory background to constitutionalisation as a global phenomenon:

> Judicial empowerment through constitutionalisation is best understood as the product of a strategic interplay between three key groups: threatened political elites, who seek to preserve or enhance their political hegemony by insulating policy-making in general and their policy preferences in particular, from the vicissitudes of democratic politics while they profess support for democracy: economic elites, who view the constitutionalisation of rights, especially property, mobility, and occupational rights, as a means of placing boundaries on government action and promoting a free-market, business-friendly agenda; and judicial elites and national high courts, which seek to enhance their political influence and international reputation. (Hirschl 2007, pp. 11–12)

Much could be said of Hirschl's general thesis, and counter-examples could certainly be produced. Hirschl's account illustrates the difficulty of keeping normative and explanatory considerations apart: his explanatory claim is clearly coloured by his normative assessment of constitutional review. In what follows I shall concentrate on the normative discussion. After clarifying the coordinates of the discussion, I shall first put forth my own version of the general defence of rights-based constitutional review and then provide a preliminary appraisal of the main critical arguments. Their relevance will then be further assessed in the context of particular institutional and doctrinal-normative types of review.

Varieties of Constitutional Review

In a normative discussion on the justifiability and legitimate scope of constitutional review, precision is needed with regard to both the object and the level of debate. First, the notion of constitutional review may intuitively be clear enough but, in effect, it comprises a wide range of institutional arrangements, as well as normative and doctrinal options. It is not at all self-evident that when discussing constitutional review, all the interlocutors are discussing exactly the same phenomenon. Secondly, discussion may proceed on different levels of generality, which easily become confused. Thus, a point relevant only for a certain type of constitutional review or merely for a particular jurisdiction at a particular historical point of time may be asserted as a general argument, purportedly delivering a death-blow to the whole idea of constitutional review. So let us try to be accurate and define the coordinates within which critical or affirmative normative arguments are deployed. I shall start with some conceptual clarifications.

First, a distinction should be drawn between constitutional and judicial review: constitutional review is not necessarily of a judicial nature, and not all judicial review is of a constitutional nature. *Judicial review* is review by the judiciary of acts of other branches of the state. It includes review of not only legislative but also executive and administrative acts. For instance, UK debates have, until recently, focused on judicial review of administration, since appraising the substantive validity of legislation has been inconceivable under the unchallenged supremacy of Parliament. In this sense, 'judicial review' is a broader concept than 'constitutional review'. On the other hand, the judiciary is not the only conceivable institutional option in constitutional review, which can also be entrusted to, say, a Committee of Parliament or to an Ombudsman. In this sense, in turn, 'constitutional review' is a more extensive notion than 'judicial review'.

Let us define 'constitutional review' as the legally institutionalised assessment of acts of public authorities in the light of the constitution by a body other than the authority itself. The review is constitutional because it uses the constitution as its yardstick. My definition comprises only explicitly regulated, *external* monitoring of constitutionality and excludes auto-control, operating as a more or less routine phase in the regular decision-making procedure of public authorities. However, it does include arrangements where the supervisory body is formally an organ of the authority under supervision but possesses distinct tasks and powers of constitutional review; here an illustration would be the Constitutional Law Committee of the Finnish Parliament.

We should not make our conceptual apparatus overly complicated. Nevertheless, two further distinctions are needed, one concerning the extent and the other the intensity of the review. The above definition, which covers monitoring the acts of all public authorities, relates to 'constitutional review' in the *broad* sense. However, critical debates have in particular concentrated on review of legislative acts issued by an elected, representative body; this constitutes the *narrow* sense of the concept. It will be the main focus of my subsequent discussion as well.

The distinction between strong and weak forms of constitutional review pertains to its intensity. This is of particular significance in analysing review of legislation, but it may also be relevant in, say, discussing the powers of an Ombudsman-like institution with regard to the executive and administrative branches. *Strong constitutional review* involves the power to strike down a statute either before or after its entry into force (*ex ante* or *ex post* control). *Ex ante* strong review includes the power to declare the proposed piece of legislation unconstitutional and to block its entry into force. In *ex post* strong review, different gradations may be discerned, depending on the legal effects of a ruling on inconsistency with the constitution. At one extreme stands the power to declare the statute ineffective and at the other the competence only to set it aside in an individual case; in the latter case, the decision entails no immediate legal effects beyond the case at hand.[6] *Weak constitutional review* includes no formal powers of defeating the will of the legislature but merely entitles the monitoring body to draw the legislature's attention to problems in the constitutionality of statutes already in force or only under deliberation.[7]

It is important to be precise about what sort of scrutiny one is discussing when discussing constitutional review. Equally important is to specify the discussion's level of generality, as well as its implicit abstractions and background assumptions. I would suggest a distinction between three discursive levels: one can address, *first*, constitutional review (either in the broad or in the narrow sense of the term) *in abstracto*; *secondly*, a certain generic model of constitutional review, say, US-type judicial review; or, *thirdly*, constitutional review in a particular country at a particular point of time, say, constitutional review in the US during the *Lochner*-era. At the first level, the focus is on the very idea of constitutional review, which is assessed in the light of some general normative criteria. But, secondly, general arguments do not necessarily possess equal relevance for all models of review, and, furthermore, some arguments pertain only to some model(s). Finally, the bearing of a viewpoint may be confined solely to a particular period in the history of a particular jurisdiction, as is exemplified by, say, the 'nine-old-men' slogan in the pre-1937 critique of the US Supreme Court.[8] It is not always easy to keep the levels of argument separate, and it may also well be that analysis of a specific type of review or even of its particular instance reveals points of a more wide-ranging purport. Nevertheless, it is important to be aware of the discursive level one is engaged with and of the transitions one makes from one level to another.

Types of constitutional review can be construed on various grounds. Below, I shall employ two kinds of criteria: *institutional* and *doctrinal-normative*. Institutional choices determine the bodies responsible for review; the conventional, albeit misleading, dichotomy of the American diffused model relying on ordinary courts and the European concentrated model of constitutional courts finds its locus on the institutional axis. By contrast, strong and weak forms of control manifest variation along the other, doctrinal-normative axis.

The weight of distinct normative considerations depends not only on the institutional and doctrinal-normative type of review but also on its constitutional

6 US constitutional review should obviously be located somewhere between the two extremes of strong review. The legal effects of a ruling on a statute's inconsistency with the Constitution depend on, firstly, whether the statute is found 'facially invalid' or merely 'invalid as applied', and, secondly, the general precedent value of decisions of the court at issue. See Tribe (1988, pp. 28–32) and Fallon (2000).

7 The above distinction is related to Mark Tushnet's discussion of strong and weak forms of judicial review. Tushnet (2003 and 2008, pp. 18ff.).

8 On references to 'the nine old men, whose total age amounts to 650 years', see Friedman (2000, p. 986).

and social context. General critical or affirmative arguments are always made against certain assumptions about the constitutional as well as the wider cultural and societal setting where review is exercised, and these assumptions simply do not possess universal validity. Relevant contextual factors relate to the vigour of the constitutional culture and the robustness of democratic structures, including the communicational and organisational networks of civil society. In what follows, I shall employ the rather crude ideal-typical distinction between *consolidated* (or 'old') and *emerging* (or 'new') *democracies*, being wholly conscious of the many transitions and gradations between the two. My main focus will be on the former, the latter, however, providing the opportunity to emphasise the context-dependence of normative argumentation.

Constitutional Review as a Custodian of the Law's Limits

I shall relate my fundamental argument for constitutional review to the perennial problem of the law's limits; a problem that every historical type of law is confronted with. The law is accompanied by the possibility of coercion; those who do not abide by its rules can be compelled to do so or at least punished for not doing so. But not all coercion in the name of law is warranted: limits exist to the justifiable human powers of making, applying and executing law.

As we noted in the preceding chapter, the issue which the modern doctrines of the rule of law and the *Rechtsstaat* have addressed is prevention of arbitrary power. Initially, the threat was seen to arise from executive and administrative power, so that the remedy was sought in submitting government officials to common-law rules (the doctrine of the rule of law) or developing administrative law as a specific branch of law and administrative judiciary as a specific branch of the judiciary (the *Rechtsstaat* doctrine). But these remedies did not actually reach the core of the problem. They aimed to bring extra-legal power within the scope of the law and to extend legal safeguards to executive and administrative acts. But the problem of the law's limits concerns, not so much extra-legal or illegal, but, rather, legally-regulated power; power in legal guise. And, gradually, both *Rechtsstaat* and rule-of-law theorists have realised that the danger can have its locus, not only in illegal or legally-unregulated executive or administrative power, but also in the very laws supposedly disciplining such power. This is the menace of what I have termed 'totalitarianism through law'. In debates on constitutional review, assuming the conditions of a majoritarian democracy, it is conventionally called the threat of *the tyranny of the majority*.

In line with all first-level normative discussion, my general defence of constitutional review is based on certain abstractions and initial assumptions. I presume what I call a mature modern legal system. Modern law is essentially positive law. Positivity entails that the traditional solution which Western law has offered to the problem of the law's limits is no longer available: these limits can no longer be conceived in terms of non-positive, natural law. The idea of the constitution as a 'higher' but still positive law is intrinsically related to the issue of the law's limits in its specifically modern shape. Through its provisions on basic rights and safeguards for their realisation, a modern constitution seeks to ward off the threat of totalitarianism through law or – to use the expression more familiar to constitutional theory – the tyranny of the majority. By the same token, the constitution aims to dissolve *the paradox of the Rechtsstaat*, consisting in the circularity of the formal *Rechtsstaat* notion: the power of the state is supposed to be restricted through law which, on the positivist understanding, emanates from the very same state power.

But, as we saw in Chapter 7, dissolution of the paradox of the *Rechtsstaat* gives rise to another paradox, which can be termed *the paradox of constitutional rights*. Rights and their safeguards derive from the constitution which, as positive law, is also susceptible to amendment, suspension and repeal. Entrenchment of the constitution, with a Bill of Rights as an integral element, provides partial but not absolute protection: if the requirements of the qualified procedure are met, constitutional limitations can be undone in a constitutionally proper manner. This is why we must extend our examination of the functioning of basic rights to their legal-cultural underpinnings. Basic rights can only fully accomplish their protective task if constitutional provisions are propped up by a supportive constitutional culture, unfolding its effects through the hermeneutical pre-understanding of legal and political actors. In a mature modern legal system, the law's self-limitation, where basic rights play a prominent role, is mainly realised in everyday legal practices; particular institutionalised procedures of constitutional review are left with merely a complementary role.

In the US debates, the case for constitutional review has often been stated in terms of *ratio* and *voluntas*, reason and will (fiat). A memorable example is Alexander Bickel's (1925–1974) comment on Felix Cohen's criticism of the equation of constitutionality with rationality. Cohen had argued that 'taken seriously, this conception … makes of our courts lunacy commissions sitting in judgment upon the mental capacity of legislators and, occasionally, of judicial brethren'. To this Bickel (1962, p. 41) retorted that 'the relevant distinction is not between rationality and lunacy but between rationality and will'. Dworkin's distinction between principles and policies and his thesis of the former prevailing over the latter is a continuation of this argument. It is tempting to argue that the legislator embodies the pole of will and policy, whereas it falls to the courts to assert the prevalence of reason and principles. Thus, constitutional review and judicial supremacy would be justified by the need to bridle through reason the free reign of will. But clearly such an apportioning of will and reason between the legislator and the courts is misleading, at least in a consolidated democracy: lawmaking does not consist merely of the uninhibited exercise of will, nor does constitutional adjudication lack its moments of will or fiat. Let us resume our examination of the role of *voluntas* and *ratio* in modern law.

First, recall that from the days of Thomas Hobbes and Jeremy Bentham onwards, the law's *voluntas* has also been related to a certain type of rationality. In the legal positivist understanding, the national legislator has treated the law as an instrument for achieving its political aims. The problem is not so much the lack but rather the truncated nature of the rationality that such a *voluntas* resorts to: it privileges *instrumental*, pragmatic reason and downplays the *ethical* and *moral* dimensions which a thick notion of practical reason includes as well. Indeed, we might argue that what makes arbitrary power arbitrary is its one-sided instrumentalism and neglect of the ethical and moral implications of the issues addressed. Conceived in these terms, the task of basic rights is to restore the pertinence of the ethical and moral aspects of practical reason and to submit instrumental reason to their control, or, expressed through Dworkin's vocabulary, to let policies be censored by principles.

But we should be very cautious against concluding that *ratio* in its thick sense could only be defended by the judiciary, perhaps aided by legal scholars, and that the legislator would only be capable of instrumentalist, policy-oriented reasoning. I have already argued that in spite of continuity in the tasks falling to the law's *ratio*, social and cultural modernisation has altered its character. The seventeenth- and eighteenth-century common-law authors, the interlocutors of Hobbes and Bentham, still embraced the notion of traditionalist, communal reason. Modern legal culture, which provides legal actors with their pre-understanding, differs from pre-modern society's legal tradition in its reflexivity and receptivity to criticism. However, when underlining the transformation of the law's *ratio*, I have implicitly presumed that the pole of *voluntas* has remained approximately the same. It is time to question this presumption.

Democracy has a contradictory impact on the law's *voluntas*. Democracy accelerates the law's instrumentalisation, as economically and socially depressed social classes and groups strive to improve their lot by political means, through legislation. The welfare state with its social interventionism did not emerge spontaneously but through deliberate political and legal decisions, facilitated by democratisation of the political system. Hence, it would appear that democracy has only bolstered the *voluntas* that the law's *ratio* is called on to temper.

But a reverse side to this development also exists. Democratisation enriches the reason allied with legislative *voluntas*; under democratic conditions, it would be a mistake to define it in exclusively instrumentalist terms. The ethical and moral aspects of practical reason can unfold their influence even in legislative procedure. Indeed, in the mature modern legal system of a consolidated democracy this is the default case. Basic-rights principles rooted in the constitutional culture form part and parcel of the preconceptions through which legal and political actors tackle their legislative tasks. Recourse to institutionalised practices of constitutional review is only the *ultima ratio* in supervision of the law's ethically- and morally-determined but still positively-defined boundaries; an exception rather than a rule.

In Chapter 2, I let Franz L. Neumann introduce the topic of the tension prevailing between the law's *voluntas* and *ratio*. Neumann sought in democratic lawmaking for reconciliation between the two poles. Jürgen Habermas has continued along the same line. With his ideal model of rational political will-formation, he has tried to demonstrate how the different aspects of practical reason can – and should! – be given their due in democratic lawmaking procedures. The model comprises a succession of diverse kinds of discourse and forms of communication: instrumentally-oriented *pragmatic discourse* where legislation is treated as a means to achieve chosen goals; *bargaining processes*, aiming at compromises between particular interests supporting divergent goals; *ethical* discourse which focuses on the values underpinning goals; *moral discourse* where pragmatically- and ethically-motivated consensus and interest compromises are assessed from a universalist standpoint; and, finally, *juridical discourse* which seeks to maintain the coherence of the legal order (Habermas 1996, pp. 157–168). Democratic lawmaking augments the rationality of legislation: it retains its instrumentalist traits, but these are held in check by the claims of ethical and moral reason. Legislation is not merely about policies but about principles as well.

This model of democratic lawmaking should not be taken as requiring that each legislative project should undergo separate, successive discursive phases focusing on diverse aspects of rationality. The phases may well be intertwined, so that distinct ethical or moral discourses, for instance, may be unnecessary. Remember that in an ideal-typical mature legal system of an ideal-typical consolidated democracy, ethically- and morally-laden basic-rights principles accomplish their censoring effect as an integral part of the constitutional culture which permeates the hermeneutical pre-understanding of political and legal actors. Hence, in the legislative process the need for distinct ethical and moral discourses typically only arises in controversial cases where the ethical and moral connections and implications turn out to be particularly problematic. Hard cases come not only before courts but before legislatures as well!

Let us assume that we have reached a consensus on the need for an entrenched constitution, including a Bill of Rights, and on the necessity to monitor the constitutionality of acts of public authorities. This consensus does not automatically extend to acceptance of *external* constitutional review. An obvious alternative is available: internal control within each branch of the government. In US debates, this has been the standard counter-suggestion that critics of judicial review have put forth, and not merely as a fruition of abstract theorising but as a wholly plausible reading of the existing Constitution. On this reading, also called the *departmental theory*, the Constitution binds all branches of government, each of which supervises the constitutionality of its own acts. This holds for lawmaking, too: the responsibility for guaranteeing the constitutionality of legislation falls to the legislature itself.[9] Actually, my account of how constitutionality is ensured in the mature modern legal system of a consolidated democracy implies the primacy

9 Larry Kramer's study of 'popular constitutionalism' demonstrates the presence of the departmental theory as an alternative to judicial supremacy throughout US constitutional history (Kramer 2004). See also Tushnet (1999).

of internal supervision. External constitutional review is meant to be merely a last resort, intervening in exceptional cases where internal supervision fails. In practice, as we know, only the legislative, executive and administrative branches are subjected to external review. Why, and by what justification?

The answer lies in the predominant policy orientation of these branches of government: their task is to initiate and undertake purposive measures, with a view to remedying social evils or to improving the living conditions of members of society. To say so is not to criticise: such policy orientation is in no way illegitimate. But while conceding its legitimacy, we should also be conscious of the quite natural jeopardy it entails: when issues are approached from an instrumentalist perspective, this easily – and understandably – leads to underrating their ethical and moral aspects. And if that happens, external constitutional review by a body which does not share the initial policy orientation comes to the rescue. This is the general argument for the role of the judiciary in constitutional review. It falls to constitutional review, as it were, to compensate for the deficiency of ethical and moral deliberations in the course of lawmaking.

The Core Case against Constitutional Review

The case for constitutional review has been made: in the mature modern legal system of a consolidated democracy, constitutional review is the *ultima ratio* in prevention of arbitrary power and in monitoring the law's limits. Let us now give the floor to the opposing party.

From its early beginnings in the late eighteenth-century United States,[10] constitutional review and judicial supremacy have been accompanied by critical debates. In the first decades of the twentieth century, the *Lochner*-era jurisprudence of the Supreme Court was a central target in the Realist attack on Classical Legal Thought. In the post-New-Deal era, the emphasis on rights-based constitutional review shifted from economic to civil rights. The civil-rights rulings of the Warren Court in the 1950s and 1960s reframed the '*counter-majoritarian difficulty*'[11] for post-Realist academic liberals: how could one maintain both judicial protection of civil rights and democratic governance? (Friedman 2001a, p. 934). In subsequent decades, the debates have shown no signs of calming down; the counter-majoritarian difficulty remains the main obsession of American constitutional theory.

10 Traditionally, *Marbury* v. *Madison*, decided in 1803, has been regarded as the Great Turning-Point, the Foundational Event of constitutional review. However, recent research has shown that in several states, constitutional review was already well established in the previous decade (Kramer 2004, pp. 35ff.).

11 This formulation of the problem stems from Alexander Bickel's *The Least Dangerous Branch* (1962), one of the canonical contributions to US debates on constitutional review. The title of Bickel's book alludes to Alexander Hamilton's defence of the institution in *Federalist 78*, which can be considered the Foundational Text of the canon.

The global trend of new constitutionalism has entailed globalisation of controversies over constitutional review. Not only in the United States but in many other countries around the globe as well, *judicialisation* (Shapiro and Stone Sweet 2002) and the ensuing *courtocracy* or *juristocracy* (Hirschl 2007) have come under attack. Schmitt is frequently drawn into present-day constitutional- and international-law debates, but the current Schmitt-renaissance does not seem to extend to his theorising about state forms and corresponding legitimacy principles. In Europe, the antecedent has rather been detected in another polemical analysis, published in the aftermath of the First World War: Édouard Lambert's attack on US-style constitutional review. Lambert's pamphlet, which came out in 1921, was instrumental in obliterating political support for the introduction of judicial *ex post* control in France. It also coined the central term for much of the subsequent criticism, not only in France but even elsewhere (Davis 1987; Stone Sweet 2003, pp. 2758–2760). The title of the book indicates the specific perspective of Lambert's attack: *Le Gouvernement des Juges et la Lutte contre la Legislation Sociale aux États-Unis*.[12] The European discussants were familiar with US *Lochner*-era experience.

Schmitt's conceptual framework may have fallen into oblivion, but substantially, the discussion has retained a Schmittian tinge: a central critical argument is that in constitutional review the judiciary overreaches its distinct legitimacy principle. In addition to its common points, criticism displays significant variation, too, depending on the particular type of review the critic is focusing on. Again, it may be difficult to separate general arguments from considerations with a more limited pertinence.

Jeremy Waldron has tried to distil the core of the case against judicial review of legislation. He has presented his case at the general level: supposedly, it is not restricted merely to the US variant but claims validity everywhere where his background assumptions are met. If they fail, he concedes that the argument may not hold. He makes four assumptions. We are dealing with

> a society with 1) democratic institutions in reasonably good working order, including a representative legislature elected on the basis of universal adult suffrage; 2) a set of judicial institutions, again in reasonably good order, set up on a nonrepresentative basis to hear individual lawsuits, settle disputes, and uphold the rule of law; 3) a commitment on the part of most members of the society and most of its officials to the idea of individual and minority rights; and 4) persisting, substantial, and good faith disagreement about rights (i.e., about what the commitment to rights actually amounts to and what the implications are) among the members of the society who are committed to the idea of rights. (Waldron 2006, p. 60)

12 *Government by the Judges and the Struggle Against Social Legislation in the United States*.

Waldron's case relies on a two-pronged argument. First, judicial review tends to obscure the real issues at stake when citizens hold diverging views about rights and to focus on 'side-issues about precedents, texts, and interpretation'. This might be called the *juridification* of rights-issues. Secondly, judicial review is illegitimate from the democratic point of view: 'By privileging majority voting among a small number of unelected and unaccountable judges, it disenfranchises ordinary citizens and brushes aside cherished principles of representation and political equality in the final resolution of issues about rights' (ibid., p. 53).

Let us start examining Waldron's case from the latter point. This is the familiar argument about the judiciary exceeding the range of its legitimacy principle and violating such constitutional fundamentals as *democracy* and *separation of powers*. This standard criticism emphasises the inevitability of political choices in rights-based constitutional adjudication. Critics argue that even when the written constitution includes a Bill of Rights, the provisions are vague and leave leeway to varying, even contradictory interpretations; the favourite reference is to heated constitutional debates on abortion in many Western countries. The problem does not consist in the abstract text of the Bill of Rights as such but in its application, which presupposes weighing and balancing, either between opposing rights or between rights and policy considerations justifying their limitation. In striking down a law, the court as a non-elected and democratically non-accountable body substitutes its own value or policy preferences for those of the legislature. If reasonable people may reasonably disagree on issues of rights, these should be decided in democratically-organised political rather than judicial procedures and by representative rather than judicial bodies. Constitutional review and judicial supremacy unavoidably contradict the principles of democracy and separation of powers. The counter-majoritarian difficulty proves impossible to solve.[13]

At first glance, the attack on constitutional adjudication on the grounds of its policy orientation may seem inconsistent: constitutional review is reproached for both too little and too extensive policy-making. The Realists condemned the conceptual deductivism of the *Lochner*-era courts and called for open policy argumentation. In the same vein, present-day critics claim that the courts tend

13 In addition to Waldron's article, representative criticisms employing the democracy argument include Tushnet (1995 and 1999), Bellamy (2007) and Hirschl (2007). Learned Hand, in his much-cited Oliver Wendell Holmes lecture, put the democracy argument very eloquently: 'it certainly does not accord with the underlying presuppositions of popular government to vest in a chamber, unaccountable to anyone but itself, the power to suppress social experiments which it does not approve … For myself it would be most irksome to be ruled by a bevy of Platonic Guardians, even if I knew how to choose them, which I assuredly do not. If they were in charge, I should miss the stimulus of living in a society where I have, at least theoretically, some part in the direction of public affairs. Of course I know how illusory would be the belief that my vote determined anything; but nevertheless when I go to the polls I have a satisfaction in the sense that we are engaged in a common venture. If you retort that a sheep in the flock may feel something like it; I reply, following Saint Francis, "My brother, the Sheep"' (Learned Hand 1958, pp. 74–75).

to turn moral and ethical or political controversies into conceptual and doctrinal problems and so camouflage the real issue. This is the first prong of Waldron's case against judicial review. Another line of criticism claims that the inescapable weighing and balancing politicises constitutional adjudication and involves judges in choices of a political nature for which they lack democratic legitimacy. The two seemingly contradictory claims of too little and too much policy-making are both invoked to renounce the justifiability of judicial review of legislation.

Critics and advocates of constitutional review hold divergent views of the controllability of judicial weighing and balancing. Constitutional doctrine has elaborated devices that are supposed to add to its objectivity or at least inter-subjectivity, the most influential of these being the proportionality test, introduced by the German Constitutional Court and subsequently adopted in many other jurisdictions. But those challenging the justifiability of constitutional review by the judiciary detect in the proportionality test the very root of judicial usurpation of political power (Manfredi 1993; Hirschl 2007). In the Critic's narrative, too, the necessity of weighing and balancing is invoked as proof of the inextricability of principles from policies (Kennedy 1997, pp. 316ff.; Koskenniemi 1999b, pp. 107–111). By contrast, the defenders of constitutional review praise the proportionality test as a guarantee of the rationality and controllability of basic-rights adjudication (Kumm 2007).

Criticism has pointed to the courts' lack of democratic legitimacy as well as the institutional competence indispensable for the policy choices allegedly involved in constitutional adjudication. Both the composition of the courts and judicial procedure reflect the aim of securing a fair trial for concrete parties; by contrast, they make the judiciary ill-suited for policy analysis and argumentation. For the US legal process-school of the 1950s and 1960s, this was a central reason for restricting the role of judicial review (Duxbury 1995, pp. 263–264), and even today it is frequently called upon (e.g. Waldron 2006, p. 77).

Waldron's core arguments are related to two general dangers which have worried critical observers of over-constitutionalisation in, for instance, Germany: the *politicisation of adjudication* and the *juridification of politics*. The former is argued to be a consequence of the judiciary's involvement in policy-making: the judiciary intrudes into areas which, in a democratic *Rechtsstaat* (a constitutional democracy), should be reserved for the democratically-elected legislature. The claim of *juridification of politics* is inherent in Waldron's accusation of judicial review transforming political into legal-doctrinal issues. But juridification and the crippling of political discourse can also – perhaps slightly paradoxically – be treated as the reverse side of the politicisation of adjudication. Constitutional considerations impose restrictions on the legislature's discretion, and legislation is increasingly seen as constitutionally determined, as the unfolding of the implications of the fundamental value choices already made at the constitutional level. This comes close to what Tushnet has called the distortion and debilitation of majoritarian legislative decision-making, proceeding through the injection of 'too many constitutional norms into the lawmaking process, supplanting legislative consideration of other arguably more important matters' (Tushnet 1995, p. 247).

In summary, the general case against constitutional review is built upon the principles of democracy and separation of powers, as well as the alleged threat of politicisation of adjudication and juridification of politics. Two possible ways are available to confront the criticism: either to continue the discussion on the general level or to question the assumptions on which the case is built and which Waldron – to his credit! – has attempted to spell out. The latter strategy implies changing the discursive level and bringing in examples drawn from particular models or circumstances of constitutional review.

On the general level, we can problematise the notion of democracy adopted in the debate on the counter-majoritarian difficulty and by such prominent contemporary critics of constitutional review as Waldron and Robert Bellamy. It equates democracy with the *majority principle*, applied, first, in elections and, secondly, in decision-making in the elected legislature. On such a view, every deviation from the majority principle violates democracy. Other conceptions of democracy, such as those embraced by Habermas and Dworkin, may lead to divergent appraisals of constitutional review.

Habermas' notion of democracy emphasises the role of discursive deliberations and the necessity of engaging civil society, particularly in debates on the ethical and moral aspects of legislative issues (Habermas 1996, pp. 287ff.). In contrast to the majoritarian view, the concept of *deliberative democracy* does not restrict the arenas for democratic processes to the legislature. No conceptual reasons exist why constitutional adjudication could not be surrounded by discourses accessible to civil society and not merely to the legal elite. Indeed, as Dworkin is prone to emphasise, the US experience provides us with illustrations of principled debates on constitutional landmark cases (Dworkin 2003, p. 345). On the other hand, a defence of constitutional review influenced by the idea of deliberative democracy readily grants the primacy of democratic lawmaking procedures. It regards rights-based constitutional review as merely a last resort, remedying the failure to address moral and ethical aspects of legislative issues at the lawmaking stage.

This view of constitutional adjudication implies a call for *judicial restraint*. As a general rule, the courts should not overturn the legislature's policy choices. The principle of separation of powers, the division of tasks between branches of government, and the corresponding institutional competences entail that, as a rule, policy-making should fall to the domain of the political departments, that is, the legislative and the executive. On the other hand, it is clear that constitutional adjudication is inconceivable without weighing and balancing either between competing rights or between rights and policy grounds calling for limitations to rights. This is not a sufficient argument for rejecting the whole idea of constitutional review, but it imposes on constitutional doctrine the task of elaborating devices which could contribute to the controllability of weighing and balancing, such as the proportionality test. In the eyes of the antagonists of constitutional review, this may signal the juridification of constitutional – read: political! – issues. But not all juridification is automatically evil; something may exist which we could term *healthy juridification*, referring to the legitimate tasks of constitutional doctrine in the functioning of the legal and political system.

Yet, despite the efforts of legal doctrine to augment the rationality of judicial decision-making, convincing reasons exist to believe that adjudication inevitably includes an intractable element of fiat; if lawmaking is not all will, neither is adjudication all reason (see below, p. 281). But in the mature legal system of a consolidated democracy, the impact of fiat is moderated by ongoing legal and public discourse that surrounds constitutional adjudication and where the merits of individual rulings are assessed.

During the *Lochner*-era in the United States, critics – many of them Realists or their precursors – attacked the courts' covert policy-making under conceptualist and deductivist camouflage. After the Second World War, with the shift in emphasis in constitutional adjudication from economic to civil rights, the focus of criticism has altered. When arguing for his case against judicial review, Waldron alludes to legislative controversies, such as those surrounding abortion, which have a conspicuous ethical or moral nature and where the policy aspect, i.e. the instrumentalist dimension of practical reason, plays a secondary role; at issue is what might be called *rights-focused legislation.* When a court strikes down such legislation, it does not invalidate the legislature's policy choices but, rather, its ethical or moral standpoints. If the lawmaking procedure has already included ethical and moral, rights-focused deliberations and if the legislature has explicitly based its decision on such deliberations, my general argument for constitutional review does not justify the court's intervention.

Abortion cases may be the most heatedly discussed instances of constitutional review but treating them as paradigmatic examples might be ill-advised. Most legislative projects aim at policy goals and pursue economic or social policies, security objectives, and so on. In standard cases, the legislative motive is primarily pragmatic, with moral and ethical considerations playing merely the role of side-constraints; the relation of pragmatic to ethical and moral aspects is exactly opposite to their respective significance for the law on abortion. And it is such standard cases that the last-resort argument addresses: the rights-issue may go unnoticed during the legislative phase and be detected only at the stage of application.

Concerns about the politicisation of adjudication are warranted; they caution against constitutional review overstepping its legitimate boundaries and reversing the explicit policy or value choices of the legislature. They do not, however, deliver a fatal blow to justifiable judicial review but serve merely as a reminder of its limits. Equally relevant is the threat of juridification of politics which can ensue from an overly 'thick' reading of the constitution. Attempts to nail down controversial policy or value choices in constitutional interpretation are prone to restrict the freedom of democratic political deliberation and decision-making. One should also be aware of the dangers of an ossified constitutional doctrine. Nevertheless, the Realist critique or Waldron's juridification argument should not be allowed to obscure the positive role that doctrine plays in ensuring the consistency and controllability of constitutional adjudication. In constitutional law, just as in other fields of law, general doctrines are needed but they should not be allowed to petrify into ideological constructions which obstruct, rather than facilitate, the framing of relevant issues.

All in all, even at the general level of discussion, I am not convinced of Waldron's case against constitutional review. He points to considerations which are relevant in examining alternative models of constitutional review, but he does not really tackle its fundamental justification as a last-resort guardian of the law's limits. Such a guardian is needed even in a society that meets Waldron's four assumptions and that roughly corresponds to what I have called a consolidated democracy. Failures to attend to basic-rights issues during the legislative phase are possible in a consolidated democracy, too. And if the assumptions do not hold in general, which still largely seems to be the case in, for instance, the new democracies of Central and Eastern Europe, such failures are ever more probable.

A different kind of argumentation is called for in countries still engaged in the process of strengthening democratic institutions, setting up a vigorous civil society, and entrenching a constitutional culture to prop up the provisions of the written constitution. Then, quite simply, Waldron's four assumptions or my own presupposition of a mature legal system in a consolidated democracy do not apply. In those circumstances a constitutional court may even substitute for a non-functioning representative democracy, safeguarding democratic values enshrined in the constitution. Kim Lane Scheppele (2005) has argued that post-communist Hungary, particularly before 1998, exemplified 'democracy through judiciary': it fell to the Constitutional Court to defend democracy in a situation where representative channels were blocked. Constitutional adjudication may also play a crucial role in forming a constitutional culture worthy of a democratic *Rechtsstaat*. Constitutional culture can only evolve through constitutional practices and discourses for which constitutional adjudication provides a central forum and incentive.

In emerging democracies, constitutional adjudication pursues specific tasks that are not equally relevant under the idealised conditions which are, consciously or unconsciously, assumed in supposedly general-level normative debates. These tasks also help to explain why post-totalitarian countries have found themselves on the crest of the post-war wave of new constitutionalism and, as a rule, opted for a strong constitutional court.

In what follows, I shall leave aside the specific problems of emerging democracies and confine my discussion to more consolidated democracies. I shall presuppose the general justifiability of constitutional review but also acknowledge the relevance of the general arguments presented by critics; here, too, I try to avoid dichotomising the issue but, rather, to comply with the methodological guideline of mediation. I shall treat the principles of democracy and separation of powers, as well as threats of politicisation of adjudication and juridification of politics, as normative yardsticks for examining particular types of constitutional review. General-level discussions usually presuppose, implicitly or explicitly, certain institutional and doctrinal choices. Often enough, the discussion relies on the dichotomy of judicial and legislative supremacy, where the former implies strong constitutional review, exercised by a judicial body. This also holds for Waldron's core case. His arguments are relevant, but their weight varies depending on the institutional and doctrinal options adopted in the system under examination. This is an additional reason for questioning the success of Waldron's pleading: even in the institutional and doctrinal respect, his purportedly general case against constitutional review rests on assumptions which do not possess universal validity.

Institutional Models of Constitutional Review

Debates on constitutional review are usually centred around three basic constitutional models: the US model of diffused judicial review; the German centralised model of a constitutional court; and the (pre-1998) British model of parliamentary supremacy which does not accept external review of parliamentary legislation. Although the case against judicial review, based on the counter-majoritarian difficulty or the democracy argument and the juridification of rights-discourse, is argued to have a more general reach, it has primarily been based on the US experience. Nonetheless, claims of politicisation of adjudication and juridification of politics are familiar in criticism of the German model, too. In addition to Germany itself, this model has been adopted in, for example, Italy and Spain, as well as most of the Central and East European new democracies. It differs from its US counterpart not only in the central institutional choice but also in the powers of constitutional review. Both models include the judiciary's power to strike down legislation. But the US model allows this only a posteriori and in the context of a concrete case, the powers of the judiciary being confined to 'cases and controversies' (Bickel 1962, pp. 113–116). The legal effects of a ruling finding an inconsistency with the Constitution hinges on whether the statute at issue is considered 'facially invalid' or merely 'invalid as applied', besides the decision's general precedent value. The German model allows both abstract *ex ante* control, preceding the entry into force of the legislation under scrutiny, and *ex post* control, linked to a particular case. *Ex post* control can be initiated in two ways: either by an ordinary court referring a constitutional issue to the Constitutional Court for a *preliminary ruling* or through a *constitutional complaint*, filed by a party to a case after all the ordinary legal remedies have been exhausted. The powers of the Court include declaring the statute at stake ineffective.

In Germany, the debate on over-constitutionalisation and the alleged 'transition from a parliamentary legislative state to a constitutional-court state'[14]

14 'Übergang vom parlamentarischen Gesetzgebungsstaat zum verfassungsgerichtlichen Jurisdiktionsstaat' (Böckenförde 1991, p. 190). See also Brohm (2001), where the term *Richteroligarkie* (oligarchy of judges) is used.

flared up quite soon after adoption of the Basic Law in 1949 and establishment of the Constitutional Court. At least from the perspective of the history of ideas, it is interesting to note that Carl Schmitt was one of the instigators of the critical discussion. The title of his article published in 1967 was vintage, concise Schmitt: 'Die Tyrannei der Werte' ('The tyranny of values'). Subsequently, important contributions have been presented by such adherents to the Schmitt school as Ernst Forsthoff (1902–1974; Forsthoff 1968) and Ernst-Wolfgang Böckenförde, whose 'Grundrechte als Grundsatznormen'[15] (1991) remains perhaps the most representative critical assessment of German constitutional review.

Critics perceive in the Constitutional Court a third legislative chamber, which has not been content with merely playing the role of a Kelsenian negative legislator but has evolved into a most significant positive legislator. With regard to the parliamentary legislature, it plays the upper hand: it is the Constitutional Court that possesses *Kompetenz-Kompetenz*, so that the German model is that of constitutional-court supremacy.

In Böckenförde's judgement, the Constitutional Court no longer confines itself to constitutional interpretation but is engaged in concretising and balancing the values and principles which it has read into the Basic Law. As a result, constitutional adjudication has undergone a process of politicisation. This has entailed a legitimacy problem: the Constitutional Court does not enjoy the democratic legitimacy which the role it has adopted in the legal order's development would require (Böckenförde 1991, pp. 185–187).

Simultaneously with and largely as a consequence of the expansion and politicisation of constitutional review, lawmaking, too, has altered its character. Legislation is turned into implementation of basic rights: what state functions or policies are to be carried out through legislation no longer depends on democratic political choices but has been determined in advance by constitutional norms. As both the parliamentary legislature and the Constitutional Court are engaged in concretising constitutional basic-right norms, the qualitative difference between lawmaking and constitutional adjudication fades away. Separation of powers, which requires organisational disconnection of enactment and application of legal norms, is blurred. So, Böckenförde concludes, the parliamentary legislature and the Constitutional Court find themselves in a situation of rivalry, which the Constitutional Court as final umpire can decide in its own favour.

German critics have attacked the Constitutional Court for disempowering not only the legislature but ordinary courts as well. Particularly through the device of constitutional complaint, the Constitutional Court has allegedly established itself as the highest private-law court.[16]

15 'Basic rights as principle norms'.

16 This criticism is summarised in the title of an article by Uwe Diederichsen: 'Das Bundesverfassungsgericht als oberstes Zivilgericht – ein Lehrstück der juristischen Methodenlehre' ('The Contitutional Court as the highest private-law court – one element of legal methodological doctrine') (Diederichsen 1998)

German constitutional development is not a result of merely institutional but also of doctrinal choices. In addition to the Constitutional Court's general activism, three interrelated doctrines, in particular, have been crucial in enhancing its position vis-à-vis the legislature and ordinary courts: the doctrines of basic-rights norms as legal principles; of basic-rights norms' horizontal effect (*Drittwirkung*); and of the state's protective duty (*Schutzpflicht*). Along with the proportionality test, these doctrines, elaborated by the court in close co-operation with constitutional-law scholarship, have had great success in the advance of the global wave of new constitutionalism. For instance, they were adopted in Finland in connection with the 1995 reform of the basic-rights chapter in the Constitution.

The German model has attained global prominence as an alternative to US-type constitutional review. However, this should not obscure the fact that post-war developments have brought about new intermediary or hybrid forms which cannot be assimilated to the conventional standard options of the US and the German variants of judicial supremacy or the traditional British model of legislative supremacy. They are often ignored in critical debates, although they can be seen as attempts to avoid the hazards of which critics have warned, while yet acknowledging the principal need for constitutional review. This holds for the innovations which Stephen Gardbaum (2001) has gathered together under the label of the *New Commonwealth Model of Constitutionalism*. He alludes to Canada, New Zealand and the United Kingdom. These are 'countries that were previously among the very last democratic bastions of traditional legislative supremacy'. Between 1982 and 1998 they 'have created a new third model of constitutionalism that stands between the two polar models of constitutional and legislative supremacy' (Gardbaum 2001, p. 709).

Canada adopted its constitutionally entrenched Charter of Rights and Freedoms in 1982. On the prevalent reading, the courts have the power to strike down laws which are inconsistent with the Charter; so far, the Canadian option follows the US model of diffused judicial review. The novelty consists in the so-called *notwithstanding-clause* of Section 33(1) of the Charter. This grants federal and provincial legislatures the right to declare that an Act or some of its provisions are to operate notwithstanding the Charter's substantive provisions on rights and freedoms. This legislative override is effective for a maximum period of five years but may be re-enacted (Section 33(3–4)). Of course, the Canadian solution is not free from problems of its own. An orthodox supporter of constitutional review would fear that the notwithstanding-clause annihilates the Charter's protective effects. On the other hand, it could be hoped that the clause would sensitise legislators' awareness of basic rights and encourage an institutional dialogue between the legislative and judicial branches. Obviously, much turns on the constitutional culture that guides the Charter's application. In practice, a convention inhibiting in particular the federal legislature from use of the notwithstanding-clause has arisen, and on Gardbaum's view, this 'has prevented Section 33 from tempering the countermajoritarian difficulty posed by an unlimited power of judicial review' (ibid., pp. 726–727; for an early critical assessment, see Manfredi 1993).

The New Zealand Bill of Rights of 1990 substantially follows the Canadian Charter but diverges from it in its treatment of the tension between constitutional review and legislative supremacy. The Bill of Rights is not constitutionally entrenched but possesses the status of an ordinary law and can be amended or repealed like other statutes. Still, it enjoys a special meta-status, because it addresses interpretation of other statutes. It imposes on the courts a *duty to interpret* other statutes in conformity with its substantive provisions: 'Wherever an enactment can be given a meaning that is consistent with the rights and freedoms contained in this Bill of Rights, that meaning shall be preferred to any other meaning' (Section 6). Again, it is obvious that the effectiveness of such a constitutionally non-entrenched Bill of Rights that reduces judicial review to an interpretive mandate hinges on factors of constitutional culture. It appears that the New Zealand Bill of Rights has played a more significant role than its formal status may have led sceptics to expect. It has also influenced legislative deliberations and deepened the legislature's attentiveness to rights. In this respect, it introduced a new institutional device which demonstrates that the institutional options available in constitutional review are not restricted to judicial bodies. Namely, it involves the Attorney-General in abstract *ex ante* constitutional review. The Attorney-General is charged with the responsibility of scrutinising bills submitted to the House of Representatives and notifying any inconsistencies with the Bill of Rights (Section 7). The Attorney-General does not possess any formal power to strike down a proposed piece of legislation. Still, the mechanism may be effective enough in enhancing basic-rights consciousness, in inducing morally- and ethically-attuned legislative deliberations, and in raising the political price which a legislative majority must pay for rights-violations (Gardbaum 2001, pp. 727–732).

The third instance of the 'Commonwealth Model of Constitutionalism' was established through the UK Human Rights Act 1998. This introduced rights-based review of legislation while at the same time deferring to the traditional notion of parliamentary sovereignty. Canada has adopted a version of strong constitutional review that includes formal judicial power to strike down pieces of legislation, while paying respect to legislative supremacy through the notwithstanding-clause. In the formal respect, the United Kingdom, in line with New Zealand, has opted for merely weak review. The Human Rights Act imposes on the courts an interpretive duty analogous to that instituted by the New Zealand Bill of Rights: wherever possible, statutes are to be interpreted consistently with the European Convention on Human Rights. If the statute does not allow for such an interpretation, the courts are not entitled to strike down an Act of Parliament. But they have the right to declare its incompatibility with a Convention-right, leaving it to the discretion of the responsible Minister whether to take legislative action. Declarations of incompatibility are not limited to statutes enacted prior to the Human Rights Act, which confers on the Act a certain entrenchedness. On the traditional reading of parliamentary sovereignty, parliament does not have the power to restrict the sovereignty of subsequent parliaments; hence the doctrine of *implied repeal* which accords a later statute primacy over a previous one in case of contradiction. The doctrine does not apply to the Human Rights Act: Convention-rights can only be amended or repealed through explicit statutory provisions. This can be argued to amount to a weak entrenchment of Convention-Rights (ibid., p. 737). It remains to be seen what the repercussions of the Human Rights Act 1998 and the turmoil in constitutional culture it has induced will be. But the sole fact of its enactment supports the claim that guarding the law's limits under the conditions of modern law calls for somehow entrenched basic rights and for some form of external constitutional review of not only executive and administrative but legislative action as well.

Common to the three examples of the 'Commonwealth model' is the endeavour to engage political actors in constitutional review and to establish a dialogue between political and judicial review. Not only in New Zealand but in Canada and the UK as well, enactment of the Bill of Rights has entailed an intensification of executive and parliamentary 'rights-vetting' through special bodies, such as the UK parliamentary Joint Committee on Human Rights (Hiebert 2004 and 2005). However, critical observers have detected signs of advancing judicialisation especially in Canada and the UK, due to judicial activism and the deference of political actors to judicial views. In practice, the borderline between strong and weak forms of judicial review has proven more fluid than constitutional documents would intimate (Hiebert 2004 and 2005; Tushnet 2003 and 2008, pp. 43ff.; Geddis and Fenton 2008).

The Finnish model of constitutional review, introduced through the new Constitution of 2000, also finds its locus among hybrid or intermediary forms. Its uniqueness lies in its particular combination of abstract *ex ante* and concrete *ex post* review.

In Finnish democracy, as in other Nordic countries, too, the parliament has traditionally enjoyed a very prominent status, including vis-à-vis the courts. For instance, its elevated position has been manifest by the high ranking of *travaux préparatoires* in the hierarchy of legal sources; higher than that of precedents of the supreme courts. Before the constitutional reform of 2000, the Finnish system allowed for no *ex post* control by the courts of the constitutionality of parliamentary legislation. Control of constitutionality consisted exclusively of an abstract *ex ante* review, exercised by the Constitutional Law Committee of Parliament.

The Constitutional Law Committee is a peculiar quasi-judicial body. Like other Committees, it is composed of Members of Parliament and, thus, displays a political character. But its deliberations are based on opinions by constitutional experts – mostly university professors – and, as a rule, the Committee abides by their view. In adhering to a legal rather than political pattern of argumentation, its reports are quite different from those of other Parliamentary Committees. For instance, reports routinely refer to constitutional precedents as settling the issue at hand, although by no means has the Committee bound itself to a strict doctrine of *stare decisis*. The experts of the Constitutional Law Committee have no official status, nor is their role even mentioned in the Constitution or the Rules of Procedure of Parliament. Still, it is quite decisive, and it is hardly conceivable that the Committee would depart from a unanimous expert view. If diversity exists among the experts, the political stance of the Members has more leeway and voting reflecting the government/opposition division occurs, although relatively seldom.

Although the Committee belongs to the institutional organisation of Parliament, its deliberations are not part of the regular parliamentary procedure. It is only called on when doubts about the constitutionality of a bill have been raised. In contrast to abstract *ex ante* review by many constitutional courts or a quasi-court like the French *Conseil constitutionnel*, the Committee has not been turned into an instrument of the opposition. On the contrary, in standard cases it is the government which, in the bill it submits to Parliament, advises the latter to consult the Committee. Initiation of constitutional review very rarely causes political controversy. The Committee's assessment is binding on Parliament. However, ever since the nineteenth century, an essential feature of the Finnish model has consisted in Parliament's power to override the Committee's ruling through a *statute of exception*: a bill which the Committee has found to be unconstitutional can still be enacted under the qualified procedure required for amending the Constitution.

The new Constitution did not bring about any formal changes to *ex ante* control through the Constitutional Law Committee. The major novelty was the introduction of concrete *ex post* control. Art. 106 of the Constitution provides that 'if in a matter being tried by a court, the application of an Act would be in evident conflict with the Constitution, the court of law shall give primacy to the provision in the Constitution'. Nonetheless, it would be hasty to conclude that Art. 106 would have epitomised a radical break in Finnish constitutional tradition, a decisive transition from the *ex ante* control of the Constitutional Law Committee in the direction of judicial review. The courts have only been entrusted with a weaker form of strong judicial review: they have the power merely to set aside a piece of legislation in the case at hand, not to declare it ineffective. As was explicitly emphasised in the *travaux préparatoires*, the primary means for the courts to contribute to implementation of the Constitution remains their duty to construe statutes consistently with constitutional provisions. The *travaux préparatoires* stressed the primacy of *ex ante* control under the new Constitution, too. Correspondingly, in its only ruling invoking Art. 106, the Supreme Court stated that 'control of the laws' constitutionality falls mainly to the Constitutional Law Committee, which in the legislative process exercises *ex ante* supervision' (KKO 2004:26). In practice, it may well be that the major alteration induced by the possibility of concrete *ex post* control will be more thorough *ex ante* monitoring. Indeed, the Constitutional Law Committee's workload, as measured by the number of its reports, has significantly increased after the basic-rights reform of 1995 and entry into force of the new Constitution in 2000.

In the *travaux préparatoires* to the new Constitution, the primacy of *ex ante* review was anchored in the requirement of an *evident* conflict established by Art.

106. If the Constitutional Law Committee explicitly states in its *ex ante* review that a controversial statute is not in breach of the Constitution, it is hardly conceivable that a court could find an evident conflict with a constitutional provision.

Parliament's power to override the Constitutional Law Committee's ruling bears a resemblance to the Canadian notwithstanding-clause. In the decades preceding the constitutional reforms of 1995 and 2000, some constitutional scholars criticised statutes of exception for weakening the protection of basic rights and for transforming *ex ante* constitutional review into a formal assessment of the required legislative procedure. In fact, the number of statutes of exception diminished considerably even before the constitutional reforms of 1995 and 2000. According to the *travaux préparatoires* to the new Constitution, statutes of exception should be resorted to very sparingly, as a rule merely when they are needed for incorporation of an international treaty or some other international-law obligation. Statutes of exception have lost most of their previous significance, and when finding a conflict with the Constitution the Constitutional Law Committee no longer contents itself with pronouncing on the procedural question, but indicates how the bill should be amended in order to remove the conflict.

In sum, the Finnish model of constitutional review has retained a notable parliamentary label through the central role of the Constitutional Law Committee. The judiciary has not acquired the dominant role which critics of the US and German models have attacked, but merely accomplishes a complementary function. Still, signs of judicialisation and a juridification of politics are detectable in Finnish development as well. After all, the Constitutional Law Committee represents a quasi-judicial element within the legislature, and its increased significance may result in a certain juridification of legislative politics. In governmental bills submitted to Parliament, an augmentation of references to constitutional basic-right provisions is visible. This reflects a heightened awareness of basic rights in the legal and political culture and, hence, in principle can be considered a positive phenomenon. Nevertheless, one should also heed the danger of juridification inherent in this development.

Intermediary forms, such as those presented above, prove that constitutional design is not restricted to a choice between the standard models: the US diffused and the German concentrated model of judicial supremacy and the British pre-1998 model of legislative supremacy. The British example warrants the claim that some sort of constitutional review is needed to resolve the perennial problem of the law's limits, and it is doubtful whether traditional British-type legislative supremacy remains a viable alternative. The hybrid forms discussed above have all in their own way attempted to address threats to democracy and separation of powers, as well as dangers of politicisation of adjudication and juridification of politics. They demonstrate that constitutional imagination can come up with innovative solutions. But the menace of *gouvernement des juges* has not vanished: recent developments in, say, the UK, Finland and France, imply that effective constitutional review is hardly conceivable without *ex post* control and without granting the courts a certain role. These countries were among the last strongholds of unquestioned legislative supremacy but they have all recently retreated from their previous constitutional positions. In Finland, the *travaux préparatoires* to the new Constitution justified complementary judicial *ex post* control as follows:

> In the (Constitutional Law) Committee, the constitutionality of laws is examined, as it were, at a general level, *in abstracto*, whereas a court assesses the issue in the context of a concrete case. Hence, it is possible that a court detects a contradiction which the Committee has not addressed at all. In such a situation, the requirement for evident conflict can exceptionally be met although the law has passed the control of the Constitutional Law Committee. (HE 1/1998, p. 164)

Judicial Activism vs Judicial Restraint

The consequences of constitutional review for relations between the judiciary and the legislature turn not only on institutional design but also on constitutional doctrines and other factors of the constitutional culture. Often enough, these factors are discussed through the alternatives of judicial activism and restraint. Though afflicted by a certain conceptual vagueness, these terms may be of assistance in a general characterisation of the dominant style in judicial review in a particular jurisdiction at a specific point of time. As the US experience shows, periods of restraint and activism may alternate in accordance, *inter alia*, with the resonance that critical normative points stressed by the opponents of judicial review find in the legal and political culture. Much may also hinge on entrenchment of cultural and sociological prerequisites of a democratic *Rechtsstaat* (a constitutional democracy), as is shown by the activist constitutional courts of the emerging democracies in Central and Eastern Europe. For its part, the activism of the European Court of Justice – the 'constitutional court' of the EU – has clearly been related to the difficulties in transnational political decision-making and the particular requirements of building up an entirely new legal system (see, for example, Stone Sweet 2004).

The degree of judicial restraint/activism is also affected by the doctrinal apparatus in use in constitutional adjudication. Even explicit constitutional provisions may play a role, such as the requirement of *evident* conflict expressly spelled out in both the Swedish and the Finnish constitutions. These constitutions have, as it were, positivised the plea for judicial restraint which was proposed in a classic formulation by James Thayer in US debates at the turn of the nineteenth century:

> It (the court) can only disregard the Act when those who have the right to make laws have not merely made a mistake, but have made a very clear one, – so clear that it is not open to rational question. That is the standard of the duty to which the courts bring legislative Acts; that it's the test which they apply, – not

> merely their own judgment as to constitutionality, but their conclusion as to what judgment is permissible to another department which the constitution has charged with the duty of making it. This rule recognises that having regard to the great, complex, ever-unfolding exigencies of government, much which will seem unconstitutional to one man, or body of men, may reasonably not seem so to another; that the constitution often admits of different interpretations; that there is often a range of choice and judgment; that in such cases the constitution does not impose upon the legislature any one specific opinion, but leaves open this range of choice; and that whatever choice is rational is constitutional. (Thayer 1893, p. 144)

More specific doctrines also exist that call on constitutional adjudication to show institutional deference to the political branches of government, such as the US *political questions* doctrine, which for instance has largely shielded foreign policy decision-making from judicial interference.[17] The European Court of Human Rights, for its part, has clothed its deference to nation-state sovereignty in the *margin-of-appreciation* doctrine, which operates as a deterrent to the court's second-guessing nation-state authorities' assessment of circumstances warranting limitations to Convention-rights (Viljanen 2003).

But, of course, doctrines also exist that have rather justified judicial activism and which, therefore, have been targeted by the critics of judicialisation. In the German critique of the *verfassungsgerichtlicher Jurisdiktionsstaat*, much has been blamed on the doctrines of basic-rights norms as legal principles with a general scope, the horizontal effect of rights, and the protective duty of the state. These doctrines have been attacked in Finnish debates on judicialisation as well. I shall discuss them against a mapping of the conceivable legal effects of constitutional rights.

Basic Rights and Their Legal Effects

The legal effects of basic-rights norms can be determined through the following alternatives:

1. subjective rights – general legal principles – constitutional commissions;
2. vertical effects in relations between public authorities and private persons, and horizontal effects in relations involving only private persons;
3. direct and indirect effects.

The distinctions call for some clarification and qualification. When adopting the German distinction between *subjective rights* and *general legal principles*

17 As is to be expected, the doctrine is highly controversial. As representative interventions, see Scharpf (1966), Tigar (1970), Henkin (1976) and Barkow (2002).

('objective-law principles'), I do not claim that all norms giving rise to subjective rights would be of a rule character. Norms establishing liberty rights, such as the right to personal liberty and integrity or the right to privacy, are partly rules and partly principles which in situations of conflict must be weighed against other basic-right principles;[18] they are rules merely in their inviolable core area (see above, p. 191). When speaking of 'objective-law principles' in the vein of German constitutional debates, I allude to general legal principles with potential relevance in all fields of law. *Constitutional commissions* oblige public authorities to secure realisation of basic-rights provisions. Such commissions may be explicit, as is often the case with constitutional provisions on social, economic and cultural rights, or they may be inferred through doctrinal reasoning from, for example, the state's protective duty. General legal principles may be derived both from provisions formulated as establishing subjective rights (liberty rights) and provisions written in the form of constitutional commissions (social, economic and cultural rights).

When guiding statutory interpretation, basic-rights norms unfold an *indirect effect*. By contrast, when a court exerts strong judicial review, at issue is an instance of *direct effect*. In addition, it is conceivable that a court bases its ruling on the Constitution in the absence of any lower-level norm; this is also a case of direct effect.

Let us now employ the above distinctions in trying to chart at least some of the alleged threats to democracy and the separation of powers which constitutional adjudication may entail.

Extension of the Scope of Liberty Rights

In the standard notion, basic rights are subjective rights that protect private individuals from arbitrary exercise of power by state and other public authorities. This notion is related to the traditional power-limiting understanding of the *Rechtsstaat* and the rule of law. And, as Böckenförde (1991) argues, this was also how basic rights were conceived in, for instance, the Weimar Republic and the deliberations leading to enactment of the German Basic Law in 1949.

Drittwirkung or horizontal effect extends the protective function of liberty rights to hierarchical power relations where both parties are private persons. Such an extension seems reasonable in the light of the often artificial and even porous boundary between the public and the private. The more private relations distance themselves from the principles of liberty and equality, constituting private law's ideological foundation, the more they obtain features typical of public law and the more warranted it is to include them in the scope of constitutional liberty rights. Not surprisingly, in Germany the *Drittwirkung* doctrine was initially adopted by the Labour Court with a view to protecting employees' political rights against

18 However, norms concerning absolute basic rights, such as prohibition of the death penalty or degrading treatment, may not possess a principle character (see above, p. 171).

encroachments by employers (Preuss 2005, pp. 23–24). The US *state action* doctrine – the American counterpart to the *Drittwirkung* – has also largely evolved through cases involving such hierarchical private relations (Chemerinsky 1985; Gardbaum 2003; Tushnet 2008, pp. 161ff.).

The recent wave of privatisation – another global phenomenon! – has endowed new significance and a novel justification to the *Drittwirkung* of basic rights, conceived as subjective rights of deterrence. If administrative tasks are privatised, the protective function of basic rights should also be 'privatised', that is, extended to apply to the recipient private organisation. One innovation of the new Finnish Constitution is to provide for such instances of privatisation. Art. 124 lays down that when public administrative tasks are delegated to others than public authorities, the law must guarantee that basic rights, legal protection, and other requirements of good administration are not endangered. When public administrative tasks are delegated under Art. 124 to entities of so-called indirect public administration, these entities are included in the public authorities directly bound by basic-right provisions.

In sum, it is reasonable to accord liberty rights a horizontal effect in hierarchically-structured private relations. Still, at least in Continental civil-law countries like Finland, it is also warranted to ask who should be entitled to decide on such an extension of the range of basic rights: should it fall to the legislature or the courts? It can be claimed that it is primarily up to the legislature, and not to the courts, to assess what types of private relations should fall under constitutional liberty rights. In delineating the public authorities that are directly bound by basic-right norms, fairly precise formal-organisational criteria are available. By contrast, when determining the reach of the horizontal effect of subjective liberty rights, such formal criteria are not on hand; substantive deliberation is needed, and the legislature may be better suited for it than the courts.

In the Finnish system, I would argue that the courts should not, as a rule, apply their review power under Art. 106 to grant direct horizontal effect to a liberty right. Given the horizontal effect's ambiguity, it is doubtful that an ordinary law could be found to be in *evident* conflict with the Constitution because of not providing sufficient protection for a liberty right in private relations. By contrast, the courts' duty to construe statutes in conformity with the Constitution encompasses the protective functions of liberty rights in private relations as well. To take an example, statutory provisions that in Finland grant employers a limited right to breach the confidentiality of their employees' e-mail correspondence should be given a narrow reading.

Social, Economic and Cultural Rights: Constitutional Commissions or Justiciable Rights?

With regard to their legal effects, social, economic and cultural rights constitute a special class. Not all constitutions include explicit provisions on such second-generation rights. For instance, in Germany the Constitutional Court has derived them – in addition to the *Sozialstaat* clause in Art. 20 of the Basic Law – from the factual prerequisites of liberty rights (Alexy 2002a, pp. 288ff.). In effect, within the whole of basic rights, the primary justification of these rights lies in the guarantees they provide for realising liberty rights aiming to protect citizens' private and public autonomy (Habermas 1996, pp. 118ff.). But this general justification does not in itself entail any institutional conclusions concerning separation of functions and powers between branches of government. Apparently, a long leap on the way of judicialisation is taken if the judiciary derives far-reaching social, economic and cultural rights from the factual preconditions of liberty rights without any direct support from constitutional provisions and if it imposes on the legislature detailed instructions as to how such rights should be realised. Equally apparent would be the threat to the policy-making powers of the democratically-elected and democratically-accountable legislature, and to the constitutional principle of separation of powers.

A crucial problem in regulating constitutional rights in general and economic, social and cultural rights in particular is to find the proper middle ground between too detailed and too vague provisions. Arguably, one central guideline is based on the distinction between preconditions of and restrictions on democracy. An integral function of basic rights is to ensure the preconditions of democratic political decision-making. These preconditions include factual guarantees for the exercise of political rights. But too detailed constitutional provisions freeze policy or value choices which should be open to public deliberation and democratic decision-making. Constitutional provisions should not impede interpretation and specification of basic rights against the backdrop of social development. Due to their dependence on available resources, the need for specification is especially conspicuous in connection to economic, social and cultural rights. Comprehensive constitutional regulation tends to reduce legislative activity to mere implementation, with the consequence of a juridification of politics.

Let us assume that we are dealing with a constitution which includes explicit provisions on social, economic and cultural rights. In defining their legal effects, the crucial distinction is that between justiciable individual rights and constitutional commissions. The wording of the constitution may and – arguably – should be clear about the intended effects. In the Finnish Constitution, only rights to free-of-charge basic education (Art. 16(1)) and to necessary subsistence and care (Art. 19(1)) are devised as subjective rights, whilst other provisions employ the language of constitutional commissions; for instance, this holds for the provision on sufficient social and health services in Art. 19(3). One option available for carrying out the constitutional commission is to guarantee the respective service or benefit as an individual, justiciable right, whose realisation is not subject to budgetary restraints. Who has the power to decide on this option?

Principles of democracy and separation of powers vindicate the primary, perhaps even exclusive, competence of the legislature. These principles must be duly heeded when determining division of labour and competence in fulfilling constitutional commissions. The courts – in Finland, the administrative courts – should respect the judgements of the legislature and, for instance, not treat as justiciable rights social or health services which the legislature has left to the care of municipalities within their budgetary means and decisions. If the courts violate this premise, they not only encroach upon the powers of the legislature but also infringe municipalities' constitutional right to self-government. The Finnish courts should not, drawing on their novel power of review under Art. 106, substitute their own view of how a constitutional commission should be fulfilled for that of the legislature; in so doing they would intrude into the policy-making domain which the Constitution has reserved for the democratically-elected legislature. Nevertheless, this does not mean that municipalities' budgetary decision-making or distribution of budgetary means in individual cases would entirely fall outside judicial control. The municipalities have a legal duty to allocate sufficient means to services whose procurement the legislature has entrusted them with. In individual decision-making, general principles of both administrative and social law should be respected, and statutory construction should conform to constitutional provisions as well; here, too, administrative courts have a monitoring role.

So in principle, it is possible to stake out a constitutionally appropriate division of labour between the legislature, the municipalities and the judiciary in executing economic, social and cultural rights, thereby paying due attention to the principles of democracy, separation of powers, and local self-government. Nonetheless, it is evident that we are moving in risky territory with regard to *gouvernement des juges*. If the judiciary assumes extensive powers to assess how the legislature has fulfilled its primary duty in implementing constitutional commissions, it is in danger of interfering with policy-making powers which in a democratic *Rechtsstaat* should be wielded by the legislature.

Basic-Rights Norms as General Legal Principles

In German debates, one of the main culprits responsible for alleged development towards a *verfassungsgerichtlicher Jurisdiktionsstaat* has been seen in the doctrine of basic-rights norms as legal principles with all-encompassing scope and entailing the duty of all state organs to contribute to their realisation. Ever since its landmark *Lüth* decision of 1958, the Constitutional Court has argued that basic-rights provisions not only create subjective rights but also express *principle norms* that manifest the legal order's fundamental values and that exert their influence in all fields of law. Basic-rights norms define the foundational order (*Grundordnung*) of not only the state but the entire society and contain, as it were, as germs the normative substance of the whole legal order. Such a conception is already implicit in the doctrine of *Drittwirkung*, introduced by the *Lüth* decision. Initially, though, reference was made merely to the effect of radiation (*Ausstrahlungswirkung*) which basic rights as an objective value order could wield throughout the law.[19]

Böckenförde argues that the doctrines of *Drittwirkung* and the state's protective duty (*Schutzpflicht*) derive from the definition of basic rights as the fundamental values or principles of the entire legal order: 'Basic rights as principle norms or value decisions point to … particular normative contents which call for their realisation; they do not function negatively but require action, the protection of these contents' (Böckenförde 1991, p. 173). Basic-rights norms imply constitutional commissions directed to all state organs and calling for their implementation through legislative, executive and administrative, as well as judicial action. Application of basic-rights norms is converted from *interpretation* into *concretisation*: the realisation of basic rights presupposes from both the legislature and the Constitutional Court not only interpretative specification of their contents but creative concretisation of constitutional value choices or commands of optimisation. The result is juridification of legislative politics and politicisation of constitutional adjudication.

Böckenförde has also tried to show that in German doctrine, no clear distinction can be made between indirect and direct horizontal effects of basic-rights principles but that the former inevitably leads to the latter. Indirect effect is realised through the general clauses of private-law legislation and statutory interpretation in general. If, however, basic rights cannot be implemented through statutory interpretation, this is not the end of their *Drittwirkung*. Thus, the German Constitutional Court has assumed the power to strike down private-law legislation for insufficient attention to basic-rights principles. The Constitutional Court has also allowed for constitutional complaints (*Verfassungsbeschwerde*) to be grounded in basic rights' *Drittwirkung*. The claimant may argue that in a private-law case, the ordinary courts have not paid due respect to a basic-right norm's indirect or direct horizontal effect. Critics, among them Böckenförde (ibid., pp. 177–180), have been concerned about the Constitutional Court becoming the final court of appeal in private-law cases and of appropriating ultimate interpretive power not only within public law but in private law as well.

The conception of basic rights as general legal principles possessing a comprehensive scope of application and providing all fields of law with their normative basis clearly manifests the constitutionalisation of the legal order. A similar tendency has been noted not only in Germany but in many other countries too: for instance, in Spain (Bon 1991), France (Favoreu 1990), and, after the 1995 basic-rights reform, even in Finland. It has significantly contributed to the general turn towards argumentation from principle in the previously rule-oriented Continental European legal systems. Should we speak here of over-constitutionalisation, leading towards a jurisdiction state? Is threatened or perhaps even partly realised jurisdiction-state development to be localised in this direction? Are proposals to introduce basic-rights-related principles into general doctrines of

19 BVerfGE 7, 198. The case has been presented by, for example, Preuss (2005, pp. 24–26).

diverse fields of law – such as criminal law, environmental law, property law, or the law of obligations – accelerating this development? Should these proposals be warded off as lapses endangering the principles of democracy and separation of powers?

The overall consequences of constitutional review result from the interplay of institutional and doctrinal factors. What repercussions the notion of basic-rights norms as 'objective-law principles' will have depends on how constitutional review is organised and how the power of the judiciary is determined. German criticism is premised on the existence of a constitutional court and the constitutional complaint as a legal remedy. The Finnish system does not include a specialised constitutional court nor anything corresponding to the German *Verfassungsbeschwerde*. Nor, too, do the ordinary courts have the power to strike down private-law legislation for its purported contradiction with basic-law principles. Yet the Finnish Constitution does contain an explicit provision on protective duty. Art. 22 of the Constitution lays down that 'the public authorities shall guarantee the observance of basic rights and liberties and human rights'. Nonetheless, it is hardly justifiable that a court could find such an *evident* contradiction between a basic-right principle and a statutory provision which would vindicate application of Art. 106 of the Constitution. The principles of democracy and separation of powers entail that the protective duty under Art. 22 of the Constitution falls primarily to the legislature: it is up to the legislature to guarantee realisation of basic-rights principles in the horizontal relations between private persons. Accordingly, the courts should fulfil their protective duty within the legislative framework and grant basic-rights principles merely indirect effects, unfolding through statutory interpretation.

Matthias Kumm has questioned the significance for the German constitution of the distinction between indirect and direct effect, invoking largely similar arguments as Böckenförde. However, unlike Böckenförde, Kumm sees the collapse of indirect into direct effect in mainly positive terms (Kumm and Comella 2005; Kumm 2006). He portrays opposition to a 'total constitution' and to private law's subordination to constitutional law as German private-law establishment's campaign to retain the high status it has enjoyed as the guardian of the *Bürgerliches Gesetzbuch* – the climax of German legal scholarship and legal culture (Kumm 2006, p. 360). Conversely, scholars from other doctrinal domains may understand expansion of the reach of basic rights as a sign of 'constitutional-law imperialism'. Again, the interlocutors' strategic interests in the power play in the field of law illuminate the context of discursive interventions. But, again, interventions can also be discussed by focusing on their illocutionary credentials.

Much can be said in favour of basic-rights principles invading other areas of law. Basic-rights connections fortify the justification of general legal principles and create conditions for a new kind of cross-boundary dialogue between the law's departments; a dialogue necessitated by the frequent cross-boundary nature of current legal problems. Furthermore, a common basic-rights foundation adds to the law's principle-based coherence. Finally, heightened sensitivity to basic rights and legal principles may lead to more overt argumentation in Continental European legal systems. Even those worried about the consequences of judicialisation from the viewpoint of democracy can hardly regard this as other than a positive development: it facilitates discursive monitoring of the court's case-law not only by legal professionals but by the media and the general public as well.

Yet to see all ordinary law as implementation of constitutional law and all adjudication as (potential) constitutional adjudication would be erroneous, too. Deference should be shown to the doctrinal traditions of the established branches of law, such as private law with its sub-fields, or criminal law. Basic-rights principles should primarily unfold their effects indirectly, through the intermediary of 'field-specific' principles. Constitutionalisation adds to the justification and institutional support of field-specific principles, and may also lead to adjustments in their normative contents, but the general doctrines of other fields of law should not be allowed to be replaced by constitutional doctrine. Otherwise, much sedimented legal *ratio* would be lost. Nor should the specialised legal competence and pre-understanding of judges and scholars dealing with other departments of law be allowed to be devalued through over-constitutionalisation.

Confrontations between Horizontal and Vertical Effects

The traditional vertical effects of basic rights, related to the liberal *Rechtsstaat* notion, and their *Drittwirkung*, obliging even the legislator, do not always sit comfortably together. Indeed, the recently-found horizontal effect may weaken the protection that basic rights offer against the power exercise of public authorities. Likewise, when basic-rights principles are taken together with the legislator's duty of concretisation and implementation, their difference from common goods and policies may be obliterated. I take as my example the *right to security*. Art. 7(1) of the Finnish Constitution states that 'everyone has the right to life, personal liberty, integrity and security'. Correspondingly, Art. 5(1) of the European Convention on Human Rights provides that 'everyone has the right to liberty and security of the person'.

'Security' is a tricky concept. It can connote either a collective good – in the sense of 'national security' or 'public safety and order' – or an individualised right to personal security. In its case-law, the European Court of Human Rights has interpreted Art. 5(1) of the Convention in line with the latter alternative. Furthermore, it has in general treated security of the person as a non-independent right, auxiliary to the right to liberty. By contrast, the Constitutional Law Committee of Finland has been inclined to understand Art. 7(1) of the Constitution in the sense of a collective good, particularly in its early post-1995 case-law. This reading is based on three argumentative steps.

First, the right to security is detached from the rights to personal liberty and integrity, and assigned independent legal relevance. This already points to the direction of a common good: it is hard to see what independent legal meaning, irreducible to the rights to liberty and integrity, could be attributed to an individual right to personal security. Secondly, the Constitutional Law Committee has invoked the horizontal effect of basic-rights norms and, thirdly, the legislature's protective duty. On these grounds, the Committee has concluded that the state – in this case the legislature – is obliged to ensure realisation of the independent right to security in horizontal relations between private individuals. In this way, public safety and order as a collective good has been elevated into a basic right with a rank equal to that of individual liberty rights. By the same move, the distinction between policies aiming at collective goods and principles focusing on individual rights has been effaced.

Even without the support of an explicit right to security, a combination of horizontal effect and protective duty can always be employed to justify, say, new powers for the police or other security authorities; such powers can always be claimed to be necessary for guaranteeing realisation of basic rights in private relations. On the other hand, police powers usually touch on basic rights purporting to protect individuals in their vertical relations with public authorities, such as rights to personal integrity, privacy, or confidentiality of correspondence. Now, the constitutional acceptability of police powers can be maintained to hinge on weighing of basic-rights principles of equal rank, although with a different locus of application along the horizontal or vertical axes. What, according to liberal constitutionalism and the traditional *Rechtsstaat* notion, was to be restricted through basic rights – executive and administrative power – is, as it were, absorbed inside the basic-rights system. In Germany, this point has been raised in criticism of the Constitutional Court's argumentation and Robert Alexy's basic-rights theory as the codification and justification of the Court's case-law (Alexy 2002a).

Although often lumped together, Dworkin's and Alexy's views on principles display significant differences. For Dworkin, the distinction between principles, related to individual rights, and policies, related to collective goods, is crucial; indeed, it provides the very basis for his taking-rights-seriously thesis (Dworkin 1978). Alexy, by contrast, tends to discard it. He has been criticised for equating principles (individual rights) and policies (collective goods) and for according them equivalent normative and argumentative weight. As an example of balancing between principles, Alexy (2002a, pp. 50ff.) has evoked a Constitutional Court case where the central issue was whether legal proceedings could be launched against a defendant whose health, and even life, could have been endangered if he had been obliged to appear in court. In Alexy's (and the Constitutional Court's) account, decisive for solution of the case was which of two principles of equal rank was accorded greater weight: the efficiency of criminal justice, or the right to life and personal integrity. Let me present a rather lengthy citation from Ingeborg Maus' critique:

> (T)his artificially induced collision of principles in individual cases … owes its existence to a concept of constitution which is diametrically opposed to the liberal constitutional concept asserted in the 18th/19th centuries. The constitution in the classic sense of the rule of law [the *Rechtsstaat* – KT] always presupposed as a

> fact the functional efficacy of the organs of the state and criminal prosecution and determined their limitations. This functional efficacy itself need not be guaranteed by a constitution, but is greatest without any constitutional regulation whatsoever … the efficiency of constitutional organs of the state cannot itself be the content of a constitutional principle, because the ratio essendi of the constitution consists precisely in restricting this efficiency … when common goods can also be regarded as principles … constitutional guarantees of freedom compete with principles which are opposite not only in terms of their content, but also in terms of their entire structure, such as the efficiency of criminal justice, the 'efficiency of the Bundeswehr' or the 'efficiency of national defence' … the 'efficiency of the enterprise and the economy as a whole'… Not only basic rights guaranteeing freedom, but also freedom-limiting state functions themselves are a measure of judicial review … the constitution loses its function of limiting the spread of government powers. (Maus 1989, pp. 197–199)

The constitutional *Rechtsstaat* doctrine involves a peculiar dialectic between collective goods and individual basic rights. On the one hand, the main thrust of basic rights – here I am alluding to first-generation liberty rights – is seen in creation of a sphere of private autonomy, secured against infringements by public authorities acting in the name of collective goods, such as public safety and order or national security. But the guarantees that basic rights provide are not – with some important exceptions – absolute: limitations are permitted, in order to promote collective goods similar to those whose purport the rights are intended to restrict. This might seem paradoxical, but the solution to the paradox is quite simple: the limitations may not touch upon the kernel (the *Wesensgehalt* of German doctrine[20]) of the right in question.

Even if we reject Alexy's levelling down of the Dworkinian distinction between principles and policies, we seem to be compelled to concede policies' (re-)entry into constitutional doctrine as grounds for limitations to basic rights. Determining their constitutional relevance certainly involves weighing and balancing, for example in applying the proportionality test. However, this weighing is not internal to the basic-rights system but involves a basic-rights principle and an external policy factor. This portrayal also corresponds to the structure of the European Convention. The Convention refers to policy standpoints, but these define acceptable grounds for limiting rights and not the rights themselves. Art. 8(1), for example, guarantees everyone the right to respect for private and family life, home, and correspondence. Para. 2 of the same article includes the limitation clause: 'There shall be no interference by a public authority with the exercise of this right except such as is in accordance with the law and is necessary in a democratic society in the interests of national security, public safety or the economic well-being of the country, for the prevention of disorder or crime, for the protection

---

20 The Basic Law includes an explicit provision (19(2)) on the *Wesensgehalt*: 'In no case may a basic right be infringed in its essential content.'

of health or morals, or for the protection of the rights and freedoms of others.' In the context of the Convention, abolition of the distinction between principles and policies would amount to eradicating the boundary separating protected rights from the grounds for restricting them.

To sum up the normative message of the preceding discussion, the horizontal effect of basic rights should not be allowed to water down their traditional *Rechtsstaat* function of creating safeguards for individuals against policy-oriented exercise of power by public authorities. When basic-rights norms as legal principles are assigned horizontal effect and when the legislator is ascribed the duty to realise them, principles acquire a policy tinge: along the way, the right to, say, liberty or personal integrity may be transformed in all but name into a policy of law-enforcement and public security.

Balancing Principles and Policies: The Proportionality Test

Arguably, a distinction between principles and policies, such as the one proposed by Dworkin, is indispensable for making sense of the protective function of basic rights. It relates constitutional review to the dimensions of practical reason and indicates the censuring role of ethical and moral reasoning with regard to an instrumental approach. If principles are collapsed into policies, as suggested by both Critical Legal Scholars and Richard Posner (see above, pp. 168–169), then the last-resort justification for constitutional review which I have espoused collapses as well. Alexy has been attacked for assimilating policies into principles. Actually, the reverse appears to be the case: he assimilates principles into policies. He defines principles as optimisation commands, which allows him to include Dworkinian policies under the concept of principles. But in his definition, he in fact attaches policy-like qualities to principles and effaces the distinction between the dimensions of practical reason (Alexy 2002a, pp. 47–48). This also appears to be the crux of Habermas' critique of Alexy (Habermas 1996, pp. 254–256).

It also seems that constitutional review cannot do without weighing and balancing, either between competing rights or between rights and grounds calling for their limitation. The limitation clauses of the European Convention on Human Rights point explicitly to the proportionality test. So does Section 1 of the Canadian Charter as well. It provides that the Charter 'guarantees the rights and freedoms set out in it subject only to such reasonable limits prescribed by law as can be demonstrably justified in a free and democratic society'. In Finland, general grounds for limiting basic rights were codified in the *travaux préparatoires* to the 1995 basic-rights reform. They include the requirements of 1) a substantive social need, 2) the necessity of the limitation for satisfying the need (the 'least-means' test), and 3) balancing the expected benefit of the limitation with its 'cost' (proportionality in the narrow sense of the term). The proportionality test is central to the 'constitutional adjudication' of the European Court of Justice, too. For instance, in competition-law cases the Court balances restrictions to market freedoms such as free movement of goods and capital with the general interest invoked by the Member State (Maduro 1998).

To many discussants, the necessity of balancing is the foremost proof of constitutional adjudication's involvement in policy-making and of the judiciary's overreaching both its principle of legitimacy and its institutional competence. It is no wonder that constitutional scholarship has spent so much effort in trying to augment the objectivity, rationality and controllability of balancing. Thus, the German Constitutional Court has been assisted by constitutional scholars in elaborating on its proportionality test. Alexy, in particular, has devoted much scholarly energy in attempting to demonstrate that weighing of principles does not rely on arbitrary, non-controllable and decisionist value or policy choices (Alexy 2002a, pp. 50–56, 100–106 and pp. 396ff; Alexy 2002b). Sceptics have not been convinced; in the eyes of one critical observer (Stone Sweet 2000, p. 98), 'balancing tests and proportionality doctrines do little more than admit, albeit in a convoluted manner, the following: that protecting constitutional rights is difficult work; that constitutional judges must possess and wield discretionary power in order for them to do this job properly; and that no firm and fast rules for protecting rights can be articulated'. For critics of constitutional review, not only are judges engaged in policy-making, with the resulting politicisation of adjudication, but, by the same token, legislative and administrative deliberations are juridified:

> If in balancing, courts necessarily become legislators and administrators, the reverse is also true: in enforcing least-means tests, courts push lawmakers and administrators into a judicial mode, requiring them to reason as the judge will, that is to consider the proportionality of their own activities. (Stone Sweet 2004, p. 11)

By contrast, supporters of constitutional review argue that such doctrinal devices as the proportionality test not only increase the controllability of balancing but also combat the trend of juridification. In Kumm's view, 'the four-prong proportionality test in particular allows courts to engage all relevant moral and pragmatic arguments explicitly, without the kind of legalistic guidance and constraint that otherwise characterises legal reasoning' (Kumm 2007, p. 2).

In the debate between critics and supporters, I am inclined to accept the critics' point of the indelible element of fiat – or *voluntas*, if you will! – that comes to the fore particularly in weighing the 'costs' and 'benefits' resulting from limitations to basic rights: simply, no unequivocal commensurable yardsticks exist for weighing exist. But, in an ideal-typical democratic *Rechtsstaat*, this inescapable decisionism is allayed by a continuous constitutional discourse to which individual rulings contribute and in which they, in turn, are assessed. This discourse should not be restricted merely to legal (and political) elites but should also be accessible to the general public, to civil society. This poses special requirements on the reasoning of bodies engaged in constitutional review; the issue should not be hidden beneath impenetrable layers of legal doctrine and concepts. Open argumentation following the stages of the proportionality test lays bare the relevant considerations on which public debate can focus. Here Kumm's de-juridification thesis hits the point.

Constitutional Scholarship: Co-Optation or Independence?

Constitutionally-entrenched basic rights and rights-based constitutional review have a legitimate role to play in the mature modern legal system of a consolidated democracy. No irresolvable conflict exists between democracy and basic rights or democracy and constitutional review. They all belong to the constitutional fundamentals of a democratic *Rechtsstaat*; they can and even should co-exist and sustain each other. Democracy is not the only justification for basic rights, but it would surely be inconceivable without the public and private autonomy which basic rights and constitutional review purport to guarantee for citizens. In this sense, safeguarding basic rights amounts to safeguarding the prerequisites of democracy as well. On the other hand, basic rights would remain only general ideas or solemn phrases on paper without democratic processes where they are interpreted and specified and where their socially and culturally varying implications are unfurled.

But this is not to say that basic rights and constitutional review entertain entirely frictionless relations with democracy or separation of powers, another constitutional fundamental of a democratic *Rechtsstaat*. We should distinguish the legal-theoretical level of justification from discussion of particular institutional and doctrinal models of constitutional review. This discussion cannot overlook the inherent tension between constitutional review and the principles of democracy and separation of powers. It is to the credit of the critics that they have drawn attention to this tension and formulated normative standards, warning signs, as it were, with which models and particular instances of constitutional review can be assessed. Nevertheless, the critics have too often ignored intermediary, hybrid models, which have been designed to avoid the pitfalls of extremes of unrestricted judicial or legislative supremacy. The rich global variety also proves how misleading it is to try to press the available institutional options into the two compartments of the US-style diffused and the German-style concentrated judicial model.

Furthermore, the critics merit tribute for deepening our awareness of the threat of juristocracy, *le gouvernement des juges* or the *verfassungsgerichtlicher Jurisdiktionsstaat*. The parliamentary legislative state has not turned into a jurisdiction state – to use Schmitt's terms – but, still, the boundaries of justifiable constitutional review must be constantly watched. Here, constitutional scholarship has a vital task to perform.

Constitutional review involves all the main legal actors of modern law: not only the legislature and the courts but scholars as well. In line with their role in other branches of law, scholars contribute to articulating and elaborating constitutional doctrine: its concepts, principles and theories. And also, in line with other branches of law, doctrine fulfils an important task in guaranteeing the consistency of constitutional law's application and in promoting normative coherence. It is hard to imagine constitutional review without the assistance of constitutional doctrine as an integral element in constitutional actors' hermeneutical pre-understanding.

Yet, constitutional law should be particularly attentive to the hazards of excessive doctrine-dependence. Doctrine should not be left to ossify but should be receptive to constant (re-)assessment in ongoing constitutional discourse, taking due note of social, cultural and political change: neither the constitutional problems nor the constitutional solutions of a late modern, post-welfare-state society are similar to those of a bygone era. Constitutional scholarship bears a central responsibility for maintaining an adequate balance between stability and renewal in constitutional doctrine. It should heed the dangers of juridification as well: doctrinal concepts and theories are needed but they should not make constitutional discourse inaccessible to the actors of civil society. Democratic control of constitutional review through public debates is a high priority if juridification is to be avoided and the tension between constitutional review and democracy managed.

In critical accounts of judicialisation, legal scholarship is often labelled an accomplice of the judiciary, assisting the latter in promoting its power at the expense of the legislature[21] and, by the same token, pursuing its own strategic interests in the field of law. However, it is easy to find counter-examples that demonstrate that such a symbiosis of or co-operation between legal scholarship and the judiciary is a contingent phenomenon and that the former may also maintain a critical stance towards the latter. Indeed, a watchful eye on constitutional review on the part of scholars is needed to combat petrification of constitutional doctrines and excessive juridification of political issues, and to reassert the boundaries of justifiable constitutional review.

Independent scholarship is perhaps more vital for constitutional law than any other department of law. But specific circumstances work against scholarly independence. Constitutional-law professors typically form an influential group of constitutional-court judges, and are actively engaged in constitutional review as counsellors or experts as well. Under these conditions, the danger of co-optation is imminent. To ward it off, traditional scholarly virtues are urgently called for!

21 Bernhard Schlink has written of '*Bundesverfassunggerichtsspositivismus*', 'which is entirely under the "spell" of the Bundesverfassungsgericht' (Schlink 1993, pp. 730–731).

EPILOGUE

Chapter 9
The Law's Farewell to the Nation State?

The Law of the Nation State

The time and space relations and conceptions which are distinctive of modern society and culture have also imbued the law. The instrumentalisation of the law, its increased use as a medium, is anchored in a linear conception of time where past, present and future are detached from each other and where social actors conceive of the future as an open temporal horizon. The acceleration of time, too, finds its expression in law. The positivity of modern law, its dependence on explicit decisions, enables its continuous changeability; this possibility is seized by the instrumentally-oriented legislator. However, modern law also possesses features that temper the pace of change. The dialectic of change and stability is, for its part, due to the law's multi-layered nature: the legal-cultural layers slow down the unremitting surface-level movement, initiated, first of all, by the legislator.

What is central to the space relations of modern society is the severance of its local ties, society's expansion beyond the community based on relationships between those present; the conclusion of social relations, not only between those present, but also between those absent. Expressed in Tönnies' terms, development has led from *Gemeinschaft* to *Gesellschaft*. The extended spatiality of modern society is manifest in the formation of nation states, accompanied, at the cultural level, by a double abstraction of the state, as Quentin Skinner (1989) puts it: the conception of the state as an entity separate from both (the rest of) society and the person of the ruler.

Modern law has been law of the nation state. The modernisation of law, its differentiation as positive law, and the emergence of the nation state were parallel and interdependent processes. Modern law has received its positive character from the decisions made by state institutions: the legislature and the courts. Even when norm-formation has bypassed the legislature, as has been the case in customary law, social norms have only acquired legal status after the courts have acknowledged their legal relevance. Furthermore, the state's coercive machinery has been an indispensable extra-legal presupposition of modern law: it has guaranteed the execution of court decisions and, thus, the law's realisation. The territorial validity of legal norms has, as a rule, accorded with state borders.

The dependence between law and state has been reciprocal. Modern, positive law would not have been possible without the legislative, adjudicative and administrative bodies of the state; but nor would the modern state have been conceivable without support from the law. The state has relied on law as an instrument in organising its institutional structure and in implementing its political decisions. The law has provided the state with a source of legitimacy as well. In this sense, *Rechtsstaatlichkeit* can be characterised as an internal *telos* of the modern state.

But the expansion of modern law's spatial horizon has not stopped at the borders of the nation state. Modern law includes a branch whose spatial dimension exceeds the boundaries separating nation states from each other: international law. But international law, too, has in many respects been tied to the nation state. The *voluntas* of international law has been essentially the *voluntas* of the nation state. On the basis of their internal sovereignty, nation states have retained control over the municipal legal order, and its application and execution; internal sovereignty has involved the exclusivity of the state's legal system. External sovereignty, for its part, has allowed for the states to participate in the international system. The traditional view defines the states as exclusive subjects and objects of international law. Norm-formation in international law has been based on bi- and multilateral treaties between nation states, and international customary law has had its origin in state practice. The legal effects of international law treaties have been confined to states as well. In accordance with its generally accepted premise, international law has not intruded into the internal domain of nation states but merely regulated inter-state relations; what transpires within state boundaries and under what norms has been of concern only to the sovereign nation state. State sovereignty has included the power to decide on the relationship between domestic and international law. Whether this adheres to the monistic or the dualistic model has depended on the constitutional choice of each individual state.

William Twining (2000) has fittingly talked about a *black-box model* as the way the relationship between municipal and international law has been conceived. In this conception, both national legal orders and international law are treated as self-contained and self-sufficient normative wholes. The law's primary principle of differentiation has been of a territorial nature.

The link with the nation state is most obvious at modern law's surface level: the lawgiver and the courts of the nation state have produced the institutional surface-level legal normative material, while state borders have determined its territorial significance. Modern legal culture, developed and articulated significantly by legal scholarship, has procured the necessary pre-understanding of legal actors and functioned as a tradition in the philosophical-hermeneutical sense of the concept. Legal culture, too, has possessed distinctive nation-state features, but at this level of the law, links with the modern form of polity have not been as self-evident as on law's surface. International law has been a special case with regard to the territorial differentiation of legal culture, too. The discourse of international law has been international discourse; this would not have been possible without shared traits in the legal-cultural pre-understanding of discussants coming from different states.

The widening of spatial horizons, typical of the modern era, has characterised development of legal culture, too. Legal culture has transformed itself from a tradition (in the historical-sociological sense of the concept) towards an expert system. Expert systems strive for universalism. Expertise does not acknowledge state borders; it is the same on either side of the border. In addition, similarities in the legal cultures of the Western world derive from the heritage of Roman law, which has left its traces not only on Romano-Germanic legal orders but on common law as well. A part of this heritage consists of the systematisation, which in Continental European legal cultures still organises legal normative material. Systematisation begins with the distinction between private and public law. Private law is further differentiated into property law, the law of obligations, and family and inheritance law. Public law, in turn, is divided into national and international public law. Corresponding to public international law, the branches of private law may include private international law.

Despite its Roman-law roots, when applied and modified in accordance with modern law, this systematisation manifests the perspective of the nation-state legislator; it purports to arrange the municipal legal order of the nation state. Two fields of law cut across state borders – public and private international law – but their location in the system of law is determined from the nation-state perspective as well. Both of them regulate relationships among nation states or their legal orders. International private law comprises the rules of choice determining what norms are applied to an issue bearing on more than one nation-state municipal legal order. Private international law itself is part of the municipal legal order of the respective nation state. And when nation states opt for either the monistic or dualistic model in the relationship between municipal law and public international law, they also define the latter's place in the law's system.

In the Romano-Germanic legal family, the foundations for modern law's general doctrines and principles of systematisation were laid during the nineteenth century. Here the role of the German historical school and the subsequent conceptual legal science (*Begriffsjurisprudenz*) was crucial. Systematisation has not, of course, remained stuck in the positions of the nineteenth century, and new branches of law with their own general doctrines have been added to the system. However, branches such as labour law, environmental law or social law have not shaken the system's nation-state premises. It is the welfare state that has engendered new fields of law such as these, and the welfare state, if any, has been a project of the nation state. Regulations typical of the welfare state have problematised the basic distinction between private and public law but they have not undermined the nation-state perspective underlying the law's divisions.

Modern law is autonomous law: as a legal order it is detached from other sets of social norms and as legal practices from other social practices. This makes it possible to examine – in the manner of Niklas Luhmann – the law as a sub-system of society, structured around its closed communicative network and relying on its specific legal code. But such an autonomous law could not have emerged without the support of modern society and modern culture. These extra-legal presuppositions have included the nation state.

Modern society, with the nation state as an integral part of it, has not only constituted modern law's extra-legal environment, it has also in a sense been effective within the law itself. Law and legal doctrine always give expression to some conception of the surrounding society. Sociologists have discussed the extent to which their conception of society has confined social relationships and processes within the boundaries of the nation state (see, for example, Beck 2004). One of the main tasks of critical jurisprudence is to reveal, or reconstruct, the implicit social-theoretical assumptions of legal theories – both dogmatic theories and 'reflexion theories' trying to capture the law's unity. Presumably, modern law's attachment to the nation state is detectable in the social-theoretical premises of legal theories too.

Modern law's ties to the nation state have set their mark on its *voluntas* and *ratio*, as well as their mutual relations. The law's primary *voluntas* has been that of the nation-state legislator. The problem of disciplining the *voluntas* has derived from the connection between law and politics, the law's instrumentalisation in the service of the nation-state legislator's political aims. The *constitution*, on the one hand, opens for the politically determined *voluntas* access to the law and thus establishes the law's positivity, but, on the other hand, it also imposes not only formal but even substantive restrictions on this *voluntas*. The constitution has been a nation-state constitution, which has crowned the hierarchical structure – *Stufenbau* – of the nation-state legal order and provided it with its formal unity. The legal order's hierarchical structure has been matched by hierarchical relations between the state organs furnished with norm-giving powers. Furthermore, the institutional *Stufenbau* of the judiciary applying the law has proffered an additional guarantee for the legal order's formal unity.

The idea of a late or second modernity, adopted in many contemporary social diagnoses, is essentially based on the observation that modern society's temporal and spatial transformations have entered a qualitatively new phase. The increasing acceleration of time, due to novel information, communication and transportation technologies and their social consequences, has also launched a new round in the liberation from space, questioning the significance of state borders in determining the territorial dimensions of social processes and relations (Rosa 2005, pp. 338ff.). The virtual space of the Internet represents the latest phase in the conquest of space. If modernisation is linked to temporal and spatial changes – to the acceleration of time and the expansion of space – the globalisation narrative is but a sequel to the modernisation narrative.

The further acceleration of time and the further expansion of space have repercussions in the law, too. I shall discuss them, first, in fields traditionally included in the nation state's internal sovereignty, and then turn to legal aspects of globalisation. However, such a distinction between internal and external may be artificial, even misleading: many of the developments eroding the state's internal sovereignty possess an international or transnational dimension.

The Fragmentation of the Nation State's Legal *Voluntas*

The democratic legislator of the nation state has employed the law as a means for achieving its political aims. It has adopted a linear and, with regard to the future, open conception of time, and conceived of society as a political project realisable in time. Such a notion of politics and law implicitly assumes that the temporality of politics and law corresponds to the temporality of other social sub-systems. In our late modern era, this assumption turns out to be increasingly problematic. Modern society is a functionally-differentiated society, and no guarantees exist for the match of different sub-systems' temporal structures. The dynamics of temporal acceleration has not affected all sub-systems similarly. The rhythms of politics and law have lingered after, for instance, rapid changes within the economy; here we have one important explanation for the state's (and the law's) withdrawal from management of the economy (Rosa 2005, pp. 391ff.). The crisis of politics involves a crisis of the law as a medium; as a means of social engineering. Legal regulation by state organs is increasingly reactive in character; instead of actively directing the functioning of other sub-systems, it responds to already realised development.

The traditional concept of the state, coined by German nineteenth-century state-law theory, was based on three elements: *state territory*, *state people*, and *state power* (see, for example, Jellinek 1914, pp. 394ff.). But it implied a fourth dimension, too: that of *state organisation*. For Gerber (1880, pp. 231ff.), for instance, the necessity of state organisation ensued from the state's free will (state power) as the basic idea of state law: this presupposed state organs that expressed and concretised the state's will. State organs did not possess a separate legal subjectivity, or their own will; they merely gave shape to the will of the state as a unitary legal person. This legal person could not have but one will; an internally contradictory state will was as implausible a thought as the internally contradictory will of an individual legal subject, a natural person. Norms of competence defined the confines within which state organs were authorised to articulate the state's will. Fundamental norms of competence, such as those confirming the separation of legislative, executive and adjudicative powers, were included in the organisational part of the constitution. Norms defining the *Stufenbau* of the legal order and the hierarchical structures of the judiciary and the administration were supposed to secure unity of state will. The formal unity of the legal order possessed an institutional support in the unity of state organisation.

Recent developments have contested the assumption of unitary state will and organisation and, consequently, the unity of the legal order. The law's *voluntas* can no longer be automatically identified with the *voluntas* of the democratic legislator. Democratic lawmaking procedure, culminating in deliberations within the representative body, requires time which the velocity of social change does not always permit. The early modern classics of political theory and philosophy already considered the executive the most rapidly reacting department of state. The legislator is primarily oriented towards the future and the judges towards the past. By contrast, the executive functions in the present, responding immediately to urgent internal and external challenges facing the state (Scheuerman 2004, pp. 38–42). The increasingly rapid pace of social processes and the incapability of the slowly functioning representative mechanisms to attend promptly to sudden regulatory needs constitute a backdrop to the growing significance of delegated legislation and emergency powers (ibid., pp. 105ff.). Delegation of legislative powers and the narrowing role of the representative body entail that lawmaking is deprived of those elements of discursive *ratio* which, in Habermas' ideal-typical democratic *Rechtsstaat*, are purported to impose procedural constraints on the *voluntas* and its instrumental reason (see above, pp. 253–254). The resulting democratic deficit cannot be remedied by attaching surrogate discursive elements to the norm-giving of the executive; the very reason for delegating legislative powers to the executive often lies in time pressures which do not allow for discursive deliberation of legislative issues.

Delegated legislation not only endangers the discursive features which political democratisation has added to formation of the law's *voluntas*. It may also threaten the unity of the legal order. Constitutions contain provisions on delegation of legislative powers and on the legal order's hierarchical structure, its *Stufenbau*. It could be argued that such provisions ensure the legal order's unity despite the mounting significance of delegated legislation. However, this unity depends on unity of state organisation. The executive branch of the state no longer constitutes such an integrated whole with its clear relations of competence and a seamless hierarchy of control as was assumed by German late constitutional state-law doctrine or Max Weber's contemporary theory of bureaucracy. Following models from the private sector, public administration has adopted new types of non-hierarchical organisational structure, as well as new types of non-legal management and control mechanisms (New Public Management). The reforms have enhanced the functional independence of administrative agencies, also as regards their norm-giving.

Public administration's increased independence has allowed for new kinds of contact with relevant private organisations. Administrative management of society is no longer based merely on legally-binding orders and money allocation; vertical power relations have, to a great extent, been replaced by horizontal co-operation, such as exchange of information and joint informal deliberations with private actors. The borderline between legally binding and non-binding management has been blurred; unequivocally obligatory hard law has been complemented by various forms of soft law. According to traditional democratic and constitutional theory, society is expected to influence the administration through the representative body and the government politically responsible to that body. Parliamentary mechanisms have been supplemented by direct connections between administration and society. This has made the boundary between public and private more porous and led to a new kind of intertwining of state and society. It has also further augmented the independence of individual administrative units – the segmentation of public administration, as it has also been called. In an empirically-oriented scrutiny, it may be more appropriate to portray administrative agencies as representatives of their respective fields of action – e.g. healthcare, education, or the economy – rather than of unitary state will. In his analysis of the Weimar political system, Carl Schmitt depicted a pluralist state which was 'totalitarian from weakness': a state whose unity was threatened by the strategic decision-making of interest-based associations (see, for example, Schmitt 1958). The contemporary expression *disaggregated state* (Slaughter 2004) also alludes to a situation where the agencies' bonds of allegiance with the private organisations of their field may be stronger than their ties to other agencies. Continental public-law doctrine seems to be moving towards rejecting the unity of state will and the state's legal personality even as legal fictions. Concepts such as 'administrative contract' and the acceptance of state organs as parties to legal proceedings may be tokens of impending doctrinal change.

Privatisation, a salient feature in public administration's development in recent decades, has also contributed to organisational fragmentation. The concept of privatisation may be employed in both a broad and a narrow sense. It may be used to cover a large variety of the novelties in public administration's internal or external relations, borrowed from the private sector: non-hierarchical forms of organisation, 'soft' mechanisms of internal management and control (e.g. result budgeting, contractual relations between administrative units, New Public Management) and the use of private-law or non-legal steering instruments. In its narrow sense, 'privatisation' connotes the transfer of public administration's tasks to private organisations. Such a transfer may include norm-giving powers, too.

In legal-theoretical debates, the fragmentation of legal norm-giving has been examined through the concept of *polycentricity*. The concept has been given various definitions, but most notably in Danish interventions it has been linked to the doctrine of sources of law (Zahle 1995). The doctrine of legal sources determines the participants in the continuous discourse on the contents of the legal order and the legal practices which contribute to production and reproduction of legal norms. 'Polycentricity' refers to a multiplication of sources of law and to the problematisation of traditional doctrine: legal discourse has acquired new participants, and interventions in this discourse by diverse participants cannot be accorded such an unequivocal weight as has been previously assumed in, for instance, Scandinavian legal theory. Polycentricity can also be manifest in different actors' adherence – and even obligation to adhere – to divergent doctrines of legal sources. Thus, local officials in social and health care may be legally obliged to comply with the instructions of local self-governing authorities, but these instructions do not necessarily enjoy the same legal significance in courts where decisions on social benefits can be appealed. Phenomena attesting to the polycentricity of legal sources have led some Scandinavian discussants to doubt whether doctrine can in general any longer be codified in the fashion proposed in the 1980s by, for instance, Alexander Peczenik (e.g. Karhu 2003).

Polycentricity is related to another pertinent topic in present legal-theoretical and legal-sociological debates: *self-regulation*. 'Self-regulation' refers to norm-generation by or with the co-operation of organisations established by the actors in the social field under regulation. The economic sector offers plenty of examples, such as good banking practice, defined by the Finnish Bank Association, good auditing practice, defined by the Chamber of Commerce, or the rules of the Helsinki stock market, approved by the company owning it, to use examples drawn from my own nation state. The list could be extended with examples from other social fields, such as the anti-doping rules of national sports associations, or codes of conduct concerning data protection.

It should not come as a surprise that the concept of self-regulation, too, has been used in different senses and that different forms and types of self-regulation have been discerned. Researchers have debated whether the concept should be confined merely to voluntary self-regulation by social actors. In its action programme for the simplification of legislation, the European Commission has included in self-regulation the practices, common rules, common codes of practice and voluntary agreements which economic and social actors, NGOs or organised groups voluntarily adopt in order to guide and organise their activities. In the examples given above, anti-doping rules clearly represent such self-regulation. In addition to 'pure' self-regulation, the European Commission examines *co-regulation* where public authorities and the relevant actors jointly and within the framework of legislation agree on more precise rules. In Finland, good book-keeping practice is defined by a board where both the authorities and private actors are represented. Co-regulation manifests the fragmentation of public administration and the networking of administrative units and private organisations. Even other criteria for classifying self-regulation could be conceived; for instance, the legal bindingness of norms, i.e. their location on a line leading from non-binding soft law to binding hard law. Given the blurring of the boundaries between soft and hard law, this might, though, be a difficult task.

Self-regulation and the polycentricity of legal sources question the assumption of unity of state will expressing itself in the law. But they do not necessarily sever the ties that connect law to the nation state. The normative doctrine of sources of law always adopts the perspective of a particular legal actor, usually that of the judge. The judge epitomises the state's standpoint, and if polycentricity of legal sources is suggestive of a disruption in the state monopoly of legal norm-production, polycentricity does not yet extend to the law's application, nor can we yet speak of a pluralism of legal systems.

Self-regulation may also be based on explicit legislative authorisation by the state, in which case it can, in fact, be categorised as delegated legislation. Thus, in Finland, the Act on Commercial Banks explicitly refers to good banking practice and the Act on Auditing to good auditing practice.

If the system of self-regulation includes not only norm-generation but a mechanism for norm-application, too, a further step away from state-dependence has been taken; a step from the polycentricity of legal sources towards the pluralism of legal systems.[1] In the light of this criterion, the Finnish cases of self-regulation in banking or auditing would not yet amount to a pluralism of legal systems: violations of good banking or auditing practice fall to the jurisdiction of state courts. By contrast, violations of the rules of the Helsinki stock market are dealt with by its Disciplinary Board, and sanctions for violations of national anti-doping rules are decided upon by the national sports associations. In private law, especially contract law, arbitration is a procedural alternative to court proceedings. However, if the law to be applied is that of the nation state, arbitration does not meet the criteria of self-regulation with regard to norm-generation.

Even self-regulation that includes sanctioning or dispute-solving mechanisms (thus giving expression to a pluralism of legal systems) usually maintains a link to the state. In most cases, the state provides the ultimate guarantee that self-regulation works, and corrects its excesses. For example, the decisions of the Disciplinary Board of the Helsinki stock market may be appealed before an administrative court, while the Supreme Court of Finland has considered itself competent to examine an appeal against suspension imposed by a national sports association for violating anti-doping rules (KKO 1998:12). Moreover, in cases defined in the municipal law on arbitration, arbitration awards may be contested before a state court. And even if access to the court is denied, the arbitration procedure remains dependent on the same extra-legal prerequisite as modern law in general: the state's coercive machinery, which ensures execution of the award.

Max Weber famously defined the state through its monopoly on the legitimate use of violence. This appears to be the last ingredient of sovereignty that a modern state obstinately clings to. It is true, though, that even here we can point to the privatisation of security services and the outsourcing of military functions. Nevertheless, the execution of legal decisions has, as a rule,[2] remained within the exclusive power of the state. This also accounts for the control that state courts exercise over non-state forms of adjudication. If execution of decisions taken within self-regulating systems is not ensured by the coercive machinery of the state, self-regulation may remain ineffective, unless it is able to rely on surrogate mechanisms securing implementation.

To sum up, it seems premature to speak of loosening ties connecting the law to the nation state and crumbling state legal sovereignty. However, the polycentricity of sources of law, self-regulation and a budding pluralism of legal systems undoubtedly challenge many of the assumptions about law, state and society in the 'hidden social theory' of legal thinking. Kelsen's hierarchy of legal norms is

1 With the concept of legal system I refer to the whole formed by the law's two dimensions: the legal order and legal practices. The independence of a legal system presupposes, in addition to a distinct normative order, specific practices establishing and applying legal norms. The possibility of such practices, in turn, requires that the norm order includes secondary norms regulating recognition, change and application of primary norms.

2 Exceptions to this rule exist too, such as private prisons in the United States.

a corollary of the state's hierarchical institutional structure, while the divisions employed in the law's systematisation have been based on separation of state and society (public/private law) and on classification of state functions (the sub-fields of public law). It is increasingly difficult to build the law's unity on grounds that presuppose a link between the law and the state, as well as the unity of state will and state organisation.

State courts appear to have retained their central role, but this does not necessarily guarantee law's unity, either. The judiciary has not been spared the fragmentation characteristic of the state's organisational development in recent decades. Fragmentation has assumed different institutional forms in different legal systems; Finland has courts with general jurisdiction, administrative courts, special courts, such as the Labour Court, and various board-like tribunals, particularly in the field of social security. The judiciary's hierarchical structure does not suffice to secure the unity of adjudication, when the judiciary is divided into multiple hierarchies with overlapping and partially unclear and contested jurisdictions. Thus, the alleged normative and institutional fragmentation of international law into semi-independent regimes has its counterparts in municipal legal systems.

Transnational Law

The most serious challenges to links between law and state arise from legal relationships transcending nation-state boundaries. Phenomena questioning the state's internal sovereignty, such as self-regulation of the economy and sports, also tend to have a transnational background and transnational links. Globalisation debates have reached the law, too. On the one hand, law itself displays signs of globalisation while, on the other hand, globalisation of other action fields requires from the law corresponding cross-boundary reactions. Globalisation may, though, be too portentous a concept for many of the phenomena under examination; it would perhaps be more fitting to talk – in the wake of Michael Zürn (1998) – of *de-nationalisation*. This concept covers even cross-boundary processes of merely, say, regional reach.

So what is globalisation or – to use the less pretentious expression – de-nationalisation about? According to David Harvey's well-known succinct definition (1989, p. 157) 'globalisation' connotes the compression of time and space. This involves not only the spatiality but also the temporality of social relations; enlargement of the locus of social interaction is matched by its acceleration. Capital investors and currency dealers not only establish contacts that pay no heed to state borders and geographical distances, but thanks to computers and the Internet, transactions are completed in the blink of an eye. The restricted spatiality of modern nation-state law does not allow it to regulate such global connections. Moreover, the temporality typical of modern law and its practices may also make it unsuitable for regulating transactions in virtual time; for example, the time of legal proceedings in state courts may simply be far too slow.

Many accounts of globalisation and its legal consequences privilege the perspective of the economy. But globalisation – or de-nationalisation – is not solely about the economy; it is not manifest only in production and exchange of goods, services and capital. Pollutants and other environmental risks, cultural influences or criminality and terrorism are not stopped by the border controls of nation states. Above, I alluded to the crisis of politics and legal regulation ensuing from the shaking of the temporal background assumptions on which the instrumentalist conception of politics and law relies: social sub-systems possess their distinct temporalities, and the time of politics and law does not necessarily mesh with the time of, for instance, the economy. The conception of politics, implicit in the law's employment in social management, is based on certain spatial beliefs as well. Society, as a project realisable in time, has been conceived of as a nation-state society. Correspondingly, the social space calling for legal regulation has been more or less self-evidently identified with the legal and political space of the nation state (Zürn 1998, pp. 54–55; Schroer 2006, pp. 189ff.). The nation state's legal sovereignty met the regulatory needs of the time when the economy was still the national economy; when criminality, too, had its nationality and the consequences of crimes occurred in the place where they were committed; and when the polluting effects of industrial or agricultural production were limited to their immediate environment. The spatial presuppositions of the instrumentalist nation-state legislator have lost their self-evident validity: the functioning of social systems – with the economy as the forerunner – pays increasingly less heed to state borders. Development has been from nation-state societies towards a world society (*Weltgesellschaft*), composed of functionally differentiated global social sub-systems (Stichweh 2000). When society undergoes a process of de-nationalisation and when, as a consequence, the social space to be regulated is no longer identical with the political space of the nation state, the law of the nation state loses its capacity to respond to regulatory needs. Nation-state regulation is not able to provide solutions to disputes arising in the global economic marketplace or fence off social dumping, threatening the foundations of the welfare state, nor can the environmental legislation of nation states prevent climate change and global warming. Legal regulation has to look for new forms or be replaced by other means of problem-solving. Even within nation states, the law has not been the only instrument in the political management of society, nor does it hold any exclusive privilege at the supra-state level; in global governance, legal regulation constitutes only one alternative.

International law has been modern law's traditional response to the need for cross-boundary regulation. As we have seen, however, international law has been firmly tied to the state in both its creation and its effects. The focus of traditional international law has been on relations between nation states, not on the cross-boundary interaction between non-state actors as has set the stage for the current debate on globalisation and de-nationalisation.

It is true, though, that the ties binding international law to the nation state are loosening. International law is still primarily law established by nation states, but negotiations on multilateral treaties in the field of, say, human rights and humanitarian law or environmental law have been opened to non-state participants, such as NGOs (but not so much as to grant them the right to vote!). This is a modest attempt to create channels for transnational civil society to participate in discourse on new norms and, thereby, to democratise international norm-giving (Lindblom 2005).

Nor do the legal effects of international law any longer concern solely nation states – the sphere of international legal subjectivity has expanded. Human rights treaties launched this development: the European Convention, for instance, creates justiciable rights for private individuals. The focus of international law's obligatory effects is still on states: as a rule, states still constitute the subjects of international legal duties. However, whether treaty obligations should be extended to non-state actors (such as transnational corporations or belligerents in civil-war-like confrontations), and how this could be done, is a highly pertinent topic in current international human-rights discourse (Klabbers 2003; Clapham 2006; Teubner 2006).

From the very beginning, international law has been afflicted by the problem of efficacy: how to secure and organise its application and execution? The problem, of course, derives from international law's ties with nation states. International courts have existed, such as the International Court of Justice in The Hague and the preceding Permanent International Court of the League of Nations. However, the jurisdiction of the International Court of Justice depends on nation states: as a rule, an alleged breach of a treaty can only be brought before the Court if the respective states have issued a declaration acknowledging its jurisdiction. The Court in The Hague resembles a permanent arbitration body, rather than a court empowered to act regardless of consent of the parties.

A new development path has, perhaps, been initiated by international criminal courts, whose jurisdiction over individual defendants does not depend on the blessing of the respective nation states. The Second World War signalled a turning-point. The Nuremburg and Tokyo trials were based on treaties concluded by the four major allied states. The courts were special courts, established only to rule in the cases defined in the treaties. The courts dealing with Yugoslav war crimes and the genocide in Rwanda and established through resolutions of the UN Security Council are more recent examples of such special courts. The problem with ad hoc courts is that they are difficult to reconcile with fundamental human-rights principles concerning fair trial in criminal law cases, such as *nulla poena sine lege*, proscribing retroactive criminal law, and the prohibition of ad hoc courts. The International Criminal Court, established by the Treaty of Rome in 1998, is a response to questions raised by ad hoc special courts with regard to human-rights principles. It is a permanent court whose jurisdiction is defined in its statute in adherence to the *nulla poena sine lege* principle, and its demand for precision and prohibition of retroactivity (Jeschek 2004). The significance of the court is tempered by the fact that only slightly more than 100 states have ratified its statute and that the United States, China, Russia, Israel and India, for instance, are not among these.

International law's efficacy problems have affected not only the jurisdiction of international courts but also execution of their decisions. Modern municipal law has been supported by the state's coercive machinery as a warranty for norms' realisation. At the international level, too, states have been extremely reluctant to relinquish their monopoly on the legitimate use of violence. As a rule, the international community does not have at its disposal a coercive machinery of its own which could guarantee international law's realisation. Even the UN does not possess permanent military or police forces but depends on the resources which the Member States have allotted to it under Chapter 7 of the UN Statute.

Even when specific dispute-solving or sanctioning court-like bodies have been established, international law's realisation remains reliant on nation states. Execution of the rulings of the International Court of Justice falls largely to the states themselves, although the Security Council can decide on sanctions against a state. In turn, sentences of international criminal courts are usually carried out in the prisons of nation states. The international prison in Schenningen may, though, attest to an emerging new practice.

Thus, treaty-based international courts are still in need of support from nation states, especially in execution of their decisions. Yet, they point to a legal development surpassing the limitations of traditional international law; towards a *transnational law* which cannot be compressed into the dichotomous categories of municipal and international law. The distinctive features of transnational law can be attached to either norm-formation or norm-application. Transnational norm-giving assumes other forms than bi- or multilateral treaties between nation states. In norm-application, in turn, the establishment of dispute-solving or sanctioning bodies beyond the control of nation states suggests the emergence of transnational law.

Of course, no watertight borderline exists between norm-formation and norm-application. Through its own case-law, a court-like body established by an international treaty develops and complements the treaty-based norms it is supposed to apply. In national legal systems as well, courts participate through their precedents in producing new legal norms. The standing of precedents in a legal system depends on the prevailing legal culture and the doctrine of legal sources it includes: we are accustomed to thinking that in common-law countries, the courts play a more important role in determining the contents of the legal order than in Continental European Romano-Germanic legal cultures. Furthermore, legislation's level of precision clearly affects the significance of precedents: the less determinate legislation is, the more leeway it leaves to norm-formation through precedents. Provisions of treaties applied by the International Court of Justice and other international monitoring bodies are usually formulated in rather general terms, and for an obvious reason: in inter-state treaty negotiations, it is difficult to reach agreement on detailed norms, so that concretisation of norms is left to treaty application.

The vague provisions of the European Convention on Human Rights have gained precision through the case-law of the Strasbourg Court. Thus, to take an example, the mere wording of Art. 6 conveys but a pallid picture of the normative contents of fair trial. European human-rights law possesses a treaty basis – the Convention and the Protocols. Nonetheless, we can speak of a transnational legal system which has distanced itself from its international law background with respect to both its normative and institutional structure. From each Signatory State, one member of the Court is chosen, and the states participate in the appointment procedure by nominating three candidates. But the final choice is made by the Parliamentary Assembly of the Council of Europe, and once appointed, the judges are not supposed to represent their respective nation states. Norm-generation through the Court's case-law, in turn, amounts to transnational lawmaking. The Court's at least partial detachment from (general) international law is also manifest in the qualified manner with which it has treated the applicability of certain provisions of the Vienna Convention on treaty law. The court has underlined the constitutional character of the European Convention and inferred from this that the Vienna Convention's provisions on reservations and international legal succession are not applicable as such.

Despite its tendency towards independence, European human-rights law has retained its interaction with the domestic legal systems of the Signatory States as well. The Convention, in line with the basic-rights provisions of national constitutions, creates justiciable individual rights. This explains the steps which national legal systems have taken to avoid conflicts between transnational and national law. Human-rights norms have been accorded binding effect in most national legal orders; hence, domestic courts play a central role in ensuring their realisation. Their position is further strengthened by the margin-of-appreciation doctrine adopted by the Strasbourg Court. According to this doctrine, it falls primarily to the domestic courts to assess whether the case at hand meets the requirements that the convention sets for limitations on rights (Viljanen 2003). Of course, contradictions between human-rights law and domestic law cannot be wholly excluded, as the rulings of the Strasbourg Court condemning the states demonstrate. However, the human-rights legal system lacks coercive machinery which would ensure execution of decisions; it is up to the states themselves to take care of this.

EU law provides another example of a legal system which has detached itself from its international-law foundation. Primary EU norms derive from international treaty law, but secondary norms, such as regulations and directives, cannot be classified in terms of international law. Furthermore, primary norms, as interpreted by the European Court of Justice, treat even private persons as legal subjects, which departs from the premises of international law. Ever since the 1960s, the European Court of Justice has characterised EU (EC) law as an independent legal order, distinct both from the municipal legal orders of Member States and from international law. Nevertheless, both normatively and institutionally, EU law remains intertwined with the legal systems of Member States. According to the prevailing conception in Finland, for instance, the municipal legal order incorporates not only directives and framework decisions duly implemented by Finnish state organs but also EU norms covered by the doctrine of direct effect. And when national courts apply EU norms, they act simultaneously as institutions of both the municipal and the EU legal system. In their latter capacity, they are obliged to comply with preliminary rulings of the European Court of Justice.

In spite of its basis in international treaty law, WTO law, too, has assumed features of a transnational legal system, resisting the dichotomy of international and municipal law. Its institutional structure includes dispute settlement panels, whose decisions may be appealed to the Appellate Body. These organs also produce normative material specifying and complementing treaty provisions. However, adhering to the traditional starting premises of international law, WTO law focuses on relations between states, and execution of decisions of dispute-resolving bodies is also left to the states themselves.

International environmental and maritime law, too, display signs of a corresponding movement away from international treaty law towards a transnational legal system. From the perspective of international law, the development has been problematised as a fragmentation which, in the view of some observers, worryingly threatens its cogency. Particular court-like bodies that do not defer to the precedents of the International Court of Justice shake its position as a guarantor of international law's unity. The qualified approach of some special courts, including the European Court of Human Rights, to the Vienna Convention on International Treaty Law, has also been seen as a danger to the coherence of international law (Koskenniemi and Leino 2002).

But whether we conceive of the ongoing process as a fragmentation of international law or as the dawn of transnational law, the growing plethora of legal sources, legal orders, and even legal systems does not mesh with the dichotomy of municipal and international law. The municipal legal order has lost its monopoly on determining legal relations involving private individuals. Even in states whose constitution defines the status of international law according to the dualistic model, transnational norms have an immediate effect, regardless of a transformative act of the national legislator. This is the case in Finland, for instance. Art. 95 of the constitution lays down that international treaties and other international-law obligations are to be incorporated into the domestic legal order through an Act of Parliament or a presidential decree. Nonetheless, this constitutional provision cannot prevent the direct effect of, for instance, EU regulations, preliminary rulings of the European Court of Justice, or precedents of the European Court of Human Rights; here, no prior decision of the national legislature is needed.

Sovereignty of the national legislator over the domestic legal order may also be diminished by excluding certain regulatory issues from its competence. This is the case in fields such as external trade and customs, which, according to the foundational treaties, fall to the exclusive competence of the EU. And even if the national legislator has retained its competence, use of this competence may have been submitted to transnational monitoring. This is the situation in environmental policy, for instance. Relations between domestic, and international and transnational regulation can no longer be conceived of through the black-box model.

The deficiency of this model is even more conspicuous with regard to transnational regulation that altogether lacks a background in international treaty law and that has emerged as a result of autonomous operation of de-nationalised social sub-systems. Discussants starting from the premises of Luhmann's autopoietic systems theory have argued that globalisation has produced fragmentation of a new type. Globalisation reiterates the *functional differentiation* which has characterised modern nation-state society: global society is differentiated into relatively independent sub-systems, and these produce their own transnational law (Teubner 1996 and 2004a; Fischer-Lescano and Teubner 2006). Hence, global law (*Weltrecht*) is not only differentiated territorially into national legal systems, but the territorial criterion has been complemented by new, functional grounds. Examples of transnational legal systems adhering to functional grounds are provided by the *lex mercatoria* of international trade, the *lex sportiva* of international sports, and the *lex digitalis* of the Internet. In each of these transnational legal systems, the applicable norms have been subsumed by neither municipal legal orders nor international law, while disputes are settled and sanctions imposed by designated transnational bodies.[3]

Lex mercatoria has evolved to provide solutions to legal disputes in international trade relations in situations where the parties, for some reason or other, do not want to apply any municipal legal order and where the rules of international private law are of no use. *Lex mercatoria* is applied by international arbitration bodies. In the beginning, the International Chamber of Commerce was the central actor of the system. It offered arbitration services and composed model contracts based on arbitration procedures. Elaboration of substantive norms applied in arbitration was, initially, dominated by European academic experts of private international and contract law. Subsequently, the role of international, especially US, law firms and consultants employed by them has grown. *Lex mercatoria* has preserved its character of 'lawyers' law' (*Juristenrecht*): international, transnational or national lawgivers have been left aside. This fact has entailed a degree of vagueness concerning applicable norms, in addition to a potential legitimacy problem. The confidentiality of arbitration has prevented formation of case-law that might remedy this deficiency – if, in general, it can be considered a deficiency! The emergence of Internet-based data banks of arbitration awards has partly redressed the situation.

The Convention on the Recognition and Execution of Foreign Arbitration Awards, together with domestic arbitration laws, provides for resort to nation-state coercive machinery in the execution of *lex mercatoria*. But support of this kind from nation states is not generally needed. Empirical research has shown that the internal sanctions of the international economic system – such as severing trade

3 For succinct presentations of these transnational legal systems, see Zangl and Zürn (2004).

relations, blacklists and boycotts, and loss of reputation – usually suffice to ensure respect for arbitration awards. It is, though, unclear what significance the mere availability of nation-state coercive execution has had (Appelbaum et al. 2001).

Lex sportiva has largely focused on combating doping. Its transnational efficacy has been backed up by the principle of the one-and-only-association and a pyramid-like organisational structure. Under the principle of the one-and-only-association, the International Olympics Committee acknowledges only one international organisation in each sport. The organisational structure of diverse sports is highly hierarchical, from the international association to basic associations with individual athletes as members. For each country, the international associations recognise only one national association. Organisations at lower levels are obliged to comply with norms established at the higher levels, such as anti-doping rules. Individual athletes and other actors in sports, such as coaches, are obliged to obey these norms either on an association-law basis – the legal figures are 'indirect membership' and 'statutes chaining' – or under a contract-law obligation.

Lex sportiva is monitored by national and international associations. In athletics, for instance, the IAAF requires that athletes participating in events under its jurisdiction acknowledge its competence. As a rule, sanctions decided by national or international associations can be appealed to an arbitral body. At the transnational level, the central actor is the TSA–CAS (Tribunal Arbitral du Sport–Court of Arbitration for Sport), established in 1983 and with its seat in Lausanne.

According to a ruling of the Swiss Supreme Court in 1993, TSA–CAS meets the criteria laid down in the Convention on the Recognition and Execution of Foreign Arbitration Awards. Hence, its decisions can be executed by nation-state machinery. However, *lex sportiva* does not usually need external assistance, because sports associations themselves possess efficient means of monitoring compliance with, say, competition bans or suspensions for violations of anti-doping rules. Indeed, sports associations tend to be suspicious of the jurisdiction of state courts, regarding these rather as a threat to the independence of *lex sportiva* and national and international sport in general. As a justification for their competence, courts have usually argued that suspension touches on the athlete's right to earn a living, which in many countries enjoys constitutional status (Lehmkuhl 2004). The Finnish Supreme Court, too, in a precedent from 1998, warranted its competence by appealing to the negative economic consequences of a suspension for the athlete.

Transnational *lex digitalis* is most developed in the regulation of disputes over domain names. The central actor in the UDRP (Uniform Domain Name Dispute Resolution Policy) is the ICANN (Internet Corporation for Assigned Names and Numbers), which is charged with international administration of domain names. ICANN is a private-law corporation with its domicile in California. The legal basis of its powers within the Internet is in fact rather unclear. In 1998, it decided to introduce the UDRP and adopted the respective rules.

In the contract of registration, domain name holders commit themselves to the procedure in situations laid down in para. 4a of UDRP Policy. The procedure can be initiated by a trademark owner on the grounds of trademark violation. The claimant is entitled to choose between court proceedings and the UDRP procedure. If the claimant opts for the latter, the defendant has no choice but under the terms of the contract of registration is obliged to accept the claimant's choice. The procedure can be portrayed as voluntary dispute settlement, where services are at present offered by, for instance, WIPO (World Intellectual Property Organisation). The UDRP procedure does not hinder subsequent appeal to a court. In court, the claimant can sue, for example, for repeal of the registration, for damages, or for a ban on use of a domain name violating a trademark. The UDRP procedure has not been considered to amount to arbitration (in the strict legal sense of the concept), and decisions have not been granted *res judicata* effect in courts. Decisions fall outside the scope of the Convention on the Recognition and Execution of Foreign Arbitration Awards as well.

In execution of decisions, *lex digitalis* does not depend on nation-state coercive machinery but can resort to electronic means of blocking use of a particular domain name. If the defendant appeals the decision to a court within a short time frame, its execution will be postponed (Leib 2004).

Fragmentation or Harmonisation

We are ready to summarise. The world of the law can no longer be conceived of under the dichotomy of municipal and international law. In the traditional view, law's empire was ruled by nation-state institutions. The nation state's legal sovereignty included the power to determine the law pertaining to both infra-state and inter-state relations. The latter were governed by international law, which, as a rule, was only binding on the state by its own consent, expressed within the framework of its external sovereignty. The legal effects of international law were usually confined to inter-state relations; infra-state legal relations fell under the nation state's internal legal sovereignty. When exceptions to the rule were made, that is, when international law was accorded legal effect within the state, this too required the state's consent. In monistic systems the constitution involved a kind of general consent, while in dualistic systems treaty provisions were, case-by-case, incorporated into municipal law through an express legislative act.

Transnational norm-giving and norm-application have detached themselves from international law, as conceived through the black-box model. Transnational law, such as EU law or human-rights law, extends its effects to private subjects irrespective of general or case-by-case consent of the nation state, and specific courts or other monitoring bodies may have been established for its application. Those normative and institutional structures which have been generated by globalised social systems themselves, without support from international treaty law, have moved even further away from nation-state control. These include *lex mercatoria*, *lex sportiva* and *lex digitalis*.

Transnational law, as well as non-state norm-formation within the confines of the nation state, have shaken the national legislator's monopoly on establishment of legal norms. By contrast, the pivotal position which the courts of nation states have occupied in modern law has not been contested to the same extent. Transnational law is still in many ways linked to national courts, in line with self-regulatory mechanisms within nation states. National courts play an important role in both human-rights and EU law, and they have also been preserved external controlling powers under *lex mercatoria*, *lex sportiva* and *lex digitalis*. Furthermore, transnational law is forced to resort to assistance from nation states in execution of the decisions of its court-like institutions, the monopoly on the legitimate use of violence being the last bastion of nation-state sovereignty. If the efficacy of transnational law can be ensured by means other than the nation state's coercive machinery, the ultimate obstacle to its growing independence will be removed. In this respect, the circumstances seem to be most favourable within the systems of transnational law that have emerged without even the initial backing of international law. The efficacy of *lex mercatoria* and *lex sportiva* is propped up by the internal sanction mechanisms of commerce and sport – severing of business relations, and competition bans and suspensions, for instance – while decisions in the field of *lex digitalis* can be instantly implemented by electronic means, by, for example, closing down a website.

Tendencies towards globalisation and transnational law are conspicuous, but they should not lead us into ignoring the many ties that still connect the law to the nation state. The law's spatial relations are undergoing profound transformations but these do not amount to total replacement of municipal by transnational law. The law's space no longer consists solely of nation-state territory, but this has by no means been abandoned, either – instead of a one and only spatial criterion, it is more fitting to speak of *multi-level spatiality*, which still includes the level of the nation state, too. Nevertheless, nation-state law's relations to other legal systems cannot be conceived of according to the black-box model. Nation-state law has lost its territorial monopoly.

The picture is not identical in all fields of law, and both international and transnational law are still reliant on backing from nation-state institutions, especially from the courts and the coercive machinery of execution. But we should note that the state no longer constitutes such a unitary actor as it appeared in the doctrine of the German late constitutional school, for instance. The pluralisation of state will and the fragmentation of state organisation also affect international relations: these are increasingly based on direct international or transnational co-operation and networking between national administrative agencies – environmental authorities, authorities for telecommunications or transportation and the like. This may have its legal basis in treaty-making competence or other international legal powers accorded to the administration (Slaughter 2004).

Our late modern legal constellation has often been examined through the prism of *legal pluralism*, a concept with its origin in legal anthropological research. According to Twining (2000, p. 83), the concept refers 'to legal systems, networks or orders co-existing in the same geographical space'. Legal pluralism is not identical to normative pluralism, which is a wider phenomenon; it may, though, be difficult to draw an exact line between the two, Twining notes. He argues that within legal pluralism, a further distinction should be made between pluralist state legal systems and non-state systems. In pluralist state systems, state courts apply different norm orders to different groups of persons. Twining's example is the Tanzania of the 1960s where state courts applied, in addition to English common law and statutes, local legislation, Islamic law, Hindu law, and local customary law. Tanzania's law was '"plural" only in the sense that the state recognized different rules for specific categories of persons, especially in such matters as inheritance, family, and some aspects of land tenure' (ibid.). The significance of non-state law is underlined by those scholars of legal pluralism who claim that 'all societies have a diversity of legal orders, of which "official" state law is only one, and not necessarily the most powerful' (ibid., p. 84). We should, however, pay due attention to the conceptual difficulties typical of the pluralism debates: how to delimit law from non-law, or state law from non-state law?

The independence of a *legal order* presupposes rules of recognition (a normative doctrine of legal sources), determining the (surface-level) norms making up the legal order. For the independence of a *legal system*, such a recognisable and definable legal order will not suffice. What is further required is institutional differentiation which manifests itself in the establishing of court-like dispute-resolving or sanctioning bodies; in the normative dimension, rules of recognition must be complemented with other types of secondary rules. It is not, however, possible, nor perhaps even necessary, to achieve precision in the separation of law from non-law and state law from non-state law. Legal pluralism is typified by interaction and porous borders between both normative orders and institutional structures. Boaventura de Sousa Santos has approached the present legal constellation from a phenomenological perspective – the perspective of legal experience – and introduced the term *interlegality*. Interlegality is not equal to legal pluralism as defined in traditional legal anthropology and 'in which the different legal orders are conceived as separate entities coexisting in the same political space'. Typical of interlegality are 'different legal spaces superimposed, interpenetrated and mixed in our minds, as much as in our actions'. De Sousa Santos argues that 'we live in a time of porous legality or of legal porosity, multiple networks of legal orders forcing us to constant transitions and trespassing. Our legal life is constituted by an intersection of different legal orders, that is, by interlegality' (de Sousa Santos 2002, p. 437).

How have late modern legal developments – transformations in the law's temporality and spatiality and ruptures in nation state legal monopoly – affected the guises which *voluntas* and *ratio* assume in law? Does the relationship between *voluntas* and *ratio* in general any longer possess the significance I have assigned to it in the preceding chapters? These are big questions, and the following comments can only be tentative.

The law's *voluntas* can no longer be unequivocally identified with the *voluntas* of the nation-state legislator. The institutional unity of the nation state has loosened, while articulation of its legal *voluntas* is no longer the monopoly of the political legislator. The *voluntas* of international treaty law has been the nation states' common *voluntas* whose contents have been specified in inter-state negotiations. In international treaty law, *voluntas* has retained the connection to politics which posed the issue of its necessary containment at nation-state level. This connection has been preserved in such a transnational political entity as the EU. By contrast, the tie between law and politics has been severed in legal systems differentiated on functional grounds and generated by global social sub-systems, such as *lex mercatoria*, *lex sportiva* and *lex digitalis*. But this has not eliminated the problem of taming the *voluntas*. The issue of power and control of power is equally pertinent in transnational as it is in international and national norm-formation and norm-application. Systems-theoretically oriented legal scholarship merits credit for many observations and insights concerning global law. Its blindspot, however, is the power inherent in functionally differentiated legal systems; its systems-theoretically tailored concepts seem to be incapable of capturing power-related phenomena.

The *constitution* has accomplished an important task in erecting barriers to the *voluntas* of the nation-state legislator. Constitutional provisions on basic rights and constitutional review, as well as constitutional culture functioning through the pre-understanding of legal (and political) actors, have been crucial for the success of this task. International-law doctrine has detected in international law, too, normative elements imposing restrictions on treaty-based lawmaking. The dramatic growth of treaty law, as well as international law's increasing fragmentation, have provided additional impetus to the debate on *jus cogens*, arguably accomplishing the tasks of *ratio* in international law. In its *Furundzija* ruling, the Yugoslav War Crimes Court (ICTY) characterised *jus cogens* as follows:

> Because of the importance of the values it [the prohibition of torture] protects, this principle has evolved into a peremptory norm or *jus cogens*, that is, a norm that enjoys a higher rank in the international hierarchy than treaty law and even 'ordinary' customary rules. The most conspicuous consequence of this higher rank is that the principle at issue cannot be derogated by States through international treaties or local or special customs or even general customary rules not endowed with the same normative forces.[4]

The Vienna Convention on Treaty Law explicitly acknowledges *jus cogens*. Art. 53 lays down that 'a treaty is void if, at the time of its conclusion, it conflicts with a peremptory norm of general international law' and goes on to explicate that 'for the purposes of the present Convention, a peremptory norm of general international law is a norm accepted and recognised by the international community of States as a whole as a norm from which no derogation is permitted and which can be modified only by a subsequent norm of general international law having the

4 *Prosecutors* v. *Anto Furundzija*, Judgment of 10 December, Case No. IT-95-17/1.

same character'. Furthermore, Art. 64 provides that 'if a new peremptory norm of general international law emerges, any existing treaty which is in conflict with that norm becomes void and terminates'. The concept of *jus cogens* is generally accepted in the theory and practice of international law, but its contents and scope of application are highly contested. According to Koskenniemi, *jus cogens* status is most often claimed for prohibition of aggressive use of force; the right to self-defence; prohibition of genocide; prohibition of torture; crimes against humanity; prohibition of piracy; prohibition of racial discrimination and apartheid; and prohibition of hostilities directed at civilians ('basic rules of international humanitarian law') (Koskenniemi 2006, p. 189 (para. 374)).

International human-rights treaties and their monitoring bodies point to the internationalisation or transnationalisation of the *Rechtsstaat* or – from a common-law perspective – the rule of law. However, international human-rights instruments are not directed towards international or transnational actors but internal power exercise by Signatory States; they complement domestic constitutional basic-rights provisions and domestic constitutional review in monitoring nation-state authorities and the *voluntas* of nation-state law.[5] Unless the measures taken by international or transnational bodies can be re-described as a nation-state authority's action, they fall outside the jurisdiction of the monitoring organs established by human-rights treaties, such as the European Court of Human Rights.[6] Paradoxically enough, humanitarian interventions by the international community have created quasi-dictatorial authorities uninhibited by human-rights instruments, such as the High Representative in Bosnia and Herzegovina or the United Nations Administration in Kosovo.

Nevertheless, human-rights treaties extend their influence on international legal decision-making beyond their immediate scope of application. They form part of the international legal environment which the principle of 'systemic integration' exhorts to heed in applying and interpreting treaty law. This principle has been confirmed in Art. 31(3) of the Vienna Convention, laying down that in treaty interpretation 'any relevant rules of international law applicable in the relations between the parties' shall be taken into account' (para. c) (Koskenniemi 2006, p. 208 (para. 413)). However, human-rights treaties possess an equal formal status to other multilateral international treaties; they have not been granted a higher hierarchical position in the norm order of international law. An exception is made only for norms of a *jus cogens* character.

It is true, though, that in the practice and theory of international law, constitutional status has sometimes been claimed for human-rights treaties. The European Court of Human Rights has appealed to the constitutional character of the European Convention when arguing that Signatory States are not entitled

5 The restricted scope of application of the European Convention is confirmed in Art. 1.

6 The legal situation will change if the European Union accedes to the European Convention on Human Rights.

to reservations on the basis of the Vienna Convention. Some scholars have defended the view that human-rights law represents the constitutional dimension in international law and, therefore, obliges the states irrespective of their consent. But in the practice of international law, *jus cogens* standing has been accorded only to some human rights norms, such as prohibition of torture, but not to human-rights law in its entirety. International law also lacks institutional procedures that could ensure the primacy of human rights over, say, WTO law.[7]

In the Critic's narrative, human-rights treaties with their monitoring bodies stand on an equal footing with other *regimes* of fragmented international law, such as WTO law or international environmental law. The Critic depicts the regimes as being engaged in a strategically-oriented jurisdictional contest: a contest over the power to define the contents of international law. International-law cases are often related to more than one regime, and their legal assessment depends on the regime from whose perspective it is examined.[8]

Constitutionalism at the level of general international law is still largely wishful thinking rather than existing practice. Constitutional discourse is more credible in the context of particular international-law regimes or such particular transnational legal systems and polities as the European Union. Whether it is possible to speak of a constitution beyond nation states even in such contexts, turns, of course, on our conceptual choices. 'Constitution' in the *formal* sense refers to a unitary constitutional enactment. The EU does not possess such a constitution, nor will it do so in the foreseeable future following the 2005 demise of the Constitutional Treaty. By contrast, it can well be argued that the EU already has a constitution in the *substantive* sense of the concept. The substantive concept alludes to the functions of the constitution in the legal and political systems. If the legal order involves norms accomplishing such functions, it is warranted to speak of a constitution in the substantive sense of the term. The founding treaties regulate not only the application and execution of EU law but also the production of new EU norms. Furthermore, EU law includes a basic-rights dimension. The European Court of Justice started to appeal to basic-rights principles as a reaction to some domestic constitutional courts' eagerness to submit EU norms for their review, and in the Maastricht Treaty an explicit provision confirmed the status of basic rights as general principles of EU law. A new phase was reached with the Charter on Fundamental Rights, which was adopted as a solemn declaration at the Nice 2000 summit and whose legal significance is confirmed in the Lisbon Treaty, replacing the failed Constitutional Treaty. Thus, EU law includes norms regulating production of new norms and ensuring basic rights, as the standard definition of a substantive constitution presupposes. The founding treaties also establish a

7 In international law debates, constitutional status has also been proposed for the Statute of the UN (Fassbender 1998).

8 In international law, the concept of regime, too, is used in various senses. See Koskenniemi (2006, pp. 65–74 (para. 123–137)).

structural coupling between the EU's political and legal dimensions in the manner required by Luhmann's notion of a constitution (see above, pp. 207–208).

The example of the EU shows that rights-based review in international or transnational law does not necessarily presuppose a universal constitution, based on international human-rights treaties, which would extend the obligatory force of treaties from nation states to international- and transnational-law entities. The *voluntas* of EU law is restricted by the EU's own basic-rights norms, whose monitoring falls to the EU's own judicial organisation. However, a constellation of 'interlegality' prevails between EU law's basic-rights norms, the European Convention on Human Rights, and national constitutions. The Treaty on the European Union attaches basic rights which count as general principles of EU law to the European Convention on Human Rights, and Art. 52(3) of the EU Charter lays down that the Convention provides the base line for defining the protection provided by EU basic rights. The Charter also includes a provision on its relation to the constitutional rights of Member States (Art. 54).

Clearly, the primary locus of power-controlling norms and practices is and should remain in the fragmented regimes of international and transnational law. Such a solution generates its own risks; the basic-rights perspective is in danger of being subjected to the system's or regime's specific function; to its 'internal *ratio*'. In the EU, this problem culminates in the tension between the four market freedoms, expressing the original economic orientation of European integration, and basic rights.

In Habermas' democratic *Rechtsstaat*, the disciplining effect of the *ratio* is supposed to be already achieved in democratic lawmaking procedures; in ethico-political and moral discourses with the public sphere of civil society as their primary stage. It is not easy to add discursive elements to international and transnational norm-formation or norm-application, as has been shown in the debates on the EU's democratic deficit and the prospects of a European civil society and *demos*. In the discussion on democratisation of international-law regimes – international environmental law, human-rights law, WTO law, and the like – the emphasis has been on NGOs – such as, say, Amnesty International, Human Rights Watch or Greenpeace. Optimistic observers have also detected signs of an emerging transnational public sphere, for which new communication and information technologies and the ensuing communicative and cultural globalisation would pave the way.

Apparently, transfer of the principles of a democratic *Rechtsstaat* to the transnational level confronts the toughest obstacles in those global legal systems which, according to legal systems theorists, are not structurally coupled so much with the political as with other social sub-systems. Norm-formation in these legal systems, too, involves power, although this is not equivalent to the political power inherent in the norm formation of the nation-state legal system. Furthermore, these transnational legal systems are confronted with problems of a basic-rights character; such as access to the Internet as an issue of freedom of speech (*lex digitalis*) or an athlete's right to compete as an issue concerning the right to earn a living (*lex sportiva*). Gunter Teubner (2004a, 2004b) suggests that the concept of constitution be detached from its link to relations between the legal and political systems; in his proposal, the constitution would refer generally to structural couplings between the reflexive mechanisms of the legal and some other social system. Such a constitutional concept would, however, deprive the constitution of its tasks in preventing the arbitrary exercise of power – tasks integral to the idea of a democratic *Rechtsstaat*.

Functionally-differentiated global legal systems, such as *lex mercatoria*, *lex digitalis* or *lex sportiva*, are not subject to general international law, nor is their norm-formation restricted by the *jus cogens* of international law. Fischer-Lescano and Teubner (2006, pp. 100–101) argue that instead of a harmonised global *jus cogens*, each system should generate its own indispositive norms, sensitive to its specific social context. But the problem remains as to how norm-formation in these systems can be induced to heed considerations that may contradict their 'internal *ratio*', that is, the specific function these differentiated systems are supposed to accomplish: how could norm-formation in, for instance, *lex mercatoria* be expected to produce environmental *jus cogens*, binding on transnational arbitral bodies?

The evidence for law's growing fragmentation and for late modern legal pluralism is irrefutable. Nevertheless, observations focusing on mounting polycentricity and pluralism capture but a part of the picture. Fragmentation is countered by harmonisation and the pursuit of coherence. The increasing significance of human-rights principles in national, international and transnational contexts shows substantive harmonisation, which should not be ignored even when examining legal development from an external, observer's perspective. The backdrop to legal fragmentation is frequently seen in cultural fragmentation and value pluralism – in the multi-cultural character of modern societies which ensues from, among other things, mounting immigration. The elevated status of human and basic rights also shows that accounts of value pluralism and fragmentation convey a deficient image of changes in our cultural landscape. *Ethical* fragmentation – the differentiation of conceptions of the good life – does not necessarily exclude the possibility of a wide-reaching consensus on fundamental *moral* principles. And, in fact, it is on the very basis of such a possibility that human-rights principles are able to exercise their harmonising effect in diverse legal contexts. It may well be that, ultimately, morals-based harmonisation exerts a more profound impact on law's development than ethical fragmentation; that law's cultural ties lie in the dimension of moral principles, rather than in the direction of ethical values. The purport of basic and human rights, such as freedom of religion and conscience or individual and collective cultural rights, is to leave conceptions of the good life to the cultural autonomy of individuals and communities.

But legal fragmentation is not incited only by a cultural value pluralism whose significance can be countered by the argument relying on the distinction between ethics and morals. If systems-theoretically oriented discussants hit the mark, a reference to cultural differentiation would not get to the crux of the matter.

The law's late modern fragmentation would, rather, result from the progress of functional differentiation, typical of modern society, and its extension to the global level. This would also account for the emergence of transnational legal systems such as *lex mercatoria* or *lex digitalis*, and, perhaps, of semi-independent regimes of international law as well.

In the systems-theoretical narrative of law, transnational legal systems are not only structurally coupled with the respective global social sub-systems, providing the stage for norm-formation; they also constitute elements of a global legal system. Teubner (2004a) argues that norms produced in other, 'non-legal' global social systems can only obtain legal validity in legal practices within the global legal system. Late modern interlegality can be examined in other conceptual frameworks, too, than that proffered by systems theory. What is important is to avoid interpreting legal pluralism in terms of a reciprocal closure of diverse legal orders or legal systems; the outdated dichotomy of municipal and international law should not be replaced by another black-box model. As de Sousa Santos (2002, pp. 417ff.) emphasises, transnational and national law, as well as state and non-state law, overlap and interpenetrate; both normative and institutional structures are interconnected by continuous flows of communication. How is this communication possible?

Self-regulation or transnational norm-formation does not take place in political fora, realising the principle of democracy. As Klaus Günther (2001) remarks, the law detached from the nation state consists largely of lawyers' law (*Juristenrecht*). In a globalising world, the language of lawyers and legal culture, which shapes lawyers' professional preconceptions, is also globalising. Günther talks about a *universal legal code* which allows for communicative links between diverse legal systems.

The concept of legal code brings to mind Luhmann's sociological legal theory, according to which the legal system, in line with other social sub-systems, is differentiated on the basis of its distinct binary code. However, the code Günther has in mind is not reduced to the Luhmannian distinction between law and non-law (*Recht/Unrecht*) but constitutes a richer legal language with normative, conceptual and methodological elements. The code involves, for instance, the concepts of rights, duties and legal subjectivity; the distinction between primary and secondary norms; the principles of strict liability and liability presupposing *culpa*; the requirement of predictability of liability and sanction; principles guiding division of the burden of proof; institutionalisation of the role of the neutral *tertius*; the principle of *audiatur et altera pars*, and so on. In particular, the human-rights related principles which Günther has included in his tentative definition of the universal legal code manifest the law's layered nature; in François Ewald's terms, the law possesses a *critical reflexive instance*, which determines the boundaries of legality (Ewald 1986). In fact, Günther enriches Luhmann's legal code with the formal determinations of law, elaborated by Habermas in his *Between Facts and Norms*, which aim at ensuring both private and public autonomy for members of society. In Günther's view, Habermas' legal philosophy – in line with the mainstream of twentieth-century legal theory and philosophy – also presupposes the democratic nation state. But Günther claims that the legal code's attachment to the nation state has been a historically contingent fact; globalisation and ensuing legal pluralism have liberated it from its previous spatial bonds and transformed it into a 'universal code of legality'.

Günther argues that the concepts and principles of the universal code were originally developed in particular historical legal cultures of the Western world: the Continental European Romano-Germanic and the Anglo-American common-law cultures. However, they have severed their ties with their cultural seedbed and undergone a process of formalisation; consequently, they can now be specified and substantiated with culturally-determined contents. Social and legal actors can employ the code in formulating their interests in legal terms, in organising their social and co-operative relations, and in regulating their mutual conflicts.

It is neither possible nor necessary to engage here in a detailed examination of the ingredients Günther suggests be included in the universal code of legality. From my own point of view, it is interesting to notice similarities between Günther's code and my interpretation of modern law's multi-layered structure. Günther's legal code is comparable with what I have called modern law's 'deep structure' (deep culture). We could contend that at its core, the globalisation of law equates with the globalisation of modern law's deep structure or – to put it in Günther's terms – the formation and spread of a universal legal code that facilitates communication across the boundaries between legal orders, legal cultures and legal systems. Following this line of argument, modern law's attachment to the nation state is a historically contingent feature, which, within modern law's layers, is located at the level of legal culture rather than that of deep structure. In turn, in the debate on epochs of law, this argument would lead to the conclusion that globalisation and increasing legal pluralism do not yet warrant a claim of the demise of the modern era. In fact, in both its pluralism and the transnationalisation of its legal-cultural underpinnings, recent legal development is reminiscent of the formative period of modern law in late-medieval Europe, before the rise of the nation state.

To sum up, our contemporary legal scene gains its colours not only from fragmentation but also from harmonisation; globalisation entails not only differentiation but also unification. It is no accident that the drift towards legal pluralism has primarily been emphasised by sociologically-oriented observers, and that the Critic's narrative reserves such an integral place for the allegedly irreconcilable fragmentation of international law and the interest-oriented, strategic power play between the regimes of international law. By contrast, normatively-arguing legal theorists tend to stick to the idea of the law's unity; this, in turn, has prompted their sociologically-minded interlocutors to employ the label of legal ideology.[9] Which side of the development predominates, fragmentation or harmonisation, appears to hinge on the point of view adopted by the discussant. Twining (2000, p. 84) notes that a concept of legal pluralism pointing to a

9 By way of representative example, see Cotterrell (1996, pp. 95ff.).

multiplicity of legal orders or systems 'shifts the main standpoint from the judge, who typically has to take a monistic view of a legal order, to external observers or to the individual or other legal subject who typically finds himself or herself governed by a variety of regulatory orders, which overlap, interact and often conflict'. From the internal perspective of the judge, the 'fiction' of unity – the striving for coherence – purports to fulfil an important normative task: to ensure formal justice, to meet the requirement that like cases be treated alike. Formal justice forms part of the legal code employed by judges and other lawyers in their legal discourse.

As I have argued, state-court judges remain vital players in the game of law, even in circumstances of mounting polycentricity and legal pluralism. Correspondingly, the participant's standpoint of the judge and the concomitant 'fiction' of unity still constitute wholly justifiable epistemological premises. But just as judges have to acknowledge the polycentricity of legal sources, legal theory must also renounce its at least implicit commitment to the self-contained legal order of the nation state. The unity of the law can no longer be conceived along the lines of a closed hierarchical order, topped by Kelsen's basic norm or Hart's rule of recognition and propped up by the institutional hierarchy of the judiciary. Nor can unity be created by a systematisation adopting the perspective of the nation-state legislator and adhering to the black-box model of relations between municipal and international law. Unity must be construed by means of substantive criteria, of the kind Günther has included in the universal code of legality.

Günther's code can be conceived of as the law's sedimented *ratio*, which functions as a tacit pre-understanding of the actors of globalised law. The law's *ratio*, too, cuts its ties with nation states; it brings coherence to the fragmentation of surface-level legal orders and the pluralism of legal systems. And if – as Günther assumes – the *ratio* sedimented into the legal code involves normative ingredients such as basic-rights principles, it also accomplishes tasks related to disciplining the law's *voluntas*.

As I have argued throughout this study, legal scholarship plays an important role in developing professional legal culture and in creating coherence in the law. Legal scholarship has reacted to the loosening of the law's ties to the nation state with proposals for new fields of law – environmental law, medical law, sports law, communications law, and so on – with their distinct legal concepts, principles and theories. These fields gather together normative material from diverse sources and norm orders, and, through their general doctrines, inject coherence into the polycentricity of legal sources and the pluralism of legal orders and systems. Often enough, they build up networks connecting researchers and research institutes from different states. Here they follow international law, the pioneer in the internationalisation of legal doctrine. They demonstrate the law's transformation in the direction of an expert system, and the expansion of legal culture's space beyond nation states. Furthermore, the internationalisation of legal education also infuses cross-boundary coherence into the law.

Bibliography

Aarnio, A. 1973. Suomalaisen oikeusteorian kehityspiirteitä. *Lakimies*, 71(3), 339–373.

Aarnio, A. 1979. *Denkweisen der Rechtswissenschaft*. Wien and New York: Springer.

Aarnio, A. 1987. *Rational as Reasonable*. Dordrecht: Kluwer.

Aarnio, A. 1997. *Reason and Authority*. Aldershot: Ashgate.

Aarnio, A. 2002. Uusi varallisuusoikeus – vai vanha? *Lakimies*, 100(4), 515–534.

Ackerman, B. 1997. Rise of world constitutionalism. *Virginia Law Review*, 83(4), 771–798.

Alchourròn, C.E. and Bulygin, E. 1971. *Normative Systems*. Wien: Springer.

Alexander, G.S. 2002. Comparing the two realisms – American and Scandinavian. *American Journal of Comparative Law*, 50(1), 131–174.

Alexy, R. 1989. *A Theory of Legal Argumentation*, translated by R. Adler and N. MacCormick. Oxford: Clarendon Press.

Alexy, R. 2002a. *A Theory of Constitutional Rights*, translated by J. Rivers. Oxford: Oxford University Press.

Alexy, R. 2002b. Verfassungsrecht und einfaches Recht – Verfassungsgerichtsbarkeit und Fachgerichtsbarkeit, in *Veröffentlichungen der Vereinigung der Deutschen Staatsrechtslehrer 61*, edited by J. Ipsen. Berlin and New York: De Gruyter, 8–33.

Allan, T.R.S. 2000. The rule of law as the foundation of judicial review, in *Judicial Review and the Constitution*, edited by C. Forsyth. Oxford: Hart Publishing, 413–420.

Allan, T.R.S. 2001. *Constitutional Justice. A Liberal Theory of the Rule of Law*. Oxford: Oxford University Press.

Allison, J.W.F. 2004. *A Continental Distinction in the Common Law. A Historical and Comparative Perspective on English Public Law*. Oxford: Oxford University Press.

Althusser, L. 1959. *Montesquieu. La politique et l'histoire*. Paris: PUF.

Ames, J.B. 1900. Vocation of the law professor. *American Law Register*, 48(3), 129–146.

Andrews, J.D. 1910. Classification of law. *Green Bag*, 22(10), 556–575.

Appelbaum, R.P., Felstiner, W.L.F. and Gessner, V. (eds) 2001. *Rules and Networks. The Legal Culture of Global Transactions*. Portland: Hart Publishing.

Austin, J. 1954. *The Province of Jurisprudence Determined and the Uses of the Study of Jurisprudence*, with an introduction by H.L.A. Hart. New York: Noonday.

Austin, J.L. 1984 (1962). *How to Do Things with Words*, edited by J.O. Urmson and M. Sbisà. Oxford and New York: Oxford University Press.

Bachelard, G. 1980. *La formation de l'ésprit scientifique. Contribution à une psychanalyse de la connaissance objective*. Paris: Vrin.

Balkin, J. 1996. Interdisciplinarity as colonization. *Washington and Lee Law Review*, 53(3), 949–970.

Barkow, R.E. 2002. More supreme than court. The fall of the political question doctrine and the rise of judicial supremacy. *Columbia Law Review*, 102(2), 237–336.

Beck, U. 2004. *Der kosmopolitische Blick oder: Krieg ist Frieden*. Frankfurt am Main: Suhrkamp.

Beck, U., Giddens, A. and Lasch, S. 1994. *Reflexive Modernization*. Cambridge: Polity Press.

Beck, U. and Grande, E. 2004. *Das kosmopolitische Europa*. Frankfurt am Main: Suhrkamp.

Bellamy, R. 2007. *Political Constitutionalism. A Republican Defense of the Constitutionality of Democracy*. Cambridge: Cambridge University Press.

Bentham, J. 1988 (1776). *A Fragment of Government*, the new authoritative edition by J.H. Burns and H.L.A. Hart with an introduction by R. Harrison. Cambridge: Cambridge University Press.

Berman, H.J. 1983. *Law and Revolution*. Cambridge and London: Harvard University Press.

Bickel, A.M. 1962. *The Least Dangerous Branch. The Supreme Court at the Bar of Politics*. Indianapolis: Bobbs-Merrill.

Bingham, T. *The Rule of Law*. [Online]. Available at: www.cpl.law.cam.ac.uk/past_activities/the_rule_of_law_text_transcript.php [accessed 10 June 2010].

Bjarup, J. 1982. *Reason, Emotion and the Law. Studies in the Philosophy of Axel Hägerström*. Aarhus: Aarhus University.

Björne, L. 1979. *Oikeusjärjestelmän kehityksestä*. Vammala: Suomalainen Lakimiesyhdistys.

Björne, L. 1984. *Deutsche Rechtssysteme im 18. und 19. Jahrhundert*. Ebelsbach: Gremer.

Böckenförde, E.-W. 1991. Grundrechte als Grundsatznormen, in *Staat, Verfassung, Demokratie*. Frankfurt am Main: Suhrkamp, 159–199.

Bon, P. 1991. La constitutionnalisation du droit espagnol. *Revue Française de droit Constitutionnel*, 5, 35–54.

Bourdieu, P. 1987. The force of law: Toward a sociology of the juridical field, translated and introduced by R. Terdiman. *The Hastings Law Journal*, 38(5), 805–853.

Bradley, A.W. 2006. The rule of law, in *Constitutional and Administrative Law*, edited by A.W. Bradley and K.D. Ewing. 14th edition. Harlow: Longman, 93–106.

Brandeis, L.D. and Warren, S.D. 1890. Right to privacy. *Harvard Law Review*, 4(5), 193–220.

Brohm, W. 2001. Die Funktion des BVerfG – Oligarchie in der Demokratie. *Neue Juristische Wochenschrift*, 54(1), 1–10.

Castiglione, D. 2001. A constitutional debate without a constitutional document, in *The Chartering of Europe*, edited by E.O. Eriksen, J.E. Fossum and A.J. Menéndez. Arena Report No 8/2001. Oslo, 75–80.

Chemerinsky, E. 1985. Rethinking state action. *Northwestern University Law Review*, 80(3), 503–557.

Cheng, B. 1987. *General Principles of Law as applied by International Courts and Tribunals*. Cambridge: Grotius Publications.

Christie, N. 1977. Conflicts as property. *British Journal of Criminology*, 17(1), 1–15.

Clapham, A. 2006. *Human Rights Obligations of Non-State Actors*. Oxford: Oxford University Press.

Cohen, F. 1935. Transcendental nonsense and the functional approach. *Columbia Law Review*, 35(6), 809–849.

Coing, H. 1969. Der juristische Systembegriff bei Rudolf Ihering, in *Philosophie und Rechtswissenschaft*, edited by J. Blühdorn and J. Ritter. Frankfurt am Main: Klostermann, 149–171.

Cook, W.W. 1907. What is the police power? *Columbia Law Review*, 7(5), 323–336.

Cook, W.W. 1928. Human rights: Review of the paradoxes of legal science by Benjamin Cardozo. *Yale Law Journal*, 38(3), 405–407.

Corbin, A. 1922. Taxation of seats on the stock exchange. *Yale Law Journal*, 31(4), 429–431.

Cotterrell, R. 1996. *Law's Community*. Oxford: Clarendon Press.

Cotterrell, R. 2006. *Law, Culture and Society*. Aldershot: Ashgate.

Craig, P. 1997. Formal and substantive conceptions of the rule of law: An analytical framework. *Public Law*, 467–487.

Craig, P. 1998. Report on the United Kingdom, in *The European Court and National Courts – Doctrine and Jurisprudence. Legal Change in Its Social Context*, edited by A.-M. Slaughter, A. Stone Sweet and J.H.H. Weiler. Oxford: Hart Publishing, 195–224.

Davis, M.H. 1987. A government of judges: An historical re-view. *American Journal of Comparative Law*, 35(3), 559–580.

Dawson, J.P. 1968. *The Oracles of Law*. Westport: Greenwood Press.

de Sousa Santos, B. 2002. *Toward a New Legal Common Sense*. 2nd edition. London: Butterworths.

Dewey, J. 1924. Logical method and law. *The Cornell Law Quarterly*, 10(1), 17–27.

Dicey, A.V. 1959 (1889). *Introduction to the Study of the Constitution*. 10th edition, with an introduction by E.C.S. Wade. London: Macmillan.

Diederichsen, U. 1998. Das Bundesverfassungsgericht als oberstes Zivilgericht – ein Lehrstück der juristischen Methodenlehre. *Archiv für die civilistische praxis*, 198(2–3), 171–260.

Dreier, R. 1981. Zur Theoriebildung in der Jurisprudenz, in *Recht – Moral – Ideologie. Studien zur Rechtstheorie*. Frankfurt am Main: Suhrkamp, 70–105.

Durkheim, E. 1950 (1895). *The Rules of Sociological Method*. 8th edition, translated by S.A. Soloray and J.H. Mueller and edited by G.E.G. Catlin. Glencoe and Illinois: Free Press.

Duxbury, N. 1995. *Patterns of American Jurisprudence*. Oxford: Clarendon Press.

Duxbury, N. 2004. *Frederick Pollock and the English Juristic Tradition*. Oxford: Oxford University Press.

Duxbury, N. 2005. English jurisprudence between Austin and Hart. *Virginia Law Review*, 91(1), 1–91.

Dworkin, R. 1978. *Taking Rights Seriously*. London: Duckworth.

Dworkin, R. 1986. *Law's Empire*. London: Fontana.

Dworkin, R. 2003. *Freedom's Law. The Moral Reading of the American Constitution*. Cambridge, MA: Harvard University Press.

Ehrlich, E. 1967. *Recht und Leben. Gesammelte Schriften zur Rechtstatsachenforschung und Freirechtslehre. Ausgewählt und eingeleitet von Manfred Rehbinder*. Berlin: Duncker & Humblot.

Ehrlich, E. 1986. *Gesetz und lebendes Recht. Vermischte kleinere Schriften*, edited by M. Rehbinder. Berlin: Duncker & Humblot.

Ehrlich, E. 2001 (1913). *Fundamental Principles of the Sociology of Law*, with a new introduction by K.A. Ziegert. New Brunswick and London: Transaction Publishers.

Ekelöf, P.-O. 1951. *Är den juridiska doktrinen en teknik eller en vetenskap?* Lund: Universitetet i Lund.

Elliott, M. 2000. Fundamental rights as interpretative constructs: The constitutional logic of the human rights act 1998, in *Judicial Review and the Constitution*, edited by C. Forsyth. Oxford: Hart Publishing, 269–288.

Ellscheid, G. and Hassemer, W. (eds) 1974. *Interessenjurisprudenz*. Darmstadt: Wissenschaftliche Buchgesellschaft.

Ewald, F. 1986. *L'État providence*. Paris: Bernard Grasset.

Fabbrini, F. 2008. Kelsen in Paris: France's constitutional reform and the introduction of a posteriori constitutional review of legislation. *German Law Journal*, 9(10), 1297–1312.

Fallon, R.H. Jr. 2000. As-applied and facial challenges and third-party standing. *Harvard Law Review*, 113(6), 1322–1370.

Fassbender, B. 1998. The United Nations Charter as constitution of the international community. *Columbia Journal of Transnational Law*, 36(3), 529–619.

Favoreu, L. 1990. Le droit constitutionnel, droit de la constitution et constitution du droit. *Revue Française de droit Constitutionnel*, 1(1), 71–89.

Fischer, W.W. III. 1992. The development of modern American legal theory and the judicial interpretation of the bill of rights, in *A Culture of Rights*, edited by M.J. Lacey and K. Haakonssen. Cambridge: Cambridge University Press, 266–365.

Fischer-Lescano, A. and Teubner, G. 2006. *Regime-Kollisionen. Zur Fragmentierung des Weltrechts*. Frankfurt am Main: Suhrkamp.

Forsthoff, E. 1968. Zur heutigen Situation einer Verfassungslehre, in *Epirrhosis, Festgabe für Carl Schmitt*, edited by H. Barion, E.-W. Böckenförde, E. Forsthoff and W. Weber. Berlin: Duncker & Humblot, 185–211.

Forsyth, C. (ed.) 2000. *Judicial Review and the Constitution*. Oxford: Hart Publishing.

Foucault, M. 1972. *The Archaeology of Knowledge*. London: Tavistock.

Foucault, M. 1974. *The Order of Things*. London: Tavistock.

Foucault, M. 1980. Two lectures, in *Power/Knowledge. Selected Interviews and Other Writings, 1972–1977*, edited by C. Gordon. Brighton: Harvester Press, 78–108.

Foucault, M. 1981. *The History of Sexuality*. Harmondsworth: Penguin.

Frändberg, Å. 1996. Begreppet rättsstat, in *Rättsstaten – rätt, politik och moral*, edited by F. Sterzel. Uppsala: Iustus Förlag, 21–41.

Fried, B.H. 2001. *The Progressive Assault on Laissez Faire. Robert Hale and the First Law and Economics Movement*. Cambridge and London: Harvard University Press.

Friedman, B. 2000. The history of the countermajoritarian difficulty. Part four: Law's politics. *University of Pennsylvania Law Review*, 148(4), 971–1064.

Friedman, B. 2001a. The counter-majoritarian problem and the pathology of constitutional scholarship. *Northwestern University Law Review*, 95(3), 933–954.

Friedman, B. 2001b. The history of the countermajoritarian difficulty. Part three: The lesson of Lochner. *New York University Law Review*, 76(5), 1383–1455.

Friedman, L.M. 2005. *A History of American Law*. 3rd edition. New York: Simon & Schuster.

Fuller, L. 1968. *Anatomy of Law*. Westport: Greenwood Press.

Fuller, L. 1969. *The Morality of Law*. Revised edition. New Haven: Yale University Press.

Gadamer, H.-G. 1993 (1960). *Truth and Method*, translated by W. Glen-Doepel. London: Sheed and Ward.

Gardbaum, S. 2001. The new commonwealth model of constitutionalism. *American Journal of Comparative Law*, 49(4), 707–760.

Gardbaum, S. 2003. The 'horizontal effect' of constitutional rights. *Michigan Law Review*, 102(3), 387–459.

Garré, R. 2005. *Consuetudo. Das Gewohnheitsrecht in der Rechtsquellen- und Methodenlehre des späten ius commune in Italien (16.–18. Jahrhundert)*. Frankfurt am Main: Klostermann.

Geddis, A. and Fenton, B. 2008. 'Which is to be master' – rights-friendly statutory interpretation in New Zealand and the United Kingdom. *Arizona Journal of International and Comparative Law*, 25(3), 733–778.

Gerber, C.F. von. 1880 (1865). *Grundzüge des öffentlichen Rechts*. 3rd edition. Leipzig: Bernhard Tauchnitz.

Giddens, A. 1979. *Central Problems in Social Theory*. London: Macmillan.
Giddens, A. 1994. Living in a post-traditional society, in *Reflexive Modernization*, edited by U. Beck, A. Giddens and S. Lasch. Cambridge: Polity Press, 110–173.
Glenn, H.P. 2007. *Common Laws*. Oxford: Oxford University Press.
Gordon, R.W. 1992. Introduction: Holmes' shadow, in *The Legacy of Oliver Wendell Holmes, Jr.*, edited by R.W. Gordon. Edinburgh: Edinburgh University Press, 1–16.
Gray, J.C. 1909. *The Nature and Sources of the Law*. New York: Columbia University Press.
Grey, T.C. 1983. Langdell's orthodoxy. *University of Pittsburgh Law Review*, 45(1), 1–54.
Günther, K. 1989. A normative conception of coherence for a discursive theory of legal justification. *Ratio Juris*, 2(2), 155–166.
Günther, K. 1993. *The Sense of Appropriateness*, translated by J. Farrell. Albany: State University of New York Press.
Günther, K. 2001. Rechtspluralismus und universaler Code der Legalität: Globalisierung als rechtstheoretischer Problem, in *Die Öffentlichkeit der Vernunft und die Vernunft der Öffentlichkeit*, edited by L. Wingert and K. Günther. Frankfurt am Main: Suhrkamp, 539–567.
Gustafsson, H. 2002. *Rättens polyvalens*. Lund: Lunds Universitet.
Habermas, J. 1982. *Zur Logik der Sozialwissenschaften*. Frankfurt am Main: Suhrkamp.
Habermas, J. 1984. *The Theory of Communicative Action Vol. 1*, translated by T. McCarthy. London: Heinemann.
Habermas, J. 1989a. *The Theory of Communicative Action Vol. 2*, translated by T. McCarthy. Cambridge: Polity Press.
Habermas, J. 1989b. Towards a communication-concept of rational collective will-formation. *Ratio Juris*, 2(2), 144–154.
Habermas, J. 1991. Vom pragmatischen, ethischen und moralischen Gebrauch der praktischen Vernunft, in *Erläuterungen zur Diskursethik*. Frankfurt am Main: Suhrkamp, 100–118.
Habermas, J. 1996. *Between Facts and Norms*, translated by W. Rehg. Cambridge: Polity Press.
Haferkamp, H.-P. 2004. *Georg Friedrich Puchta und die 'Begriffsjurisprudenz'*. Frankfurt am Main: Klostermann.
Hale, M. 1971. *The History of the Common Law of England*, edited by C.M. Gray. Chicago: Chicago University Press.
Hand, L. 1958. *The Bill of Rights. The Oliver Wendell Holmes Lecture*. Cambridge, MA: Harvard University Press.
Hart, H.L.A. 1959. Scandinavian realism. *Cambridge Law Journal*, 17(2), 233–240.
Hart, H.L.A. 1980 (1961). *The Concept of Law*. Oxford: Clarendon Press.

Harvey, D. 1989. *The Conditions of Postmodernity – An Inquiry into the Origins of Cultural Change*. Cambridge and Oxford: Blackwell.

Hattenhauer, H. (ed.) 2002. *Thibaut und Savigny. Ihre programmatischen Schriften*. 2nd edition. München: Vahlen.

Hayek, F.A. 1982. *Law, Legislation, and Liberty Vol. 1*. London: Routledge & Kegan Paul.

Heck, P. 1909. Was ist die Begriffsjurisprudenz, die wir bekämpfen? *Deutsche Juristenzeitung*, 1456–1461.

Hegel, G.W.F. 1952 (1820). *The Philosophy of Right*, translated by T.M. Knox. Chicago: Encyclopaedia Britannica.

Helin, M. 1985. Käsitteistä päättelemisestä, in *Juhlajulkaisu Simo Zitting 1915–14/2–*, edited by J. Tepora. Vammala: Suomalainen Lakimiesyhdistys, 82–92.

Helin, M. 1988. *Lainoppi ja metafysiikka*. Vammala: Suomalainen Lakimiesyhdistys.

Henkin, L. 1976. Is there a political question doctrine? *Yale Law Journal*, 85(5), 597–625.

Herget, J.E. and Wallace, S. 1987. German free law movement as the source of American legal realism. *Virginia Law Review*, 73(2), 399–456.

Hermanson, R.F. 1878–1879. Om juridisk konstruktion i statsrätten I–II. *Tidskrift utgifven af juridiska föreningen i Finland*, 1–32 and 457–616.

Heuschling, L. 2002. *État de droit – Rechtsstaat – Rule of Law*. Paris: Dalloz.

Hiebert, J.L. 2004. New constitutional ideas: Can new parliamentary models resist judicial dominance when interpreting rights? *Texas Law Review*, 82(7), 1963–1987.

Hiebert, J.L. 2005. Rights-vetting in New Zealand and Canada: Similar idea, different outcomes. *New Zealand Journal of Public and International Law*, 3(1), 63–103.

Hirschl, R. 2007. *Juristocracy*. Cambridge and London: Harvard University Press.

Hobbes, T. 1971 (1681). *A Dialogue between a Philosopher and a Student of the Common Laws of England*, edited and with an introduction by J. Cropsey. Chicago: Chicago University Press.

Hobbes, T. 1976 (1651). *Leviathan*, edited with an introduction by C.B. MacPherson. Harmondsworth: Penguin.

Hobsbawm, E. 1983. Introduction: Inventing traditions, in *The Invention of Tradition*, edited by E. Hobsbawm and T. Ranger. Cambridge: Cambridge University Press.

Hoeflich, M.H. 1986. Law & geometry: Legal science from Leibnitz to Langdell. *American Journal of Legal History*, 30(2), 95–121.

Hoeflich, M.H. 1989. Savigny and his Anglo-American disciples. *American Journal of Comparative Law*, 37(1), 17–38.

Hohfeld, W.N. 1913. Some fundamental legal conceptions applied in judicial reasoning. *Yale Law Journal*, 23(1), 16–59.

Hohfeld, W.N. 1916. Fundamental legal conceptions as applied in judicial reasoning. *Yale Law Journal*, 26(8), 710–770.
Holmes, O.W. Jr. 1870. Codes, and the arrangement of the law. *American Law Review*, 5(1), 1–13.
Holmes, O.W. Jr. 1872. The arrangement of the law. Privity. *American Law Review*, 7(1), 46–66.
Holmes, O.W. Jr. 1880. Review article. *American Law Review*, 14(3), 233–235.
Holmes, O.W. Jr. 1897. The path of the law. *Harvard Law Review*, 10(8), 457–478.
Horwitz, M.J. 1994. *The Transformation of American Law 1870–1960. The Crisis of Legal Orthodoxy*. New York and Oxford: Oxford University Press.
Hull, N.E.H. 1999. *Roscoe Pound and Karl Llewellyn: Searching for an American Jurisprudence*. Chicago and London: Chicago University Press.
Jääskinen, N. 1983. *Historiallisen koulun oikeustiedekäsitys*. Helsinki: Helsingin yliopiston yleisen oikeustieteen laitos.
Jackson, J.H. 2004. Effektivität und Wirksamkeit des Streitbeilegungsverfahrens der WTO, in *Verrechtlichung – Baustein für Global Governance*, edited by B. Zangl and M. Zürn. Bonn: Dietz, 99–118.
Jellinek, G. 1914 (1900). *Allgemeine Staatslehre*. Berlin: O. Häring.
Jeschek, H.-H. 2004. The general principles of international criminal law set out in Nuremberg, as mirrored in the ICC Statute. 2 *Journal of International Criminal Law*, 38–55.
Jhering, R. 1884. *Scherz und Ernst in der Jurisprudenz*. Leipzig: Breitkopf & Härtel.
Jowell, J. 2006. Parliamentary sovereignty under the new constitutional hypothesis. *Public Law*, 562–579.
Jowell, J. 2007. The rule of law today, in *The Changing Constitution*, edited by J. Jowell and D. Oliver. 6th edition. Oxford: Oxford University Press, 5–24.
Kalman, L. 2001. *Legal Realism at Yale 1927–1960*. Union: Lawbook Exchange.
Kambartel, F. 1969. 'System' und 'Begründung' als wissenschaftliche und philosophische Ordnungsbegriffe bei und vor Kant, in *Philosophie und Rechtswissenschaft*, edited by J. Blühdorn and J. Ritter. Frankfurt am Main: Klostermann, 99–113.
Kant, I. 1983 (1786). Metaphysische Anfangsgründe der Naturwissenchaft, in *Immanuel Kant. Werke in zehn Bänden. Band 8*, edited by W. Weischedel. Darmstadt: Wissenschaftliche Buchgesellschaft, 11–135.
Kantorowicz, H. 1962. *Rechtswissenschaft und Soziologie. Ausgewählte Schriften zur Wissenschaftslehre*. Karlsruhe: C. F. Müller.
Karhu, J. 2003. Perusoikeudet ja oikeuslähdeoppi. *Lakimies*, 101(5), 789–907.
Kelsen, H. 1911. *Hauptprobleme der Staatsrechtslehre entwickelt aus der Lehre vom Rechtssatze*. Tübingen: J.C.B. Mohr.
Kelsen, H. 1929. Wesen und Entwicklung der Staatsgerichtsbarkeit. *Veröffentlichungen der Vereinigung der deutschen Staatsrechtslehrer 5*. Berlin and Leipzig: De Gruyter, 30–123.

Kelsen, H. 1989 (1960). *The Pure Theory of Law*, translation from the 2nd German edition by M. Knight. Berkeley, Los Angeles and London: California University Press.

Kennedy, D. 1976. Form and substance in private law adjudication. *Harvard Law Review*, 89(8), 1685–1778.

Kennedy, D. 1997. *A Critique of Adjudication*. Cambridge and London: Harvard University Press.

Kennedy, D. 2006a. Three globalizations of law and legal thought: 1850–2000, in *The New Law and Economic Development*, edited by D. Trubek and A. Santos. Cambridge: Cambridge University Press.

Kennedy, D. 2006b. *The Rise and Fall of Classical Legal Thought*. Washington, DC: Beard Books.

Kennedy, D.W. and Fisher, W.W. III. 2006. *The Canon of American Legal Thought*. Princeton: Princeton University Press.

Kern, S. 2003. *The Culture of Time and Space 1880–1918*. Cambridge, MA: Harvard University Press.

Kiefner, H. 1979. Lex frater a fratre. Institution und Rechtsinstitut bei Savigny. *Rechtstheorie*, 10(2), 129–141.

Kimball, B.A. 1999. Warn students that I entertain heretical opinions, which they are not to take as law: The inception of case method teaching in the classrooms of the early C.C. Langdell, 1870–1883. *Law and History Review*, 17(1), 57–140.

Klabbers, J. 2003. (I can't get no) Recognition: Subjects doctrine and the emergence of non-state actors, in *Nordic Cosmopolitanism: Essays in International Law for Martti Koskenniemi*, edited by J. Petman and J. Klabbers. Leiden: Martinus Nijhoff Publishers, 351–369.

Kocourek, A. 1934. Classification of law. *New York University Law Quarterly Review*, 11(3), 320–348.

Komiteanmietintö (Committee Report) 1917:7. Helsinki 1917.

Koselleck, R. 1984. *Vergangene Zukunft*. 3rd edition. Frankfurt am Main: Suhrkamp.

Koskenniemi, M. 1985. General principles: Reflexions on constructivist thinking in international law, in *Oikeustiede Jurisprudentia XVIII*. Vammala: Suomalainen Lakimiesyhdistys, 117–163.

Koskenniemi, M. 1999a. Letter to the editors of the symposium. *American Journal of International Law*, 93(2), 351–361.

Koskenniemi, M. 1999b. The effect of rights on political culture, in *The EU and Human Rights*, edited by P. Alston. Oxford: Oxford University Press, 99–116.

Koskenniemi, M. 2004. Legal universalism: Between morality and power in a world of states, in *Law, Justice and Power: Between Reason and Will*, edited by S. Cheng. Stanford: Stanford University Press, 46–69.

Koskenniemi, M. 2005. Epilogue, in *Apology and Utopia*. 2nd edition. Cambridge: Cambridge University Press, 562–617.

Koskenniemi, M. 2006. Fragmentation of International Law: Difficulties Arising from the Diversification and Expansion of International Law. Report of the Study Group of the International Law Commission, Finalized by Martti Koskenniemi. UN Doc. A/CN. 4/L. 682 (13 April 2006).

Koskenniemi, M. and Leino, P. 2002. Fragmentation of international law? Postmodern anxieties. *Leiden Journal of International Law*, 15(3), 553–579.

Kramer, L.D. 2004. *The People Themselves. Popular Constitutionalism and Judicial Review*. Oxford: Oxford University Press.

Kronman, A. 1983. *Max Weber*. Stanford: Stanford University Press.

Kronman, A. 2001. *The Lost Lawyer*. Cambridge and London: Harvard University Press.

Kuhn, T. 1967. *The Structure of Scientific Revolutions*. Chicago: Chicago University Press.

Kumm, M. 2006. Who's afraid of the total constitution? Constitutional rights as principles and the constitutionalization of private law. *German Law Journal*, 7(4), 341–369.

Kumm, M. 2007. Institutionalising Socratic contestation: The rationalist human rights paradigm, legitimate authority and the point of judicial review. *European Journal of Legal Studies*. [Online], 1(2). Available at: www.ejls.eu/2/26UK.pdf [accessed 10 June 2010].

Kumm, M. and Comella, V.F. 2005. What is so special about constitutional rights in private litigation? A comparative analysis of the function of state action requirements and indirect horizontal effect, in *The Constitution in Private Relations: Expanding Constitutionalism*, edited by A. Sajó and R. Uitz. Utrecht: Eleven International Publishing, 23–32.

Laband, P. 1888. *Das Staatsrecht des deutschen Reiches. Band I*. Freiburg: Akademische Verlagsbuchhandlung.

Lambert, É. 1921. *Le Gouvernement des Juges et la Lutte contre la Legislation Sociale aux Etats-Unis*. Paris: Giard (Marcel).

Landis, J. 1938. Landis: A foreword to 'law and literature'. *Yale Law Journal*, 48(3), 489–507.

Legarre, S. 2007. The historical background of the police power. *University of Pennsylvania Journal of Constitutional Law*, 9(3), 745–796.

Lehmkuhl, D. 2004. Der lange Schatten staatlichen Rechts: Verrechtlichung im transnationalen Sport, in *Verrechtlichung – Baustein für Global Governance*, edited by B. Zangl and M. Zürn. Bonn: Dietz, 179–197.

Leib, V. 2004. Verrechtlichung im Internet: Macht und Recht bei der Regulierung durch ICANN, in *Verrechtlichung – Baustein für Global Governance*, edited by B. Zangl and M. Zürn. Bonn: Dietz, 198–219.

Leiter, B. 2007. *Naturalizing Jurisprudence. Essays on American Legal Realism and Naturalism in Jurisprudence*. Oxford: Oxford University Press.

Lenaerts, K. 2003. Interlocking legal orders in the European Union and comparative law. *International and Comparative Law Quarterly*, 52(4), 873–906.

Lindblom, A.-K. 2005. *The Legal Status of Non-Governmental Organisations in International Law*. Cambridge: Cambridge University Press.

Llewellyn, K. 1930. Realistic jurisprudence – the next step. *Columbia Law Review*, 30(4), 431–465.

Llewellyn, K. 1931. Some realism about realism – responding to Dean Pound. *Harvard Law Review*, 44(8), 1222–1264.

Llewellyn, K. 1960. *Common Law Tradition: Deciding Appeals*. Boston: Little Brown.

Llewellyn, K. 1969 (1930). *Bramble Bush*. 3rd printing. Dobbs Ferry: Oceana Publications.

Llewellyn, K. 2008. *Jurisprudence: Theory and Practice*, with a new introduction by J.J. Chriss. Piscataway: Transaction Publishers.

Luhmann, N. 1983 (1968). *Legitimation durch Verfahren*. Frankfurt am Main: Suhrkamp.

Luhmann, N. 2004. *Law as a Social System*, translated by K.A. Ziegert. Oxford: Oxford University Press.

Lundstedt, V. 1929. *Obligationsbegreppet. Förra delen*. Uppsala: Norblad.

Lundstedt, V. 1956. *Legal Thinking Revised*. Uppsala: Almqvist.

Lyles, M. 2006. *A Call for Scientific Purity: Axel Hägerström's Critique of Legal Science*. Stockholm: The Ohlin Foundation for Legal History.

Määttä, T. 2000. Monitieteisyys ympäristöoikeudessa – oikeustieteen sisäiset ja ulkoiset yhteydet oikeustieteellisen tutkimuksen haasteena. *Oikeus*, 29(3), 333–355.

MacCormick, N. 1981. *H.L.A. Hart*. London: Edward Arnold.

MacCormick, N. 1984. Der Rechtsstaat und die Rule of Law. *Juristenzeitung*, 39(2), 65–70.

MacCormick, N. 2005. *Rhetoric and the Rule of Law*. Oxford: Oxford University Press.

MacCormick, N. 2006. *Institutions of Law. An Essay in Legal Theory*. Oxford: Oxford University Press.

MacCormick, N. and Weinberger, O. 1986. *An Institutional Theory of Law*. Dordrecht: Kluwer.

MacIntyre, A. 1988. *Whose Justice? Which Rationality?* London: Duckworth.

Macpherson, C.B. 1962. *The Political Theory of Possessive Individualism*. Oxford: Oxford University Press.

Maduro, M.P. 1998. *We the Court. European Court of Justice and the European Economic Constitution*. Oxford: Hart Publishing.

Maier, H. 1986. *Die ältere deutsche Staats – und Verwaltungslehre*. München: DTV.

Mäki-Petäjä-Leinonen, A. 2003. *Dementoituvan henkilön oikeudellinen asema*. Vammala: Suomalainen Lakimiesyhdistys.

Makkonen, K. 1959. Ajatuksia juridisen kielen loogisesta analyysista. *Lakimies*, 56(1), 49–72.

Makkonen, K. 1965. *Zur Problematik der juridischen Entscheidung*. Turku: Turun yliopisto.

Makkonen, K. 1967. Der Ausdruck 'subjektives Recht' in der juristischen Sprache, in *Studia in honorem Otto Brusiin, Ius humanum*. Turku: Turun yliopisto, 112–123.

Mallory, John A. 1902. Philosophical classification of law, *American Law School Review*, 1(5), 137–142.

Manfredi, C.P. 1993. *Judicial Power and the Charter. Canada and the Paradox of Liberal Constitutionalism*. Norman and London: University of Oklahoma Press.

Marx, K. and Engels, F. *Manifesto of the Communist Party*. [Online]. Available at: www.socialistparty.org.uk/manifesto [accessed 10 June 2010].

Maus, I. 1989. Die Trennung von Recht und Moral als Begrenzung des Rechts. *Rechtstheorie*, 20(2), 191–210.

Nelken, D. (ed.) 1997. *Comparing Legal Cultures*. Aldershot: Dartmouth.

Neumann, F.L. 1967. *Demokratischer und autoritärer Staat. Beiträge zur Soziologie der Politik*. Frankfurt am Main: Europäische Verlagsanstalt.

Neumann, F.L. 1980. *Die Herrschaft des Gesetzes*. Frankfurt am Main: Suhrkamp.

Nörr, D. 1994. *Savignys philosophische Lehrjahre*. Frankfurt am Main: Klostermann.

Nuotio, K. 1998. *Teko, vaara ja seuraus*. Vammala: Suomalainen Lakimiesyhdistys.

Palmer Olsen, H. 2005. *Magtfordeling*. KØbenhavn: Jurist- og Økonomforbundets Forlag.

Paschukanis, E. 1969 (1929). *Allgemeine Rechtslehre und Marxismus*. Frankfurt am Main: Suhrkamp.

Pihlajamäki, H. 2004. Against metaphysics in law: The historical background of American and Scandinavian legal realism compared. *American Journal of Comparative Law*, 52(2), 469–488.

Plotner, J. 1998. Report on France, in *The European Court and National Courts – Doctrine and Jurisprudence: Legal Change in Its Social Context*, edited by A.-M. Slaughter, A. Stone Sweet and J.H.H. Weiler. Oxford: Hart Publishing, 41–76.

Pocock, J.G.A. 1989. Burke and ancient constitution: A problem in the history of ideas, in *Politics, Language, and Time. Essays on Political Thought and History*. Chicago and London: Chicago University Press, 202–232.

Posner, R. 2007. 'How to skip the constitution': An exchange. *New York Review of Books*, 54(1), 63.

Postema, G.J. 1989. *Bentham and the Common Law Tradition*. Oxford: Clarendon Press.

Postema, G.J. 2002. Classical common law jurisprudence I. *Oxford University Commonwealth Law Journal*, 2(2), 155–180.

Postema, G.J. 2003. Classical common law jurisprudence II. *Oxford University Commonwealth Law Journal*, 3(1), 1–28.

Pound, R. 1908. Mechanical jurisprudence. *Columbia Law Review*, 8(8), 605–623.

Pound, R. 1910. Law in books and law in action. *American Law Review*, 44(1), 12–36.

Pound, R. 1911a. Scope and purpose of sociological jurisprudence I. *Harvard Law Review*, 24(8), 591–619.

Pound, R. 1911b. Scope and purpose of sociological jurisprudence II. *Harvard Law Review*, 25(2), 140–168.

Pound, R. 1912. Scope and purpose of sociological jurisprudence III. *Harvard Law Review*, 25(6), 489–516.

Pound, R. 1921. *The Spirit of Common Law*. Francestown: Marshall Jones Company.

Pound, R. 1924. Classification of law. *Harvard Law Review*, 37(8), 933–969.

Pound, R. 1939. Public and private law. *Cornell Law Quarterly*, 24(4), 469–482.

Pound, R. 1940. Administrative law: Its growth, procedure, and significance. *University of Pittsburgh Law Review*, 7(4), 269–282.

Pound, R. 1944. Administrative law and the courts. *Boston University Law Review*, 24(4), 201–223.

Powell, T.R. 1919. The police power in American constitutional law. *Journal of Comparative Legislation and International Law*, 1(1), 160–174.

Pöyhönen, J. 1981. *Oikeudellisista teorioista*. Helsinki: Helsingin yliopiston yleisen oikeustieteen laitos.

Pöyhönen, J. 1988. *Sopimusoikeuden järjestelmä ja sopimusten sovittelu*. Vammala: Suomalainen Lakimiesyhdistys.

Pöyhönen, J. 2000. *Uusi varallisuusoikeus*. Helsinki: Kauppakaari.

Prewo, R. 1979. *Max Webers Wissenchaftsprogramm*. Frankfurt am Main: Suhrkamp.

Preuss, U. 2005. The German Drittwirkung doctrine and its socio-political background, in *The Constitution in Private Relations: Expanding Constitutionalism*, edited by A. Sajó and R. Uitz. Utrecht: Eleven International Publishing, 23–32.

Puchta, G.F. 1850. *Cursus der Institutionen*. Leipzig: Breitkopf & Hartel.

Rabban, D.M. 2003. The historiography of late nineteenth-century American legal history. *Theoretical Inquiries in Law*, 4(2), 541–578.

Rammstedt, O. 1975. Alltagsbewusstsein von Zeit. *Kölner Zeitschrift für Soziologie und Sozialpsychologie*, 27(1), 47–63.

Raz, J. 1979. The virtue of the rule of law, in *The Authority of Law. Essays in Law and Morality*. Oxford: Oxford University Press, 210–229.

Reichel, J. 2006. *God förvaltning i EU och i Sverige*. Stockholm: Jure Förlag.

Reimann, M. 1989. The historical school against codification: Savigny, Carter, and the defeat of the New York Civil Code. *American Journal of Comparative Law*, 37(1), 95–120.

Reimann, M. 1993. A career in itself. The German professiorate as a model for American legal academica, in *The Reception of Continental Ideas in the*

Common Law World 1820–1920, edited by M. Reimann. Berlin: Duncker & Humblot.

Ricoeur, P. 1970. *Freud and Philosophy. An Essay on Interpretation*. New Haven and London: Yale University Press.

Rodriguez, D.B. 1997. Jaffe's law: An essay on the intellectual underpinnings of modern administrative law theory. *Chicago-Kent Law Review*, 72(4), 1159–1186.

Rosa, H. 2005. *Beschleunigung. Die Veränderung der Zeitstrukturen in der Moderne*. Frankfurt am Main: Suhrkamp.

Ross, A. 1946. *Towards a Realistic Jurisprudence*. Copenhagen: E. Munksgaard.

Ross, A. 1956. Tû-tû. *Harvard Law Review*, 70(5), 812–825.

Ross, A. 1958. *On Law and Justice*. London: Stevens and Sons Limited.

Rückert, J. 1984. *Idealismus, Jurisprudenz und Politik bei Friedrich Carl von Savigny*. Ebelsbach: Verlag Rolf Gremer.

Rümelin, M. 1907. *Bernhard Windscheid und sein Einfluss auf Privatrecht und Privatrechtswissenschaft*. Tübingen: Schnürlen.

Savigny, K.F. von. 1981 (1840). *System des heutigen römischen Rechts. Band 1–2*. Second reprint Berlin 1840. Aalen: Scientia.

Savigny, K.F. von. 2002 (1814). Vom Beruf unsrer Zeit für Gesetzgebung und Rechtswissenschaft, in *Thibaut und Savigny. Ihre programmatischen Schriften*, edited by H. Hattenhauer. München: Vahlen.

Scharpf, F.W. 1966. Judicial review and the political question: A functional analysis. *Yale Law Journal*, 75(5), 517–596.

Scheppele, K.L. 2005. Democracy by judiciary, or, why courts can be more democratic than parliaments, in *Rethinking the Rule of Law after Communism*, edited by A. Czarnota, M. Krygier and W. Sadurski. Budapest: Central European University Press, 25–61.

Schermers, H.G. and Waelbroeck, D.F. 2001. *Judicial Protection in the European Union*. The Hague: Kluwer Law International.

Scheuerman, W.E. 1997. *Between the Norm and the Exception. The Frankfurt School and the Rule of Law*. Cambridge, MA and London: MIT Press.

Scheuerman, W.E. 2004. *Liberal Democracy and the Social Acceleration of Time*. Baltimore and London: Johns Hopkins University Press.

Schlegel, J.H. 1995. *American Legal Realism and Empirical Social Science*. Chapel Hill: University of North Carolina Press.

Schlink, B. 1993. German constitutional culture in transition. *Cardozo Law Review*, 14(3–4), 711–736.

Schmitt, C. 1934. *Über die drei Arten des rechtswisssenschaftlichen Denkens*. Hamburg: Hanseatische Verlagsanstalt.

Schmitt, C. 1935. Der Rechtsstaat, in *Nationalsozialistisches Handbuch für Recht und Gesetzgebung*, edited by H. Frank. München: Akademie für Deutsches Recht, 3ff.

Schmitt, C. 1958 (1933). Weiterentwicklung des totalen Staates in Deutschland, in *Verfassungsrechtliche Aufsätze*. Berlin: Duncker & Humblot, 359–365.

Schmitt, C. 1967. Die Tyrannei der Werte, in *Sekularisation und Utopie*. Erbracher Studien. Ernst Forsthoff zum 65. Geburtstag. Stuttgart, 37–62.

Schmitt, C. 1985. *Politische Theologie*. 4. Aufl., unveränd. Nachdruck d. 1934 erschienenen 2 Aufl. Berlin: Duncker & Humblot.

Schmitt, C. 1987. *Der Begriff von Politischen*. Text von 1932 mit einem Vorwort und drei Corollarien. Unveränd. Nachdruck d. 1963 erschienenen Aufl. Berlin: Duncker & Humblot.

Schmitt, C. 1988a (1923). *The Crisis of Parliamentary Democracy*, translated by E. Kennedy. Cambridge, MA and London: MIT Press.

Schmitt, C. 1988b (1940). *Positionen und Begriffe. Im Kampf mit Weimar – Genf – Versailles 1923–1939*. Unveränderter Nachdruck. Berlin: Duncker & Humblot.

Schmitt, C. 1996 (1927). *The Concept of the Political*, translated and with an introduction by G. Schwab with a new introduction by T.B. Strong. Chicago and London: Chicago University Press.

Schmitt, C. 2004a (1932). *Legality and Legitimacy*, translated and edited by J. Seitzer with an introduction by J.P. McCormick. Durham, NC and London: Duke University Press.

Schmitt, C. 2004b (1934). *On the Three Types of Juristic Thought*, translated by J.W. Bendersky. Westport, CT and London: Praeger.

Schmitt, C. 2004c (1922). *Political Theology. Four Chapters on the Concept of Sovereignty*, translated by G. Schwab, foreword by T.B. Strong. Chicago and London: University of Chicago Press.

Schmitt, C. 2008 (1928). *Constitutional Theory*, translated and edited by J. Seitzer, foreword by E. Kennedy. Durham, NC and London: Duke University Press.

Schmitt-Dorotic, C. 1921. *Die Diktatur*. München und Leipzig: Duncker & Humblot.

Schröder, J. 1976. Savigny's Spezialistendogma und die ‚soziologische' Jurisprudenz. *Rechtstheorie*, 7(1), 23–52.

Schröder, J. 1979. *Wissenschaftstheorie und Lehre der 'praktischen Jurisprudenz' auf deuschen Universitäten an der Wende zum 19. Jahrhundert*. Frankfurt am Main: Klostermann.

Schroer, M. 2006. *Räume, Orte, Grenzen. Auf dem Weg zu einer Soziologie des Raums*. Frankfurt am Main: Suhrkamp.

Searle, J. 1988 (1969). *Speech Acts*. Cambridge: Cambridge University Press.

Sedley, S. 1995. Human rights: A twenty-first century agenda. *Public Law*, 386–401.

Shapiro, M. and Stone Sweet, A. 2002. *On Law, Politics, and Judicialization*. Oxford: Oxford University Press.

Siegel, S.A. 2001. John Chipman Gray and the moral basis of classical legal thought. *Iowa Law Review*, 86(5), 1513–1599.

Siltala, R. 2000. Fragmentteja, osa III: Mistä puhumme, kun puhumme oikeudesta. *Oikeus*, 29(4), 473–492.

Simpson, A.W.B. 1981. The rise and fall of the legal treatise: Legal principles and the forms of legal literature. *University of Chicago Law Review*, 48(3), 632–679.

Singer, J.W. 1982. Legal rights debate in analytical jurisprudence from Bentham to Hohfeld. *Wisconsin Law Review*, 6, 975–1060.

Skinner, Q. 1989. The state, in *Political Innovation and Conceptual Change*, edited by T. Ball, J. Farr and R.L. Hanson. Cambridge: Cambridge University Press, 90–131.

Skinner, Q. 2002a. *Visions of Politics. Volume I. Regarding Method*. Cambridge: Cambridge University Press.

Skinner, Q. 2002b. *Visions of Politics. Volume II. Renaissance Virtues*. Cambridge: Cambridge University Press.

Slaughter, A.-M. 2004. *A New World Order*. Princeton: Princeton University Press.

Speziale, M. 1980. Langdell's concept of law as science: The beginning of anti-formalism in American legal theory. *Vermont Law Review*, 5(1), 1–37.

Stichweh, R. 1992. Motive und Begründungsstrategien für Wissenschaftlichkeit in der deutschen Jurisprudenz des 19. Jahrhunderts. *Rechtshistorisches Journal*, 11, 330–351.

Stichweh, R. 2000. *Weltgesellschaft. Soziologische Analysen*. Frankfurt am Main: Suhrkamp.

Stone Sweet, A. 2000. *Governing with Judges. Constitutional Politics in Europe*. Oxford: Oxford University Press.

Stone Sweet, A. 2003. Why Europe rejected American judicial review and why it may not matter. *Michigan Law Review*, 101(6), 2744–2780.

Stone Sweet, A. 2004. *The Judicial Construction of Europe*. Oxford: Oxford University Press.

Taylor, C. 1985. What is human agency?, in *Human Agency and Language. Philosophical Papers I*. Cambridge: Cambridge University Press, 15–44.

Terry, H.T. 1910. The arrangement of the law. *Green Bag*, 22(9), 499–513.

Terry, H.T. 1917. Arrangement of the law. *Columbia Law Review*, 17(4–5), 291–308 and 365–382.

Teubner, G. 1989. How the law thinks: Toward a constructivist epistemology of law. *Law and Society Review*, 23(5), 727–757.

Teubner, G. (ed.) 1996. *Global Law without a State*. Aldershot: Ashgate.

Teubner, G. 1998. The two faces of Janus: Rethinking legal pluralism, in *Law and Power. Critical and Socio-Legal Essays*, edited by J. Uusitalo, Z. Bankowski and K. Tuori. Liverpool: Deborah Charles, 119–140.

Teubner, G. 2004a. Global private regimes: Neo-spontaneous law and dual constitution of autonomous sectors?, in *Public Governance in the Age of Globalization*, edited by K.-H. Ladeur. Aldershot: Ashgate, 71–87.

Teubner, G. 2004b. Societal constitutionalism: Alternatives to state-centred constitutional theory?, in *Constitutionalism and Transnational Governance*, edited by C. Joerges, I.J Sand and G. Teubner. Oxford: Hart Publishing, 3–28.

Teubner, G. 2006. The anonymous matrix: Human rights violations by 'private' transnational actors. *Modern Law Review*, 69(3), 327–346.

Thayer, J.B. 1893. The origin and scope of the American doctrine of constitutional law. *Harvard Law Review*, 7(3), 129–156.

The Federalist Papers. 1961. Edited and with an introduction by C. Rossiter. New York: NAL Penguin.

Thoma, R. 1978 (1910). Rechtsstaatsidee und Verwaltungsrechtswissenschaft, in *Der bürgerliche Rechtsstaat*, edited by M. Tohidipur. Frankfurt am Main: Suhrkamp, 499–524.

Tigar, M.E. 1970. Judicial power, the political question doctrine, and foreign relations. *UCLA Law Review*, 17(6), 1135–1179.

Tolonen, H. 1991. Rules, principles and goals. *Scandinavian Studies in Law*, 35, 271–293.

Tolonen, H. 1992a. *Korko, raha ja sopimus*. Jyväskylä: Lakimiesliiton kustannus.

Tolonen, H. 1992b. Menneet ja nykyiset käsitteet oikeuden ja yhteiskunnan aatehistoriassa. *Oikeus*, 21(2), 126–143.

Tontti, J. 2004. *Right and Prejudice. Prologomena to a Hermeneutical Philosophy of Law*. Aldershot: Ashgate.

Tribe, L.H. 1988. *American Constitutional Law*. 2nd edition. New York: The Foundation Press.

Tridimas, T. 2005. *The General Principles of EU Law*. 2nd edition. Oxford: Oxford University Press.

Troper, M. 1995. Constitutional justice and democracy. *Cardozo Law Review*, 17(2), 273–297.

Tuori, K. 1987. General doctrines in public law. *Scandinavian Studies in Law*, 31, 177–197.

Tuori, K. 2000. *Kriittinen oikeuspositivismi*. Helsinki: WSLT.

Tuori, K. 2002a. *Critical Legal Positivism*. Aldershot: Ashgate.

Tuori, K. 2002b. The 'Rechtsstaat' in the conceptual field – adversaries, allies and neutrals. *Associations*, 6(2), 201–214.

Tuori, K. 2004a. En sista tillflyktsort för polisens allmänna befogenhet? *Tidskrift utgiven av juridiska föreningen i Finland*, 140(3–4), 492–516.

Tuori, K. 2004b. The many senses of European citizenship, in *Europe in Search of Purpose and Identity*, edited by K. Nuotio. Helsinki: Forum Iuris, 51–88.

Tuori, K.T. 2007. *Ancient Roman Lawyers and Modern Legal Ideals. Studies on the Impact of Contemporary Concerns in the Interpretation of Ancient Roman Legal History*. Frankfurt am Main: Klostermann.

Tushnet, M. 1995. Policy distortion and democratic debilitation: Comparative illumination of the countermajoritarian difficulty. *Michigan Law Review*, 94(2), 245–301.

Tushnet, M. 1999. *Taking the Constitution away from Courts*. Princeton: Princeton University Press.

Tushnet, M. 2003. New forms of judicial review and the persistence of rights- and democracy-based worries. *Wake Forest Law Review*, 38(2), 813–838.

Tushnet, M. 2008. *Weak Courts, Strong Rights. Judicial Review and Social Welfare Rights in Comparative Constitutional Law*. Princeton and Oxford: Princeton University Press.

Twining, W. 1985. *Karl Llewellyn and the Realist Movement*. London: Weidenfeld and Nicholson.

Twining, W. 2000. *Globalisation and Legal Theory*. Evanston: Northwestern University Press.

Ulrich, C.U. 1935. A proposed of classification for the law. *Michigan Law Review*, 34(2), 226–256.

Undén, Ö. 1928. Några synpunkter på begreppsbildning inom juridiken, in *Festskrift tillägnad Axel Hägerström den 6 september 1928*, edited by H. Larsson et al./Filosofiska och Juridiska föreningarna i Uppsala. Uppsala: Almqvist & Wiksells Boktryckeri-A-B, 167–177.

Van Caenegem, R.C. 1973. *The Birth of the English Common Law*. Cambridge: Cambridge University Press.

Van Caenegem, R.C. 1993. *Judges, Legislators and Professors. Chapters in European Legal History*. Cambridge: Cambridge University Press.

Viljanen, J. 2003. *European Court of Human Rights as a Developer of the General Doctrines of Human Rights Law. A Study of the Limitation Clauses of the European Convention on Human Rights*. Tampere: Tampere University Press.

Viljanen, V.-P. 2001. *Perusoikeuksien rajoitusedellytykset*. Vammala: Suomalainen Lakimiesyhdistys.

Von Oertzen, P. 1974. *Die soziale Funktion des staatsrechtlichen Positivismus*. Frankfurt am Main: Suhrkamp.

Waldron, J. 2006. The core of the case against judicial review. *Yale Law Review*, 115(6), 1346–1407.

Watson, A. 1985. *The Evolution of Law*. Baltimore: Johns Hopkins University Press.

Weber, M. 1963 (1920). *Gesammelte Aufsätze zur Religionssoziologie*. Tübingen: J.C.B. Mohr.

Weber, M. 1978 (1922). *Economy and Society*, edited by G. Roth and C. Wittich, translated by E. Fischoff et al. Berkeley: University of California Press.

Weber, M. 1988 (1922). *Gesammelte Aufsätze zur Wissenschaftslehre*. Tübingen: J.C.B. Mohr.

Wiecek, W.M. 1998. *The Lost World of Classical Legal Thought. Law and Ideology in America, 1886–1937*. Oxford: Oxford University Press.

Wilhelm, W. 1958. *Zur juristischen Methodenlehre im 19. Jahrhundert*. Frankfurt am Main: Klostermann.

Wilhelm, W. 1969. Savignys überpositive Systematik, in *Philosophie und Rechtswissenschaft*, edited by J. Blühdorn and J. Ritter. Frankfurt am Main: Klostermann, 123–136.

Wilhelmsson, T. 1992. *Studies in Critical Private Law*. Dordrecht: Kluwer.

Wilhelmsson, T. 1997. A Jack-in-the-box theory of European community law, in *Law and Diffuse Interests in the European Legal Order*, edited by L. Krämer, H.-W. Micklitz and K. Tonner. Baden-Baden: Nomos, 177–194.

Wilhelmsson, T. 2001. *Senmodern ansvarsrätt*. Helsingfors: Kauppakaari.

Wilhelmsson, T. 2004. Yleiset opit ja pienet kertomukset ennakoitavuuden ja yhdenvertaisuuden näkökulmasta. *Lakimies*, 102(2), 199–227.

Wittgenstein, L. 1966. *Philosophical Investigations*, translated by G.E.M. Anscombe. 2nd edition. Oxford: Basil Blackwell.

Yale Law Journal. 1938. 47(4).

Zahle, H. 1995. The polycentricity of the law or the importance of legal pluralism for legal dogmatics, in *Legal Polycentricity. Consequences of Pluralism in Law*, edited by H. Petersen and H. Zahle. Aldershot: Ashgate, 185–200.

Zangl, B. and Zürn, M. (eds) 2004. *Verrechtlichung – Baustein für Global Governance*. Bonn: Dietz.

Zitting, S. 1952. Omistajan oikeuksista ja velvollisuuksista I–II. *Lakimies*, 50(2), 387–401 and 501–531.

Zürn, M. 1998. *Regieren jenseits des Nationalstaates*. Frankfurt am Main: Suhrkamp.

Index

For Product Safety Concerns and Information please contact our
EU representative GPSR@taylorandfrancis.com Taylor & Francis
Verlag GmbH, Kaufingerstraße 24, 80331 München, Germany